The United States Jaycees Foundation

Uplift

What People Themselves Can Do

Prepared by

The Washington Consulting Group, Inc.

Olympus Publishing Company Salt Lake City, Utah

ISBN: 0-913420-38-7 (Paper)
Library of Congress Catalog Number: 74-81131

Printed in the United States of America

The information published herein was obtained through a
grant with the Office of Economic Opportunity, Executive
Office of the President, Washington, D.C. 20506. The
opinions expressed herein are those of the authors and
should not be construed as representing the opinions or
policy of any agency of the United States Government.

Contents

FOREWORD   vii
   M. Carl Holman

PREFACE   ix

ACKNOWLEDGMENTS   xi

INTRODUCTION   xiii
   Susan A. Davis

1 ECONOMIC DEVELOPMENT   2

The Humphreys County Union for Progress Farmers
   Cooperative   4
The Franklin Dairy Co-op   8
Tract Handcrafts   12
The Self Help Action Center   15
Kah-Nee-Ta Vacation Resort   21
The Warm Springs Sub-Assembly Plant   25
Fine Vines   30
The Dineh Cooperatives   34
The Southeast Alabama Self-Help Association   37
Appalachian Fireside Crafts   42
The Knox County Community Development Corporation   47
Cornucopia   53
The Christian Community Progress Corporation   59
Sisseton-Wahpeton Oyate Tokataya Ptewanuyanpi
   Ecahyapte   62
The Mexican American Council for Economic Progress   65
The Missouri Delta Ecumenical Ministry   72

2 EDUCATION   80

Break Free   82
The Center for Environmental Education   90
The "Now" People Program   93
The Harlem Consumer Education Council   97
The Patch   102
La Raza   105

Homemaker Skills   107
The Committee for a Comprehensive Education Center   112
Operation LIFT   117
The Watts Summer Festival   121
Tabernacle Tutorial   125
The Bi-Lingual Broadcasting Foundation   129
East Harlem Block Schools   133

3   EMPLOYMENT OPPORTUNITY   138

The Inner City Auto Repair and Training Center   146
Homeworkers Organized for More Employment   140
Urban Talent Development   150
The Epicurean Kitchen   156
Young People of Watts   161
Hispanic Rug Weaving   165
Miracle Workers   168
The Afro-Urban Institute   172
United Community Construction Workers   175
The Vocational Development Center for the Handicapped   179
Home, Inc   182
The SEMCAC Senior Services Program   185
Appalachian Craftsmen   188
SWEAT Associates   191
Community-Action-Newsreel   196
The Watts Job Clearing House   201
Urban Youth Action   204
United Graffiti Artists   208

4   HOUSING   214

The Roxbury Action Program   216
Operation Better Block   220
The Ocean Hill–Brownsville Tenants
   Association   224
Jeff-Vander-Lou, Inc.   229
Interfaith Adopt-a-Building   233
Menno Housing/Tabor Community Services   238

5   SOCIAL SERVICES   246

People United For Self-Help   248
Action House   252
Centro Mater   256

The Organization of People Engaged in the
  Neighborhood   261
The Portland American Indian Center   266
Women in Distress   270
The B.O.N.D. Community Crisis Center   274
The Southwest Community Enrichment Center   276
St. James Baptist Church   280
Youth For Service   284
Our Lady of Fatima Mission Center   289
The Help One Another Club   294

6 HEALTH SERVICES   298

Hope House   300
La Clinica de la Raza   305
The Community Care Association   309
The Green Bay Area Free Clinic   315
Hope Harbor   319
The People's Free Medical Clinic   324
St. Jude Home   327
Walden House   331
The Chicano Community Center   335

7 OFFENDER REHABILITATION   338

The New Directions Club   340
Job Therapy   350
Awareness   354
SCAN Volunteer Services   358
We Care   363
H.I.R.E.   366
Mother Goose   369
Project Inmate Human Rights   373
Operation SHARE   377
Social Advocates for Youth   381

8 COMMUNITY ORGANIZATION   388

The Tremé Community Improvement Association   390
The South Arsenal Neighborhood Development
  Corporation   395
The Allenville Water Company   398
The Davidson Community Center   403
The Scott Area Action Council   407
The Equal Justice Council   413

The Arkansas People's Corporation for Self Help   420
Block Partnership   424
The People's Club   429
Arkansas Community Organizations for Reform Now   434
Guadalupe Center   439
Virginia Assemblies   444
The Committee for Community Controlled Day Care   448
People's Free Way   452
The Afro-American Cultural Center   455
The Southern Mutual Help Association   458

Foreword

Martin Luther King Jr. used to say, "You can't expect people to pull themselves up by their own bootstraps when they haven't any boots." It was his way of telling affluent Americans of what it means to be poor and disadvantaged in this country. It was also his reminder to the poor indicating what they needed to start with to build a better life.

Dr. King would be pleased to see that the disadvantaged are indeed making great strides to become self-sufficient. People are learning to unite, to organize, and to find practical ways of meeting their own very pressing needs for jobs, for social services, for education, for better housing, etc. They are indeed learning to create their own "boots"—through creating hundreds of successful self-help projects in our inner cities and rural communities.

Although self-help necessarily involves a great deal of trial and error, it also leads inevitably to self-education. And the intrinsic value of the research presented here through Project UPLIFT is to encourage this educational process. For the first time, people involved in successful self-help efforts are sharing their experiences on a large scale to encourage others to follow in their footsteps and to help others to avoid their mistakes. Furthermore, we have here a means whereby society as a whole can gain new insights into the role it could play in assisting our disadvantaged citizens, while preserving the pride and dignity of all individuals.

M. CARL HOLMAN
President
The National Urban Coalition

Editorial Note

This book has been prepared—under a grant from the Office of Economic Opportunity to the United States Jaycees Foundation—by The Washington Consulting Group, Inc.

The book represents one phase of Project UPLIFT, an ongoing research effort to identify, analyze, and disseminate self-help program ideas throughout the United States in order to further the development of the self-help movement.

For additional information write to:

Project UPLIFT
The Washington Consulting Group, Inc.
1800 Wisconsin Avenue, N.W.
Washington, D.C. 20007

Preface

"Self-help" essentially means what people themselves can do. And what increasing numbers of disadvantaged people are now doing throughout the United States is developing and operating their own—nongovernment—projects to deal with the myriad problems that have long afflicted their communities.

New business enterprises, farm cooperatives, health clinics, job-training programs, drug and alcohol rehabilitation centers, housing programs, multi-purpose community organizations— these and other self-help projects demonstrate the remarkable achievements of small groups of people who, in the words of one self-help project leader, "had nothing . . . [and] went ahead and built on that."

The existence, let alone the success, of many such projects seems to have been largely unknown until very recently, not only to the public at large but also to people at all levels of government. What is more, there has been little communication among the self-help projects themselves, which means they have not had the opportunity to learn from one another's experience.

The principal purpose of this book, therefore, is to make all segments of society aware of both the scope and success of the burgeoning self-help movement, as well as to spur the development of new self-help projects and to help bring about a dialogue among the existing ones.

The book describes, in nontechnical language, one hundred of the most representative and successful self-help projects in existence. It is inevitable, though, that these stories have already been overtaken by progress, for the hallmark of the best self-help projects is their ability to adapt and change as needed. Nevertheless, it is hoped that an updated and expanded version of this book will be published in order to add the stories of other successful projects, and to keep the American people abreast of the growth and accomplishments of the self-help movement.

Acknowledgments

A number of people and organizations deserve special mention for their help in the preparation of this book.

We particularly wish to thank Alvin J. Arnett, director of the Office of Economic Opportunity, and Gary McNaught, director of the United States Jaycees Foundation, for their assistance.

A large measure of the credit for the initial phase of Project UP-LIFT belongs to the hundreds of Jaycees who spent considerable time and effort locating self-help programs in their communities.

A particular note of thanks goes to The Boys' Clubs of America, The Center for Community Change, The Committee on Religion in Appalachia, the National Association for the Advancement of Colored People, The National Center for Voluntary Action, The National Council of La Raza, The National Urban Coalition, Save the Children Federation, United Way, United Fund, and The Council of Eastern Native Americans.

Thanks also go to the more than sixty other regional and national service organizations that contributed their assistance.

We also wish to thank the members of Project UPLIFT's Review Board: Louis R. Bruce, co-director, The Council of Eastern Native Americans; Dr. Raul R. Cuadrado, chairman, Medical Technology and Health Services, Florida International University; Mrs. George W. Romney; Monsignor Geno C. Baroni, president, The National Center for Urban Ethnic Affairs; M. Carl Holman, president, The National Urban Coalition; Edward R. Lucero, chairman of the board, The Colorado Economic Development Association; Theresa F. Cummings, executive director, Springfield and Sangamon County [Ill.] Community Action, Inc.; and, Dennis E. Jordan, chairman, the United States Jaycees Foundation.

A note of thanks also goes to Development Alternatives, Inc., for its assistance in developing methodology and analyses.

We are also grateful to the many professional writers and photographers who supplied us with on-the-spot reports and pictures for the book, as well as to the editorial team headed by Steven R. Christensen, Paul Elliott, and William E. Howard.

And lastly we wish to acknowledge the contributions of the members of the hundreds of self-help projects included in our research efforts, and in particular the detailed help—and patience—of the one hundred projects described in this book.

Introduction

SUSAN A. DAVIS
Director, Project UPLIFT

The late President Franklin D. Roosevelt once remarked, "As new conditions and problems arise beyond the power of men and women to meet as individuals, it becomes the duty of the Government itself to find new remedies. . . ."

Although government has enjoyed a measure of success in improving the social conditions of most Americans, a number of problems affecting disadvantaged citizens seem too large or complex for government alone to correct.

But if these problems represent a bureaucratic frustration for public officials, they certainly constitute a very real difficulty for the more than 25 million disadvantaged Americans whose poverty is both product and producer of a social and economic environment that seems to offer little hope for solutions.

This difficulty is compounded by the fact that disadvantaged citizens are estranged or isolated from the mainstream of society. Their financial position is insecure, many of them live in homes that are substandard, they constitute the largest portion of the unemployed, and they have found the basic amenities of a healthy life to be a luxury. For them, the system—the mechanism that produces for most Americans a comfortable life of economic security, adequate housing, proper health care, and full employment—remains either a mystery or a mirage.

But disadvantaged people are not helpless. No contemporary view of poverty is complete unless you consider what is being done by a large number of people who want to move from the periphery of society into the mainstream. Their stories tell of the collective efforts of small groups of disadvantaged people getting together to solve their own problems. While their chronicles are widely separated by distance and type of activity, they all find some common ground in the understanding of what people themselves can do.

UPLIFT

Although members of the general public, as well as people in government, have long been aware of self-help initiatives undertaken by disadvantaged citizens, there has been no detailed information available until recently on the scope and success of the self-help movement. A number of elementary questions—such as how many self-help projects exist, how did they get started, how are they funded, how are they organized and for what purposes, who do they help, and how successful have they been?—had never been the subject of study or analysis.

UPLIFT, sponsored by the United States Jaycees Foundation, was launched in mid-1973 to begin to find answers to these and other questions about the self-help movement. As the initial phase, representative and successful self-help projects were selected for case study to provide a basis for identifying analyzing, and disseminating successful self-help program ideas throughout the United States.

The project was made possible by a grant from the Office of Economic Opportunity to the United States Jaycees Foundation. The research for the foundation was directed by The Washington Consulting Group, Inc., which also prepared this book.

UPLIFT's initial step of identifying ongoing self-help projects was accomplished by distributing some 10,000 project kits to the nearly 7,000 chapters of the United States Jaycees and to 75 other major service and community organizations across the nation. Using these kits, the organizations provided UPLIFT with data on close to one thousand self-help projects, together with information about the existence of many more.

Rather than simply publish its findings in statistical form, UPLIFT felt that the most effective way to provide both the general public and all levels of government with a clear understanding of the achievements and potential of the self-help movement would be to publish the stories of one hundred of the most representative and successful projects. Such an approach, it was thought, would also make it possible to at least suggest, if not pin down, some of the more elusive qualities of the projects and their members—such qualities as dedication and purpose, a sense of commitment, the ability to organize volunteers and programs, and the will to confront and overcome adversity.

In screening projects considered for this book, the UPLIFT staff was assisted by specialists in the field of social action.

Their combined recommendations were then submitted to a board of review, which made the final selection.

The one hundred projects discussed in this volume are intended to be representative of both the scope and success of the self-help movement. They serve in effect as representatives for the hundreds of other worthy projects that could not be included.

In order to structure the book for the convenience of the readers, the project accounts have been arranged according to eight functional areas, each of which is accorded a separate chapter: economic development, education, employment opportunity, housing, social services, health services, offender rehabilitation, and community organization.

It is important to realize, though, that many of the projects are active in more than one functional area. Furthermore almost all of them, in one way or another, contribute to the economic welfare of local residents.

Summary of Findings

A representative profile of successful self-help projects emerged from UPLIFT's research showing that, while unique in their approaches to common problems, successful self-help projects share a number of basic qualities.

To begin with, successful self-help projects may resemble federal and state anti-poverty programs, but their origins are rooted in independence. They are not substitutes for government programs; they are unique alternatives that have evolved as a way of meeting continuing and unsolved needs within a given community.

Almost without exception, the successful self-help projects reported in this study began as a result of meeting internal needs, rather than responding to outside intervention. Self-help projects have evolved in disadvantaged communities and they have done so in answer to disadvantaged needs, and at the direction of disadvantaged people.

Some self-help groups completely shun government support and its attendant controls. Others incorporate minimal government grants into their projects, but maintain a balance that heavily favors private support.

While government-instituted programs rely on paid staff, self-help projects more often rely on volunteers. (Analysis revealed that self-help projects utilize an average of seventeen volunteers for every paid worker.) And when many volunteers are willing to give their time to a project, it is an indication that the endeavor is valued by the community. Moreover, most of these volunteers, as well as the paid staff, come from the local neighborhoods, which means the projects have strong ties within their own communities and they can create roles and responsibilities for the people themselves.

Nearly all the projects were organized by persons living within the community they served. Strong leadership and the quality of the staff are particularly important in projects that have to deal with the policies of local officials in order to succeed.

The average operating period of the selected projects is close to five years so far. This means that these projects as a whole have had time-tested experience in overcoming problems of planning and financing, as well as of meeting continuing needs within their communities.

The analysis also revealed that the successful self-help project tends to be one having the following features:

• The enterprise is self-sustaining and is often a spur to the development of community programs.

• There are tangible benefits for the community (i.e., improved quality of life, more social services, increased employment opportunities, increased income, better health facilities, better housing.)

• The ratio of private to public monies is high.

• The project was community-initiated and remains community-controlled.

• There is significant cooperation and integration with other community organizations.

• There is effective leadership, effective use of volunteers, and sound fiscal management.

Summing up, the representative successful self-help project shows a strong reliance on volunteerism, independence, and a significant input from the disadvantaged themselves.

The Evolving Story of Self-Help

The first-year results of UPLIFT suggest that a great many low-income and other disadvantaged people recognize the potential that self-help holds for them. And the actual number of self-help projects in existence points to a self-help movement that promises to be the basis for significant social change.

It is crucial, therefore, to make sure that this change can be brought about without destroying the essential self-help characteristics of local individual initiative and independence.

Both fostering and preserving the self-help movement are related directly to the need for increased awareness, understanding, and cooperation among the various segments of society. The people in positions to give outside assistance to self-help projects need to be aware of the self-help organizations in their community and to know what these groups are seeking to accomplish.

This also requires a new attitude on the part of the many people involved in social action who mistakenly view self-help as a process of "letting the poor fend for themselves." Self-help needs links to sophistication; it needs to be sophisticated itself.

For their part, many disadvantaged people need to learn what resources are actually available to them, as well as how to mobilize these resources and how to form effective alliances with service organizations, churches, business, and government. They also need to know more about other successful projects within the self-help movement and to develop means of sharing experience, knowledge, and ideas with those other projects—as well as with disadvantaged communities not yet active in the self-help movement.

If people's abilities and social conditions are to be improved through self-help, and if the strengths of the self-help movement are to be preserved, then it is essential that the movement itself organize and support a coordinated national effort. Such an effort could, as some project members have suggested, include a national self-help service organization. Making full use of assistance from the private and public sectors, the self-help movement could, through its own service organization, play several important roles:

Public Awareness. The organization could conduct a nationwide campaign to make all segments of society aware of the potential of the self-help movement. The campaign would be a continuing effort designed to generate more interest in, and financial support for, self-help organizations.

Resource Materials. The organization could develop a resource unit to supply technical information as well as the "how to'' rudiments to people seeking to learn how to improve or begin projects. Based on the data already collected, manuals and training films could be developed to provide instruction and guidance in the development of each major functional type of self-help project.

Systems Bank. Projects need counseling by both outside experts and experienced project members in such matters as how and when to incorporate, fund-raising strategies, making and marketing products, and the techniques of community organizing. A systems bank operating on a regional basis could give the projects a ready source of expertise and guidance.

Funding. A self-help service organization could effectively work for the acquisition of funds from private and public sources to further the self-help movement.

Training Seminars. Training seminars of both a general and specialized nature could be organized as an effective way of sharing and communicating ideas. Such an undertaking would not only involve self-help project members as both teachers and participants, but would also be coordinated with the systems bank as needed.

It is imperative that the self-help movement be neither organized nor wholly serviced by government or any outside organization. Self-help projects are not—and cannot be—a rigid network of identical programs imposed on or handed to the people. The worth of the projects rests in their individuality and independence and natural growth within their local communities.

Some two centuries ago a number of disadvantaged American colonists, struggling under the British yoke, banded together and proved what people themselves can do. Today, as the United States nears its 200th birthday, it is appropriate for Americans to reconsider the past and future of their country. And in doing so, they would do well to reflect on the words of a 19th-century writer named Samuel Smiles:

"The spirit of self-help is the root of all genuine growth in the individual; and, exhibited in the lives of many, it constitutes the true source of national vigor and strength.''

UPLIFT

What People Themselves Can Do

CHAPTER 1

Economic Development

The United States is a divided nation. One segment consists of a well-to-do society enjoying the highest standard of living the world has ever known. The other is an impoverished society that bears a large proportion of the country's ills—a society of privation, deterioration, indifference, and neglect.

Closing the gap between the two societies has traditionally been an unattractive proposition to the middle and upper classes that control the country's supply of capital, technical know-how, and managerial experience. And many government programs to help build the other America have failed either because they tried to impose ready-made solutions or because they turned over implementation to local people who were too inexperienced.

A new approach has emerged in recent years—the self-help economic development project. Throughout the country, low-income and other disadvantaged people are setting up and managing their own enterprises, pooling their economic resources, determining their own priorities, and demonstrating that they can obtain and channel government and corporate assistance.

There are native Americans, for example, who, after relying for decades on white-controlled trading posts, are now operating their own cooperatives. There are rural blacks in Mississippi who have found that they can make money owning their own feed and supply corporation instead of being at the mercy of the local monopoly. There is the small Southern town where half of the black women were on welfare until a minority-controlled company was started that paid them decent wages.

Food and supply co-ops, minority-owned banks and credit unions, and craft enterprises—all of these demonstrate the potential of the self-help economic development project.

Most of America's economic power is still in the hands of the elite. But the small-scale economic development project in the hands of the local community is proving to be an effective tool for the members of the other America as they strive to gain a foothold in the marketplace.

*It was time to become part of America. We
wanted to have some voice in the community. We
wanted to better our conditions. And by uniting
together we felt like we might be able to.*

Humphreys County Union for Progress Farmers Cooperative

Belzoni, Mississippi

A farmers' cooperative that started in a tiny backroom office is helping rural blacks in the Mississippi delta break the chains of economic servitude that have been their lot since the Civil War.

Operating with little government aid, the Humphreys County Union for Progress and its cooperative have brought a previously unknown degree of economic security to almost a hundred farm families. They have provided the things that many Mississippi black farmers have been used to not having—credit, reasonably priced supplies and fertilizers, equipment and machinery, and a more stable market and earnings for their crops.

On the map, and in spirit, Humphreys County lies deep within the Mississippi delta, some 70 miles northwest of Jackson. Two-thirds of its 14,600 residents are black and most of them live on farms or in small communities. The largest community, Belzoni, has only about 3,200 inhabitants. Agriculture is the main source of income for half of Humphreys County's people. According to the 1970 census, however, only 119 blacks are farmowners, and their land holdings average only 40 to 80 acres per unit. These owners are supposedly on the top of the black economic ladder in the county, yet their median income was only $862 in 1969; a man could earn more working in the underwear factory in Belzoni or as a truck driver on a big plantation.

Twenty-five years ago the economic opportunities for blacks in Humphreys County were even worse. In those days, soon after World War II, a number of blacks left the county to look for work in the cities, especially Northern cities. But some men, such as Ernest White, remained, hanging on to the small farms they owned and struggling to keep their families together. White attempted to build up his farm, but fought against heavy odds. In 1954, at a time when many whites were still unwilling to see blacks participate in the electoral process, White registered to vote. The result was that he lost his bank credit, and then had his name removed from the voter rolls. Despite these difficulties, he managed to develop his property into a well-run, 120-acre farm. But the white-controlled Humphreys County cooperative never asked him—or any other black farmer—to join.

Time passed, and conditions in Humphreys County did not improve appreciably.

So five years ago, Ernest White and a few other black community leaders in the county decided to organize. In White's words:

"It was time to become a part of America. We wanted to have some voice in the community. We wanted to better our conditions. And by uniting together we felt like we might be able to."

Humphreys County blacks began organizing on a formal basis, with some help from the Mississippi Action for Community Education of Greenville, which helped train two fieldworkers to canvass the county and enroll members.

Some 850 members were enrolled by the end of 1969 in a new organization that became known as the Humphreys County Union for Progress (HCUP).

At the time that HCUP was organized, the black farmers in the county were having problems obtaining both farm supplies and loans. What is more, they were also being forced to pay very high prices for what supplies they did manage to get.

The members of HCUP discussed the problem at length. Ten of them, including Ernest White, met in December 1969 to discuss one possible approach: the creation of their own cooperative. They had many reservations and some fears about their business ability and lack of experience, but against those drawbacks they weighed the advantages to be gained from a collective effort that would help them acquire both economic and political power. The group sought legal assistance from the North Mississippi Rural Legal Services (funded by the Office of Economic Opportunity), and in March 1970 the cooperative was formally chartered as the Humphreys County Union for Progress Farmers Cooperative.

The cooperative began with somewhat limited resources—a $950 loan from the Greenville community group, 80 farmer members, plus an experienced fieldworker, an accountant, and an office manager. It carried on its business out of a backroom in a building rented by HCUP. Fertilizer, seed, and other supplies were kept in a member's barn.

With $450 from the first loan, the cooperative bought stock in the Mississippi Chemical Corporation of Yazoo, both to be able to purchase fertilizer and also to obtain the rebates that are part of the delta farming system—a part previously limited to whites.

Even with that small investment, the cooperative saved its members $6 a ton on ammonium nitrate, in addition to obtaining the patronage rebate. These kinds of savings were persuasive evidence. "We would go from community to community," recalls Ernest White, "and show the farmers what they could do if they united together and the savings that they could make if they combined their efforts."

The co-op had a remarkably successful first year. It handled sales of $35,000 in supplies and products to the farmers, and it ended the year with a $2,500 profit.

Determined to expand its activities, the co-op secured $20,000 from a private foundation and set about establishing its own storage and warehouse buildings, plus offices for the co-op and the Humphreys County Union for Progress. The members used $6,000 to buy a site in Belzoni, and then spent $10,000 to build a 5,000-square-foot structure for crop and fertilizer storage.

An arrangement was made whereby almost all the farmer members would keep half their rebates in the co-op to fall back on in a bad crop year. That decision paid off in 1972. With late rains and floods, the harvests of both cotton and soybeans were way below normal levels. The co-op had a paper debt of $22,000. Its fertilizer surplus provided the margin for survival. It sold $11,000-worth of fertilizers to co-ops in neighboring counties, and so weathered the year with total sales of $46,518 and rebates and earnings of $5,487.

Despite the 1972 setback, the co-op's annual sales figures were good. The high point was reached in 1973, when the organization achieved a $7,100 profit on sales of $55,000. The profits, as usual, were distributed among the members, largely in patronage rebates.

Beyond the co-op's balance sheet are the individual co-op members. Consider, for example, the experience of a typical small farmer, Tommy Nalls.

A 40-year-old father of ten, Nalls has managed, thanks to the cooperative, to buy a mechanical cotton picker.

"If the cotton is just right," he says, "I can pick as much cotton in a day as we used to pick by hand in a month. My family appreciates it, too, because there's no more bending over. That's a job—bending over picking cotton."

For farmer Nalls' account books there are benefits too. As he says, "I can get it much cheaper here [at the co-op]. I buy fertilizer, oil for my tractors and picker, cottonseed, and poisons.

"Fertilizer cost me $59 in the co-op, and then I get the $12 rebate. In town I would have paid $63 and no rebate."

Securely on its feet now, the co-op is branching out into other ventures. It has established a store in the predominately black community of Louise, offering staple food items and vegetables at a 5-percent discount to co-op members. And it has set up a record shop in Belzoni, where young people can buy tapes and records at discount prices.

There are more ambitious plans for the future. The co-op, for example, hopes to launch a supermarket in Belzoni, and to build bulk liquid-fertilizer storage facilities.

It will take time before the co-op can put together all the money it needs for those and other plans. What it has established in abundant supply now is self-assurance among its members.

And economic power has led to growing political power. The fear that made blacks take their names off the voting lists twenty years ago is gone. Today, blacks are running for county and city offices, as well as voting for them.

"We haven't won," Ernest White says, "but we have a political voice now, and we expect to use it."

Money saved from the co-op will allow farmers to repair their houses.

*We began on a wing and a prayer. No funds,
no experience—just enthusiasm.*

The Franklin Dairy Co-op

Detroit, Michigan

• A mother with seventeen children buys her weekly supply of dairy products—including thirty-four half-gallons of milk—for $22.82.

• A retired factory worker is now able to afford not only milk but real orange juice on his limited monthly income.

• Fresh eggs and enough milk for five growing children are on the weekly menu of a mother trying to stretch her welfare check.

All of these Detroiters have something in common. They are inner-city black residents who shop at the Franklin Dairy Co-op—and all are happy to see their food dollar go so far.

The co-op opens its doors each Wednesday. It is manned by volunteers who sell milk, eggs, cheese, and other products at reduced prices. If the mother of seventeen children had purchased the same amount of milk at one of the small neighborhood grocery stores in the area, she figures it would have cost her over $30—more than 25 percent above what she paid at the co-op.

The co-op has the benefit of occupying rent-free quarters in the Franklin Settlement building, an old Victorian structure in the middle of Detroit's prime poverty area. It is an area of narrow streets and rundown buildings situated between the downtown business area and a wall of highrises erected under an urban renewal program, with scattered gaps of cleared spaces awaiting low-income housing to be built someday.

Until the co-op started, residents of the area were wholly dependent for food on small, family-owned stores. And the small stores, because of low sales volume and high losses, put a high markup on their goods. The people had little choice as to where they bought food, for the supermarket chains had already begun moving their stores out toward the city's boundaries and beyond.

Complaints about high prices in low-income areas won the attention of the Mayor's Committee for Human Resource Development (MCHRD), as the city's anti-poverty agency is known, in 1968. The agency made a decision to help launch a cooperative food store to serve the people of the Franklin Settlement area.

Jeanice Edwards was called upon to put the self-help project together. In twenty years of community involvement, she had gained a reputation for always being on hand to round up food, clothing, or a place to stay for a family in need. She also knew how to round up volunteers.

She organized some volunteer help, and they were soon making decisions on work schedules, store hours, and finding a dairy supplier. Some of them thought home delivery was essential, at least for the elderly, but that idea was discarded as impractical.

"We began on a wing and a prayer. No funds, no experience—just enthusiasm," recalls Jeanice Edwards.

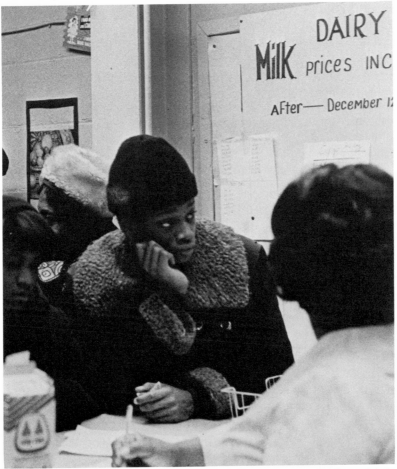

Bargains bring shoppers to Detroit's Franklin Dairy Co-op. Complaints about high prices in low-income areas prompted the local cooperative food store to offer quality dairy products at cut-rate prices.

The newly founded co-op did have one advantage, though. The free operating space on the first floor of the Franklin Settlement meant no rent, no utility bills, and no overhead.

Like any business, the co-op found some routines workable and others not. One of the first lessons it learned was that a good check doesn't always go with an honest face. The organizers voted unanimously for strictly cash transactions, plus the use of food stamps.

Bookkeeping presented more headaches. From the beginning the co-op kept business records, but did not treat the matter with great importance. Consequently it was a shock when bills began to pile up faster than they could be paid. The solution was to assign a salaried MCHRD community worker to keep the books.

Having established a good dairy products line, the co-op decided to expand its operations in 1970, with the introduction of vegetables to be sold on the same bulk-buying basis. This experiment, though, was not destined to succeed. Women volunteers could not cart heavy sacks of potatoes and other vegetables from the produce terminal to the co-op. Furthermore, as the rising prices of fresh commodities filtered down to the nation's stores— and the co-op—the demand for fresh vegetables tapered off. Consequently the co-op ended its vegetable sales in June 1973.

At one point some customers began returning spoiled milk to the store. It was then that the shoppers and the co-op workers discovered that the dairy was bringing them unsold products that had been removed from other stores. The co-op acted quickly, and soon made arrangements for delivery with another dairy.

Satisfaction with present service and an absence of major problems—other than the universal one of rising prices—have been the picture since then. Jeanice Edwards says unhappily that she has had to call several meetings to shift prices upward.

Funds available through federal programs were an attractive idea to the co-op participants, and they applied for and received two federal grants in 1972. And a $435 grant from the New Detroit Committee, Inc. bought a mimeograph to help fill a stipulation in one of the federal grants that the co-op assist consumer education by distributing hints, budgets, and bulletins about food.

The feeling that the co-op is a true neighborhood operation persists as some families forced to move by urban renewal return to shop there. The Franklin Dairy Co-op means more than dairy products to the people of inner-city Detroit. Assessing the co-op's effectiveness over the past six years, the director of Franklin Settlement says he finds people who shop at the co-op take advantage of other services at the Franklin center. In a neighborhood where people can watch their past disappear with the swing of demolition cranes, the co-op and the settlement serve as gathering places to reestablish common bonds.

And seeing the results in grocery savings is real proof it can and does pay to market cooperatively.

Members talk optimistically of expanding their operation to canned goods, produce, toilet articles, and even clothing. But government budget cuts threaten further funding, as well as MCHRD's ability to provide free room, utilities, and bookkeeping.

There may be a new struggle ahead. But Jeanice Edwards believes the co-op is too well established to go out of business. As she says, "There are always ways of finding floor space rent free or at low cost when you have something the people really need."

I sat around for years looking at my family, and wondering how my people were going to make it. . . . I think this Tract cooperative will help us out because it's something we can do.

Tract Handcrafts

Webster, South Dakota

The old fashioned quilting bee is bringing new prosperity to a hard-pressed area of South Dakota.

"Orders are pouring in every day," says Gladys Knudson, president of Tract Handcrafts, Inc. And she adds, happily, "We have to keep hiring more and more people to take care of the backlog."

The orders are for handmade quilts, and they are being placed by 350 major department stores around the country. The high-quality colorful patchworks come in thirty-eight distinctive designs, ranging from contemporary to traditional Sioux, German, Russian, and Scandinavian—designs that reflect the heritages of the women who are making them now in Day, Marshall, and Roberts counties, in the northeastern part of the state.

Since production began in 1971, the quilts have grossed more than $650,000 for the quilt makers, all of whom are from low-income families; 20 percent of them, including Gladys Knudson, are residents of the Lake Traverse Indian Reservation of the Sisseton-Wahpeton tribe of the Sioux Indians.

Tract Handcrafts owes its existence to a series of events that began with an economic survey of the area undertaken in December 1970 by a tri-county resource and development program funded by the Office of Economic Opportunity. Robert Pearson, who was one of the program's coordinators, says attempts had already been made to attract outside industry to the area. But they had failed.

"We decided instead," he says, "to concentrate on working with what was already here—the native skills of the people—and to find and develop a market for those talents."

One of the VISTA (Volunteers in Service to America) people assisting in the survey, George Whyte, noticed that many of the women, both Indian and non-Indian, were skilled quilt makers.

"I was fascinated by the artistry of the designs," he says, "but also with the care and workmanship evident in their creations."

Whyte started by organizing a series of meetings to determine whether the women wanted to join a quilt-making cooperative. He was surprised by the turnout in Webster and seven other small communities. Altogether more than 500 women showed up, including Gladys Knudson, whose age and lack of formal training would have prevented her finding a job in most other industries.

At the meeting in Webster, she said: "I sat around for years looking at my family, and wondering how my people were going to make it. Everything just seemed to get harder for us, no matter how hard we tried. I think this Tract cooperative will help us out because it's something we can do."

Gladys Knudson's decision to donate her time and sewing machine to get the project rolling inspired others at the meeting. Before long, every sewing machine in the area was donated or loaned to the fledgling cooperative.

Whyte, Pearson, and the local junior chamber of commerce were quick to gauge the extent of community support, and they spent weeks canvassing other businessmen, civic clubs, and churches for building space. They also took the initiative in working out certain basics, such as establishing the membership as a nonprofit cooperative, soliciting funds for larger machinery, and searching for a market.

The quilts that Whyte had seen during the survey had been pieced together from parts of other household articles—drapery, linens, and used clothing. These recycled fabrics were not plentiful or consistent enough to use in large-scale manufacturing. To provide for a large and ready supply of materials, the Northeast South Dakota Community Action Program transferred $38,000 to Tract Handcrafts.

A concerted drive by five churches netted Tract $19,000 in less than six months. In addition the American Lutheran Church made a grant of $20,000. All of the money collected in 1971, the first year, was spent on wages and materials.

Buyers proved to be much harder to obtain than materials. In June 1971, Pearson and Whyte took a traveling quilt display to the major Eastern department stores in an attempt to establish outlets for Tract's wares. It was a frustrating experience. The buyers at the stores would not see the quilts or the Tract men. "As we now know," Pearson says, "unless the product's name is well-known, or the buyer knows the representative personally or by reputation, there is no opportunity to do business."

Stopping by Dayton's in Minneapolis, Minnesota, on their return trip, Pearson and Whyte managed to impress the sales manager of the store with their display. Still, no sale was made in that the store's buyer was on vacation.

Several weeks later Dayton's sales manager phoned Pearson and advised him to contact a prominent manufacturer's representative, Park B. Smith, of New York. Pearson was told that Tract could be assured of success if Smith took them as a client.

"Naturally, we had our doubts after our experience with the stores. But we had nothing to lose, and called him. It proved to be the most fortunate contact we ever made," says Whyte.

Park Smith arrived in South Dakota on Labor Day, 1971. He liked what he saw, and he spent four days with the Tract staff evaluating their organization and planning two products displays for a New York exhibition in November. Smith was skeptical that Tract would be able to meet the November deadline.

Smith explained that the New York market showings attract both American and foreign buyers who come to select merchandise for the next season and to see what is new in home furnishings. In anticipation of the crowd of buyers, the Tract members voted unanimously to change their corporate status from non-profit to profit.

The next four weeks in the work center were hectic. Tract borrowed $25,000 from the local community development corporation for materials. "They worked tirelessly, day and night, just to meet the show deadline. It was exhausting and beautiful labor to behold," recalls Pearson.

Tract's quilts were not only presented at the show but they were a great hit. *Home Furnishings Daily*, a trade newspaper, said: "The freshest idea in home furnishings in 100 years."

Over $50,000-worth of Tract merchandise was ordered at the show by some of the country's best department stores, and one such store, Lord & Taylor's of New York, gave the collection one of the biggest promotions in the store's history.

This New York success was a fine debut for a group that had such a difficult time making inroads into a seemingly closed market. Tract's perseverance—and good luck—had paid off.

Tract Handcrafts managed to break even in 1972, with orders totaling $260,000. In 1973, buttressed by $150,000 in Small Business Administration loans, Tract reached $400,000 in sales.

There remains a constant need for working capital to fill in the gap between production costs and payment for merchandise, but the staff and workers are optimistic.

"I'm very confident of the future," Whyte says, "I think within two years we will be the largest quilted bedspread manufacturer in the United States. It's destiny, given the dedication of the workers."

The Self Help Action Center is something else.
It's for those who cannot afford the frills
but need the food.

The Self Help Action Center

Chicago, Illinois

One hot July afternoon a pair of farmers drove into the parking lot of Antioch Missionary Baptist Church with a pickup truck half-filled with eggs, fruit, and vegetables.

An hour later the truck was empty, and the farmers had $300 in their pockets, nearly twice what they would have received for the same produce at a regular farm market. And the dozen or so Chicago families who bought the food spent more than $175 less than they would have in the supermarket.

This impromptu food fair in 1968 was strictly an experiment. But it was the start of what has grown into a remarkable food-for-the-poor program organized as the Self Help Action Center (SHAC). This nonprofit Chicago group carries cooperative buying to the ultimate—eliminating not just some but *all* the middlemen who make up the food price chain between barnyard and city dinner tables.

Starting with the Antioch Missionary Baptist Church, SHAC has formed hundreds of food-buying clubs that deal directly with small farmers in the Chicago area. The chief organizer of the clubs is Dorothy Shavers, a former teacher, who conducts food fairs around the city, bringing organizations into contact with farmers who want to sell to them directly. Like the city folks who feel they are paying too much at the store, the farmers feel they are being shortchanged by the middlemen.

"We're not against supermarkets and the middleman," Dorothy Shavers adds. "There is nothing wrong with a wide selection of prepared, portioned, and packaged food, neat aisles, uniformed checkout girls and delivery-boy convenience. That's great for those who can afford it. It provides a lot of jobs, as checkout girls and delivery boys, for poor people.

"The Self Help Action Center is something else. It's for those who cannot afford the frills but need the food."

The SHAC idea dates back to 1966, when Paul Horvat, a Slovenian immigrant who had come to the United States fourteen years earlier, watched a television news report about small Midwestern farmers burning their crops in protest against low prices. On the same show he heard black militants complain about the high prices in Chicago's inner-city markets.

Horvat, then 65 years old, had recently retired from the day-to-day operation of an enormously successful landscaping business he had built up in just ten years. So he had the time to see what could be done about these two seemingly unrelated food-supply conditions.

What Horvat found when he visited small farmers and the inner-

Dorothy Shavers, the chief organizer of SHAC's food-buying clubs.

city poor startled him. It was a situation nearly identical to one that had landed him in jail (for the first of several stays) as a teenager before World War I in what is now Yugoslavia.

"It was like in my old country fifty years ago and more," he explains. "The farmers in my village of Bratonei were paid one dinar for the apples in their orchards. But the city people were paying as much as ten dinar for the same apples. What happened to the nine dinars? They went to the man who owned a cart and carried the apples to town. Communications were not so good then, and nobody in the village knew what happened in the city. It was the sort of abusive treatment that made Communism sound good to the peasants."

As a teenager, Horvat organized the neighboring farmers to carry their own fruit and vegetables to market, where they collected five and six times what they had been paid by produce buyers. That worked well until the buyers complained to the police, and Horvat, as the ringleader of the farmers' action, was jailed for two weeks. Thus began a long and colorful career of political dissidence in which Horvat was twice condemned to death, only to escape each time, and served in the underground during World War II before finally fleeing Eastern Europe for the United States.

Horvat's curiosity of 1966 persisted. Off and on for two years he traveled from ghetto to farm to ghetto, studying the familiar, parallel problems. On vacation trips to Florida he stopped along the way and talked to farmers, always finding them struggling with the economic dilemma of modern farming—get bigger or get out!

Horvat was at home in the farming communities. But in Chicago's mostly black inner-city areas, he encountered more suspicion and hostility than he had expected. Still he kept going back, visiting different neighborhoods each week, meeting civic leaders and ministers, ward politicians and businessmen.

"Do you know that within twenty miles of where we are standing there are farmers who cannot find decent markets for their food?" he was fond of asking.

One of those who listened in 1968 was the Reverend Wilbert Daniels, pastor of the Antioch Missionary Baptist Church. "Okay," the minister agreed one day, "let's see you get those farmers of yours in here with some of that food. We'll sell it right off the church parking lot."

It was as much a challenge as it was an invitation.

Two weeks later Horvat arrived with his two farmers and their half-loaded pickup truck. The congregation of the church followed up by forming a co-op food club to buy from the same two farmers every two weeks.

Suddenly, before he had even thought of a name for the program, it was launched. Horvat had found the device necessary to bring farmers and hungry city people together.

At the time of the first parking lot fair, Dorothy Shavers was working as a special education teacher in the public schools.

"I knew that many of the retardation problems that I was dealing with were caused by prenatal malnutrition of the mother," she explains. "So when I heard about what Mr. Horvat was doing I got in touch and offered to work for the program, at first just on Saturdays."

She was exactly the boost the program needed—a black woman to establish almost instant credibility in the black communities that were Horvat's primary target areas. An unexpected benefit turned out to be a handful of black farmers that she knew in the Kankakee area. They helped enhance the program's first impression at food fairs in black areas.

Dale Wittner

In the more than four years since becoming a full-time SHAC worker, Dorothy Shavers has produced from four to eight food fairs a month, usually under the auspices of a church, a block club, a community center, a parent-teachers' association, or some other organization. If these demonstrations elicit an interested response, she returns with a second show a week or two later, and then attempts to recruit the leadership for a food co-op.

If one is formed, she undertakes to give a four-week training course tutoring volunteers in the operation of a co-op. Over the years many co-ops have gone out of business soon after starting for lack of sustained volunteer workers or other essential resources—hence the special emphasis on training.

Of the hundred or so clubs begun under SHAC auspices that have survived, more than two-thirds are now independent, having established their own farm contacts. This is SHAC's goal. On the average there are fifteen to twenty young co-ops not fully independent but in the process of making their own buying contacts. The remaining fifteen or so are totally dependent on SHAC, relying on Paul Horvat and Dorothy Shavers to handle all farm negotiations and transactions, including problems with food stamps.

But even where SHAC acts as a third party in the transaction, meticulous care is taken to avoid any increase in price to consumer co-ops. What the farmer charges is what the co-op pays, no more. The same is true when ordering must be done from the commercial market in winter. SHAC never adds a markup.

SHAC was incorporated in 1972, and Horvat personally underwrote all costs until 1972. That year the Freedom from Hunger Foundation contributed $17,100 to provide a paid staff. Dorothy Shavers worked for a full year without salary after resigning her teacher's appointment. Even now the annual payroll for director Shavers, a secretary, and two farm organizers is less than $25,000.

From June 1972 through October 1973 the center's costs were covered by the Freedom from Hunger Foundation grant and an additional $10,000 from the Campaign for Human Development. The Illinois Human Resources Commission contributed $1,100, and miscellaneous other contributions added another $900.

But as the program expanded, increasing in volume from $195,000 to $443,000, it became clear that its best chance of survival was not in annual funding appeals that would leave SHAC dependent on foundation grants. Instead an appeal was made to Catholic Charities of the Archdiocese of Chicago, which, in October 1973, just as the last of the grant money was running out, agreed to take over all administrative costs, including salaries.

Looking back over her years with the program, Dorothy Shavers concedes: "There have been discouraging times. Like the morning I went down to the storage room and found it had been broken into again. This time the burglars took 180 cases of eggs. Do you know how many eggs that is? It's 64,800 eggs—over $4,000 worth even at our price. Well, first I cried. Then I called all the buying clubs and told them to get ready for an eggless week. Then I got my sense of humor back and called the police. I told them to be on the lookout for thieves with high cholesterol and egg on their faces.

"But seriously, it's the good times—the smiles and the laughs and the *happy* tears—that I remember, not the bad times."

Dale Wittner

Because of our success in running the village, we
knew we could do bigger things.

Kah-Nee-Ta Vacation Resort

Warm Springs Indian Reservation, Oregon

The tribal council of the Warm Springs Indian Reservation was wrestling with a very difficult decision. The federal government had just awarded the 1,800 members of the tribe a total of $4 million for the loss of their Columbia River salmon-fishing grounds, which were disappearing for good under the rising waters of the reservoir of a new hydroelectric power dam.

What should they do with the money?

They knew that other tribes receiving reparations for lost fishing rights were dividing up all the money among their members. But Warm Springs' tribal manager, Vernon Jackson, argued against taking such a course. He wanted to put the money in a bank and use it to develop alternate economic resources that would benefit the entire tribe. Other council members disagreed.

"Vern had terrific opposition," recalls the present manager, Kenneth Smith. "There was tremendous pressure on the council to distribute it all as a dividend."

Ultimately the council members arrived at a compromise. They decided to distribute $1 million to the members and put the other $3 million in the bank.

This has proved to be a farsighted decision, for since that fateful day in 1958 the residents of Warm Springs Indian Reservation have achieved considerable success in the world of business. Investment of the banked money, together with effective use of their human resources, have given the Indians several flourishing enterprises that now provide employment for many tribal members and generate a total payroll of more than $5 million annually. The profits are being used for child care, education, housing improvement, rehabilitation of alcoholics, and other programs aimed at promoting tribal welfare.

The Indians own and run:

● Warm Springs Forest Products Industries, a lumber mill purchased for $4.9 million in 1967 with the help of a bank loan

● The Warm Springs Sub-Assembly Plant, where electronic components are assembled for major industrial corporations

● Kah-Nee-Ta Vacation Resort, a complex of cottages and other facilities built around bubbling hot springs, plus a recently completed 90-room convention lodge, valued at a total of more than $6 million

Two earlier steps enabled the tribe to make good use of its government award. The first, in 1938, was incorporating as the Confederated Tribes of the Warm Springs Reservation. "Incorporation gave us the necessary tools to handle our own affairs," says Smith, "placing the Bureau of Indian Affairs in an advisory position rather than telling us what to do."

The second step came in 1958, while the decision was pending on what to do with the reparations money. The tribal council commissioned Oregon State University to do a detailed study of the reservation's human and natural resources. The university study made it clear that the Indians needed to embark on a plan for economic development.

The tribal council, in considering economic possibilities, decided to buy back a small resort that had been built on the reservation at the hot springs 11 miles north of the town of Warm Springs. A physician who had worked at the reservation had bought the site from the Indians in 1935 for $3,500. He had erected a small lodge complete with bathing pool, which came to be patronized by people with medical ailments who believed in the curative powers of the hot springs.

The repurchase question was put to a general vote in 1963, and the members approved the idea—although the price of the property was now $165,000.

Next the council proposed spending $750,000 to expand the resort. This idea, though, was turned down by the members in another election held to resolve the matter.

"Our people didn't want to open our reservation to the public," recalls Smith. But Vernon Jackson was a persuasive manager, and his renewed campaign in favor of the development resulted in victory in a second tribal election.

"We opened in 1964 and have been financially successful since," says Smith. "Presently, we have an investment of $1 million in the Kah-Nee-Ta Village complex, which consists of thirty-one cottages, bathhouses, three pools, a restaurant, snack bar, house trailer space, camping area, picnicking area, miniature golf course, craft shop, riding stable, and twenty-one teepees."

Teepees? "Large, handcrafted, they may be rented to accommodate as many as ten occupants each," a promotional brochure explains. Designed to lure the non-Indian tourist, it goes on:

"These are traditional Indian teepees, with a wood floor and fire pit in the center. Dew flaps around the sides control extremes of temperature, summer or winter. The teepees require the use of sleeping bags and camping facilities, but they may be securely closed at night."

Neither traditional teepees nor modern trailer homes are out of place at Kah-Nee-Ta Village. As the brochure stresses, "Every effort has been made to combine modern and pleasant vacation facilities with the colorful culture of the tribes."

The combination has been successful, attracting visitors from many parts of the country. But within a few years of its opening, the tribal council had begun to realize, as Ken Smith says, "that the resort was profitable, but it was rather seasonal." This meant that the profits were seasonal, as well as that the employees were without jobs in the winter.

The tribal manager, Vern Jackson, had an idea. He had read a study showing that Oregon was in need of facilities to handle conventions of 200–300 people for between three and five days. So why not an addition to Kah-Nee-Ta Village aimed at catering to the convention business? After all, conventions are held at all times of the year, and what better place than an Indian reservation with a dry and sunny climate. And year-round operation would mean year-round earnings and year-round employment.

"Because of our success in running the village," says Smith, "we knew we could do bigger things."

The bigger thing turned out to be a 90-room convention and resort hotel called Kah-Nee-Ta Lodge, about a mile down the Warm Springs River from the village. It was opened in June 1972. Unfortunately the man who had conceived the idea did not live to see its realization; Vern Jackson died in 1969.

The lodge was built at a total cost of $6.2 million, with $5 million of that being financed through a loan and a grant from the Economic Development Administration (EDA). It is an eyecatching building made largely of wood (much of it coming from Warm Springs' own lumber mill), with a full complement of meeting rooms, lounges, dining rooms, and so on. There are also outdoor facilities, including tennis courts, a golf course, a semi-enclosed swimming pool, and hiking trails.

The lodge did not prove to be an immediate financial success. Largely because of slack times in the convention business, the lodge did not meet expenses in 1973. Nevertheless Ken Smith is confident that it will succeed.

His fellow Indians at Warm Springs all share his confidence. In

December of 1973 they voted $1.6 million in funds for an expansion program. This will be combined with a second EDA grant of $600,000 to add 55 guest rooms to the hotel and enlarge the main banquet room and cocktail lounge, as well as to build four new tennis courts and lengthen the golf course to 18 holes. Smith says the expansion will enable the resort to handle both large and small conventions.

The Kah-Nee-Ta Vacation Resort—which encompasses both the village and the lodge—has given the Indians of Warm Springs an opportunity to broaden their economic base and tap the Pacific Northwest's tourist trade potential. More importantly, perhaps, it has given them the opportunity to develop their managerial and business skills, and thereby contribute actively to the general welfare of the confederated tribes.

Kah-Nee-Ta Lodge is a year-round hotel and convention center.

*I think part of our success was that we didn't try
to start big, didn't try to take on too much at once.
We felt our way along pretty slowly at first,
learning the tricks of the trade.*

The Warm Springs
Sub-Assembly Plant

Warm Springs Indian Reservation, Oregon

The sparsely populated semidesert of central Oregon, on the eastern flanks of the Cascade Range some 60 miles southeast of Portland, is an unlikely place for an electronics plant.

More unlikely to an outsider is that the plant is run by a 33-year-old reservation-born Indian with only one year of college. But this situation seems unlikely even to the supervisor himself, Everett Miller, who had planned to be a diesel mechanic.

Yet this enterprise with Miller at the helm does indeed flourish —in a former dairy barn on the Warm Springs Indian Reservation.

The reservation is 564,000 acres of mostly rock and juniper, set aside in 1855 for the Wasco and Warm Springs tribes. The land is too dry to farm, too dry for much of anything except marginal stock-raising—a gift of the white man to the Indians.

Making any kind of living in such a setting is difficult. But the Indians are as resourceful as they are industrious. In 1964 the tribal council opened Kah-Nee-Ta Village, the nucleus of what has become the Kah-Nee-Ta Vacation Resort, which caters principally to non-Indian visitors.

But the resort is 11 miles from the town of Warm Springs, where most of the reservation's 1,800 Indians live. Commuting is a problem for mothers who need employment and have the additional responsibility of caring for small children.

In the late 1960s the tribal council was becoming increasingly worried about many of these women who headed households. Some were being forced to resort to public welfare to support themselves and their families.

"They were widowed, or perhaps the father was crippled and no longer could work," Miller says. The problem was aggravated by the fact that some frustrated mothers were turning to alcohol.

Casting around for a solution, one member of the 11-man tribal council suggested starting a manufacturing enterprise.

"There was some talk," says Miller, "of an umbrella factory." That fell through, though, and the council turned to Tektronix in Portland, broaching the seemingly wild idea of a subplant in Warm Springs. Tektronix is one of the nation's leading manufacturers of oscilloscopes. The firm is noted for the high quality of its product, achieved by rigid quality control on the production line.

In September 1968 the land use and industrial development committee of the tribal council met in Portland with Tektronix officials, and a month later the Tektronix officials met with the council in Warm Springs. On December 15, 1968, the firm agreed to a one-year trial of a subassembly plant on the reservation.

The tribe at this point didn't even have a place to put it. "There was really only one building that was available," says Miller.

That was the old barn, 50 feet by 30 feet, which had been the machine shop for the reservation's utilities department.

The tribal council loaned its new enterprise—the Warm Springs Sub-Assembly Plant—$10,000 to remodel the structure. Workbenches were built and intensive lighting put in. Air conditioning was installed. "We paid back the loan within the first year and haven't borrowed since," Miller says proudly.

To learn how to assemble the components the new plant was to produce, Miller and two reservation women—Maxine McKinley and Adeline Miller—went to Portland to be trained. They became part of Tektronix's trainee class at no cost to the company. To pay for their travel and expenses, the council appropriated $2,000.

Upon their return from Portland, Adeline Miller recalls, "We hired five ladies and started teaching them, one thing at a time." That was February 10, 1969, when the plant opened.

During 1969 the work force grew to an average of thirteen. The figure was fifteen during 1970 and 1971, leaping to twenty-seven during 1972, and dropping back to twenty-three during 1973.

The employees, all women but for Everett Miller, range in age from 19 to 55. They have all had at least some schooling, ranging from the fifth-grade level to college. Their pay scale at the reservation plant ranges from $1.75 to $2.43 per hour.

Miller has been fortunate in having had a generally stable work force in the plant's formative years. He says one of his employees who has a serious nervous problem is nevertheless successful at the plant. Another who came to work with a drinking problem "has kind of straightened out and is doing pretty well."

Indeed, in the first three years of operation there were only two "turnovers"—Miller's euphemism for firing. The stability of the work force was exceptional until late 1972, when there were a number of "turnovers," many due to absenteeism.

During that critical year of 1972, the plant lost $4,847 compared with a loss of $1,769 in 1971 and a profit of $16,109 in 1970.

"I had given them [the workers] a raise because of inflation, and we had twenty-seven employees, the most we've ever had," Miller says. Profits skidded to losses—"I really don't know what happened," he says, but he made a drastic managerial decision. He slashed the work force to seven.

Gradually it was restored to an average of twenty-three during 1973, when the plant turned $15,000 in profits over to the council.

The Warm Springs Sub-Assembly Plant has been most successful in producing oscilloscope components for Tektronix. And that success has helped the plant win contracts from other companies as well.

For example, it now assembles cable units for voice scramblers for Boeing in Seattle. And it does work for North Pacific Products, a toy manufacturer in the community of Bend, about 60 miles south of Warm Springs. Its work for North Pacific consists of assembling the plastic propeller driving mechanisms of rubber-band-powered model airplanes, and plastic tails for kites.

The Warm Springs plant still does the bulk of its business with Tektronix. Its 1973 gross was $128,700, of which $111,350 came from Tektronix, $7,350 came from Boeing, and $10,000 came from North Pacific.

Everett Miller has been a major factor in the development and operation of the Warm Springs plant.

After graduation from Madras High School, near Warm Springs, Miller enrolled at Oregon Technical Institute at Klamath Falls. Following a year there studying to be a diesel mechanic, he left for two years in the U.S. Army, and upon his discharge he returned home to work on the Warm Springs Indian Reservation.

Employed at the reservation sawmill as a laborer, he was always thinking of trying to better himself. Then one of his sisters told him that the tribal council was looking for a supervisor for a new enterprise. He was interested, and was among eight people who applied.

When the council, after extensively interviewing the 28-year-old, chose him for the job, he almost felt like backing out because, as Miller recalls, "every one of the other applicants had a better education than I did."

Today he admits that "I really didn't know what I was getting into." The closest thing he had to any business education was accounting in high school—"and I got that by accident," he laughs. "I wanted to be a mechanic."

But, Miller says, that bit of accounting proved to be valuable in his role as a businessman—"At least I knew the terminology."

Today, after five years of running a business, Miller is back in school learning accounting and managerial skills for two hours a week. He attends a class taught at the reservation by a business teacher from Central Oregon Community College at Bend.

Everett Miller's skill as a supervisor is reflected in the award given to the plant in November 1973. The Warm Springs operation was cited by Boeing as one of ten recognized by Boeing as its most outstanding subcontractors.

"There was a minimum of rejections," says Jerry Day, Boeing purchasing agent, in making the award, "and a maximum of good performance."

The Boeing and North Pacific contracts are fulfillment of a prediction made in March 1969, just as the Warm Springs operation was getting under way. Wayne Roberts, industrial specialist in Portland with the Bureau of Indian Affairs, said at the time: "When the tribe can look to corporations like Tektronix, which really believe in helping minority groups to gain job skills, it opens many doors. Hopefully the Warm Springs plant will grow and seek contracts with other companies."

A measure of Tektronix's trust is that it has never signed a contract with the Warm Springs plant.

"It was and still is a verbal contract," Miller laughs. "Nothing was ever written down.

"I think part of our success was that we didn't try to start big, didn't try to take on too much at once. We felt our way along pretty slowly at first, learning the tricks of the trade."

If we can take a low-skilled person, teach him a job, pay him a decent salary, and run a business for profit, others may decide to get into business.

Fine Vines

Greenville, Mississippi

There had been one distressing failure after another—Freedom Village, a crafts center; Strike City, an attempt at teaching displaced farm workers to make bricks; the Graflex Project, a lavishly financed training venture to give local people job skills.

Then there had been the vegetable-processing enterprise, the self-help housing program, and the concentrated employment programs; they, too, had fallen by the wayside.

Every effort made by the people in the Greenville area to improve their economic well-being seemed destined only to deepen their despair. Lack of jobs was and is a serious problem in this part of the Mississippi delta, especially for black people and most of all for black women.

At last, though, the pattern of business failure is being broken. A garment-manufacturing project—Fine Vines, Inc.—has escaped the blight of failure and is now flourishing as a black-owned and black-run economic enterprise. What's more, to the delight of both the community and local officials, the project has managed to obtain 90 percent of its work force, mostly women, from the local pool of people on public assistance rolls.

"I think it's great that women finally got involved in business," says city councilwoman Sarah Johnson. "Fine Vines not only serves a purpose in the community, but it also encourages people in other counties and states."

The corporation owes its initial success mostly to a group of representatives of fourteen civil rights and church organizations and civic groups. Determined to work for the economic development of the Mississippi delta, these people organized the Delta Foundation, which was incorporated as a nonprofit, tax-exempt enterprise in 1969. The group members began their endeavor by embarking on a study of the reasons behind all of the previous failures. They found that most of the other projects had been too ambitious and too unrealistic, as well as lacking in both the professional management and technical skills needed to start them.

Consequently the members of the group embarked on a much more methodical approach to developing a new project.

The foundation solicited the assistance of outside industry to help it to select an enterprise that, from the start, would have a fighting chance of succeeding. Ten companies formed an advisory team, which drafted a list of standards and requirements to determine the nature of the future enterprise:

● The social priorities (providing employment for the poor) have to be compatible with the economic objectives (operating a profit-making concern).

● The enterprise must accommodate low-skill-level employees.

● The project should employ as many people as possible and be designed so all receive training in skills and managerial tasks.

● There should be a low initial capital investment per employee.

● The products manufactured should be exportable and not compete with existing local industry.

● There should be ready access to raw materials.

● The project should allow a quick turnover of capital so the organization can start other projects without heavy refinancing.

"We have to establish a business that can at least break even," was the way that project counselor Vance Nimrod phrased it at the time. Applying its criteria, the advisory team came up with nineteen possible choices. After more screening and deliberation, it was decided to establish a plant that would produce blue jeans.

"Jeans seemed realistic," Nimrod recalls. Furthermore, it was agreed, the plant would not attempt to sell the denim jeans through retail outlets; rather, it would sell them to a wholesaler.

Having selected the type of project to be set up, the Delta Foundation embarked on a search for funds. It was fortunate in being able to secure a loan of $346,000 from a Greenville bank—the largest commercial loan ever granted a black-operated enterprise by a Mississippi bank. As the bank's senior vice-president commented, "We were very impressed with the low-profile, businesslike approach of the organization. They presented us with a well-prepared loan request. We were only too happy to oblige."

The project's organizers were also able to secure grants from a Presbyterian church and the Office of Economic Opportunity, together with a loan from a private foundation. All told, the organizers raised $736,000 in funds to start the new plant.

Now came the complex task of setting up a plant and putting it into operation. Drawing on the advice and resources of the advisory companies, the foundation brought in two experienced consultants to set up the factory. In addition it also acquired quarters for the new plant (barracks on a former air base), plant equipment, and denim and other supplies. And it interviewed many applicants until it had enough qualified local people to enable it to start.

In October 1970 the Greenville area acquired a new business enterprise when production began at Fine Vines, Inc. (As any black street dude knows, "fine vines" are sharp-looking clothes.)

The operation of the plant proceeded smoothly, although there were the initial difficulties in maintaining the quality of the product.

Then near-disaster struck. First, the firm that had said it would buy every pair of jeans the plant could produce cancelled its contract. This left Fine Vines with $35,000-worth of jeans in inventory and no place to sell them. To make matters worse, the general manager—one of the two consultants—looked over the situation and decided his own future would be more secure elsewhere.

This was the critical point in the development of the enterprise. As Charles Bannerman, now chairman of the board of the Delta Foundation, says, "We could stop production, lay off the work force, and look for new outlets for the product. Or we could continue production and hope to market the product ourselves."

Since shutting down would have caused a loss of faith as well as jobs in the community, the foundation continued production and formed its own marketing firm, Delta Sales Corporation. This proved the right step. Delta Sales sold all of the jeans in the inventory, and subsequently went on to build up a yearly sales volume to retailers of $1 million in several product lines. Arrangements were also made for Fine Vines to not only market its jeans through Delta Sales but also to sell some directly to the J. C. Penney Company for sale under Penney's label.

In 1972 the Delta Foundation established a new holding company, Delta Enterprises, which took over Fine Vines stock. This arrangement enabled the Delta Foundation to maintain its nonprofit status and, using the profits generated by Fine Vines, to subsequently back more new businesses.

Fine Vines reached the profit-loss break-even point in 1973. "Its sales for that year were over $750,000 and, if denim shortages and the energy crisis don't get too severe, sales should be substantially higher in 1974," observed financial comptroller Bennie Marshall that year. And by that time the plant had a total of about 100 employees, and it anticipated that it would add twenty to fifty more workers during 1974.

Although the blue jeans plant has still not made money for the Delta Foundation, it has nevertheless more than doubled the annual income of its employees, many of whom had previously lived on only $1,800 per year. Working at the plant has also given the employees skills that they can eventually use to seek better-paying jobs with other companies.

Fine Vines has also proved that, despite past failures, economic self-help can succeed in the Mississippi delta. One measure of that success is that the Greenville bank that originally lent money to the project recently offered to extend a line of credit to Fine Vines; normally it is the industry that takes such a proposal to the bank, not vice versa.

And Scott Daugherty, assistant director of the foundation, sums up both the beliefs and hopes of the project when he says:

"If we can take a low-skilled person, teach him a job, pay him a decent salary, and run a business for proift, others may decide to get into business."

The blue jean operation has also met with widespread approval from officials in the area.

As Pat Dunne, mayor of Greenville, says, "Fine Vines is one of the best developments in our city. Everything I can say about them is positive. More than 90 percent of their employees were on welfare and now they are all contributing to the tax rolls. They are strictly an example of the free enterprise system at its best."

Fine Vines general manager Clarence Antoine says, "The two biggest lessons I have learned are, (1) don't try to make it by the skin of your teeth, and (2) don't be too ambitious. You must be sure to leave a margin to cover unforeseen incidental costs and be willing to meet your failures and cope with them when they come up."

In other words, apply the same practical business principles to a self-help project that are employed by hard-headed businessmen to make any enterprise go. This is how Fine Vines has succeeded where so many of its predecessors failed.

Indians, especially Navajos, had been tragic victims for years of a system they could neither control nor understand. Pure and simple, they were getting ripped off.

The Dineh Cooperatives

Navajo Indian Reservation, Arizona/New Mexico

Indians on the Navajo Indian Reservation are struggling for control over their economy, long dominated by the white man's system of trading posts. The Indians, for a change, may be winning, because a system of Indian-owned and operated cooperatives seems to be taking root in the Navajo territory.

The reservation, the largest in the United States, covers some 25,000 square miles of semiarid land in eastern Arizona and western New Mexico and is the home of about 135,000 Navajos. Most of the people are poor, unemployed, and living in substandard housing. Being far removed from department stores and other conventional businesses, they are forced to rely on the trading posts on the reservation as a source of food and supplies and as a market for their farm goods and handicrafts.

The trading posts have been the economic backbone of the reservation for decades. They have been a good business for their owners and operators, all of the posts on the reservation doing a combined business of close to $20 million a year. The posts have not proved to be as profitable for the Indians, as documented in a 1973 Federal Trade Commission report. High prices, credit abuses, garnisheeing, withholding of government and welfare checks, refusal to negotiate Navajo checks for cash—all were allegedly practiced. An Indian, for example, was allowed credit at only one post on the reservation. Credit was usually granted only if the trading post was given control over the Navajo's check. He was, in effect, tied to the trading post.

"Indians, especially Navajos, had been tragic victims for years of a system they could neither control nor understand. Pure and simple, they were getting ripped off," says a Navajo social worker.

Navajo attempts to gain more control of their economy had been ill-starred. In the 1950s they tried to establish competitive trading posts, but their lack of business experience doomed the ventures. A uranium mine was opened on one reservation, but failed and left the area a ghost town. A proposed auto trailer plant at the same site also failed. No self-help projects, with the exception of one very small semi-welfare program, were attempted.

The grievances and discontent were there, but little specific was done about them until 1971, when a group of Indian craftsmen complained they were being cheated by some trading posts. The idea of a cooperative came out of discussions among a group of young men working on the reservation. The principal instigator was Robert Salabye, an Indian social worker with the Navajo aid organization Dinebeiina Nahiilna Be Agaditahe (DNA). Joining him were VISTA member Jon Colvin, DNA attorney Robert Hilgendorf, and Miller Nez, who had had previous co-op experience.

The first step was to sell the tribal councils on the idea. They had to be persuaded that cooperatives, unlike so many earlier Indian business efforts, would not fail.

There were other problems as well. In October 1971 the national economy was in a tailspin, which like many business downturns, hit the Indians severely. Fierce resistance was also expected from the trading post monopoly.

"When we first got together," Salabye recalls, "there was a collective feeling of helplessness."

DNA and the Navajo Office of Economic Opportunity helped tackle some of the basic legal work. In December 1971 a Navajo Co-op Association was established. The name was later changed to "Dineh Cooperatives, Inc.," using the Navajos' name for themselves. At the same time the legal aid office on the reservation had persuaded the Los Angeles office of the Federal Trade Commission to investigate the trading post monopoly.

By September 1972 major funding had come through. The Campaign for Human Development of the U.S. Catholic Conference made a $34,650 grant and Food Advocates of the University of California at Berkeley made a $15,840 grant to cover co-op staff salaries.

Co-op backers took a calculated risk by avoiding both the state tribal councils and Bureau of Indian Affairs (BIA) for land use approval. Instead they obtained permission to build co-ops from local councils. Going to the BIA for permission, they feared, would delay the co-ops for two to five years. The BIA and state councils never tried to stop the co-ops, however.

To no one's surprise, the trading posts threatened to cut off credit and other services to any Indian using the co-ops. This harassment, although initially effective even with the co-op board members, lessened as the Dineh Co-ops began taking root. The trading posts have obviously lost business to the co-ops, but they have never revealed any figures.

By the end of 1972, eight co-ops were operating. The number has now grown to eighteen, and seven are self-sustaining. Selling food, dry goods, hay, arts and crafts, and gasoline, the co-ops serve almost 8,000 Indians a month. Average monthly sales are almost $65,000. The co-ops pay annual wages of almost $160,000 on annual sales of more than $750,000.

Grants have increased, but more importantly the co-ops are becoming part of the Southwest business community and economy. One example is their membership in Associated Grocers, which gives Dineh Cooperatives access to major wholesalers. Bread companies and other wholesalers have also discovered the co-ops can provide them with far more outlets.

The Dineh Co-ops are now managed and operated almost entirely by the Indians. All volunteers and paid staff come from the Navajo nation. State employment programs are training store managers. Co-op credit unions are encouraging Indians to save money. Co-op board members are obtaining business experience that will eventually benefit the entire reservation.

Navajo life is being changed in other ways, too. Co-ops have replaced trading posts as gathering and social centers.

"The co-ops have brought a lot of people together," Salabye says. "For many it has given them a new excitement and enthusiasm about themselves and their future."

There is some concern that Indian habits may be changing too fast, perhaps to the detriment of Navajo culture. Navajos, for example, have always lived by the sun.

"Now," says Salabye, "they are opening and closing on time. I don't know if that's good or bad yet."

The co-ops hope to expand. There are plans, for example, to establish an automobile cooperative on the reservation, since Indians have frequently been overcharged when buying cars in communities off the reservation.

Whether that plan goes through depends partly on the energy shortage. The reservation has been suffering gas shortages for both cars and generators. Some stores might be forced to close if sales drop too low.

The overall mood, however, is buoyant and optimistic. The Navajos are taking control of their economy. And the key to that change is proving to be the Dineh Cooperatives.

People—no matter what their past economic,
social, or political status—can improve
themselves by working together.

The Southeast Alabama
Self-Help Association

Tuskegee, Alabama

Houston Everett clapped his hands and beamed happily as the auctioneer banged his hammer and called out: "Sold for $49.94!" It was a record high price for a feeder pig in Everett's co-op.

Everett is one of more than a hundred small farmers who have found a healthy new source of income: raising pigs to be sold to pork buyers for fattening and processing. The farmers are members of a feeder-pig marketing and management cooperative started in 1969 by the Southeast Alabama Self-Help Association (SEASHA), a tax-exempt, nonprofit organization that operates in a twelve-county area of southeastern Alabama.

Since 1969 the pig cooperative has grown from nothing to a flourishing business. The first pig sale netted a total of $76 for four pigs. By early 1974 the co-op's pigs were bringing an average price of $27 each. On January 14, 1974, for example, the co-op sold 555 pigs for $15,348, with buyers coming from three states in addition to Alabama.

Hope and despair have been riding a seesaw in Alabama's Black Belt counties for generations. Most of the poor blacks, because of inherent racial prejudices, could not utilize existing social service programs. This sentiment is reflected in the thoughts of one community volunteer: "It seems that in our area poor people are made to feel unwanted and unwelcome in what they attempt to do to gain support for their families." In the late 1960s, as the civil rights movement gained momentum in the rural South, hope began to gain the upper hand when the Tuskegee Institute's Community Education Program (TICEP) initiated a self-help plan for a community development organization called SEASHA. TICEP was an Office of Economic Opportunity (OEO)-funded program in which Tuskegee Institute students tutored the children of poor families in surrounding counties. The tutors also helped with other family problems.

SEASHA's director, John Brown Jr., was on the TICEP staff at

the time. "My job," he recalls, "was to form parent-tutor organizations to deal with the results of poverty, malnutrition, and disease that impaired the child's ability to learn. The same parent-tutor groups became the nucleus for SEASHA's county branches when we decided to start the self-help program after TICEP lost its OEO funding at the end of 1967."

Since then, SEASHA has grown in size to approximately 6,000 members, each of whom pays $1 for a lifetime membership. The organization's young and aggressive staff of thirty-three is headquartered in a small building and a house trailer in Tuskegee. The staff is supplemented by some people from VISTA (Volunteers in Service to America), who are serving as field workers. These same volunteers have helped SEASHA's staff to identify community needs and to recruit low-income people to utilize SEASHA services. As Taylor Harmon, SEASHA's assistant director says, "We work together like a family, helping each other as needed."

SEASHA currently runs three major programs: the feeder-pig co-op, a credit union, and an economic development component aimed at providing technical assistance to existing small businesses and developing new business ventures. Future plans include the institution of a low-cost housing project.

Two farmers from each of the twelve counties in the area were selected to start the feeder-pig project. They attended classes conducted in each county by Tuskegee Institute, and received basic information in swine husbandry, necessary facility construction, and veterinary medicine.

The participants were granted five-year loans of up to $2,500 to purchase a boar and ten gilts (young female hogs) and to purchase materials for building farrowing and feeding pens. In 1971 the loan amount was doubled so the sponsored farmer could initially purchase more livestock.

The project has been so successful that a feed mill has been set up to provide farmers with feed at cost. And a new marketing center has been erected nearby for conducting the monthly pig sales. SEASHA anticipates that the pig cooperative will become financially self-sufficient in the next two years.

The credit union is SEASHA's answer to farm stores and finance companies that have kept low-income people continually in debt. Directly involving the membership in its operation, the credit union teaches members how to save and borrow wisely. Counseling services are provided by the staff, offering guidance in general money matters and family budgeting.

Although the first year, 1969, was rocky, in the last two years the credit union has doubled its assets, reaching a high in December 1973 of $102,525. Membership now totals over 1,254 people.

In 1973 the SEASHA credit union was granted a certificate of permanent share insurance by the Bureau of Federal Credit Unions, certifying that each member's share is insured to a maximum of $20,000. The organization also received the Thrift Honor Award for 1973 from the National Credit Union Administration. The credit union is a strong and growing element of SEASHA, and it too is expected to be totally self-supporting. An indication of its promise is the decision by the board of directors to declare a dividend of 5 percent on shares for the calendar year 1973.

SEASHA's economic development program has proven to be the most demanding and the most rewarding of the different projects. In addition to providing technical assistance to small, black businesses in the twelve-county area, SEASHA's staff has made known available private and government monies and management expertise. This well-designed technical assistance program, relying upon the fine resources of Tuskegee Institute, can offer the necessary assistance for the establishment of minority business ventures that strengthen the impoverished economic base of southern Alabama. Since its inception, the two staff members have helped ten new businesses get on their feet. Several new applications are currently being processed by the Small Business Administration.

Economic development implies employment, and SEASHA performs an additional service to the community, acting as an informative clearinghouse for both employer and employee between black and white. Under SEASHA's directions the unskilled worker may successfully obtain an on-the-job training contact. During the 23-month period ending November 1973, SEASHA was responsible for 242 direct job placements and 85 indirect placements. Field workers give individual attention to the unskilled workers, accompanying them to the employer agencies and assisting them in finding their way through all the red tape, as well as in dealing with various legal matters.

In the area of low-cost housing, its newest field of interest, SEASHA is pulling together a consortium of talent in the fields of architecture, construction, sociology, finance, and management. The goal is to provide a complete housing delivery system for low-income rural residents in the twelve-county area.

Plans call for construction of a low-cost housing unit in Coosa County, to begin when sufficient low-interest federal loans have been approved. The housing staff also has started on the initial stages of a federally funded research program on low-cost housing.

With the feeder-pig project and the credit union approaching self-sufficiency, will SEASHA, in its entirety, also become self-supporting in the future?

"That's not in our planning," says John Brown. "SEASHA is a development corporation to launch new enterprises. The feeder-pig project and the credit union will be spun off when they become self-supporting. We'll replace them with new responsibilities, which we hope will also become self-supporting. SEASHA's equity share in each spin-off will provide capital for new projects. Eventually we hope to lick poverty."

SEASHA clearly has a long way to go to meet these ultimate goals, but, in the few years of its life, it has proven, as Brown says, "that people—no matter what their past economic, social, or political status—can improve themselves by working together."

SEASHA farmers receive valuable advice on land and crop management.

We were better off not to have government funds.
They tell you how to use them, and it all ends up
in a lot of overhead. . . .

Appalachian Fireside Crafts

Berea, Kentucky

A chain saw salesman happened upon William McClure in Berea, Kentucky, a while ago, using one of his company's saws to skillfully roughcut a buckeye bowl from a log. He took some photographs and asked the mountain craftsman if the company could use them in advertising.

The salesman suggested the ads would not only sell chain saws but would also be good for the buckeye bowl business. The shallow bowls of buckeye wood have long been used in the "hollers" of Appalachia to let bread dough rise, and their graceful shape has come to be prized as decorative tableware by cityfolk.

The bib-overalled McClure agreed the photos would make nice ads. But he said the buckeye bowl business was about as good as he could handle. He said he could use a new chain saw, though.

The saw man held out for mutual advertising, but he wasn't able to make a deal with the Kentucky farmer.

William McClure, 52 years old and the father of thirteen children, has been a subsistence farmer in Rockcastle County most of his life. He turned to woodcarving seven years ago to make extra money, and he has since learned something about letting his talent go cheaply. He recently recounted how he had a hard lesson along those lines from the federal government:

"They was going to set up this woodworking shop at Mount Vernon and use some men from Rockcastle County to make minibarns. Well, we got funded—$50,000, I think—and a few pieces of machinery, and we all donated time to set up. We hauled coal free and one thing and another.

"But it ended up with all the money in two or three people's pockets, and there wasn't enough left to make a go of it. They was making $10,000–15,000 a year and we was getting $1.69 an hour. Mostly we spent our time running back and forth to see if they had anything for us to do."

On the other hand, McClure has learned that working by himself in crafts has its drawbacks, too. "When I started out, I only sold a few items," he says. "When I'd been in it awhile, orders started picking up and the next thing I knew I was losing them because I couldn't keep up. Sometimes it might be six months before you can collect, too."

Consequently McClure scoffed when Jerry Workman made a business proposal to him, even though he had known Workman when he was with the Kentucky Guild for Arts and Crafts. Workman was now with Appalachian Fireside Crafts, Inc., and interested in walnut and buckeye bowls. He told McClure that he thought he could use thirty a month.

"I said, 'Lord have mercy, you'll never get shut of them'," McClure recalls, still a little incredulous three years later. "But I started turning them out, though, and I've been going ever since."

What McClure didn't understand at first is that Workman had special backing—a group of men and women who had organized under the name of Appalachian Fireside Crafts (AFC). Like McClure, the AFC members had a bent for traditional mountain crafts and a need for supplemental cash that could be earned

Warren Brunner

without going too far from home. The organization's founders, in fact, were mountain women who wanted to sandwich money-making activity in with looking after their children and taking care of other household responsibilities.

Five such mothers in Kentucky's rural Wolfe County came up with the idea in a 1968 meeting with a fieldworker for the Save the Children Federation (SCF), well-known for over four decades for its services on behalf of children around the world. Why not make craft items and sell them? It was a notion that sounded good and it caught on.

Charles Wesley, who heads the federation's Berea office, relates how the project got off the ground:

"The first thing we decided was that all the money would go immediately to the families. We didn't want a lot of equipment, because we wanted to keep costs down, and we decided on natural materials."

The project was geared to the federation's child-sponsorship program (in which donations are solicited by SCF and go directly from an outside sponsor to a child's family), and it did not use money from any other source.

"We were better off not to have government funds. They tell you how to use them, and it all ends up in a lot of overhead without support," says Wesley.

The women, with some SCF instruction, started working on Christmas wreathes of pine cones and other materials from the woods. And Jerry Workman—on loan from SCF to administer the project—got authority to "risk the money right there." He guided participants in setting quality standards, and when the first wreath met them, its maker was paid on the spot.

"A lot of shops have tried to get these people to work for consignment sales, but that's no good," Workman says. "They use you. You risk effort and materials, and they risk shelf space. Sometimes you wait months. Then, if it doesn't sell at all, they're not out anything—but you are."

SCF thought it could avoid those shortcomings with immediate payments that could be recouped later with craft sales. The risk was, of course, that the crafts wouldn't sell and the federation would be out the money.

But of course, SCF didn't want to do that, not only because it would lose federation money but also because that wouldn't really alleviate the problem in the long run. So, working with the crafts project people, Workman set out to make sure they had more than a "make-work" program. They kept the standards high.

Workman helped develop the project along with eleven area

women and William McClure. The project was formally organized in March 1971, with SCF's backing, as a nonprofit corporation, Appalachian Fireside Crafts, Inc. All of the board members were craft producers, and they set a policy of letting the marketplace decide what would be produced. They also decided to market their wares by making use of direct mail advertising.

In 1969 the only items offered were the pine cone wreaths, and they brought in a total of $9,000 in sales. Broadening out the next year to such craft items as quilts, cornshuck and cloth dolls, pillows, and woodcarvings, AFC boosted its annual sales to about $30,000 in 1971 and to $62,000 in 1972.

During the past few years, AFC has not only increased its sales but has also spread to a much wider area. The craftmakers now represent close to 200 families living in twelve Kentucky counties and one Tennessee county.

There have been problems along the way, of course. For example, members of the standards committee were reluctant to reject crafts made by their friends, even if the goods were shoddy. "It took maybe six months to straighten that out," Workman says.

Project members soon saw that inferior craftsmanship would ruin things for everybody, and they decided slower producers should get more help on technique. They also established a smaller, tougher quality control committee.

Various decisions had to be made as the project grew in membership and in craft lines. Should quilting material be given to the women, for example, or sold to them at wholesale and covered in the price of the quilt? (The latter was the ultimate route, because it avoided minimum-wage complications.) And growing problems with financial records led to employment of a full-time bookkeeper.

The AFC board of directors—chosen on a one-man, one-vote basis by the membership—presently plans to build a $70,000 headquarters and warehouse near Booneville, Ky. Sales are up and the company is looking forward to hiring its own full-time manager and ending its financial dependency on the federation. "There's support for that overhead now," Wesley says.

The support is made up of people like Joyce VanWinkle, of Rockcastle County, who finds it "awfully easy to sit down and just make a pillow while the baby plays on the floor." And the support is there because Appalachian Fireside Crafts has given the people a chance to fulfill their basic needs as they could not before. Incomes are still low, but the many talents of the mountain craftspeople are gaining wider recognition across the country.

People can solve their problems if they're earning
their own living. It also increases self-respect.
Who has self-respect if he has to have his hand
out for a welfare check?

The Knox County Community Development Corporation

Barbourville, Kentucky

Knox County, in southeastern Kentucky, is one of those text-book examples of Appalachian poverty that used to be shown on the television evening news during Appalachia's period of national "discovery" in the 1960s. But when the frontier of social discovery moved on, Appalachia and Knox County disappeared from the national scene.

No interstate highway or passenger train passes through Knox County. Most of its people live in remote hollows near places with such names as Salt Gum, Bailey Switch, and Stinking Creek. As a reminder of technology at work in rural America, giant bull-dozers level mountaintops to get at rich seams of coal, and much of the county's population shuttles between the Kentucky hills and the demeaning slums of Michigan and Ohio in search of jobs.

In the midst of this grim mountain setting, however, is a genuine success story of poor people making a go of three commercial en-terprises. These businesses are operated by the Knox County Community Development Corporation (CDC).

The name makes it sound like a venture that's kept alive by unending injections of federal funds. But it isn't. The CDC is a profit-making, expanding operation that received only minimal federal assistance at the outset and is now completely self-suf-ficient. The corporation's three enterprises are

- a furniture factory, whose 220 employees manufacture up-holstered living room furniture
- the Hill Country Hickory House, a popular restaurant
- Kentucky Krafts, a log cabin souvenir and gift shop adjacent to the restaurant, selling crafts made both within and outside Knox County

"If you want people to start making decisions for themselves, they have to be economically free. Jobs seemed like a good place to start," explains Hollis D. West, president of the CDC and, since 1967, executive director of OEO's local office, the Knox County Economic Opportunity Council.

"My personal feeling," he adds, "is that people can solve their problems if they're earning their own living."

Adds West, who is 43 and a southern Illinois native trained to be a schoolteacher: "It also increases self-respect. Who has self-respect if he has to have his hand out for a welfare check?"

The CDC had its beginnings in a grouping of both some people participating in programs launched in economically depressed areas in 1964 and 1965, plus professional staff personnel from the Knox County Economic Opportunity Council.

A worker in the CDC's furniture factory

Much of the early enthusiasm for the CDC and many of the ideas that led to the corporation's beginning came from talks between local poor people and staff members at Knox County's twelve community centers formed under OEO's community action program (CAP). Throughout the brief history of the CDC, the poor people of Knox County have constituted approximately 70 percent of the membership of the CDC's 13-member board of directors. The corporation's general membership numbers about six hundred people, who elect the members of the corporation's board of directors; membership is open to anyone for a $1 membership fee. At least 60 percent of the CDC's board of directors and general membership must be low-income people, according to the organization's corporate regulations.

Early leaders of the CDC who searched for ways to create jobs in Knox County pondered several earlier failures of CAP-inspired attempts to produce jobs. The rural community of Kayjay, for example, had to scuttle a plan to make brooms when it discovered that its sparsely populated area lacked the manpower for large-scale production and marketing. Residents of Lost Fork of Stinking Creek tried to develop a picnic area, only to find that it would go unused because Lost Fork is so remote that it is truly "lost."

"The people learned something from those failures," recalls Helen Schalet, West's assistant. "Mountain people are very independent and self-reliant, and they wanted to have their own programs at their own community centers. But they learned that to be effective, they were going to have to join a countywide effort."

The critical decision during the period of the CDC's inception related to the type of business that the CDC was going to concentrate on. "We wanted something that was 'labor intensive'—something that produced a lot of jobs—even though it might not be the most profitable business," Helen Schalet says.

Large-scale manufacturing of handicrafts was ruled out for that reason—not enough jobs. A proposal to put people to work sewing on a contract basis was rejected because the CDC would be left without a product of its own to sell if the contractors reneged.

Furniture production was finally chosen, according to CDC officials, because it requires a good deal of labor, because wood and other raw materials are available in Knox County, and because furniture is a commodity that remains in steady demand.

The crafts shop, Kentucky Krafts, which had opened in 1968 as the Knox County Anti-Poverty Arts and Crafts Store, was incorporated into the CDC in 1971, and the Hill Country Hickory House restaurant was opened in 1972. Both projects, it was felt, would provide some employment and important community services, and both were expected to prove profitable. (The restaurant has not yet turned a profit—partly, perhaps, because hopes of adding motel rooms to the facility were dashed after the city of Barbourville, the county seat, refused to extend sewer lines to the place.)

Another CDC enterprise, Kentucky Krafts Manufacturing, was phased out in 1972, because CDC officials decided crafts and toy production did not produce enough profits or employment.

Federal funding, which came to the CDC indirectly from OEO, was required for early construction and development expenses.

"Basically our projects have been funded on the expectation that if we could get them started we could keep them going," Helen Schalet says. "We've proven this to be valid because all operating costs have been covered from our own funds, and grants have been used only for high construction and equipment costs."

Knox County business and political circles have often failed to realize that the CDC is profitable and self-sustaining. The CDC's continuing existence is frequently attributed erroneously in Barbourville to life-saving contributions of federal money.

Nevertheless there is growing acceptance of the CDC outside Knox County's poor community. This improvement in public relations is credited by CDC officials largely to the efforts of Jesse D. Lay, superintendent of the Knox County school system and chairman of the CDC's board of directors. As superintendent, Lay represents the largest employer in the county and therefore, like most eastern Kentucky school superintendents, is one of the most powerful political figures in the county.

"I've been for this kind of thing from the beginning," Lay says. "It's done more for Knox County than anything I know of."

Lay notes that an offshoot of the CDC's success has been better education for Knox County's poor children: "When the parents are getting along and making a little money, they're in a better frame of mind to see that their kids go to school."

Important as Lay's support has been, the CDC has gained general public acceptance largely by simply succeeding. From a 1971 net profit level of about $48,500, the CDC jumped to net profits of $133,000 in 1972 (23.3 percent of net sales).

The CDC plans to build an additional furniture factory, which will employ 150 people and produce convertible sofa-beds. In addition, CDC leaders hope to soon develop a distributorship for their products in southeastern Kentucky, northeastern Tennessee, and southwestern Virginia.

"People on our payrolls are spending their money at local businesses, and this is new money from outside the county injected into the local economy," West says. The CDC enterprises, particularly the furniture factory, have created a labor base of trained workers; two light industries established factories in Knox County largely because of the labor potential. The factories may eventually employ a total of 500 people. "We're starting to get credit from the public for some of these things," Helen Schalet explains.

The best gauge of the CDC's success, however, has been its impact on its employees.

Before landing a job with the furniture factory as a woodstainer, Melvin White was an unemployed construction worker living in dilapidated housing.

"I carried my water in a bucket from a well," White recalls. "Now I have running water. I've added a room to my house, I've improved my lot, and I've added a lot of appliances."

The CDC's employees have gained intangible things like respect and pride that may be more important to them than material gains. As Charlie Hobbs says of local merchants, "When I don't have a good job, I can't get any credit. Now I have credit, and they'll treat me like a human being." Al Brafford was an unemployed coal miner with a bleak future before he joined CDC's payroll: "I just don't know what would have happened if this job hadn't come along, but the future's looking mighty good now."

Hollis West and his associates aren't trying to kid anyone that they have a final solution to poverty. As West says, "That's still going to take massive funding." But he believes the CDC invites imitation. The ingredients, West believes, are:

● no-strings-attached government or private financing to get started

● a level of organization that can command local respect and draw upon local ideas and talent

● a broad enough following to be able to exercise local political power

● professional managerial help

● careful consideration of what products can be produced at a profit in a given community

"We've proven that people with little background, training or experience can be trained to run a business with indigenous leadership and indigenous people," West notes.

"And that can be done anywhere."

We were all so excited—I think we expected that in another year there wouldn't be any hungry people left in Chicago . . . But what we didn't have then was any idea of how to run a business of this size.

Cornucopia

Chicago, Illinois

Chicago's sprawling South Water Street Market is a circus of the wholesale food business. Unkempt and seemingly uncontrolled, it is a teeming terminal for the transfer of food products from the farm and processor to the supermarket and consumer.

In the pre-dawn light, truckers compete in obscene earnest for the inadequate dock space along the warehouse quays to accommodate their trailer rigs. Here ethnic loyalty still counts for a penny or two off the price of a case of tomatoes. And here, too, the difference between fresh vegetables and yesterday's leftovers can be concealed cleverly enough to fool even the farmer.

It is, in short, no place for the amateur. Nor was it the place for the stream of family station wagons and small vans that suddenly began contending with the big trucks, as a horde of buyers representing food cooperatives seeking relief from high prices descended on the market in the late 1960s.

The co-op buyers were treated with amused patience at first by the market regulars. But as their numbers increased, slowing both trade and traffic, they were made to feel unwelcome—by word and higher prices. Co-op buying soon turned into a weekly ordeal for the co-op members who had to go to the market.

As the friction grew week by week, it wasn't long before leaders of the various co-ops decided there had to be a better way. The co-op movement itself seemed threatened. A task force was formed—mainly young people representing co-ops sponsored by the Lutheran Welfare Services of Chicago—and it soon struck upon the idea of a co-op of co-ops, to be called Cornucopia.

Instead of each club sending a buying team to the South Water Street Market each week, the co-ops would telephone their orders to Cornucopia, and a few days later they would go to a central facility to pick up their goods. Rather than dozens of inexperienced and market-shy buyers stumbling from one wholesaler to another in faint hope of bargains, one expert buying team from Cornucopia would purchase for all the co-ops, arriving at the market once or twice a week with the purchasing leverage of a supermarket-sized order.

As conceived by the task force, Cornucopia would go beyond just filling the immediate needs of existing co-ops, most of which were located in low- and middle-income white-dominated areas of the city. A secondary objective would be encouragement and organization of new food-buying clubs in the inner city, where the need to stretch food dollars is greatest and organizational resources are most limited. The task force also envisioned a companion program of informal education in nutrition, home economics, and organizational leadership for the successful co-ops.

Many of those plans formulated in 1971 by the task force have been realized, but not without great difficulties.

Cornucopia is now a cooperative federation, a joint venture of food-buying co-ops scattered around Chicago and even extending into the suburbs—most of them being co-ops sponsored by churches, community centers, block clubs, and the like. While Cornucopia is chartered in Illinois as a nonprofit corporation, the member co-ops function as a cooperative, electing the corporation's directors and officers. The paid and volunteer staff, on the other hand, functions as a collective that controls the day-to-day operations of the warehouse facility.

Currently Cornucopia serves 67 member co-ops or clubs and, through them, it benefits an estimated 5,400 people. As membership has increased, the percentage of client families with incomes below the federal poverty guidelines has increased dramatically— from less than 5 percent in 1972 to more than 35 percent in 1974. A high percentage of the co-ops that have formed and been admitted to Cornucopia have been in Chicago's lowest income areas.

As envisioned by the task force in 1971, Cornucopia was not a project to be undertaken on a shoestring. A warehouse had to be rented. A truck was necessary. Walk-in coolers were a must for storing perishables. Office furniture, food bins, cash registers— the list of needs seemed endless. An early proposal to finance the project with subscriptions from member co-ops was quickly dropped for fear of scaring off the very member clubs whose loyalty (and volume business) would be essential to success.

Start-up costs alone were expected to run as high as $20,000. And the most realistic projections anticipated that Cornucopia would operate for at least a year without meeting its own costs.

Therefore the task force turned to the Cook County poverty program for assistance.

The poverty agency already was sponsoring several buying clubs, meal programs, and a cooperative store—each of which was struggling with inefficient and undependable sources of supply. Instead of an outright grant, the agency agreed to fund Cornucopia for a year under a service contract by which Cornucopia

Cornucopia's warehouse is a distribution center serving an estimated 5,400 people through a total of some 67 individual co-ops.

agreed to supply the agency's existing groups. It was a windfall. Not only did Cornucopia gain additional member co-ops at a critical time but $33,515 as well.

Those early days are remembered fondly by Cornucopia's founders. Claudia Meyer, a prime mover of the task force, is now the program's full-time staff coordinator. "Suddenly we had all this money and it seemed as if it could never run out," she recalls.

"After almost a year of hard work and dreaming, we were about to get off the ground. We were all so excited—I think we expected that in another year there wouldn't be any hungry people left in Chicago. . . ." That was the vanishing edge of innocence.

"We on the task force may have been a little naive," she now concedes. "We had our political and economic philosophies all in order. But what we didn't have then was any idea of how to run a business of this size. And whether it was a word we liked or not, that's exactly what we had—a business. There's a lot more to it than just 'help your brother'. There's pricing, storage, accounting, legal problems, funding. . . ."

As the task force fanned out across the city to find a warehouse, there was a temptation to look first along a north-south line that ran through downtown Chicago and connected most of the existing co-ops. "But if part of our mission was *really* to encourage food clubs in the black inner city as well as in the medium- and low-income white areas where most of us had roots, then we had to move the warehouse search west, into the black neighborhoods," Claudia Meyer says.

"We knew that could cost us support from a few of the smaller existing clubs, from people who simply would not feel safe coming into an all-black area every week with a substantial amount of money. But at least *they* could come. Those in the real poverty belt are too immobile to come out to us. If we were going to reach them it could only be by setting up shop on their doorstep. It was a very hard decision. We wanted to do it, but we also wanted to assure that Cornucopia worked. Looking back now, all of us are proud of the way we went."

"People in this part of town are cynical about projects like this," she continues. "They have seen storefront projects come and go. We felt Cornucopia would gain a measure of credibility just by keeping its doors open a few months and not making a lot of promises that later got broken. Once we accomplished that, and once the neighborhood people realized what we were up to, we figured it would be easy to organize them into co-ops. And that's exactly what has happened. What's more, we didn't lose a single one of our original co-ops because of moving west."

An early advantage of the decision to put the warehouse on the city's West Side was the availability of commercial building space at a reasonable rental. Shells of many manufacturing premises had stood abandoned since the fiery disturbances of the late 1960s. The task force finally settled on a 16,000-square-foot warehouse in the 2800 block of West Lake Street—under Chicago's elevated rapid transit tracks. It was a bargain at $1,250 a month.

In January 1972, Cornucopia was incorporated. The next month the initial contract and money came through, the warehouse was found, and squads of food co-op faithful from around the city were coerced into showing up there one Saturday to paint the facility and wrestle the big coolers into place. By mid-March the doors were open, and Cornucopia was in business.

The costs of starting up left barely $13,000 in the bank—far too little capital to get such a large operation launched. That became especially clear when unforeseen circumstances gouged into the reserve. Some co-ops ordered and then failed to pick up (or pay for) their food. To introduce itself to the neighborhood, Cornucopia opened its doors Saturday afternoon and sold the week's unclaimed produce to individuals. That worked well until an audit revealed that enormous amounts were being stolen. The audit, plus an armed robbery that netted the robbers the week's receipts, convinced the staff to hire Brinks—at an additional cost of $100 a week. Spoilage cut far more deeply than expected into revenues and costs for everything from utilities to mousetraps ran far higher than had been anticipated.

At the start Cornucopia marked up food only 10 percent, hoping that would be enough to cover its operating expenses. By December 1972, though, after just ten months of operation, the new venture had not only spent its initial poverty agency contract money but also another $30,000 grant from the Freedom from Hunger Foundation—and $5,000 beyond that; making a grand total of more than $68,000. Cornucopia was broke, forced to increase its markup to 20 percent.

At the higher markup, savings were reduced on the average to about 18 percent of supermarket prices. The savings ran higher on some items, such as fresh fruits and vegetables, and lower on others. But the reduction was sure to cool the enthusiasm of member co-ops. Would there be a rebellion in the membership? Would they simply turn back to shopping for themselves at South Water Street Market again—or, worse yet, abandon the cooperative movement altogether?

The Cornucopia newsletter, a gazette of recipes mixed with sidewalk politics, played a major role in encouraging the co-ops to stick with the federation. It explained the difficulties in great detail, begged both patience and outside help in the form of ideas and volunteers to cut costs, and promised to increase the savings again just as soon as Cornucopia seemed self-sustaining. The newsletter pointed out that Cornucopia's success depended on volume, and that the surest way to guarantee its success was to up the size of weekly orders and to encourage more co-ops to join.

The young staff also did some belt tightening. The average monthly payroll of nearly $5,000 was cut to less than $3,500 in 1973. (All paid staff members earn $3.00 an hour, or $120 a week for a full 40 hours, although few ever claim a full 40 hours.) At the same time the wholesale value of food dispensed rose by almost 50 percent—from $202,000 in 1972 to $299,000 in 1973. Small economies in the security service, the truck leases, and even a two-month reduction in the rent were negotiated. Cornucopia was in a desperate, survival period. Foundation money dried up, and to make matters even worse, Cornucopia lost its bid for tax-exempt status.

Replacing staff members with volunteers was not easy. "The first loyalty of the co-op members was to their individual co-op, not to Cornucopia, and each of them had a hard enough time getting time and muscle donated," Claudia Meyer recalls. "They all knew we had a big paid staff, so they were a little cynical when we came around begging for free help at the warehouse." But again a straightforward explanation of the seriousness of the dilemma produced good volunteer crews on the critical Thursdays, Fridays, and Saturdays when the warehouse is busy with pickups.

If Cornucopia's survival depends on volume, it indirectly depends on an attractive and tempting shopping list. It is hoped that 1974 will see volume double to $600,000, both through the addition of new co-ops and increased sales to the existing ones.

"We can sell more to each co-op either by encouraging them to expand membership or by offering for sale a larger part of their food needs," Claudia Meyer observes. "The first approach depends on them. The second depends on our ability to successfuly stock more things."

The order list has already grown enormously. Besides the expected red Delicious apples (at 29 cents a pound when they are 35 cents to 45 cents in stores) and tomatoes (at 25 cents in midwinter), it now goes on to include everything from ham hocks (88 cents) and bratwurst ($1.32) to eggs (71 cents a dozen), roasted peanuts (54 cents), and munster cheese ($1.25).

"Port Salut? Oh, yes sir, right over here—$1.27 a pound. And happy eating."

The storefronts were boarded up. Glass and bottles lay broken on the pavement, smashed like the lives and hopes of many who lived nearby.

The Christian Community Progress Corporation

Menlo Park, California

Five years ago the intersection of Willow Road and Newbridge Street in the Belle Haven area of Menlo Park was an urban wasteland. The storefronts were boarded up. Glass and bottles lay broken on the pavement, smashed like the lives and hopes of many who lived nearby. And Belle Haven was an area seething with as much racial hatred as almost any ghetto area in urban America. Few white people would have dared trying to walk down the street.

Clarence Towers

Today the intersection of Willow Road and Newbridge Street is the site of a shopping center, where blacks and whites shop under the sign of the Christian Community Progress Corporation (CCPC). The sign shows a white hand touching a black one.

A black minister with strong powers of persuasion, working with white clergy and backed by local businessmen, put together the corporation as a nonprofit, interracial organization. Running as much on enthusiasm as on money, it is trying to train and employ young people in the community, as well as ease tensions and racial friction.

The black minister and guiding force behind the organization is the Reverend Albert Williams, pastor of the Second Baptist Church in nearby San Mateo.

"I saw the need," Williams says, "for blacks and whites to work together in a close relationship—going to church, building up a rundown neighborhood, bringing the community together."

Seeking out white audiences, Williams responded to a call from a white minister who was looking for two blacks—one anti-white extremist and the other not—to address his congregation. After Williams gave his views, he was besieged by church members wanting to know how they could help in the black community. They said they could not believe such poverty and physical and human destruction existed.

"So I showed them; I took them on a tour," Williams explains. "That was the beginning of CCPC."

Williams had ideas for the riot-wrecked intersection of Willow Road and Newbridge Street, envisioning a shopping center, stores, and job-training projects. The local community certainly needed shops; the closest shopping center was three miles away.

The minister began translating his ideas and the community's needs into action by buying up property around the intersection. From chuch groups he raised the $10,000 down payment needed for the $100,000 parcel. That was just the beginning. Williams went on to obtain contributions from private citizens, church members, and businessmen, with one individual giving $35,000.

With the money came help from professional construction companies, as well as volunteers for painting, cleaning, and lighter chores. The corner of Willow and Newbridge became engulfed in a flurry of building and repairing activities as the wreckage of the intersection was transformed into a shopping center.

The first two businesses to be opened at the new shopping center were the Crossroads Market (July 1970) and a laundromat with thirteen washers and eight dryers (late 1970). Both enterprises are wholly owned and operated by CCPC.

Subsequently CCPC leased space in the center to a hamburger stand, appliance store, dress shop, shoe-repair shop, realty office, beauty parlor, and barber shop. CCPC kept rents as low as possible, but did so on condition that the shops operate training programs as part of their rental agreements.

While the contractors were putting up the brick and mortar walls in the shopping center, Albert Williams was trying to bring down other walls in the area—walls of hatred and divisiveness.

"Many black groups didn't believe in the white man," Williams says. "They felt that the white man would come in and want to control it [the center]. The blacks felt we were going the wrong way."

Typical of such people was Norman Morgan, one of the young blacks who came off the street and joined the volunteer workers.

"Five years ago," says Morgan, "I wouldn't sit in the same room with a white person, let alone talk to them."

After five years no one claims Belle Haven is a perfect picture of racial harmony and tranquility. Yet there seems to be little dispute that real changes for the better have occurred.

Williams thinks the project has at least shown community residents that something can be done to alleviate poverty. He also thinks that tensions have eased.

He is pinning many hopes on the small job-training projects in the new stores. Currently there are five trainees at the appliance store. And the dress shop is training both dressmakers and sales personnel. In addition, professionals in the leased shops, such as the butchers, managers, and repairmen, give instruction after regular business hours.

With unemployment widespread among the young, these efforts are at least making a small dent. But few in the community seem to have any illusions that the project at its present scale and money levels can do much more.

Williams is candid about financial problems. Bad checks passed at the Crossroads Market are a serious problem for the corporation. And Williams acknowledges that the books are not in good shape—but then there is not enough money to hire a full-time accountant.

CCPC clearly faces difficulties, but it now does so in a community that lives in relative harmony. More than money is in balance at Willow and Newbridge.

"We started off uphill," says Albert Williams, "and goodwill is the only thing that's keeping us going."

Even so, thanks to the shopping center project, goodwill is one commodity that is in growing supply in Menlo Park.

I hope these cattle can be as helpful to us as the buffalo were to our grandfathers.

Sisseton-Wahpeton Oyate Tokataya Ptemanuyanpi Ecahyapte

Lake Traverse Indian Reservation, South Dakota

Where herds of buffalo once roamed the land, young people of the Sisseton-Wahpeton Sioux tribe are now raising new strains of prime beef cattle as part of an ambitious program aimed at solving the principal economic problems facing the tribe.

Two of the most serious problems are lack of income and lack of jobs. The tribe's average per capita income, for example, is only about $650 a year. And the unemployment rate, which varies from season to season, averages 71–91 percent over the year.

A third major problem has been the exodus of young adults. The population of the reservation has declined about 30 percent over the past decade, as young Sioux have left to try life in the cities—a trend that, unfortunately for the reservation, has been helped along by the Bureau of Indian Affairs' relocation program of manpower training and employment.

The young cattlemen are all members of an organization called Sisseton-Wahpeton Oyate Tokataya Ptemanuyanpi Ecahyapte ("Future Ranchers of the Sisseton-Wahpeton Sioux"). The chief purpose of S.W.O.T.P.E., as it is known, is to develop scores of competent, self-employed ranchers over the next decade and thereby improve living conditions on the Lake Traverse Indian Reservation. A successful cattle-raising venture will mean more income, more jobs, and more people staying on the reservation.

There are many large ranches on the 900,000-acre reservation, but most ot them are white-owned. Over the years the Sioux have lost (through homesteading) or sold off much of this land and are now down to about 107,000 acres, most of it fertile pastureland containing many lakes and creeks. Sioux men by and large have not been successful in starting their own ranches. Individual allotments of land have been too small, and the men have been unable to obtain bank loans to meet operating costs.

In 1935, the Bureau of Indian Affairs operated a program designed to alleviate the effects of the Depression on the Sioux.

Families were provided with ten cattle each, but the grant did not cover fencing, feed, machinery, or training. This oversight made maintenance of the herds impossible, so the project had to be abandoned.

For close to three decades Indian participation in agriculture was almost nonexistent on the reservation. Then the tribal health council began trying to interest the people in raising livestock as part of a proposed 4-H club program.

In June 1968 the council applied to Heifer Project, Inc., for assistance. Heifer Project, an international organization that donates livestock to children from low-income families, eventually approved the application, but the reservation did not receive any livestock until October 1971.

The long-awaited stock—18 heifers, 15 young female pigs, and 35 sheep—were distributed to fifty-five children from twenty-five reservation families. Each of the recipients signed a contract whereby his stock's first offspring would be given to the health council to be distributed to other children.

Encouraged by the success of their children's 4-H projects, the adults decided to form a livestock enterprise that would give the whole tribe a sense of purpose for the present and hope for the future. A key person is this decision was Irene Gronau, the head of the tribal health council. As she says, "Over half our tribe is under 16 years of age. Our young people have always had vital and responsible places in our tribe. They were protectors and providers. Our youngsters want to help out. We have had to find ways to let them, and at the same time we have to do something about their future."

Consequently, in February 1972, Sisseton-Wahpeton Oyate Tokataya Ptewanuyanpi Ecahyapte was incorporated as a nonprofit enterprise. A five-person board of directors was elected.

In November of that year the Campaign for Human Development of the U.S. Catholic Conference loaned S.W.O.T.P.E. $100,000 for the purchase of 230 head of cattle.

The cattle were distributed to twenty-three eligible families. To be eligible a family had to have sufficient feed, shelter, and fencing on hand before obtaining any of the stock.

S.W.O.T.P.E.'s plan was to operate a sort of revolving live-stock plan. Each participant family was to receive ten cows and have them for four years. The family would keep all ten cows for the first year and then return three of them to S.W.O.T.P.E. after the calves had been weaned during the second year. Three more cattle would be returned in the third year, and the remaining four in the fourth year. Each participating family would assume full ownership of its calves, while the corporation would recirculate the breed cattle to new members.

The breeds of cattle selected for this project were two strains developed in Europe—the Gelbvieh and the Chianina. Both of these breeds are noted for their ability to put on weight rapidly while growing to maturity—a valuable quality in beef cattle.

The members of S.W.O.T.P.E. undertook to use a progressive breeding program designed to give the corporation excellent breeding stock within a few years. Furthermore they acted in the knowledge that the market price for each generation of the cattle will increase along with the purity of the strain.

Meanwhile the members of S.W.O.T.P.E. had received funds from the Freedom from Hunger Foundation to enable them to buy needed agricultural equipment. The corporation used these funds to buy a tractor, a rake, and a baler in order to be able to produce hay for the livestock.

Another grant from the Campaign for Human Development in 1973 enabled the members to further improve the facilities on their ranches, as well as to purchase much-needed machinery and other equipment. The grant also carried funds that enabled S.W.O.T.P.E. to hire a paid project coordinator.

The number of families participating in the cattle-raising project is increasing year by year. Irene Gronau believes that the total number of people involved in the program will reach more than 450 within a decade—which is to say, some 40 households will have become self-supporting through their ranching efforts.

In addition to the direct benefits to be obtained from raising cattle, the members of the corporation are also discovering that they can profit from their dealings with local non-Indian ranchers and farmers. Since the S.W.O.T.P.E. members now need their pastures and fields for their own livestock, they can—and do— charge the non-Indians considerably more for renting land.

Sisseton-Wahpeton Oyate Tokataya Ptewanuyanpi Ecahyapte has proved itself to be a successful economic venture that has won widespread acceptance on the reservation—and not just among the younger people. As one elderly member of the tribe reflected, "We have been so anxious for a program like this that will help the economy here . . . and develop the good things the tribe has."

S.W.O.T.P.E. represents a real hope for the future. As one rancher said when he received his stock, "I hope these cattle can be as useful to us as the buffalo were to our grandfathers."

We wanted a piece of the American pie, but how
do you gain access to the resources locked
up in ivory towers?

The Mexican American Council
for Economic Progress

Austin, Texas

José Uriegas is a changed man—at least outwardly.

He has swapped his faded blue jeans for a business suit and tie. He no longer shouts his anger from the streets at the financial power structure. Instead he deals with it directly in the board rooms of bank presidents and business magnates.

Five years ago, as a civil rights activist, Uriegas bore the label of a "militant confrontationist." He was blackballed from teaching in his hometown schools. And he is still fighting for the same goals— for social and economic equality for Mexican Americans. But to achieve them, he has discovered, has meant transforming himself into a business wizard. It has not been easy. When he speaks now, though, Uriegas can do so with the confidence and authority of a man who has helped establish an organization that has founded 200 new businesses in south Texas and has $1 million in grants to its credit—an organization known as the Mexican American Council for Economic Progress (MACEP).

MACEP is a product of years of hope and effort—compounded with frustration, anguish, and anger—on the part of Uriegas and its other founders. It is also a product of the belief that economic power is the answer to the social injustices bred by poverty.

Now the hope and promise for thousands of poor people throughout south Texas, MACEP had its origins in the minds and hearts of twelve angry young men—ten Mexican Americans and two Anglos—who refused to accept the Chicano condition as unchangeable. Two of them were José Uriegas and Arturo Casillas.

Born in the small south Texas town of Uvalde, José Uriegas grew up accustomed to hard work. As a youth, he put in long hours as a migrant laborer while trying to get as much education as possible in the public schools. With the help of his family, he then managed to put himself through college, where he acquired the credentials to teach school.

While teaching school in Uvalde, Uriegas grew increasingly concerned about reform for his people. Making a successful bid for election to the city council, he became the first Mexican American to play an active role in the city's government. But his eagerness for reform did not set well with the conservative Anglo community, and he was soundly defeated for reelection. And the Anglos' disapproval of his politics spread to his professional life: Uriegas soon found himself out of a teaching job as well.

These setbacks served only to increase his determination to fight for an improvement in the substandard living conditions being endured by the Chicano communities. So it was that Uriegas became an outspoken leader in the civil rights movement of the 1960s. Later he found another path of opportunity when he got a supervisory job with VISTA (Volunteers in Service to America).

Meanwhile, in another south Texas Chicano community, Arturo Casillas was fighting his own way up from the pit of poverty. Reared in the urban barrio of Corpus Christi, Casillas came out of the public schools prepared for college, but the money simply wasn't available so he had to forego a college education.

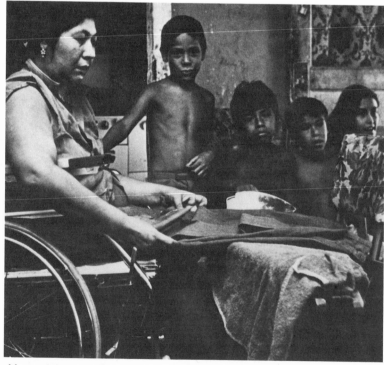

Mike Lacey

Many of the poor Chicanos of south Texas look to MACEP for assistance.

Casillas married young and moved from job to job, working with his hands to support his family. He developed a successful business with the purchase of a newspaper route, and began turning his attention to the idea of social change through organization. Consequently he became involved in a Corpus Christi garbage workers' strike, which, although it failed, did give Casillas both experience and acceptance as a leader. He then threw himself into the civil rights movement, which bred in him a combination of ambition, hope, commitment, and a growing disenchantment with the way things were. Deciding that he should put all of his efforts into his beliefs, Casillas left his financially successful job, took a cut in pay, and began as a VISTA supervisor.

In south Texas, as in other parts of the country, VISTA brought many people and ideas together, and it thereby gave birth to programs and projects that were to flourish independent of the mother organization. One such project was created in 1969 by Uriegas and Casillas, and their friends, who anted up a grand total of $1,200 ($100 each) to incorporate the Mexican American Development Corporation (MADCO). MADCO was to be a consultant group aimed at helping Chicanos help themselves through acquiring and using the power of money. As José Uriegas says, "In order for the general standard of living in the barrio to rise, the whole economic outlook must change. As long as available jobs continue to be low-pay, low-incentive, and involve unskilled employment, employee turnover and unemployment will be high. As long as the barrio residents must deal with Anglo proprietors who channel their money out of the community, the economic status in the barrio will remain the same."

Harmon Lisnow, one of two Anglos in on the founding of MADCO, puts it even more succinctly: "We knew we had to gain access to power to bring about change, instead of confronting it all the time. We wanted a piece of the American pie, but how do you gain access to the resources locked up in ivory towers?"

MADCO was not able to provide the answer, for the fledgling consultant firm failed to take off. As Casillas, Uriegas, and the others discovered, the business was simply not there for inexperienced consultants. So MADCO fell dormant.

But not so the men intent upon developing Chicano economic power. In 1970 they started the Mexican American Council for Economic Progress, a nonprofit organization designed to help Chicanos begin or expand businesses of their own. MACEP would accomplish this goal, the founders hoped, by actively seeking grants, loans, and contracts on behalf of Chicano businesses, and by offering all those businesses a variety of technical assistance, and training (which MACEP would obtain, in turn, from established institutions throughout south Texas).

MACEP began slowly, carefully feeling its way through the maze of obstacles that lie in wait for all new enterprises.

One of the first problems the council faced was obtaining funds just to get started. Deciding the best approach would be to seek small donations from many would-be givers, the founders undertook a door-to-door campaign among the churches, large businesses, and banks of Corpus Christi. Their efforts paid off to the tune of $66,000—not a huge sum but certainly sufficient to put MACEP on its feet and also to give it the means to seek out federal government funding.

Another problem confronting the council was the need for business expertise. A major factor in MACEP's surmounting this difficulty was the presence of Arturo Casillas. In addition to his experience with his own business, he was one of the first Chicanos to take advantage of a training program sponsored by the National Council for Business Opportunity. That program gave him the skills needed to put together loan packages from financial institutions to finance new business ventures.

MACEP began its first economic development program in Corpus Christi. In 1971 the Economic Development Administration came through with a $68,000 grant for MACEP to set up the Corpus Christi Economic Development Corporation.

Although the principal milestones in MACEP's short history have involved government agencies, the council's greatest strength and influence are in the assistance it gives to individual businessmen, principally minority group businessmen. More than 200 businesses have opened or expanded as a result of MACEP involvement, creating an estimated 2,000 new jobs and a conservative estimate of $8 million in incomes. The success-to-failure ratio of MACEP-aided businesses is phenomenal: only one out of sixty-eight fails, as compared to the national new business failure ratio of eight out of ten.

Basically MACEP helps individual businessmen by first compiling feasibility studies, together with complete records of assets, liabilities, and equities, in a prospectus. This package is then taken to a bank where it is used to secure a loan for the establishment of a business.

A business established through MACEP belongs entirely to the individual, but MACEP provides technical assistance in establishing the business and trains the owner and personnel to make it prosper. As a business becomes self-sustaining, the business-man is encouraged to pay for the assistance that he receives from MACEP. Such ongoing help includes managerial aid, technical help, and further financial assistance if needed.

Obviously, not all of the business ideas presented to the council are sound, so part of MACEP's function is to screen out the unacceptable ones. Less than 15 percent of the original applicants actually receive loans, according to Casillas, because many don't have the slightest idea as to their potential market, the money they will need to start, or any other business-related factors.

"People come in very excited about their business idea and want to start right away, like today or tomorrow," Casillas says, adding that many expect to get rich quick. "They don't know they are going to have to work ten-to-sixteen hours a day for the first few months just to break even."

As a business develops, the owner must continue to educate himself in the total business structure. As Casillas puts it, "A

Mike Lacey

This south Texas laborer is a Chicano who now has a piece of the economic pie, thanks to the efforts of MACEP.

plumber knows how to be a good plumber, but if he wants to start a plumbing business, he must learn to stop being a plumber and become an administrator. He must hire other plumbers and turn his attention to profit-and-loss statements, breakeven points, and wages. It's impossible for the businessman to be completely versed in every aspect of a business, but he must at least be familiar with them."

Funding has played a major role in the three-year development of MACEP, for, as grants and contracts are obtained, the organization grows. Support from the major financial institutions outside the barrios has enabled businessmen inside the Mexican American communities to establish themselves—MACEP's goal.

MACEP is currently exerting a widespread influence throughout south Texas. In Austin, for example, Mexican American merchants, due to the encouragement of MACEP, have formed a Mexican American Chamber of Commerce to promote Chicano businesses in the community. And people in Houston, Uvalde, and other rural and urban communities increasingly request the council to duplicate its work in their areas.

Individuals also show signs of benefiting socially as well as financially from the council's efforts. One man in the town of Alice, for instance, whose failing business was saved through MACEP, has since begun new hiring practices. In the past he would hire the cheapest labor possible, including "wetbacks" at 10 cents an hour. But he has now developed a social conscience and pays decent wages to Mexican Americans in the community. And other Mexican American businessmen in various communities have become aware of the needs of others in the barrio, and their hiring practices prove it.

With each program development, the horizons of MACEP have expanded. There is no contract it will not seek, even if that means training new personnel to earn it. And every time MACEP goes through a business process, the staff acquires more expertise and raises the level of its knowledge. Within an estimated five years MACEP people hope to have as much business savvy as any sophisticated organization in the nation.

MACEP's remarkable progress enabled its founders to revive MADCO in 1972 with the hope of eventually becoming self-sustaining through the profits of MADCO contracts. In addition to its general expansion anticipated for the years ahead, the council also envisions the formation of a Minority Enterprise Small Business Investment Corporation (MESBIC). Such an enterprise would provide financial assistance for those who lack the equity to begin businesses on their own.

The whole focus of MACEP is and will continue to be to bring about social change through economic self-sufficiency.

"We believe," says José Uriegas, "that if we can produce a cash flow in the minority communities, people will be able to get the necessities they need. We realize that most minority problems are related to money, and if we're going to change that, we need to get away from the Christmas-basket approach."

The MACEP approach has meant learning and adopting established business and government financing techniques. It has also meant some outward changes in the attitudes of its organizers—but it has paid off in a slice of the economic pie.

Mike Lacey

A migrant family packs possessions in the only thing it owns.

Poor people, like everybody else, need capital. . . . In this area they even need it to be admitted to hospitals.

The Missouri Delta Ecumenical Ministry

Hayti, Missouri

"In a way, last year was our worst year—and also our best," William L. Jones was telling the group of farmers seated around the table. This was the annual board meeting of the Bootheel Agricultural Services Incorporated Cooperative (BASIC), being held in a weatherbeaten shed amid the soybean fields of the "Bootheel" of southeastern Missouri.

Jones, the president of the cooperative, continued: "Because of the floods, we could not plant on time. Only five or six members raised vegetables. The remaining acreage was planted in soybeans, and we made over $8,000 profit after gathering only half the beans."

This was encouraging news to the men at the table, all of them ex-sharecroppers and tenant farmers. Their cooperative had been losing money ever since it started in 1967. Now, with a profit for the year 1973, it looked as though their hard work and determination were paying off—and the bad times were behind them.

And in looking back over those times they knew they could not have survived if it hadn't been for the co-op—and especially for the Missouri Delta Ecumenical Ministry (MDEM). It had been MDEM that had started the co-op, that had covered their financial losses during the lean years, that had given them advice and encouragement and hope for the future.

The Missouri Delta Ecumenical Ministry is an interfaith social action agency dedicated to improving the economic conditions and overall quality of life in the poverty-stricken area known as the Bootheel.

The three counties that make up the Bootheel form a narrow band of fertile bottomlands along the Mississippi River. But the fertility of the land is of small consequence, for the Bootheel, according to the U.S. Department of Agriculture, happens to rank as one of the worst poverty pockets in the United States.

The poverty of the tri-county area stems largely from the mechanization and consolidation of the local cotton farms during the past two decades. The farms now have little need for many field hands, let alone any tenant farmers or sharecroppers. And the area offers little else in the way of employment opportunities. So the people are forced to seek public assistance and eke out a livelihood by taking whatever low-paying jobs they can find. Consequently most of the families in the area have incomes of less than $3,000 a year—well below the federally designated poverty line. In fact, a third of them subsist on about $1,000 a year.

These were the conditions observed by an Episcopalian minister, William Chapman, in the mid-1960s, when he made a study of the tri-county area to determine what could be done for and by the people. Together with other local ministers and interested citizens, Chapman organized the Delta Pilot Program to work with the poor people, to help them identify and meet their own needs.

In 1969 the organizers formally incorporated their project as a nonprofit, tax-exempt corporation known as the Missouri Delta Ecumenical Ministry. Since then the organization has grown to become one of the largest church coalitions operating in rural America, with funding being provided by the Protestant Episcopal Church, the United Presbyterian Church in the U.S.A., the Presbyterian Church in the U.S., the United Methodist Church, the Roman Catholic Church, the United Church of Christ, and the American Lutheran Church. In addition, some funds are also provided by private corporations and national trade unions.

MDEM's ultimate goal is to eliminate poverty in the area. And the way to do that, in the words of Richard Male, executive director, "is to organize programs and make them stand on their own, from both a managerial and financial point of view. The hands of the poor are potentially the best resources in the world. But they first must have something to grab onto as they work toward self-sufficiency."

What they should grab onto, MDEM believes, are organizations that enable them to act and wield power collectively—organizations owned and operated by the people themselves.

The people, too, clearly believe in this approach to their problems, for MDEM has been remarkably successful in developing and/or maintaining a number of self-governing organizations.

The Bootheel Agricultural Services Incorporated Cooperative, now the oldest organization under the MDEM banner, was organized in 1967 by a small group of local people aided by members of the original Delta Pilot Program. The program supplied the funds for startup costs (including the cost of farm equipment).

BASIC now has about a hundred member families. They grow vegetables and other crops in order to provide food for themselves, as well as to have a surplus that can be sold for cash. So the cooperative provides them with a modest additional income—at least in a good year such as 1973.

The member families work together in raising cash crops on multi-acre fields. And each family also grows vegetables on its own small plot of land; it can then keep some of its produce and sell the rest. The crops sold by the co-op are marketed in the St. Louis area and also locally (one customer being an MDEM-affiliated cooperative supermarket).

In addition to providing both food and income for its members, BASIC serves as a seasonal source of employment for several local families. It hires people from outside the co-op—often people whose only other source of income is public assistance—to work as field hands during harvest-time.

The cooperative grows all of its crops on land that is rented. This is not a matter of choice, though, for BASIC simply cannot afford to buy its own land—of which it needs about a hundred acres. As Bill Jones says, "Land around here is very expensive. Prices now are between $600 and $1,000 per acre."

Nevertheless land ownership ranks as one of BASIC's major goals. In Rich Male's words, "A crucial factor in BASIC's need for land is the psychological effect it will have on its members, few of whom have owned anything more than a $300 car that is ten years old. A person needs a bona fide stake in the society if he is to be expected to take an active role in building it. The ownership would give BASIC and its members a dignity they have never felt before. It would be something tangible, something to increase their sense of independence."

Another major MDEM project is the Bootheel Credit Union (BCU), which was organized in 1971. Located in the town of Hayti, BCU helps meet one of the basic needs of the poor people of the Bootheel. In the words of BCU's manager, Noma Fisher:

"Poor people, like everybody else, need capital. They need it for housing, food, education, clothing, and everything else. In this area they even need it to be admitted to hospitals. These fees run as high as $150—far beyond the means of the average poor family.

"The people have limited access to capital. There have been no community-owned or controlled financial institutions, and commercial banks are out of the question for most of the poor because of the tight lending policies and because most banks don't

Bootheel resident visits the credit union in Hayti.

make loans under $500 anyway."

Consequently a group of local residents, aided by MDEM, decided to organize a credit union. It wasn't easy. To begin with, as Noma Fisher points out, the people were not accustomed to saving money, they were not aware of the high interest rates charged by finance companies, and they frankly didn't know that a credit union offers many advantages.

So the group set up courses designed to educate the local people about interest rates, installment purchasing, and the financial pitfalls of buying from high-pressure, door-to-door salesmen. And it organized a planning committee of ten members, nine of whom were either poor or had come from low-income families.

The credit union was formally chartered in July 1971 and opened its doors in October of that year. With initial funding of $10,000 from the Fund for Fifty Million, a Presbyterian group, BCU spent several months recruiting members.

Initially, though, the poor people were reluctant to take part in the credit union activities. As Noma Fisher recollects, "Some of the welfare recipients felt that, if it was discovered that they had $5 in the credit union, their checks would be cut off. We had to assure them that it was perfectly legal to have money in the credit union, that we were working *for* them, not against them, and that our files were confidential, anyway."

Since that time there has been a considerable change in the people's attitude.

"People now feel that they own the credit union," Noma Fisher says. "They also feel free to talk over all sorts of problems with us. And they now tend to pass the word about the benefits of belonging to the organization."

She also believes that BCU has increased the feeling of unity among the Bootheel's residents.

"By being a member of the credit union," she says, "the residents show a common bond. They know that it doesn't matter whether you have $5 or $50 in the organization—you're all members and you're really investing in the community. You're helping the community, yourself, and others."

The credit union currently has more than 600 members. They own more than $107,000-worth of income-producing shares. Since 1971 they have been granted close to 500 loans for such purposes as health care, home improvements, school needs, clothing, cars, and consolidation of bills. The credit union members are charged only 1 percent interest per month on their unpaid loan balances. And they receive free budget counseling and free income tax advice.

Although the credit union has expanded steadily, it has still not reached the point where its deposits exceed its demands for loans. Its assets total more than $118,000, but it has made loans amounting to about $174,000.

"Membership savings are not enough to meet the demands for loans," Noma Fisher says. "The reason we can't make it on membership deposits alone is because this is a low-income area. We need more outside support in terms of additional payroll deductions and deposits."

Payroll deductions for credit union shares are already being made by more than a dozen local businesses and factories, and BCU is busy drumming up support throughout the tri-county area for additional deposits. BCU is also planning a branch office in Kenneth, the largest city in the area. These approaches, BCU hopes, will bring the credit union closer to realizing its goal of 4,000 members by 1976.

Housing in Missouri's Bootheel is some of the worst in the country.

Another MDEM-affiliated project is the Howardville Area Cooperative Enterprises (HACE), which was organized in 1971 to develop a community-based cooperative shopping center. HACE's first accomplishment was the establishment of a supermarket.

Like most projects that MDEM has helped organize, the supermarket took plenty of planning, and it wasn't seriously discussed until the residents were certain they wanted it.

"Before we moved along with the project, the community had to show some commitment," Rich Male recalls. "We told them that if they wanted a supermarket, they'd have to work for it. Too many concepts fail because people who are asking for the project have no real interest in it. In this case, the residents raised $2,000 through small sales and they purchased 2.6 acres of land. After that we were convinced that they really wanted the project and, since they had made an investment, they would support it."

The supermarket was opened in 1973, representing a total investment of close to $100,000. Since then more than a hundred local families have become members of HACE, for they, like MDEM, have come to recognize that the store meets a basic community need.

As Rich Male says, "Before the residents got their own supermarket a lot of people who didn't have adequate transportation had to travel as far as 25 miles to shop. And they had to pay as much as $5 to get a taxi or neighbor to make the trip."

Henrietta Grant, the local woman who manages the supermarket, believes that HACE can expect a considerable increase in membership. We get a lot of community support, but some people are so accustomed to buying all their goods at a particular store that it's hard to get them to change their shopping pattern. We have to convince them that this is their store, that they only have to purchase five shares of stock to become full-fledged members."

Since 1971 the Missouri Delta Ecumenical Ministry has also been instrumental in the founding of a number of other projects:

• *Health and Welfare Rights*, which was started so volunteers could work with welfare recipients on health and welfare issues.

• *Local Leadership Development*, which is aimed at having MDEM staff members work with other people in the community in order to develop new leadership.

• *The Health Advisory Committee*, which works with local people in the area of health education, with the goal of eventually establishing a community-controlled health facility.

• *The Neighborhood Improvement Force*, which operates in local neighborhoods in order to help deal with such common problems as substandard housing and poor drainage.

• *Missouri Delta Community Corporation*, which finds permanent jobs for migrant workers.

• *The Bootheel Ministries for Better Mental Health*, which conducts educational programs in the field of mental health.

• *The Bootheel Area Legal Assistance Program*, which serves the local two counties of the Bootheel region and offers assistance in consumer and tenant-and-landlord problems, and conducts a legal education program for area residents.

MDEM realizes that it must begin projects only at the rate that residents are willing to accept them.

"We must develop programs according to the dictates of the community," Male says. "We must never impose our values on the community. Sometimes what we want and what the community

Home for one Bootheel family is an abandoned school bus.

wants are two different things. But we must listen to the people, let them determine what their needs are, and work with them according to their priorities."

It's not always tangible success stories that convince MDEM that it is making a dent in improving the lot of the poor. Sometimes it's the change in attitudes that does it.

There was the time, for example, when an elderly woman approached an MDEM official after a somewhat heated meeting with county welfare officials and said: "You know, for over fifty years I have been trying to say what is really on my mind about the welfare system. This is the first time that I have had the nerve."

MDEM officials and the people of the Bootheel feel that MDEM's multifaceted approach has taught poor people one basic lesson—to be self-sufficient. As Rich Male says:

"We're teaching the people how to work for themselves rather than relying on others to do the work for them. We're providing an economic alternative and meaningful employment opportunities.

"It gets back to the basic question—are you providing things for people, or are you helping people to learn to help themselves?"

CHAPTER 2

Education

Being born into poverty can handicap a person educationally almost from birth. Crowded living conditions, malnutrition, absence of one or both parents, and poor health care set a pattern for the child even before he or she starts school. The disadvantaged home deprives him of the necessary prerequisites to formal schooling—intellectual and sensory stimulation. And the confinement of an urban slum or the drawbacks of rural isolation can impede his development as a human being and deprive him of a chance to obtain a good education—and a rewarding life.

Education has traditionally been the responsibility of the state. But all too often the state-controlled public school system seems too rigid to deal with the problems of the disadvantaged—for example, reading skills that are deficient or never developed; the lack of bilingual classes for students of Spanish or Asian descent; the lack of adult education for people who got a later start in life.

All of these problems and more constitute a crisis in U.S. education that few public school systems can completely resolve.

The self-help education program can be an alternative to the inflexibility and insensitivity of public schooling. A community- or neighborhood-controlled education project can teach English as a second language to functionally literate adults and children. Another program can be rooted in preserving the cultural inheritances of a minority group or the preservation of a traditional skill or craft that is threatened by extinction.

Self-help projects lure dropouts back to learning, teach ghetto housewives how to shop wisely, and bring career information to children cut off from the future in inner-city slums.

The mutual-assistance education program that fosters self-help can also supplement the public school system by helping an individual to increase his capacities to succeed in high school, college, or vocational school.

Being disadvantaged is a handicap, but the person who has an opportunity to be part of a self-help education program has one of the best chances of a good life in the mainstream of society.

*We had no mastermind, no strategy. . . . We
looked at what we needed and scrounged around
until we got it.*

Break Free

New York, New York

Maurice Weir was a dropout. But he decided on a course of action that appealed to very few of his fellow dropouts on New York's Lower East Side: someday he would not only complete his education but would go back to work within the system.

Today, as an adult armed with an education, Maurice Weir is working with the system—not as a teacher in the traditional network of public schools, but as executive director of a private organization named Break Free. This is a nonprofit organization that was begun in 1969 to help high school dropouts on the Lower East Side to "break free" of the slum cycle by finishing high school and going to college.

Break Free was originally a component of Young Life, a surburban Christian organization that began to involve itself in the problems of the Lower East Side in the mid-1960s.

Young Life worked with gang leaders, as one worker put it, "trying to get them to trade switchblades for bibles." Some of the Young Life people, though, believed that education should be given priority over religious conversion. Consequently Break Free, then staffed by community leaders, decided to break away from Young Life and become a secular organization.

Break Free's first efforts were directed toward helping the talented but insecure students who, for one reason or another, have lost their way in the huge, impersonal public high school system. These are the students who perhaps think of going on to college but rarely get there, either because they drop out of high school or because they make no effort to get into college. As one of Break Free's leaders has noted, "Slum kids just don't know where to apply, or don't have the application fees. Even if they get into a school, they're afraid to go away—afraid of discrimination and hostility. Or they might get scholarships, but they won't have the money to get to the school; or they feel their poverty background so keenly that they're embarrassed because they don't have any really decent clothes. It's easier for them not even to try."

Break Free decided to concentrate on giving some of the Lower East Side dropouts a chance to complete their high school education in a good education environment. During the 1969–70 school year, Break Free took about thirty youngsters and placed them in a private preparatory day school in New Jersey. In the spring of 1970, though, economic problems threatened to close the school. This meant that not only would Break Free's students lose credit

Break Free students get a second chance to complete their educations.

for their work but six of them would not get the diplomas they expected in June. Break Free decided to meet the crisis by organizing a core of volunteer teachers to finish out the term. It persuaded a local church to donate basement space and it got a private preparatory school in New York City to administer the exams and give extended accreditation. The result was that the six students graduated with diplomas.

But that still left two dozen students with no place to go the following fall. That July the Break Free staff decided to try to create a permanent school. Don Schwartz, the only remaining member of the original board of directors, recalls that "we plotted some figures, then trooped over to Morgan Guaranty, whose urban affairs office had been funding the street academies on the Lower East Side. They told us to get everything else together, and they'd see."

Maurice Weir, who grew up in Harlem and on the Lower East Side, and had taken over leadership of the organization a few months before the crisis, insists, "We had no mastermind, no strategy.... We looked at what we needed and scrounged around until we got it."

The scrounging, however, required immense tact, and multiple written and verbal proposals. With Morgan Guaranty Trust's tentative support, the staff went to the New York City Board of Education, which helped to procure state urban aid funds (appropriated for remediation of educational problems associated with poverty) to hire teachers.

"I went to the Foundation Library every day to pore through the list of foundations to find additional sources of financial support," Weir says. "Everyone went to all sorts of meetings—community meetings, church meetings. The Collegiate Reformed Dutch Church decided to support the project and give us space—two floors of an office building located in Wall Street, just outside the community, at $1 a year."

Various other schools agreed to give the Break Free school extended accreditation.

Break Free also looked to its own community for support. Streetworkers hung out on the streets and on basketball courts, and knocked on doors. Larry Hester-Bey, Break Free's head streetworker, organized a mothers' group to provide community support.

Break Free leaders approached the disparate communities of the Lower East Side—the blacks, Puerto Ricans, Chinese, Italians, and Jews—to sell the idea of the school being a community project that would include everyone. "But there was really no credibility problem," says Hester-Bey. "Almost everyone involved in the program grew up in the community—they knew us, trusted us, and, because of that, supported what we decided to do."

"We began to learn that organizations which could not give money would give in kind," Weir notes. "Morgan Guaranty also contributed financial advice and legal services. Schools contributed books. Weyerhaeuser Company Foundation contributed lumber. We hired a carpenter, and we set to work painting, making repairs, building partitions for rooms in the school."

The people working directly for Break Free also gave in kind. Recalls Weir: "There was no money for salaries yet—our teachers and staff gave up good jobs to live off their savings, or they drove taxis, sold cosmetics, parked cars, worked by night to support themselves while they worked to build something they believed in.

You know, you don't get teachers like that by advertising in *The New York Times.*"

Weir himself was under great pressure. As Jackie Robinson, hired as a teacher that fall and now assistant headmaster, observes, "Maurice spent a lot of sleepless nights worrying about how to put it together. He had to make all the decisions. He didn't work overtime, he worked double time."

With double time, the school managed to open that October, a month late in the school year. Don Schwartz remarks, "It was phenomenal. The school went from idea to reality in just three months, in just 90 days."

The setting is unlikely: two floors of a nondescript battered office building, for which two signs—"Wall St. Pen Repair: Authorized Station" and "Rondell's: Watch Repair" are landmarks for those emerging from the bowels of the subway onto the dark, narrow street. Furniture is old office furniture contributed by the Exxon Corporation; plywood partitions separate offices; a curtain draped over a rope separates a large room into two classrooms. There is no coatroom, so students use old-fashioned coatracks that stand in the administrators' offices. There is no library, for there is no large collection of books. The school originally wanted to replace textbooks with primary works, but limited financial resources have meant that teachers take what they can get. In Elaine Choy's chemistry class, for example, she has to make do without a laboratory of any sort, and her students use as many as five different texts. As she says, "Try assigning reading and homework using five different texts."

Yet Break Free's Lower East Side preparatory school is one of New York's more successful alternative schools. It is a school that takes in the "hopelessly undisciplined" or so-called "stupid" public school dropouts. It is a school where 80 percent of the students finish a college preparatory program. It is a school where almost 85 percent of its graduates go on to college.

Individuals on the staff are reluctant to single out any particular reasons for the school's success. But outside observers can at least draw their own conclusions. Some of these conclusions are as follows:

● First there is the school's size: there are 191 students now, a small school by New York City standards. And with a staff of about fifteen, the school has a good teacher-to-student ratio—about one to twelve.

● The school, which operates on the trimester system, has an accelerated program that allows students who are already several years behind to earn their diplomas as quickly as possible.

• The school day is short, lasting from 8 a.m. to 1:30 p.m. This is accomplished through discarding homeroom, lunch, and study hall, thereby allowing students to hold jobs after school.

• The curriculum is tailored to meet the special needs of the students, most of whom belong to minority groups. About 40 percent are Chinese (a number of them being non-English-speaking Hong Kong immigrants), 25 percent are black, and 25 percent are Puerto Rican.

• Many of the teachers are bilingual. Furthermore an important distinction is made between teaching English as a second language and teaching courses bilingually. Bilingual teaching assumes proficiency in a native language, while many New York-born Puerto Ricans speak only so-called street Spanish.

• There is emphasis on basic skills and remedial work.

• Many of the staff come from the community or have experience in community or youth work. Most are young, many of them being under 30 years of age.

• The teachers are expected to keep themselves up to date through outside work or courses.

• The headmaster and assistant headmaster are each required to teach one course a term, so that administration doesn't get too removed from the students.

There are obviously other success factors as well. All teachers, for example, try to develop self-confidence and a sense of self-worth in the students. Jim Murphy, the headmaster, suggests that this helps avoid the traditional discipline problems and lack of motivation found in dropouts: "The students who come here have had histories of failure. We try to give them a history of success.

Another staff member asserts that "it is practically impossible to underestimate the students' lack of experience. Many have never been out of their immediate neighborhoods. It's difficult to imagine the amount of fear a ghetto kid would have going uptown, let alone walking into someplace like a museum."

Consequently teachers make it a point to include practical information about the outside world in classes. A recent schedule change now leaves each Wednesday free as Activity Day—students go on field trips to learn about the subjects they study and possible careers. Occasional weekend trips show them alternatives to urban slum living. Joan Hightower, a former participant in Break Free's program and now a college senior, declares, "We would see suburban houses on TV, but we always thought they didn't exist. When I went to school in Albany, it was like a dream—I saw what other minority people had, and I began to think that I could have it, too."

Important also is the recognition that most of these students have had little contact with the conservative, middle-class view of what people should and shouldn't do. So the school, as the assistant headmaster, Jackie Robinson, says, "accords them all the rights of ordinary citizens in our society." Students have the right of free speech and expression in the school and in the school publications. Habits judged irrelevant by the college process,

such as smoking or chewing gum, are also held irrelevant by the alternative school. Students have a real voice and real power in the school. An advisory group makes recommendations on school policy and disciplinary action before it is taken. Two of the seats on Break Free's board of directors belong to students, who have full voting rights.

Furthermore the school tries to meet some of the special non-educational needs of its students. A cooperative child care center, for example, is being organized to allow mothers without child care to go to school.

A staff of streetworkers, currently four full-time and two part-time people, deals with what have been traditionally called "personal" problems. Such matters, as is recognized by the streetworkers, are frequently the causes rather than the effects of academic failure. So it is that the staff thinks it important to help the students deal with family problems, drugs, pregnancy, and financial difficulties.

The streetworkers are all community people. Larry Hester-Bey stresses the importance of having had experience with such problems. "We've been there; we know. And they know we know. When the father comes home, instead of helping with the housework, he beats the mother. When you're scrounging for food, wearing last year's sneakers in the snow, and have inadequate medical attention—you're going to school after that? Social workers fresh out of college just don't know what it's like."

The school cooperates with local methadone programs, health and welfare agencies, and the police. Larry Hester-Bey insists, "It's important to have community contacts, and to deal with problems honestly and frankly. It's important, when a kid thinks he's got VD, to simply say, 'Go see Dr. so and so'. Or when someone tells you he's on drugs, it's important to deal with the problem and not just lecture. Or to go straight to the parents when you need to—because you *know* momma and poppa personally; now, that's validity."

Streetworkers visit the homes of students once a term. Like administrators, they are on a first-name basis with the students. Jackie Robinson points out, "The school has a history of breaking down barriers between students and teachers. You mustn't necessarily see yourself as a teacher or youth worker—but rather as a person." Also, like the administrators, their doors are always open, they are always accessible, and available for "just rapping." Don Schwartz evaluates their role: "A streetworker can say, 'I'm not your teacher, coach, disciplinarian; I'm your friend'. It helps these people overcome the feeling of being lost in a vast impersonal system." Streetworker Denise Mohica concurs: "These aren't my students, they are my friends."

Streetworkers and staff are also aware of their function as role models. Butch Newlin, the counseling supervisor, explains: "You notice I wear a coat and tie to work. The only people these kids ever see dressed up are pimps and pushers—you got to give them a sense of alternatives. These kids have to be encouraged until they are self-motivated—and just the way you carry yourself may be a motivation." As Larry Hester-Bey says of his job, "This isn't a function, it's a way of life."

Break Free students, when asked how the school is primarily different from the public schools they've abandoned, say "People here care."

Ronald Granger, a Break Free graduate entering college in the fall of 1974, says, "I was told all my life I was worth nothing. They made me feel like I was worth something. They bust their asses to keep you in line, so the least you can do is keep your nose clean. They made me want to try. Also, you know that you're out on your ear if you don't."

Students with more than eight absences a term are suspended. Students are constantly aware that the school is voluntary, and that there are many applications for each place available. "But the students are beautiful, they're the least of our problems," observes Hester-Bey.

Break Free's success has been extraordinary. Among its other credits, it won the Exxon Community Leadership Award for 1973. Nevertheless it is precisely that kind of success, however, that threatens the school's individuality.

"Everybody loves a winner," comments a staff member. The school's size has almost doubled in the last year, and it is expected to swell to almost 500 students by 1975.

Furthermore the Break Free school has been designated as an accredited New York City public high school, and it has accepted public funding. But receiving accreditation means giving up some identity and freedom. It also means being a little more careful if not conservative—in the front office and in the classroom.

But Maurice Weir is optimistic. The school is scheduled to move from its office building to a former bank nestled among Wall Street's skyscrapers, a few blocks away. A bit institutionalized? Maybe. But Weir knows the expanded facility promises hope. He concludes with a quiet air of determination, "We're certainly going to give it a try."

Those people respect our kids and try
to teach them about the modern world.
That's good for them.

The Center for
Environmental Education

Pine Ridge Indian Reservation, South Dakota

At a small alternative learning center on the Pine Ridge Indian Reservation, students are working on art and science projects, operating a printing press, and publishing a weekly newspaper. They are also learning the traditional values of their Oglala Sioux heritage. Indeed the entire purpose of the center is to imbue Indian children with understanding and respect for their heritage and culture. As a school it is not only an alternative but a challenge to the nearby Bureau of Indian Affairs (BIA) school, which aims at assimilating the Indian into the white man's culture.

Government efforts to assimilate the Oglala date back more than a century, to when the Pine Ridge reservation was set up. In the post-Civil War era the Indians at Pine Ridge, as elsewhere around the country, came under the control of government officials who advocated an educational system that would in effect prepare Indian children for a life on the fringes of white society rather than in the midst of their own culture.

This approach to Indian education has persisted to the present day. It is estimated that approximately 33 percent of all Indians of school age are currently attending U.S. government-run boarding schools and day schools, and about 35 percent are placed in foster homes, adoptive homes, or institutions. Very few are placed in Indian homes, very few have a chance to attend Indian-run schools (partly because there are very few such schools).

Such a policy is viewed by Indian activists as a denial of Indian children's rights to benefit from the teaching, counsel, and experience of their own parents and their own people—rights that have to be freely available if American Indians are to survive as people.

So it is that the BIA school at Kyle, one of the chief communities on the Pine Ridge reservation, is viewed with disfavor and distrust by many Oglala. These people look instead to a bold new experiment, the Center for Environmental Education, which views itself as a means for reuniting families and preserving Indian identity.

The center began as a part of a reservation-wide project sponsored by University Year in Action (UYA), a university work-study program that is run by Action, a federal agency. Learning centers were established early in 1972 in some forty-five communities scattered across the reservation, with UYA volunteers (many of them Indians) being assigned to each of the centers.

This program continued without any difficulties until the spring of 1973, when many of the students, together with five UYA volunteers, were arrested for participation in the takeover of Wounded Knee village undertaken by the activist organization known as the American Indian Movement. Subsequently the Pine Ridge tribal council requested Action to discontinue the program. The agency complied in June, and by September all funding of the Pine Ridge program had been discontinued.

But several of the UYA volunteers, as well as other people on the reservation, were unwilling to accept the idea of closing down the Indians' chief hope for an Indian-oriented education program.

"We had to go on," recalls Walter Gallacher, a University of Colorado sociology professor active in the UYA program at Pine Ridge. "We had too much of ourselves invested in the kids. Many of them looked to us as the only vehicle by which they could come to terms with this society."

Gallacher and four other UYA members stayed at Kyle in order to set up an independent project for the reservation children. A board of directors composed of students and parents was elected to steer the enterprise. And the project was named—and formally incorporated as—the Center for Environmental Education.

The principal project of the Center for Environmental Education is the Kyle Learning Center, which is housed in a once-abandoned building about half a mile from the center of the Kyle community.

After the students leave the nearby BIA school at 3:30 p.m., they flock to the learning center to watch television or participate in an art or science project.

Instruction at the center is informal. The hundred or so students, aged 6 to 20, select their own areas of interest and establish their own learning pace. Special meetings, discussions, and lectures are arranged, much of which emphasize Indian culture.

The students' parents are virtually unanimous in their support of the learning center. As the mother of one student said, "I'd rather have them there than on the roads or anywhere else. Those people respect our kids and try to teach them about the modern world. That's good for them."

The center's staff is very much concerned about the interaction between the center and the rest of the reservation. At times when the center is not very busy, Gallacher and his staff make it a point to visit the homes of the students, and they also frequently attend community business, social, and ceremonial functions.

The administration of the BIA school has so far ignored the learning center and has not offered any assistance. The center itself is not as interested in attacking the policy and operation of the BIA as it is in demonstrating a workable alternative to the BIA approach. The main difference in philosophy is that the center believes that the Sioux are people with a future as well as a past, and have many contributions to make to the modern world.

Although the learning center is housed in an old building, it is scheduled to eventually move into a 50-foot-high geodesic dome currently under construction. When completed the dome will be used for classes, crafts, shop activities, recreation, and meetings.

The dome is a very important project to the students, for it represents a circle, which is a sacred symbol of the Oglala people; they believe that the "power of the world always works in circles." And perhaps with the dome such power will come to them.

The Center for Environmental Learning also operates the Medicine Root Press, which was begun with an offset printing press, printing supplies, and darkroom equipment donated by UYA.

The Medicine Root Press was set up to provide educational materials and also on-the-job training for the students. Some have been trained to operate the press and darkroom equipment. Two of the trainees have secured printing jobs with a Denver firm. The students are paid for their work at the press from funds raised by selling calendars, Christmas cards, and stationery, and by doing small printing jobs for the reservation and local businesses.

In addition the center writes, prints, and distributes the *Shannon County News*, a weekly publication with a circulation of 1,500. This is the only paper printed and distributed on the reservation. Although the paper barely breaks even, the students gain by learning writing techniques, and the community gains by having a reliable source of local and topical information.

While it is still a young and growing enterprise, the Center for Environmental Education has already proved itself to be a practical alternative to the white-oriented educational system that has been imposed on the American Indians for more than a century. And it has proved that Indian adults working with Indian youngsters strengthens both the community and the culture.

I've seen youngsters with no idea of what to study
in high school. . . . I have a son here too, and I
don't want him to get caught up in that.

The "Now" People Program

Los Angeles, California

Once a month the fifth- and sixth-graders at West Athens Elementary School in the Watts section of Los Angeles eagerly await their special guests. The visitors may be professional athletes, musicians, educators, engineers or politicians; one month the guest list may include Johnny Otis and his band, the next month it presents Jim Thomas, a McDonnell Douglas engineer who amazes the children with a mammoth model of a DC-10. The visitors come from all walks of life, but they have one thing in common: each of them has made a success of his or her career.

The person who brings these people to the students of West Athens is Amanda Curry, the director of the "Now" People Program, and a mother who knows about life and crowded schools in a low-income area such as Watts.

"I don't want to see any more kids get caught in the failure cycle of ghetto children," says Mrs. Curry. "I've seen youngsters with no idea of what to study in high school. Besides, I have a son here too, and I don't want him to get caught up in that."

Breaking the so-called failure cycle is an important part of "Now" People. Instead of the traditional Career Day given to high school seniors, "Now" People reaches into the elementary school and tries to capture the interest of fifth- and sixth-graders before they lose interest in further education.

"Youngsters aren't getting enough from school," says Amanda Curry. "When parents or students realize this, it's generally too late. "Now" People is their headstart."

To keep the program going, Mrs. Curry frequently badgers well-known personalities and reminds them of their duties to the community. "Why don't you," she asks, "come out and rap two or three hours with these children?" While the recent response to her pleadings has been good, she has not always been so fortunate.

"At the very beginning," she recalls, "the experience of trying to do a program like this was somewhat traumatic." She consulted with educators, and child psychiatrists, policemen, school principals, and other community people of south-central Los Angeles.

"I just was trying to give them a fair idea of what I had in mind," she says. But her ideas tended to fall on deaf ears—perhaps not so much deaf as skeptical. But she persisted, even though it meant conditioning herself to deal with possible failure when it came to actually getting people to come to the school to talk with the youngsters.

"I was so afraid I would be turned down by celebrities," she remembers. "I had to psych myself out and be prepared that no one would help."

As it turned out, Mrs. Curry's cushion against fear was never really needed. For the first program, for example, she sent out invitations to six guests—and a total of thirteen came to the school to talk with the kids!

"We suddenly discovered," she says, "that a lot of people really wanted to come and participate. And besides," she laughs, "we soon found we could capitalize on professional jealousy. If one person knew the other was coming to the school, we'd have both of them show up."

The "Now" People Program was incorporated as a nonprofit community service organization. The intent was to remain separate from the school but utilize planning sessions that involved school administration, teachers, the School Community Advisory Council, the parent-teachers' association, and the administrative complement of the "Now" People Program.

The "Now" People Program has produced varied, interesting and even startling results, as the visiting "now" people interreact with the kids of West Athens.

When some local politicians made an appearance before one of the classes, for instance, they found that their normal approach to a fifth-grade audience didn't work. "They wouldn't let those guys off the hook," recalls Jim Thomas, the McDonnell Douglas engineer who, since his own workout with a West Athens class, has taken an active interest in the program and now assists Amanda Curry. As Thomas notes, "The kids began to badger them. They were convinced that each politician had a 'lackey' on the payroll." He pauses. "Let's just say it was an illuminating session."

In another session the kids got a chance to use a computer terminal. Linked to a standard telephone circuit, the terminal enabled the youngsters to "talk" with a distant computer.

Amanda Curry believes one of her best sessions was when she invited some law-enforcement officers. A total of thirty-two policemen and sheriff's deputies—twice as many as invited—showed up, black and white, and they brought with them a variety of displays and rescue units and motorcycle squads.

"They were so patient with the kids," Mrs. Curry says. "They answered everything that was asked." Before the day was over, the children had "adopted" a Los Angeles county sheriff.

The procedures used for presenting visiting speakers are

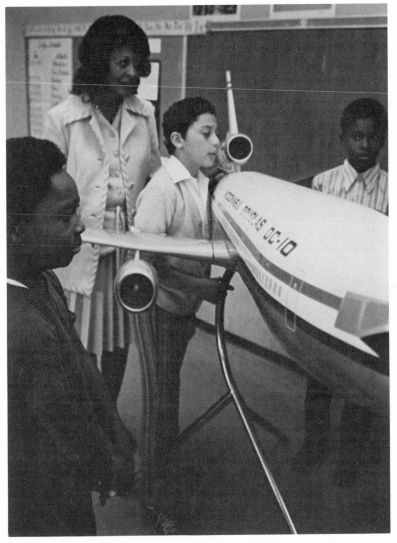

"Now" People's Amanda Curry brings the exciting world of jumbo jet aviation to a group of elementary school students in Watts.

simple. The "Now" People Program is divided into eight monthly presentations organized around the categories of law enforcement, communications, science, business, politics, arts, medicine, and sports. A single topic is taken up each month with three separate speakers invited to attend. Having three different people helps to give the children a broader exposure to different opinions and emphases, as well as more diversified insights into various topics.

Once selections have been made, speakers are requested to send a brief outline of their present occupation and educational background along with a picture of themselves for display in the school library. The outlines and pictures are posted, and identical materials are distributed to the teachers of the classes involved in the program.

The speakers are assigned individual classrooms to set up their displays, if any, and to conduct the sessions. When it is his turn, the speaker tells, in a brief introduction, something about his childhood, his schooling, and his job. Then follows a question-and-answer session, which gives the students the chance to engage in an enthusiastic and meaningful dialogue with their guest. The students attend each session in groups of approximately thirty or forty. After 45 minutes, each group rotates to another room for the second of three presentations, and so on.

Amanda Curry describes "Now" People as an "intensive motivational" program for the future. She envisions the program expanding to all school areas—not simply as an experimental program at West Athens. She believes it is essential that the boys and girls of today be given a chance to help decide what to do as the men and women of tomorrow. As she points out, "The senior high school Career Day is a grand idea . . . but it starts too late when the senior is already too far advanced to be able to take full opportunity of his education. He is already unmotivated. Or he's frustrated realizing that he can't pursue a field he'd now like to follow because he hadn't planned ahead for it. 'Now' People is designed to grab the attention of the wonderfully energetic youngsters, follow them every few years through school with the parents' full knowledge of the program, too, and keep them interested right up to final Graduation Day."

In the meantime the "Now" People Program continues to grow. It currently reaches some 1,500 students in West Athens and two other elementary schools. All these youngsters, Mrs. Curry believes, need encouragement in developing their full potential as human beings, and, as she likes to say, " 'Now' People offers a sensitive, direct, and economic approach to this end."

Too many people are afraid to do anything
because they don't feel "qualified" . . . . All you
need is confidence in the rightness of your cause.
The rest of it will fall into place.

The Harlem Consumer
Education Council

New York, New York

In February 1973 the New York State Public Service Commission told the New York Telephone Company to stop victimizing ghetto residents by forcing them to pay a pre-installation deposit fee. This victory for low-income consumers was largely the result of the persistent efforts of a diminutive, 54-year-old black woman named Florence Rice, who runs the Harlem Consumer Education Council. Far from equipping herself to do battle on legal technicalities, she simply upstaged all the well-prepared industry lobbyists and lawyers with her eloquent common sense. Commandeering the witness stand at the public service commission's hearings, she obliterated their statistics and charts with stories of real-life people, and demanded that the phone company discriminate against "one and only one class of subscribers—the class that won't or don't pay the bill!"

After years as a domestic and garment-industry worker, Florence Rice became a low-level participant in one of Harlem's most flourishing enterprises: consumer exploitation. She became a credit investigator for one of those disreputable Harlem furniture stores where varnished flakeboard and plastic "brocade" elegance is available to poor people on "easy credit terms"—at what really amounts to a 300–400-percent markup. At that time Mrs. Rice had a good friend named Elizabeth White, who worked on commission as a door-to-door salesperson for a company that specialized in a fraudulent fur-remodeling scheme.

"We both reached a point where we couldn't take it any more," Florence Rice recalls. "Living in Harlem, we knew we couldn't avoid getting ripped off, but we couldn't use that as an excuse to do it to other folks."

"It was like suddenly we woke up," small, soft-spoken Elizabeth

White adds. "We looked around us, and we saw people being cheated in so many ways. But we knew that nobody but us who live in Harlem cared enough to do anything."

This was in the pre-Nader year of 1962, at a time when "consumerism" had not yet entered the American vocabulary. Deceptive sales and credit practices, and the use of misleading contracts and advertising "puffery" had spread to all major levels of the U.S. economic scene, but nowhere was consumer fraud more blatant and more widespread than in the nation's urban ghettos. And although efforts have been made by both the public and private sectors to curb such abuses, the condition persists in Harlem and other disadvantaged areas.

There are several reasons for this, according to Richard Givens, regional director of the Federal Trade Commission (FTC). A ghetto resident generally has less education than the average citizen, so he can be an easy mark for a fast-talking salesman. And the low-income person is often forced to make major purchases at whatever place is willing to give him credit, and he has little choice in the terms offered to him.

For the merchants who have made a great deal of money out of extending credit to the poor, it pays off to continue using shabby sales and collection practices, for they know their customers.

"Many of the worst frauds are deliberately aimed at those who are least likely to complain," Givens notes. Of the 50,000 consumer complaints received yearly by his office, over 85 percent are from middle- and upper-income people, he estimates.

"If a merchant fails to deliver an electric toothbrush to one of these people, the consumer immediately sends angry letters to the newspaper editor, the Federal Trade Commission, the attorney general, his congressman, and the United Nations," says Givens. "But to the poor, being ripped off is just a part of life."

The consumer problem is complicated in Harlem, as it is in many other ghetto areas, by a racial factor that aggravates the economic condition. Although 90 percent of Harlem's residents are black, most of the area's businesses—and just about all of its major retail outlets—are owned by nonresident whites, according to David Caplovitz, author of *The Merchants of Harlem*. It was Caplovitz who, in an earlier work entitled *The Poor Pay More*, prepared the first major study to prove that poverty-stricken slum dwellers are routinely charged more for the same items than are the people who live in middle-class neighborhoods.

It was against this background that the Harlem Consumer Education Council began to evolve in 1962. The evolution was an informal process, for Florence Rice and Elizabeth White had no interest in devising grand schemes, nor in developing any agenda or drafting any statements of purpose; they simply decided it was essential to do something.

Their first step was a form of self-education—a conscious effort to gain an awareness of "the perils of shopping." As Mrs. Rice recalls, "We read stacks of consumer publications, did some comparison shopping, and talked to all kinds of people."

She began to develop contacts, through letter-writing and informal meetings, with activists in the consumer-protection field—writers, attorneys, and government agency heads.

"Soon, my friends were coming to me with their consumer problems," she smiles. "I would go to the merchant and demand a fair settlement. Or I'd call the Federal Trade Commission and state attorney general to get some legal teeth into the case. Sometimes I'd call a reporter if it seemed that the problem was widespread and needed publicity."

The project's first formal activity was a day-long consumer-education conference at which several experts and government officials were slated to speak. Only four people attended the program. Undaunted, Florence Rice has continued to conduct such a conference once a year. Although community residents still attend in only miniscule numbers, the conferences are well-attended—by representatives of agencies and organizations from all over the metropolitan area, and even from neighboring states.

In addition to annual conferences, Mrs. Rice periodically conducts smaller-scale workshops. In the fall of 1973, for example, she set up and ran a food action seminar to discuss "who's really in control, who's really running up the prices in Harlem."

Florence Rice's growing expertise and willingness to work hard rapidly earned her a widespread reputation in her neighborhood, and people whom she had never met began to bring their complaints to her. For four years she worked out of her apartment, amassing information, contacts, and a grateful constituency. In 1966 a local community organization provided her with office space; subsequently HCEC moved into a dilapidated storefront just off Harlem's major commercial thoroughfare, 125th Street.

"We've never stopped raising hell," Florence Rice states. The organization's continued ability to raise hell has been greatly helped by its refusal to become a highly structured bureaucratic entity. Under Mrs. Rice's guidance, it operates in a loose, improvisational manner, taking on whatever tasks seem important at the moment, recruiting people to help out when necessary, and scrounging for money and supplies on a hand-to-mouth basis.

"Too many people are afraid to do anything because they don't feel 'qualified' to run something the way things are 'supposed' to be run," Mrs. Rice, a high school dropout, remarks. "Hell, I'm no professional. All you need is confidence in the rightness of your cause. The rest of it will fall into place."

Thus HCEC is truly an indigenous community operation, one that reflects the unabashed, earthy style of Florence Rice. Its history is not one of systematic plans and programs. Rather, much of Mrs. Rice's achievement has been on a one-to-one level, and countless individuals have gained awareness and knowledge from her. Florence Rice now ranks as one of the most vigilant and credible spokesmen for New York City's low-income consumers.

"I think of myself as a teacher—with no classroom and no time-card," Mrs. Rice explains. "If you're really an activist, you're always working, in every encounter, in any setting. It's not just teaching people how to buy; it's teaching them to think, to have confidence, to demand their rights in all their affairs." She goes on to say that it is this kind of activity—"planting seeds and watching people bloom"—that can't be put in a grant proposal, but that is ultimately the most rewarding.

HCEC also teaches by doing. For instance it has also organized the picketing and boycotting of several local businesses, principally those where sales practices or pricing have been found to be unethical. In 1966, in one of it most ambitious efforts, HCEC undertook a comparison of prices in neighborhood supermarkets, and subsequently picketed several national chain stores that were charging exorbitant prices in their Harlem outlets. And dozens of welfare recipients were bused to cooperative grocery stores to dramatize the advantages of cooperative buying.

The council has also used press conferences and widespread leafleting to alert consumers about various sales schemes. Florence's Rice's vigorous harangue against a flourishing food-freezer fraud, for example, has been credited with putting that operation out of business. Door-to-door selling, appliance repairing, and buying on credit have all been covered in HCEC's information campaigns. And a major consciousness-raising campaign has been undertaken that involves a "consumer's pledge" to consult a lawyer or consumer-protection agency before signing any retail contract for the purchase of merchandise when buying on credit.

Several major new laws and regulations dealing with consumer problems have been passed since HCEC began its work in 1962.

The Federal Trade Commission (FTC), for example, has exhibited increased interest in the problems of poor consumers; the state attorney general is in the process of opening a Harlem office;

New York City's 4-year-old department of consumer affairs has established two consumer-complaint centers in the Harlem area; and the Harlem Better Business Bureau prides itself as being "more than just a public relations arm of the merchants," according to its director. Furthermore Harlem now has a small claims court. This has an innovative community advocate program, in which paraprofessionals are available without charge to counsel consumers in actions against merchants.

Despite the mushrooming of government power and programs in the consumer field, the importance of Florence Rice's work in Harlem has not diminished. This is largely because, except for efforts such as that of the Harlem Consumer Education Council, consumer militancy remains largely a middle-class phenomenon in New York City as in the rest of the country.

Mrs. Rice does more than teach and talk to the low-income consumers of Harlem. Through her colorful, down-to-earth testimony in public hearings, particularly on utilities, she has also given them their first major representation in such forums.

But what does she know about, say, public utilities?

"At first, people said, 'How can you go in there and speak on utilities—you're no expert'," Mrs. Rice recalls. "But, I figured, there's already plenty of folks with charts and figures. I have the only kind of facts that makes sense to me, and that's trying to live and stay out of debt in Harlem. That's what I'm an expert in."

But she needs and relies on other qualities, too.

"Florence has the precious attribute of credibility in the community and in the power structure," notes syndicated consumer columnist Sidney Margolius, who goes on to comment, "Her commitment is derived from deep personal ties to the people whose experiences she shares."

"She has a remarkable network in Harlem," adds the Federal Trade Commission's Richard Givens. "She doesn't just sit in her office and wait for people to come in; she goes out and digs up complaints from consumers who have been damaged, but who would never complain to a government agency."

Any realistic assessment of HCEC's work would have to conclude that the organization's victories have been somewhat limited, and that, for most of Harlem's consumers, living conditions are pretty much as they have always been.

But Florence Rice remains convinced about the need for her endeavors and the value of her work. As she likes to say:

"Planting seeds, spreading awareness, getting us on the record—it's slow, but it's real.

"Self-help projects can't fail. The victory is that you're trying."

What it gets down to is opening new worlds for
these kids, letting them know they, too, can write
a song, or play a guitar, or draw a picture, or
figure out how to use the library—that they
can do those things, and that those things
are not just for other kids.

The Patch

Atlanta, Georgia

Debra Smith is 14 years old, the daughter of a white textile mill hand, and she lives in a hard-scrabble neighborhood of frame houses built a stone's throw from the mill.

The mill and Debra's home, close to downtown Atlanta, are in a community that has long been known as Cabbagetown (because the vegetable was once a mainstay of family dinners there).

For the past two years Debra Smith has been stopping after school at a house called the Patch, two blocks from the mill.

"I like it because there are a lot of things to do there," she says. "Some people say it doesn't teach anything, but how would they know? They never come to the Patch. I think it teaches people things if they would learn."

Debra Smith and about seventy-five other children ranging in age from 8 to 16 make the Patch—which was created by Cabbagetown people themselves, not by outsiders—as much a part of their neighborhood and their lives as the textile mill itself.

"Traditionally, Cabbagetown has been somewhat of a closed community resisting any kind of program that agencies deem beneficial to the neighborhood," says Esther Lefever, a young, former public school counselor who is director of the Patch.

The Patch is not designed to replace the public school classes that Cabbagetown's children attend. The center's art, music, and writing classes, its rap sessions that sometimes take up the latest community problem but are just as likely to end up talking about the location of, say, India—these build on the public school base.

"Our purpose," explains Esther Lefever, "is threefold. First, to provide each individual youth with an increased awareness and understanding of himself and his environment through one-to-one relationships and small group interactions. Second, to teach basic survival skills, like reading, math, and social behavior. And third, to provide a base for community self-help."

"What it gets down to," says Joyce Brookshire, a Cabbagetown native and full-time but only partially paid worker at the Patch, "is opening new worlds for these kids, letting them know they, too, can write a song, or play a guitar, or draw a picture, or figure out how to use the library—that they can do those things, and that those things are not just for other kids."

Kids acquire increased awareness of one another at the Patch, where new worlds are opened to them in their own neighborhood.

A few years ago many of the kids of Cabbagetown spent their after-school hours in the streets. They were bored and looking for something to do—which usually turned out to be either dangerous or illegal or both. This naturally worried their parents.

Joyce Brookshire and Esther Lefever heard about the parents' complaints in the course of their work at nearby elementary and high schools, where they were community liaison counselors. "It was the first time the people in Cabbagetown themselves wanted to do something together," Esther Lefever recalls.

In June of 1971 the Patch opened its doors in a three-room house. By the fall the house was being swamped with young visitors, so the Patch closed temporarily that winter to find larger quarters. "We could have lost—we almost did—the community support at that point," says Esther Lefever. "It's a careful line to draw, and the community could easily have thought we were giving up, that it wouldn't work.

"But we kept talking it up, going into the homes, getting ideas for new programs when we would reopen, and the community stayed with us."

When the Patch reopened in larger quarters, it expanded from being a three-days-a-week open house to being a children's learning and resource center that is open on weekdays from 10 a.m. to 7 p.m. for recreational activities, classwork tutoring, and also art, music, and craft classes. It also acquired a library—actually a mini-branch of the Atlanta public library system, complete with a librarian. And arrangements were made to provide counseling services to help youngsters deal with personal troubles.

The Patch, which has been used by more than 200 neighborhood children since 1971, keeps many Cabbagetown parents involved, scheduling them as volunteers, even if only for an hour a week. Together with the staff, the parents organize street festivals and flea markets, which not only reinforce community involvement in the project but also add a little money to the Patch's general fund.

The only government money involved in the Patch's $19,000-a-year budget is $6,000 from the city of Atlanta. This sum is used to pay two-thirds of the librarian's salary; the remaining $3,000 is paid by a donation from a private family foundation in Atlanta.

The remaining $10,000 of the project's budget is acquired from a variety of sources. The local mill management and the mill employees' fund regularly donate several hundred dollars. And a number of businesses and private service organizations have made cash donations and have contributed office, recreational, and educational equipment.

"But the key to our success has been the community," says Joyce Brookshire, who also edits the Patch's monthly newsletter. "When the community said it wanted something like the Patch, no outsiders stepped in and did it for them, took it away from them. They started it, run it, and will keep it."

*It was hard to teach them that writing is work
that is paid for.*

La Raza

Appleton, Wisconsin

Once a month a small newspaper is distributed to the growing number of former migrant farm workers who have settled in Appleton, Wisconsin, and the surrounding communities. The newspaper is bilingual and is called *Adelante Raza* ("Onward, People").

The newspaper is published by La Raza, Inc., a self-help organization for Chicanos, and it is an important means of creating a sense of community among the 3,400 Mexican American settlers who are scattered over a six-county area. The newspaper provides both inspiration and information about the many services offered by La Raza to help its constituents to become self-sufficient amid their new surroundings. Most of the ex-migrants still live in rural camps. Many are poor and uneducated, and suffer from having to try to pick up English as a second language.

La Raza's services range from programs for preschoolers to an alcoholic referral program.

The agency's first venture—the tutoring of Stevens Point school children by university and high school students—started shortly before La Raza was incorporated in 1971.

Sister Ann Kilkelly, one of La Raza's founders, launched the tutorial program, she says, to help children overcome the shock of discovering in school that "Spanish isn't good enough any more." The tutors go into the youngsters' homes twice a week to help with both reading and language. They also serve as an important link between the schools and parents unable to read English.

The program has grown from 12 tutors and 35 children to 75 tutors and nearly 200 students today. All the costs are borne by a Stevens Point school district.

At its center in Appleton, La Raza is conducting a summer program for youths to help them develop communications skills, including writing for the newspaper. They also learn radio broadcasting and filmmaking.

During the summer of 1973 this program had 175 participants taught by 46 paid and volunteer staff members. The program has been funded for $39,000 by Title I of the Elementary and Secondary Education Act.

Mariá Sánchez, the newspaper's volunteer editor, says the students were paid $2 an hour "partly so they could convince their parents the program was as worthwhile as working in the fields." She adds that some of the youths didn't consider interviewing people for stories to be work, and, she says, "It was hard to teach them that writing is work that is paid for."

La Raza had its start as a state-supported self-help agency in the little farming town of Wautoma, some fifty miles from Appleton. It was headed by Martino Martinez, a college-trained sociologist, who has since gone on to direct La Raza's alcoholism referral program. Martinez enlisted the aid of Father Pancho Oyarbide.

A year after his arrival the priest was contacted by Patricia Santos, the wife of an Appleton physician, and she asked him to expand his efforts by creating an organization in Appleton. La Raza came into being in 1971 with Oyarbide as its head.

The priest readily concedes he is no administrator of offices and that he finds all the paperwork frustrating. "In this society," he says, "if you don't write it down it isn't worth anything." What he prefers, he says, is the "oral tradition" of the Chicanos. And when he moves among the people, Oyarbide makes eloquent use of this tradition to bring them together and to inspire them.

"If you give food to people today," he says, "they are hungry tomorrow. You don't give them food, you show them how to get it. And you have to do that as a group."

La Raza is financed by donations from churches and local charities, and its budget has grown to nearly $100,000 a year. This includes a $30,600 award from the Campaign for Human Development, which is funded by the U.S. Catholic Conference.

La Raza's projects also include a day nursery, an emergency loan fund, legal aid, and a translation service to assist Chicanos in court and in their dealings with other public agencies.

In 1973 a La Raza group staged three public forums called "Strangers in Our Homeland", which began with music, plays, and poetry describing the history and agonies of Mexican Americans. The forums then went on to explore labor and farm issues and problems with schools and social services.

Father Oyarbide believes that La Raza's most significant contributions have been social and psychological.

"There has been a gain by our people of knowing who you are and who can help you," he says. "That is the accomplishment."

*I guess the real thing is that they get to
know us and trust us as friends. Once you start
working in the same kitchen with a person or sit
in the living room with her, there's a
certain bond of friendship and trust that
automatically begins to develop.*

Homemaker Skills

Pittsburgh, Pennsylvania

Her admirers call Cora Raiford the "miracle worker" of Pittsburgh's Homewood-Brushton district because of her ability to
brighten the drab lives of the poor.

During the last five years she has become a friend, a teacher
and confidante to more than a thousand people—poor people
who have long been victims of poverty, imprisoned without hope
in the city's slums.

She has touched their lives through compassion and caring,
through helping them and teaching them. She has taught them
about decorating their homes, about stretching the family income,
about flower arranging and ceramics. She has given them lessons
in sewing, knitting, cooking, and the art of candle making. But
what she does best is to help people learn about the most important art of all—the art of living.

Cora Raiford's story is a large part of the story of a special program started in the late 1960s called Homemaker Skills. It was
launched by ACTION-Housing, Inc., which is a privately funded
self-help agency founded in 1957 to provide new and rehabilitated
housing for low- and "no"-income families.

"It's one thing to take people out of the slums and give them a
place to live," says ACTION-Housing's executive director, William
Farkas. "But it's something altogether different to expect them to
know how to live once they've gotten a place."

The challenge of the Homemaker Skills program, continues
Farkas, is "to find out how in the hell we can deliver the myriad of
services and abilities people must have to maintain homes at near
or below poverty levels—so that they can live with the dignity and
pride of their more affluent neighbors."

Homemaker Skills concentrates its efforts in two low-income areas of Pittsburgh. One is the Homewood-Brushton district which is predominately black; the other is the Perry-Hilltop district, about one-third black, on the city's North Side. Although AC-TION-Housing says the program is available to the general community without regard to place of residence or income level, the primary thrust of Homemaker Skills is clearly directed toward families living in new or rehabilitated housing that is sponsored by ACTION-Housing and other nonprofit leasing enterprises.

The twin driving forces of Homemaker Skills are a pair of dedicated, energetic women: Cora Raiford, who works in the Homewood-Brushton area, and Aurelia Demus, who is active in the Perry-Hilltop area.

"They, not us, make Homemaker Skills tick," says Jonathan Zimmer, director of supportive services for ACTION-Housing.

What makes the approaches of Cora Raiford and Aurelia Demus tick is sensitivity. Both know the problems of poverty. Both have seen the deterioration of their neighborhoods and communities. They have different ways of going about it, but they both know how to develop a sense of self-confidence and dignity in the "ladies" of the program.

Their constant reference to "ladies" reflects the importance they attach to human dignity in their overall attack on the problems. A lady is a symbol of achievement, and to Cora Raiford and Aurelia Demus all the women in Homemaker Skills are ladies.

The Homemaker Skills program provides the ladies with free classes in a great variety of subjects. These include the basics of homemaking, such as sewing, cooking, and interior decorating, as well as more advanced topics, such as nutrition, budget stretching, upholstering, and art.

"Our hope is to build the necessary skills for people to live in public housing so that they can become self-sufficient," says Farkas. "This is the real bread and butter of housing programs."

It is also what sets ACTION-Housing apart from other housing programs.

Homemaker Skills classes are conducted on an informal basis, without rigid structuring. In general they have had no official beginning or ending point. Some participants tend to drop out after reaching a certain level of skill, while others continue to attend over a long period of time. The classes are held in a variety of places—in the four Homemaker centers, in the homes of the "students" themselves, or some other place.

All of the class sessions are kept free of anything that would lead to them being mistaken for welfare or social development programs. Cora Raiford and Aurelia Demus want to make it instantly clear that they are homemakers, not caseworkers. Theirs is a one-to-one relationship with each lady, not a teacher-student or caseworker-client relationship.

"I guess the real thing is that they get to know us and trust us as friends," says the soft-spoken Aurelia Demus. "It really becomes a social situation when they begin sharing all their problems with us. Once you start working in the same kitchen with a person or sit in the living room with her, there's a certain bond of friendship and trust that automatically begins to develop."

Both Cora Raiford and Aurelia Demus come by their talents naturally. Mrs. Demus has been sewing or knitting all her life. And Mrs. Raiford says, "I can't remember when I couldn't sew or read a pattern. I love to cook, and any kind of art work I see I want to try." She is an experienced home economist who learned her craft at Tuskegee Institute in Alabama.

The Homemaker Skills program has gone far beyond just knitting, sewing, cooking, and other routine skills. Mrs. Demus, for example, has added a charm class for teenage girls, is experimenting with cooking courses for boys, and has started special piano and music classes for adolescents and adults.

One of the most exciting new ideas she has brought to the Perry-Hilltop area is a course in junk art—the art of making such things as wall hangings and centerpieces from bottle caps and coat hangers. The course is being taught by Dorothy Richardson, a long-time civil rights worker and the person who got Aurelia Demis involved with ACTION-Housing in the first place.

A Homemaker Skills student learns sewing techniques.

Cora Raiford has also expanded her offerings to include classes in candle making and foliage arrangement. Tutorial classes for boys have been launched. And even the men of the neighborhood have become involved in the basics of plastering, upholstering, and home repairs.

The results of Cora Raiford's classes can be found throughout the homes in the Homewood-Brushton area. One woman, for example, did all her own drapes and curtains, turning her home into a showpiece for the rest of the neighborhood. Both her pride and reputation are now spreading, as others follow her example.

One interesting result of Homemaker Skills' success has been that Allegheny County Community College has called on Mrs. Raiford to teach a special ten-week, 30-hour creative home economics skills course right at her Tioga Street Center. "Our hope," says Zimmer, "is that a college certificate will stimulate some of the people involved in Cora's program to go on to other areas of eduction and training."

Homemaker Skills operates four centers, two in Homewood-Brushton and two in Perry-Hilltop. The centers themselves reflect the creativity of the Homemaker Skills program. Cora Raiford, for example, has converted the Tioga Street center—an abandoned sheet mill—into a veritable rose garden of homey pleasantness. Combining her own work with that of her participants, she has completely revamped the inside with bright and decorative wall hangings, attractive furniture, and colorful foliage arrangements.

All of the centers are beehives of activity throughout the week, with a variety of activities in full swing on any given day. Consider a typical evening at Aurelia Demus' three-story thatched row house headquarters on Charles Street. The center is filled to overflowing. Eight women ranging in age from 21 to 86 are on the second floor for their regular sewing class. A group of neighborhood men are meeting on the first floor to discuss furnace maintenance with an expert from one of the local gas companies. And the third floor is jammed with teenagers talking about a school project, as their record player blares forth the music of Aretha Franklin and Roberta Flack.

And this is how Aurelia Demus likes it. "When we're busy," she says, "that means we're reaching people," and she goes on to recall her very first sewing class in a makeshift trailer two years ago—when only two people showed up.

Some of the participants are turning their new-found talents to profit-making ventures.

A woman in Mrs. Demus' sewing class, for example, has begun making turbans, for which she has found a good market. And then there is Ann McCoy, one of the veterans of Cora Raiford's program, who has learned how to make fancy napkin holders using empty detergent bottles. In 1973 she sold over one hundred of her popular creations to friends and neighbors for Christmas gifts.

"It would have cost $5 to get something that pretty at a store," says one woman. "Ann only charged $3."

The Homemaker Skills program offers classes in candle making.

Funding is a continuing problem for both Homemaker Skills and ACTION-Housing. Although Homemaker Skills has largely been supported by private foundations, these sources are beginning to dry up somewhat.

As Cora Raiford puts it: "We've had to beg, borrow, and steal to get the necessities, such as stoves, refrigerators, sewing machines, and other materials. So far the supply has been ample."

But with or without equipment, Homemaker Skills will go on.

"By itself," admits Zimmer, "it has not solved all the problems associated with poverty. Far from it. We are never satisfied and feel much more can be done. But through people like Cora Raiford and Aurelia Demus we have improved the housekeeping and maintenance skills of the residents we serve in our more than one thousand housing units. This in turn has begun to provide a beneficial impact on the quality of life in our housing developments and the community as a whole."

*We decided to just go ahead and open a school—
not wait until the board put up the building. Just
open a school on our own and try to demonstrate
what we were talking about.*

The Committee for a Comprehensive Education Center

New York, New York

The first thing that strikes a visitor about Park East High School, located in what was once a music school in East Harlem, is that the walls are bare. No graffiti.

One also learns that the student body of 475 tends to get along without drugs and without violence.

But there are other, more important differences that set Park East apart from most New York public schools.

Park East is an experiment in alternative education. It is the city's only community-controlled public high school, the creation of a handful of resolute women who formed the Committee for a Comprehensive Education Center to find the most effective way to educate their children.

Essentially the school is aimed at providing educational alternatives to youngsters who otherwise may be assigned to traditional schools—with inflexible curricula and with few or no resources to provide the personal attention and special help that students need to develop their own interests and skills.

"We want to give these kids what they need—not what some curriculum guide says they should have," explains Thelma King, the school's director (the committee does not care for the title "principal").

Park East's student body is generally the same as that of any of the city's larger high schools.

The youngsters are mostly from low-income homes, and the majority of them are black and Puerto Rican (at Park East the proportions are blacks, 40 percent; Puerto Ricans, 40 percent; and whites, 20 percent). At Park East, however, all of the students are young people who have asked to be enrolled there. Many have been there since the school first opened in February 1971 in the basement of a local church.

Park East is what is called an "ungraded, trackless" school. It has basic academic requirements for graduation—demonstrated proficiency in reading, writing, and mathematics—but it allows students to design their own programs and follow their own interests at a pace they set themselves.

What most of them need is help with reading, writing, and mathematics. For example, like students in many New York schools, a high percentage—perhaps 85 percent—of Park East's students do not have the reading proficiency needed to pass standardized tests for high school graduation.

Therefore, before they enroll, incoming students are thoroughly tested, and their performance is evaluated. Then, a special program is designed, in consultation with them, to ensure that they will acquire the basic reading, writing, and mathematical skills. Once they've satisfied the basic requirements, they can pursue their own interests in selecting courses, individual work-study programs, and "internships" in careers they are considering.

So far, the staff and community leaders who worked to establish Park East are pleased with the results of their innovative program. Of the fifty-seven students who formed the school's first graduating class in June 1973, forty-eight went on to college, two entered nursing school and seven accepted permanent jobs in firms where they had served their career internships.

Despite this impressive record, though, the center still has a long way to go before it realizes the dreams of the community leaders who decided a decade ago that they should have some control over the kind of public education available to their children, and that they also wanted a center to extend comprehensive social services to area residents.

The idea for an innovative education center originated when mothers active in a local parents' association became interested in a board of education decision to build a new high school on Manhattan's Upper East Side.

"We heard that the board was going to build a new school. Most of us with children in junior high school decided that we should have some say about where the school was located and what kind of facilities it would provide," recalls Elizabeth DiTrapani, one of the community activists who is responsible for the education center's establishment.

The parents' group then learned that one site under consideration was the abandoned Ruppert Brewery in Yorkville, which stretches north from 79th Street to East Harlem and encompasses the Upper East Side from Fifth Avenue to the East River. In real contrast with East Harlem, with its majority of low-income blacks and Puerto Ricans, Yorkville is a well-to-do, almost-all-white neighborhood that includes an affluent middle-class population, plus some upper-middle-class and lower-middle-class groups.

The parents' association learned that a Yorkville community planning board was already planning for renewal of the brewery site and seeking a commitment from the board of education to construct the East Side new school in the Yorkville area. Subsequently the association came to support the planning board's attempt to locate the school in the Ruppert renewal area.

In 1966 the board of education agreed to the Ruppert location, and the planning board designated a committee to help design the school. This committee envisioned the new school as a community center to funnel a variety of social services to East Harlem and Yorkville residents. And it was this group that began considering the kind of education young people would be getting at the new school.

Out of the committee's deliberations came a proposal for community control of the new school. Although New York's elementary and junior high schools are "decentralized" (that is, controlled by local school boards in the various sections of the city), all the high schools are operated by the central board's Office of High Schools.

"At the time, parents had no influence at all over which public school their children would be assigned to, let alone the kind of education available," Elizabeth DiTrapani explains. "But we were dissatsified with the system and began to discuss the kinds of alternatives there could be. We wanted to see what we could do about providing the kind of school that would best meet the needs of the students."

Once its plan was formulated, the committee began seeking support from the board of education and the community. "We wanted to work within the system and help devise a new kind of public school," says Mrs. DiTrapani. "We needed the board's approval and the community's support."

In 1968 the board designated the proposed Ruppert school as the city's pilot "comprehensive" high school. It officially asked the committee to help develop plans for the new structure. Armed with the board's approval, the committee began recruiting supporters in the two communities that would be served by the new school—East Harlem and Yorkville.

The committee reorganized itself, hired a planning staff, and decided upon a name for itself—the Committee for a Comprehensive Education Center (CCEC).

"I think our first crucial decision was that we couldn't do the planning without expert help," Mrs. DiTrapani recalls. CCEC recruited two professionals—George Conroy, a teacher who had spent most of his life in East Harlem, and Byron Stookey, a Harvard graduate who had academic planning experience at the University of California at Santa Cruz.

"Byron and I didn't know when we were hired that the committee had only enough money to pay us for a few weeks," says Conroy, now deputy director of the school. "They ran out of money, so we worked unsalaried for a couple of months."

Stookey recalls initial efforts to mobilize community support for the center: "We decided to have a weekend-long workshop. We lined up all sorts of participants—invited everybody. We got people to stand at the subway station handing out flyers, got cooks to cook up things. We were going to spend the day discussing the new high school and then have a big celebration in a local schoolyard.

"Well, only about nine people showed up. It was a disaster, but it taught us something. We had nothing concrete to offer at the time. Nothing people could relate to. All they saw was another hustle. After that, we decided to just go ahead and open a school—not wait until the board put up the building. Just open a school on our own and try to demonstrate what we were talking about."

That decision was made in 1970, and thereafter CCEC found it easier to involve the community. "We found," Conroy remembers, "a lot of blacks and Puerto Ricans from East Harlem working with us. I never saw that kind of activity in this community before."

"We all worked together in those days," he says. "The kids, their parents, the staff—we renovated the place, painted it. We all felt a part of it—that the school really belonged to us."

When the school did open, it was on a shoestring budget. Money promised by the board of education hadn't arrived, so the original financing consisted of a state grant of $70,000 (made available under the Vocational Education Act) and a Ford Foundation grant of $108,630. Since then, money from the board of education has been used to operate the school. CCEC meets all operating expenses with funds it receives under its contract with the board ($244,420 for the 1973-74 school year), although the board itself assumes the responsibility of paying the salaries of the regular licensed teachers.

CCEC is still looking for money to provide the community services it wants to offer through the center. It did operate an early learning (day care) center for 18 months, but ran out of money and had to close the facility temporarily.

It also wants to open several "group homes" for youngsters who otherwise may be institutionalized. But in this case, too, it has been unable to come up with enough money to carry out its plans.

An effort to seek out and aid needy families in the community was dropped because of a lack of funds and because it got lost in the shuffle as CCEC concentrated on operating both the high school and an adult education component offered in conjunction with the regular high school program.

"We decided against a separate adult education program at night," Stookey explains. "Instead, any adult in the community may enroll for any class offered at the school. Since the school is open from 8:30 a.m. until 10 p.m.—with classes scheduled straight through—adults can attend at their own convenience."

In 1974, a total of 100 of Park East's 475 students were students enrolled in the adult education program.

CCEC is under pressure to prove that its innovative school is accomplishing what it set out to do. When its original three-year contract with the board expired in 1973, the contract was renewed for only one year.

"They could decide that they've had enough of this experiment," says project director Gilbert Belaval. "They could just cut us off and take over the operation of the high school themselves."

Elizabeth DiTrapani is also somewhat pessimistic about the future: "We only got the board's approval in the first place because we made a nuisance of ourselves, refused to take 'no' for an answer, and refused to be discouraged by the bureaucracy and all the red tape. But we did have some sympathizers on the board in those early days. Most of those people are no longer there, and their replacements don't really understand what we are all about."

The board's indifference—some call it hostility—toward the project is the determining factor for the future. But despite the uncertainty, CCEC is proceeding with plans to reactivate the day care center, open a group home, and expand the school.

CCEC already has convinced the board to scale down its original plan for a school for 4,000 to a school for 2,000, and to disperse facilities throughout East Harlem and Yorkville instead of concentrating them at the former brewery site.

That alone is a significant achievement. If the committee can maintain its relationship with the board as the center continues to expand and as the new school building goes up, it ultimately will prove its point—that a determined community can and should have influence over the schools within its boundaries, as well as on the kind of education its children receive.

I wanted to go back to high school, but it's
hard to face people and let them know you
have this handicap. So I came here.

Operation LIFT

Dallas, Texas

Raphael grew up in a Spanish-speaking family and never mastered English well enough to graduate from high school. He dropped out and became a spray painter at a Dallas auto body shop. Today, at 25, he is once again in the classroom—studying English in hopes of going to El Centro Community College so he can learn business administration.

Raphael is one of the students enrolled in classes conducted by Operation LIFT (Literacy Instruction For Texas), which is a Dallas-based self-help literacy program intended for adults and conducted by volunteer teachers. Raphael's reasons for joining LIFT are fairly typical:

"I wanted to go back to high school, but it's hard to face people and let them know you have this handicap. So I came here."

Others join for the reason expressed by an older man: "I found my son coming home from school and reading better than I can."

"What we try to do for our students is teach the basics of reading and writing," says Margaret Hirsch, LIFT's director. "Some are shy and lacking in confidence because they don't have the skill to even fill out a driver's license application. We want to make all of our students as self-reliant as possible."

LIFT functions without a schoolhouse of its own. Instead its classes are formed on request in a neighborhood and are held in a convenient place, such as a church basement or meeting hall—where, if the teacher is lucky, there is a blackboard.

"The way it usually works is that we get a call from a man or woman who has heard about us and they inquire about setting up a class," says Margaret Hirsch. "We try to get them to sign up five or ten people, and when we think we have the nucleus of a class, we put out a notice on the radio saying when it will start and invite others to join. This way we go to where the need is."

Currently there are about 600 students in the twenty-one LIFT classes being held in the city and county around Dallas. Not all of the students are Mexican Americans. About one-third of them are, and the rest of the participants are evenly divided, some black and some white. The classes are open to all people wanting to learn to read, write, and speak fluent English and to gain confidence in dealing with the business world around them.

Many of the 100 or so volunteers are retired teachers; others come from business or elsewhere in the community. "Very often people go into LIFT teaching," says Margaret Hirsch, "because they think it is glamorous or will produce quick results. But they quickly find out different. It is hard work. They find they must become personally involved with their students and be patient and compassionate as well.

"We had one woman who made her students feel uncomfortable because she didn't want to 'stoop' to their educational level. Others don't know how to handle occasional flareups, like when one student downgrades another. But generally we do very well with our volunteers."

And the volunteers also tend to be enthusiastic about their participation in LIFT. Jim Brooks, a manager for a large computer firm, has been a LIFT teacher for a year. He says, "I like the people. They're trying hard. I get excited when one of my students realizes one day he's reading without any problem."

Each volunteer teaches a minimum of two 2-hour classes per week. Some classes have more sessions, and they may be held either in the daytime or at night. Students furnish their own books and transportation, but otherwise the instruction is free. A typical class has about thirty students, with three to four teachers to provide individualized instruction.

To overcome the sensitivity of students about their linguistic deficiency, LIFT teachers are instructed to treat them as politely as possible—even to the point of being rather formal. This is intended to create an atmosphere of mutual respect. Teachers also keep a close eye on attendance. If a student misses two consecutive classes, the teacher telephones and says, "We miss you."

"For our students who lack the basic skills and who have difficulty coping with the world, we mix in a lot of practical advice," Mrs. Hirsch says. "We take them on imaginary trips to the doctor's office, to the grocery store, to the welfare agency, and we teach them what they need to know to get along in those places.

A LIFT student does an exercise in his bilingual workbook. LIFT classes in the Dallas area involve 600 students in twenty-one courses. ▶

We give them practical advice—like not endorsing their pay-checks until they are ready to cash them at the bank."

Each weekday Margaret Hirsch conducts a 20-minute class over a local television station that covers roughly the same course content that is presented in the neighborhood classes. This broadcast helps stimulate enrollments in the individual classes, but is otherwise independent of them.

LIFT was started in 1961 as a pilot project of the National Council of Jewish Women, which was intent upon trying to do something about the rising number of illiterate people in the Dallas area, then estimated at 45,000. Pat Peiser, president of the council's Dallas section at the time, says the council's impetus came from the Foundation for World Literacy, as well as a desire to help the disadvantaged. The foundation had devised instructional techniques based on televised films and supplemented by classroom instruction that were being used successfully in Memphis, Tennessee, for adult illiterates. This system was employed in the pilot project, which had 200 students and was continued until 1964. At that time a new curriculum was developed by Margaret Hirsch, who had taken over the direction of LIFT in 1963.

Margaret Hirsch, a refugee from Nazi Germany, grew up in Australia and has lived in Dallas since 1949. Over the past decade she has made LIFT an expression of her own personal philosophy: "If you've been lucky enough to get an education, you've got an obligation. Most of the good volunteers feel education is something to share."

Margaret Hirsch is not at all fazed by LIFT's critics, who claim that the students would be better served by paid professionals, and who point out that the number of illiterates in the area has doubled since the project began.

Margaret Hirsch simply responds by saying that the population also has grown enormously in that period, and the public schools haven't been able to cure the problem. Moreover, she adds, "we would get less work done with paid teachers—that would take away from the whole idea of LIFT."

She is presently trying to expand the program. Finding money is difficult, however (LIFT currently gets along on an annual budget of $3,000, the money coming from individual donations and foundations).

"But a little progress is better than none," she says, firmly. "The need is so great."

People have been sold a bill of goods that money
is the key to a successful project. The real source
of success is people, and the one thing even
the poorest community in American has is people.

The Watts Summer Festival

Los Angeles, California

Outside the Watts Summer Festival offices, the rain is a steady curtain of water and the air is uncharacteristically cool. Inside, a giant heater blasts hot air around cubicle-like offices in what was once a large store. Tommy Jacquette hardly notices. He is slumped in a high-backed executive chair behind a massive, cluttered desk, his hands folded across the white T-shirt that is a part of his daily dress (the other parts being khaki workpants, old boots laced only halfway up, and a black hat adorned with a "Taking Care of Business" button).

"Well, who knows," Jacquette says after a glum momentary silence, "Maybe there won't be a festival this year anyway."

The executive director takes off his hat, flips it on the desk, and runs a huge hand through his mop of hair. "We use a lot of electricity and gasoline during festival week," he continues, rising out of the chair by unwinding his long, lanky body and raising his arms high above his head, hands entwined. "If we can't get the gasoline we need, we'll be pumping bicycles to pull the floats."

Jacquette's pessimism no doubt reflects the mood of an ugly day. But if the Watts Summer Festival succumbs to the energy crisis, it will not be inappropriate, for he spent most of January 1974 organizing an all-day seminar on the energy crisis and its impact on minority communities in Los Angeles. Moreover, the success of the yearly week-long August festival—commemorating what Jacquette prefers to call the revolt (not the riot) of August 1965—makes it possible for the Watts Summer Festival organization to take on a variety of new ventures. Among these are the energy seminar, a food-distribution program for needy families, a cash prize essay contest for school children (the subject being unknown black heroes), a program to contribute to student funds in Watts schools, and preparing a monthly newspaper.

In the months that followed the August 1965 disturbances (a

confrontation that left 35 dead, 883 injured, and more than $200 million worth of property in rubble and ashes), the outside world, perhaps shamed by the conditions that had sparked the upheaval or afraid that next time the fire might spill out of the narrow confines of Watts, poured millions of dollars into the long-neglected ghetto. Like flowers that emerge in California deserts only after infrequent rains, dozens of programs and agencies suddenly blossomed in the Watts wasteland.

But despite this sudden show of concern by the outside world, community workers—black professionals as well as volunteers who gravitated toward these newly founded organizations—felt a subtle, undefined depression permeating Watts. Along Central Avenue, where unemployed men, outwardly impassive, talked in small groups on street corners, as well as in the side streets where women gathered on the front steps of old, weatherbeaten frame houses, there seemed to be an inescapable feeling that the 1965 outbreak, although it might have been justified and might have brought some money and attention to Watts, had somehow robbed black people of something and that it had established violence and looting and arson—in short, "fury"—as the black man's last and only recourse.

"Something had to be done to show the positive side of the community, something that would stress to people the black cultural heritage," says Jacquette, a high school dropout who once served time for burglary. "Some of us who had gotten involved in the various agencies decided a festival might be the right thing."

Community workers who discussed the need for a morale-boosting event decided the festival would feature concerts, parades, and carnival rides. But more importantly, the festival would include exhibits and shows featuring black art and handicrafts. Social agencies of all kinds would be invited to set up booths in the festival grounds, where Watts residents, who hate to battle the impersonal city bureaucracies, would be able to find out about the old and new services and programs open to them.

"Once we decided on a festival," recalls Jacquette, who at the time was doing volunteer work for a church group in Watts, "we decided that the Jordan High School Alumni Association would be best suited to run the festival, because they had an established organization. We went to the mayor's office for help in cutting red tape to get parade permits, and to the county board of supervisors for permission to use a park that belongs to the county."

The Los Angeles business community was canvassed for financial support. The Schlitz brewing company found $40,000 in its coffers to support the festival's musical activities. Coca-Cola came up with $10,000 to support a junior olympics competition. The Olympia brewing company donated $10,000. Norton Simon gave $1,000. IBM and Xerox gave $500 each.

These companies were—and in fact still are—involved supporters of the festival. But, Jacquette says, the prime ingredient in the festival's success has always been having community volunteers.

"People have been sold a bill of goods that money is the key to a successful project," Jacquette says. "The real source of success is people, and the one thing even the poorest community in America has is people.

"Once we decided on a festival, we contacted everybody in the community—Black Panthers, the churches, the Watts Community Labor Action Committee, the Sons of Watts, the Mothers of Watts, welfare rights organizations. We let everybody know we wanted their help.

"People came in and we formed committees, appointed chairmen and foot soldiers. We gave them no formal training. Just told them the broad outlines of what we wanted and let them develop everything from there. . . . Everything was done spontaneously."

Since those early days the Watts Summer Festival has matured, moving toward being a more structured organization (but, as Jacquette interjects: "We still have to be impulsive, to be quick on our feet"). Since 1968 the Watts Summer Festival has been incorporated, has hired a small but full-time administrative staff, has streamlined its board of directors, and has moved into permanent headquarters in a building given to it by the Episcopalian diocese.

Not everything, of course, has gone smoothly. The shine on the Watts Summer Festival, for example, has been tarnished from time to time by its inability to come to terms with the question of security at the week-long festival. Organizers recognize the need for some kind of law and order at an event that has drawn up to 200,000 people, but neither Jacquette nor any one else has been able to find a solution acceptable to all parties. The presence at the festival of police officers and men from the county sheriff's office has alienated vocal (and influential) groups in the black community, which regard these law-enforcement agencies as enemies of minority people. On the other hand the festival's attempt to use Watts youths to keep order at the festival have rankled conservative members of the black and white communities—especially when there have been disturbances involving the youths.

Another problem facing the Watts Summer Festival is that the current organization may also be harboring the seeds of a future leadership crisis. In 1971 the organization applied for and got a $165,000 grant from the federal Model Cities program. But the check came with a proviso: Jacquette, the high school dropout who had obviously not had the benefits of even a rudimentary education, much less the sophisticated training allegedly necessary to administer a sizable chunk of federal money, had to step aside in favor of a supposedly more "expert" administrator chosen by Model Cities. Under this arrangement, though, the Watts Summer Festival rang up its first loss in six years of operations (a $27,000 loss to be exact) and almost folded permanently.

Explanations vary. Some observers blame the bureaucratic mentality of the Model Cities administrator and his staff—all of them black, by the way, which perhaps illustrates the leveling influence of bureaucracy. The Model Cities people, it was felt, were not up to coping with what was essentially an operation dependent on its street wisdom for success. Other observers point out that Jacquette, who in a compromise agreement remained with the festival organization in a minor capacity, did not go out of his way to give the new management team his full assistance.

As the grant was only for 90 days, the Model Cities people soon left, and Tommy Jacquette resumed his position as executive director. Even so, the episode left its mark on the organization, prompting it to give serious thought to restructuring itself so as to make it less vulnerable to outside influences.

The most pressing problem currently facing the Watts Summer Festival is one confronting a number of other self-help projects around the country: the dwindling sources of financial support.

The 1972 festival, because it included a concert that resulted in the successful movie "Wattstax," managed to gross as much as $1.5 million. These earnings have provided some hedge against future expenditures, in addition to sustaining other projects.

The Wattstax benefit concert packed 100,000 people into Los Angeles' Memorial Coliseum for six hours of headliner entertainment. The Stax record organization syndicated an album of the concert, with proceeds going to the festival. Performances during the week included contemporary jazz, dance, and drama. Smaller in scope, these exhibitions of black culture featured local artists.

The Watts Summer Festival is ambitious. Continuation of previous efforts, though, will require even more resources.

"Part of it," sighs Jacquette, "is the economy. Things have gotten progressively worse since 1969, and people say that they just don't have the money anymore. But part of it, too, is that seven or eight years ago people were willing to give money because they thought that for a couple of bucks they'd buy ten or twenty years of calm. But the ashes have cooled, and they have forgotten."

At the heart of each Tabernacle Tutorial
program . . . is the belief that education
and training are essential if the community
is to become self-sustaining.

Tabernacle Tutorial

New York, New York

All along the eight blocks from the subway station to 1174 Bedford Avenue, abandoned stores and buildings line the garbage-strewn sidewalks. Hurrying past the boarded-up doorways and broken windows, a small girl carrying schoolbooks stops in front of number 1174.

The building's doors swing loosely, handleless and graffiti-marked, bumping with each gust of wind against a mound of hard-packed snow. Pausing only for a moment in the cold, the girl slips quickly through the doors—and into another world.

Outside is bleak, desolate Bedford-Stuyvesant, a great sprawling slum that covers block after block of south Brooklyn.

Inside there are school children crowded around Formica-topped tables, reading and writing in workbooks. Adults sit with them or move from child to child, answering questions, asking questions, listening, helping, encouraging.

This is Tabernacle Tutorial, a couple of large, warm, cluttered rooms serving as storefront playground, study hall, community resource, and haven.

In the back, inside a small office formed by thin plywood partitions, sits the Reverend Gracie Havenwaller. She is the founder and director of Tabernacle Tutorial.

About nine years ago, when Gracie Havenwaller was unable to find a place to leave her infant son during the day so she could work, she decided to open a small day care center in her apartment for herself and other Bed-Stuy mothers. Before long she had acquired many children and a number of adult volunteers. Her apartment quickly became overcrowded, so Tabernacle Day Care managed to raise enough money to pay the rent on a storefront at 1174 Bedford Avenue.

While operating the center, Gracie Havenwaller came to realize that, as she says, "The children of the community needed a place to study after school, a place where they could be warm and get help with [their school] work." She also came to believe that both adults and teenagers in Bed-Stuy needed help in acquiring job skills. Determined to do what she could to help, she marshalled her resources, lined up more volunteers, and, in 1969, started Tabernacle Tutorial.

At the heart of each Tabernacle Tutorial program—and its programs range from remedial reading to carpentry—is the belief that education and training are essential if the community is to become self-sustaining.

For children the center offers the opportunity of remedial study after school and on Saturdays.

Save the Children Federation

A youthful trumpeter in a Bed-Stuy parade put on by Tabernacle Tutorial

For adults there are both academic and technical classes, from basic subjects needed to pass high school equivalency tests to cooking, upholstery, sewing, and carpentry. More esoteric subjects are introduced from time to time as qualified teachers become available. Swahili, for instance, is now in the curriculum because a visitor from Kenya who came to look was persuaded by the director to stay and take on an active teaching role.

A major factor in the progress made by children at the center is simply that they have a place to go when their parents are working, instead of returning home to empty apartments. Another factor is that, in a community where many fathers are absent from the home altogether, the presence of male volunteers at the center strengthens the children's understanding of both family life and the adult world ahead of them.

Tabernacle Tutorial provides the people of Bed-Stuy with considerably more than just classroom experience. Staff members take the children on trips to the zoos and other places throughout New York City. They operate an informal counseling and referral service for local people seeking housing, jobs, and information on a great variety of subjects. And they solve individual problems by making use of their good relations with local government agencies and politicians. As the director says, "Everybody's always coming in, looking for help." And at Tabernacle Tutorial, they are able to get the help they need.

The center's emphasis on education and training covers the volunteers as well as the students. Most of the fifteen or so volunteers are currently enrolled in college or high school classes themselves. And many of them have learned or taught themselves certain skills so as to be able to teach others at the center. One woman, for example, who used to be on welfare, taught herself how to type and she now teaches typing to others, in addition to doing secretarial work at the center.

Ever since the day care program was started in 1965, funding was a recurrent problem for Tabernacle. There were times when the rent on the building was paid only after the director took up a collection among the local people. And most of the supplies and tools needed at the center were donated or loaned by individuals in the community.

The starting of Tabernacle Tutorial in 1969 placed even greater demands on the organization's meager resources. But Gracie Havenwaller approached the Community Development Foundation (CDF), and that organization, recognizing the worth of the center's activities, contributed a number of small but essential grants.

In 1973 the Save the Children Federation (SCF), a sister agency of CDF, entered into an agreement with Tabernacle Tutorial whereby it would "sponsor" some 125 children (close to a third of the center's total enrollment), giving the center $2,500 each quarter to cover the cost.

It was also in 1973 that the day care program moved out of the Bedford Avenue building and into a newly renovated building a few blocks away. In doing so it also changed hands, for it was taken over in its entirety by the City of New York, which had come to recognize it as one of the best day care centers currently operating in the metropolitan area.

Of the many changes that Tabernacle Tutorial has brought to the community of Bed-Stuy, perhaps the most exhilarating and impressive is a sense of motivation and power among the people. The power is certainly not massive, but it is there. When low-income people begin to change their own lives, to take control of their own destinies, and to speak up for themselves, then progress has been made in the community. And when people who have been helped or trained return to help others, as has happened at Tabernacle Tutorial, then the center is not just a building or its services. It is a reflection of the community's determination and pride and hope.

Al Clayton

*It has served the dual purpose of giving the
Anglos an awareness of the Chicanos and the
Chicanos an awareness of themselves.*

The Bi-Lingual
Broadcasting Foundation

Santa Rosa, California

"We thought we were the only Mexican people living here," says
Jose Mireles, describing his family's sense of isolation after moving to northern California from Mexico several years ago.

But Mireles soon discovered how many poor Mexican and Mexican American families lived in the farming communities around
Santa Rosa, some 60 miles north of San Francisco. And he discovered that it was mostly a strong language and cultural barrier
that kept them apart from the mainstream of society—and consequently from a chance of bettering their lives.

Determined to do something for his people, Mireles linked up
with a group of fellow Chicano students and together they established a unique assistance project designed to break down the
barrier, to educate the people, and to reduce that all-too-common
sense of isolation.

What the young Chicanos did was to organize the Bi-Lingual
Broadcasting Foundation to own and operate one of the country's
first bilingual, bicultural, noncommercial educational FM radio
stations.

The innovative efforts of radio station KBBF have given the Chicanos of northern California a new outlook on life and a voice in
the affairs of the region. Irrespective of whether they can read or
write English—or Spanish—they now have a link with the outside
world, as well as ties that help bind together their many once-iso-
lated Chicano communities scattered throughout the area. And
they now have the means of reaching beyond their present situation through the radio station's on-the-air bilingual education
classes, its programs about job opportunities and health care,
and its discussions dealing with all kinds of consumer problems
and personal problems.

The radio station has also been directing some of its programming at the other residents of northern California, principally the

dominant Anglo community, to give them an idea of the presence, needs, and potential contributions of the thousands of Chicanos who are living in their midst.

If KBBF has proved to be the key to bilingual learning in northern California, then radio education has become the door to bicultural understanding. In the words of Jose Mireles, who is now only in his mid-20s and currently serves as director of the station, "Education has brought people closer together and helped them understand themselves; and it has helped others understand the Mexican American."

The idea of starting a radio station came to Mireles and his fellow founders as a result of their wanting to provide Spanish-language news and entertainment to the area's Chicanos, many of whom are uneducated, low-income farm workers. The students rejected the idea of a newspaper because they knew that a lot of farm workers either couldn't read or were too tired to do so at the end of the workday.

So they turned to the idea of reaching the people by radio. Subsequently they started a successful Spanish-language program on a local commercial station. But one short program a day did not constitute the voice of the people.

So their next step had to be a noncommercial station of their own—one that would be heard throughout the day and one that would not have to worry about or be hindered by the requirements laid down by commercial advertisers.

Having identified their goal, Mireles and his colleagues went in search of funds and assistance. Their first boost came from California Rural Legal Assistance (CRLA), which helped them set up the nonprofit Bi-Lingual Broadcasting Foundation, Inc. in June 1971. Next they organized a board of directors made up of Chicano educators, community leaders, a local television station executive, a CRLA attorney, a Head Start mother, and also a number of Chicano farm workers.

A $5,000 grant from a private foundation enabled the foundation to hire Guido del Prado as full-time director, and he took over the principal chore of raising funds. One of the organizations he approached was the Campaign for Human Development (a foundation sponsored by the Catholic church) which came through with a $65,755 grant. Other foundation, business, and personal contributions subsequently brought the total to $120,000. A site for the station was found in Santa Rosa, where some surplus federal land was made available to the foundation. And equipment and technical help were either donated to the fledgling station free of charge or provided at cost.

With the physical requirements for a station satisfied, Del Prado went to the Federal Communications Commission to apply for the necessary FM noncommercial broadcasting license. The application was approved.

In 1973, two years after the corporation was chartered, KBBF went on the air with a 1,000-watt signal that could reach people within a hundred miles and more of its mountaintop transmitter.

But the KBBF staff quickly discovered that the station's problems were only just beginning.

The supporters and board members were unified on the idea of a radio station," Mireles explains, "but once it was on the air, the program content became quite an issue."

The establishment Mexican Americans on the board wanted to avoid controversial programming. "They wanted us to be more professional—meaning not so abrasive," Mireles recalls. Staff members on the other hand wanted to stick to the original purpose of the radio station—reaching and serving poorer, isolated Mexican Americans, even if that meant airing programs that would not be to the liking of the establishment.

The dispute came to a head some six weeks after KBBF's opening. A sign was posted on a locked chain-link fence around the studio building: "This station is closed pending action by the Board of Directors."

A compromise was eventually worked out, but not before most of the original board members and the station's director, Guido del Prado, had resigned their positions.

The station is now operated by a staff of sixteen. Seven are paid by the foundation, two are volunteers, and seven are Neighborhood Youth Corps trainees.

The station is currently on the air each day of the week from 6 a.m. until midnight, broadcasting each of its programs first in Spanish and then in English.

The station has a varied format. Its programs include:

● newscasts, including in-depth discussions of major news stories (based on the legwork of KBBF's own reporters and volunteers from Chicano associations in the area, as well as on news picked up from shortwave broadcasts by overseas radio stations)

● classes designed to give the Chicanos a working knowledge of the English language

● practical information on health care available in the nine-county area, plus a series of question-and-answer sessions on such issues as prenatal and child care, low-cost nutrition, and

preventive medicine, plus an on-the-air referral service
- issues important to the Chicano community, with a wide range of guests and panel members discussing such matters as the energy crisis, welfare problems, and the economy
- spot announcements that alert the sometimes unsuspecting Chicano to legal injustices and consumer frauds; these spot ads also provide job information and important tips on available services in the area
- youth programs, undertaken in cooperation with the Neighborhood Youth Corps, to provide young people (Chicanos and members of other minority groups) with a channel to reach a large audience of their own age with news and discussions
- an experimental children's program that presents its young listeners with a variety of information and materials relevant to the Chicano experience
- a plentiful selection of Latin music and entertainment

The Bi-Lingual Broadcasting Foundation is also involved in expanding the Chicano community's foothold in the world of broadcasting. It has, for example, started a training program for low-income youths in the broadcasting field. And ten of the foundation's students have already received third-class radio broadcasting licenses, and more are being trained in such skills as oral communication and technical familiarization.

Money remains the chief problem for the station, which operates on a yearly budget of only about $50,000. This is simply not enough to provide all the services the group would like to offer the Chicano community. The station has developed a membership program, with an annual fee of 50 cents per membership for individuals and $100 per membership for organizations. With only 360 members (most of them individuals), though, the station knows it must find other sources of funding.

Despite the money problems, the station's backers remain enthusiastic and optimistic. They are in the process of developing a series of programs and classes that could be packaged and sold to other stations. This would not only provide the station with additional sources of revenue but it would help develop a sense of unity among widely scattered Spanish-speaking communities.

The Bi-Lingual Broadcasting Foundation has proved to be a useful tool in combating prejudice, ignorance, and illiteracy in northern California. More fundamentally, perhaps, it has served the dual purpose of giving the Anglos an awareness of the Chicanos and the Chicanos an awareness of themselves. As a KBBF staff member once remarked, "Many didn't know there were Chicanos out there until we started broadcasting."

*Hey you guys, the attitude is to help each other
learn, not beat each other down.*

The East Harlem Block Schools

New York, New York

The beginnings were modest enough. A group of parents in East Harlem, a neighborhood on the Upper East Side of Manhattan, got together and set up a bilingual day care center in 1965.

When the children grew too old for the nursery, a first grade was added. The following year a second grade was added. And in succeeding years other grades were added, other programs were started, and existing classes were subsequently expanded to accommodate new students.

The East Harlem Block Schools (EHBS) now constitute a community educational complex that offers the area educational services ranging from day care through high school equivalency and college programs for adults associated with EHBS.

The schools are supported by the community and controlled by the parents, who also work in them as teachers' aides to help give their children an alternative to the city's public schools.

The Block Schools' administrative offices, two floors of a little blue building on East 111th Street, are alive with activity. Upstairs in a narrow blue shoebox of a room are a wall of desks, end to end. Two typewriters clatter nonstop amid the steady stream of scheduled and unscheduled arrivals of parents, teachers, students, directors. The air is filled with half a dozen conversations in Spanish as well as English; a meeting convenes spontaneously as three chairs are pulled around a desk. People greet each other warmly, with unselfconscious affection.

Downstairs are two small meeting rooms which double as classrooms for the adult programs. At a weekly directors' meeting the same men and women who had been laughing and teasing each other upstairs soberly discuss the school's responsibility regarding a disruptive child whose parents are uncooperative. The general concensus is that EHBS really does not want to adopt an attitude of "you've got to do this or that" toward any of its parents. In eight years of operation no child has ever been suspended.

Judi Macaulay is the Block Schools' third executive director, and the first parent to become executive director. Asked how long she's been with the school she answers, "I came here when my son was in the second grade. Now he's in the sixth grade. That's my calendar."

The two bywords at the Block Schools are parent control and teacher accountability. Any parent of a child in the Block Schools can easily become a staff member, committee member, or board member, and ultimately all decisions including school policy and hiring and firing of personnel come from the parents themselves. In addition, each school has a parent coordinator who is responsible for maintaining communication with the parents of children in that school. Both teachers and parent coordinators are expected to make home visits during the course of the year.

H. Villafana

EHBS consists principally of the East Harlem Block Nurseries and the East Harlem Day School (which plans on leveling off at the eighth grade). The nurseries and day school are located in six different buildings in East Harlem. The nurseries and lower school (grades one through four) are permanently housed in storefronts on Madison Avenue and on East 106th Street. The Middle school—grades five, six, and seven—are in temporary quarters at the East Harlem Protestant Parish Study Center and the Church of St. Edward the Martyr.

The doors of the three Madison Avenue storefronts open into brightly lit schoolrooms full of sounds and colors. Number 1726 Madison is Block II, one of the two nurseries. At street level are three classrooms, a parent-teacher room, and kitchen facilities. Downstairs is a huge basement for indoor play.

While the children spend a quiet rest hour, Sonia Medina, director of Block II, meets with parents and staff. They are discussing their observations of other day care centers where problems have arisen between professional teachers and parent staff members. The director says, "Some parents have been very good as teachers—very creative, very human, and the teacher becomes threatened." The group agrees they should avoid this mistake.

On 106th Street east of Third Avenue is Block I, the original Block Schools storefront nursery. Here as in Block II there are facilities for three-, four-, and five-year-olds. The center is open all day, from 8 a.m. until 6 p.m. There are sixty children in Block I, and about fifteen new three-year-olds are added each year from a waiting list of well over two hundred names.

Down the street from Block II on Madison Avenue is the storefront that houses the first and second grades of the day school. The two grades are combined, yet they are divided into two classes—so there are kids from both grades in both classes.

In a nearby storefront are the third- and fourth-graders. They too are organized into two classes of combined grades. One of the classes has been given the task of writing poems. The teacher's instructions on the board are to write a "lie poem" with suggestions for subjects such as animals, places, colors. The children bend over their work as they write, then sit up, read aloud to each other and laugh.

Ken Dawson, director of the day school, explains the reasons behind combining the classes: "It gives us flexibility in assigning the kids so we can prevent stagnant relationships from developing. Each kid has a greater variety of children to relate to. Also, it gives us two sets of teachers working with each age group. Ordinarily, the fifth, sixth, and seventh grades meet together. They're split up now because of the space problem. Next year, when the eighth grade is added, we'll have to re-divide."

In each EHBS classroom there are two teachers—one professional teacher and one parent teacher. The professional teacher is usually the head teacher, and the parent teacher is his or her assistant; in one class of third- and fourth-graders, though, a parent teacher so impressed the school with her work that she was promoted to head teacher and a professional was hired as her assistant.

The academic curriculum is chosen from what the directors and staff consider to be the best commercial material available, supplemented by their own ideas. The nonacademic curriculum is determined to a great extent by the skills and interests of individual teachers. The middle school has an activities program from 2 p.m. to 3 p.m. each day. The students are given a choice of activities, which include swimming, basketball, karate and dance.

In the gym at St. Edward the Martyr the sixth- and seventh-grade boys are practicing basketball. Two adults oversee the exercise. Dawson says of the men: "John's a teacher, Ray's a parent who volunteers." There's some scrambling on the court and John calls out, "Hey you guys, the attitude is to help each other learn, not beat each other down." His words are reinforced a hundred ways each day throughout the Block Schools.

The high school equivalency program at EHBS is open to all staff members, board members, and parents associated with the Block Schools. The program is offered in cooperation with the Bronx Community College's office of continuing education. EHBS's college program, open to the same people is offered in cooperation with Bank Street College and Empire State College.

Throughout their history the Block Schools have enjoyed good working relationships with other neighborhood service organizations and community groups. When the middle school lost its building, the teachers canvassed the neighborhood and in one day returned with a dozen offers of temporary housing, many of them being for housing that was rent free.

Ruth Herrera is a caseworker for Afro-American East, a group that deals primarily with the problems of unwed teenage mothers and fathers. She is also a Block Schools parent. Mrs. Herrera describes how EHBS and Afro-American East serve each other: "In a community crisis we work closely with the Block Schools. There are many deprived children in this neighborhood. Sometimes the families break up because young mothers can't care for them. When we can place the kids in our schools, and provide their mothers help, it's possible for families to stay together."

As a Block Schools parent she sums up the feeling that sustains the school: "What holds people together? Well, the idea that there can be an alternative to the oppression of public education holds us together. We're bound by a desire for good education for our children, for a good learning system."

In the early days of planning the Block Schools its founders made tongue-in-cheek references to a future "East Harlem University." With every day of operation the Block Schools bring that dream closer to a reality.

A Block Schools nursery child enjoys the solitude of a rest period. ▶

3

Employment Opportunity

The opportunity to obtain and hold a good job is a basic feature of a democratic society. Yet this opportunity has long been denied to millions of disadvantaged Americans.

Although most of them are indeed poor, the disadvantaged people of America are not discriminated against simply because they are poor. Rather they are victimized because of other factors, such as being a woman or a member of a minority group, being an ex-convict or parolee, being under the age of 22 or over the age of 45, being physically or mentally handicapped, and being without a high school diploma or job skills or work experience.

Many disadvantaged people do work, but their jobs tend to be low-paying, unskilled positions that are often only part-time or seasonal. And being at the bottom of the economic ladder, they are often subject to dismissal and rarely have job security.

One major reason for the severity of the unemployment problem among disadvantaged people is that there are simply not enough job opportunities in the areas where they live. And they do not have the means to commute to other places.

Another reason is that they rarely get the chance to acquire the skills needed to land either better jobs or any jobs. Vocational schools tend to be out of their reach, and few of them get the opportunity to develop useful skills through on-the-job training.

Throughout the country, though, there are now various self-help employment projects that are giving jobs and training and hope to the disadvantaged who want to work but have been either ignored or rejected by business and government.

Residents of an Appalachian village, for example, have found a way to profit from their traditional skills through making crafts for urban markets, inner-city youths provide training and jobs for themselves by repairing cars.

In our society an individual is expected to contribute to the economy in order to share in its benefits. For the disadvantaged person willing to make that contribution, a self-help employment project often means a step toward a better job and a better life.

We don't want to make money so we can leave.
We just want enough money so we can stay.
Besides, when you have a little bit of land you're
never really poor.

Homeworkers Organized
for More Employment

Orland, Maine

Despite local jetports that put the area within an hour or two of most Eastern cities, despite the lure of the interstate highway system's intersection-free efficiency and high-speed curves, many of Maine's summer visitors still prefer the leisurely drive up the coast along U.S. Highway 1. Following the rise and fall of the rocky landscape and maintaining a discreet distance from the sea, the coast road picks its way carefully from town to town, feeding secondary roads down to the shore as it goes.

To the summer visitor heading for Maine's stellar attraction, Acadia National Park, the highway promises the charm and beauty of northern New England, together with the temptation of those irresistible Down East antique stores, country inns, and gift shops. And to the visitor stopping in the small community of Orland, some 30 miles short of the national park, the highway offers a chance to glimpse a unique social experiment that is known as Homeworkers Organized for More Employment (H.O.M.E.).

The visitor pulling in at H.O.M.E. finds a trim collection of buildings that houses a well-stocked craft shop. He is soon inside, looking over the store's selection of quilts, toys, dried-apple dolls, and other handmade goods. Perhaps, if he has the time and curiosity, he wanders about the other buildings in the complex. A quick tour of them reveals a shoe-repair shop, a wholesale clothing operation, a pottery class, and a group of some twenty-five adults intent upon completing their high school education.

But such a tour does not reveal all the people touched by H.O.M.E.'s activities—unless it includes a trip to the austere, weatherbeaten, neighborhood farmhouses, where the rural families who make the store's crafts are working for a better life.

H.O.M.E., it turns out, is much more than a gift shop.

It was in the late 1960s that a group of Roman Catholic nuns moved to the Orland area to start their own hermitage. As they

could not hope to find local work to support themselves in an area where jobs were and are in such short supply, they turned to another, novel way of supporting themselves. They arranged to do work at home for a shoe factory in Belfast, on the western shores of Penobscot Bay.

When the nuns began to receive more than enough work for themselves, they recruited additional workers from the Orland area to handle their increased workload. The program was a success, but it was not to last. The business downturn of 1970 struck throughout New England, and the Belfast shoe factory shut down.

This was a serious blow to the nuns and their helpers, but they did not give up hope. They had proved that it was possible to make money working at home. They had proved that there was an alternative to abandoning the land and looking for work in the big cities—a trend that has afflicted many areas of rural America.

The Orland community was determined to keep alive the idea of home production.

"It was like striking a match to a flammable material," recollects one of the nuns about the effect of the idea. "There was a real need in the community. We knew by the response to the home work that there was a great need of income. These people had skills and a contribution to make."

With property and a house donated by a relative of one of the nuns, the H.O.M.E. cooperative was started and incorporated in June 1970, with a charter that stated the aim of the organization: "To present an alternative to welfare living by improving the quality of life for rural families."

"We started selling a little bit of everything," says Sister Lucy, the director of H.O.M.E. "It was just a cut above a church bazaar."

That situation changed in time, though, as the store began to concentrate on its popular items and drop the others. Increasing numbers of tourists stopped off at H.O.M.E., and before long the "bazaar" image was a thing of the past. In its first year of operation, the store grossed $16,000. Sales during the second year amounted to $39,000, and in the third year they topped $49,000.

In 1972, about two years after opening the store, the cooperative ventured into the wholesale clothing business, despite the fact that initially it had neither the experience nor the business knowledge to grapple with the complex marketing practices involved in such an operation. Optimism and hard work have paid off, though, for the wholesaling of women's dresses now grosses over $34,000 a year.

The Orland store proved so successful that the cooperative made efforts to expand its business by opening satellite stores elsewhere in coastal Maine. Expansion, however, resulted in a considerable increase in costs, so H.O.M.E. decided it would be wiser to close down the additional stores. Currently the group does operate one other store (in addition to the one in Orland) in Bangor, a major regional center some 20 miles to the north.

The sale of handicrafts benefits both H.O.M.E. and the home-workers. By agreement, 75 percent of the sales price of each item sold goes to the maker, who is paid monthly. Depending on the store's sales and the worker's productivity, the amount of money a craftmaker receives each month ranges from $10 to $1,500. At last count, some 900 craftmakers had earned money through their cooperative effort with the store.

Being able to earn money rather than rely on meager welfare handouts has meant a great deal to the rural families living in the Orland area.

"It sure does help," says Annie Stethan, of nearby Bucksport. "I hadn't worked for years until my husband retired. Then we had to do without a lot of things, like a hot-water heater. Now we don't have to worry as much."

The worry has been reduced because Mrs. Stethan regularly earns money from the sales of her quilts. In 1973, for example, she made over $1,500. And the quilt-making is now a family affair, occupying both her and her husband; he cuts the squares and she sews them together.

So it is that working at home produces other benefits for such people as the Stethans, in that it helps give them a renewed interest in life, a rekindled pride in workmanship and production, and relief from the boredom of retirement or enforced inactivity.

The group of nuns found, in meetings with the crafters, that the Orland community had an interest in and a need for much more than a simple economic arrangement with a craft store. Like rural areas elsewhere in the country, Orland had been bypassed or ignored in many ways having to do with education and social welfare. Many people, especially women, in the Orland area had, for one reason or another, quit school before graduation. And some had never had an opportunity to learn about family planning or modern child-rearing practices or health care. And what is more, it turned out, some of the people interested in trying their hand at making handicrafts and selling them through the H.O.M.E. cooperative store actually did not know how to make them. Consequently, before joining the enterprise, they would first have to learn the necessary handcrafting skills.

The people's interest and need could be summed up in one word: education. So H.O.M.E. began an education project.

At about the same time that H.O.M.E. was thinking about what to do to provide educational opportunities, a local Catholic priest and teacher named Father Claude Vachon was wondering what to do with a currently unused schoolhouse—unused because the parochial school had had to be closed down.

Arrangements were made, and Father Vachon began classes again—this time for the young adults and older people of the area.

The first classes were aimed simply at teaching craft skills to the people who wanted to participate in the craft-store program. Gradually, though, other courses were added. These included "personal enrichment" courses, along with diploma courses, which were certified by the state department of education.

As Father Vachon would not be able to handle all the teaching load himself, H.O.M.E. recruited a number of volunteer teachers, including members of VISTA (Volunteers in Service to America).

The search for teachers was initially more successful than the search for students. As Father Vachon recalls, "We had forty-five more volunteers the first year than we had students." Although some local people had clearly expressed an interest in learning, and many needed it, only a few were actually willing to risk any of the non-craft courses at first.

"Remember," says VISTA volunteer Jacqueline Mitchell, "that these people basically distrusted any and all institutions. They considered them all useless."

Nevertheless the barriers of distrust were gradually torn down, and students came to outnumber their teachers. The school currently has about 400 students, most of them women, who range in age from 16 to 59.

The H.O.M.E. school has managed to do more than simply offer instruction in a variety of prescribed subjects. On an informal level the students have also learned much about social relationships (after all, H.O.M.E. is a cooperative). And in particular they have gained a better sense of themselves. As Jacqueline Mitchell says: "Their self-esteem is established by accomplishing something."

H.O.M.E. looks to the future for further accomplishments. One of its major projects, already under way, is a craft center for sewing, weaving, leatherworking, pottery making, and other crafts. VISTA workers and other volunteers are currently working on a large open building to house the center. As Sister Lucy notes, "It will be a living village where crafts will be made and sold. A museum is also planned to preserve the culture of these people."

H.O.M.E.'s Marion Bridges is skilled at the intricate art of weaving.

Another projected H.O.M.E. program is the sheep cooperative, which is being planned to assist local people who are still trying to eke out a basic livelihood on family-owned farms. Explains Sister Lucy: "The idea is to use the land to raise sheep for their wool, which will be shorn and used locally, and then to sell the meat directly, eliminating the middleman."

The relative isolation of rural Maine, as of the rest of Appalachia, has preserved a lifestyle that is out of the mainstream of American life in the 1970s. In many ways these people are to be envied, for they have their land and the lifestyle of an era that most Americans have forgotten.

But isolation can also mean poverty. Jobs are scarce, goods and services few. And opportunities and services, routinely available to city dwellers, are not readily available.

The people of H.O.M.E. are practical enough to recognize the best and worst aspects of rural life. Giving people the opportunity to work in their homes ensures the future stability of the community without sacrificing a lifestyle tied closely to living on the land. Promoting and nurturing traditional crafts not only benefits the people who produce them but maintains a living heritage that won't be relegated to the musty archives of a museum.

"We don't want to make money so we can leave," states one H.O.M.E. craftsman. "We just want enough so we can stay. Besides, when you have a little bit of land you're never really poor."

Mobil's contribution was worth much more because it gave recognition and stature for the first time to thirty-five young people who had been accustomed to getting attention by making trouble. It also gave them courage to ask for more.

The Inner City Auto Repair and Training Center

Milwaukee, Wisconsin

"We keep cars running—that's our trip," says Terry Brulc, standing on a lot cluttered with aging automobiles and reverberating with the sound of engines being revved up by intense young mechanics.

The lot is the headquarters of the Inner City Auto Repair and Training Center, which the 30-year-old Brulc manages. It is the scene of brisk activity in an otherwise forlorn neighborhood on the South Side of Milwaukee.

Brulc brings to his job a lot of hustle, plus a wealth of experience that spans working as an experimental mechanic, organizing labor strikes, and dabbling in radical politics. And despite his flip talk, he is more interested in salvaging lives than automobiles.

In a sense, that is what the center has become—a salvage yard for teenagers who have trouble with reading, writing, and the law. They have turned the auto repair center into a recreational hangout as well as a school for mechanics and a place to earn some money. They have done it with self-help enterprise, and some have even learned to read and write in the process.

It all began in 1971, when Brulc joined the staff of Milwaukee's Inner City Development Project, a federally funded network of neighborhood social service centers. He was assigned to the South 16th Street center and told to work with young people.

"I said 'great'," he recalls, "and started rapping with the kids hanging around the place." They were around because the South Side is woefully lacking in places for young people to gather, let alone pursue interests that could brighten their lives and lead to opportunities for finding worthwhile employment.

Many of the youths, Brulc soon discovered, were car freaks. They wanted to know why it wasn't possible for the government to provide them with a place to work on their machines. Brulc didn't have the answer to that one, but he did have an alternative—the backyard and alley of the place where he lived.

But that did not work out. The neighbors complained about the noise and the beer cans littering the yard. The car freaks were forced to relocate.

Brulc learned of a boarded-up service station owned by the Mobil Oil Company in the neighborhood. Knowing the ways of dealing with management, he wrote to the president of the company requesting that the station be turned over to his group of young people—The Associates, as they called themselves.

Inner City Auto Repair salvages young lives as well as broken cars.

"A month later they sent out a guy with a lease for a dollar a month," Brulc said, happily recalling the first big boost for the project. The company cleaned up the lot, tore out the storage tanks, paved and rewired the property, put in a furnace, and overhauled the air compressor.

"It must have cost $12,000 at least," Brulc recalls.

But Mobil's contribution was worth much more because it gave recognition and stature for the first time to thirty-five young people who had been accustomed to getting attention by making trouble. It also gave them courage to ask for more.

Brulc wrote letters to foundations and businesses. The youths scouted local firms. And everyone had an assignment to procure a particular item needed at the center.

Inexperience and poor education hampered them at first. "It took one guy two weeks to get an eight-foot stepladder because he didn't know how to talk on the phone," Brulc says.

But they learned, and eventually tools and equipment began to arrive. Parts selected by the young people from magazine ads were donated by firms for the asking. Another big assist came from the Allstate Insurance Company in the form of a $7,200 contribution. This meant that some youths could be put on a payroll and that emergencies could be met.

At that point the only wage earner in the group was Terry Brulc, who was—and is still—collecting a $6,000 annual salary from the Inner City Development Project.

Gradually the project has taken on three distinct functions. It is now, in effect, three centers in one:

1. An auto repair co-op—learning mechanics work on the vehicles of low-income neighbors at considerably less than standard commercial rates. They also take care of the cars of other community groups and agencies, notably the United Farm Workers, Vietnam Veterans Union, and other co-ops.

2. A skill development and job-training center—the volunteer staff conducts classes in mechanics for students in area schools, for dropouts, and for adults. The schools give credit for the courses. All forty-nine students who had graduated from the center by 1974 found jobs as mechanics.

3. A recreation center—hundreds of neighborhood teenagers regularly drop in to talk about cars; how to build hot rods and funny cars, as well as how to race them. Some who have no cars of their own come in just to socialize and soak up mechanical lore. The center is so popular that Brulc has had to limit visitors to about two hundred a month.

All the paid work at the center is supervised by Brulc and youths who have qualified as expert mechanics. His top hand is an 18-year-old who dropped out of high school after three years and now is responsible for scheduling, supervising, and running the shop.

Brulc says the youth has gained such a reputation for fixing hot rod engines that it is not at all unusual for someone to come in with little more than a box of parts and say to the fellow, "Hey, man, build me a motor."

Brulc adds: "I'm sure that in a couple of years he'll be making very good money."

The center's director can tell any number of other individual success stories:

• There is one 17-year-old, for example, who joined The Associates in 1971 and learned to read, write, and fix autos at the center. He has returned to Texas, where he is now a freshman in high school and is currently working as a trained mechanic in order to help support his family.

• One self-employed youth has purchased a tow truck and is using the center as a base for his service.

• Another "graduate," now about 30, is going into business for himself and is seeking loans to buy a $39,000 car hauler.

• A member of the original group was arrested for stealing a car and keeping it for five days (backgrounds of car theft are common among The Associates). Brulc persuaded the court to put the 15-year-old on probation instead of shipping him off to a state school for boys. The youngster has since stayed out of trouble. Brulc, in fact, contends that the center helps reduce a high incidence of car theft in the area because it provides cars for youngsters to use on a controlled basis. There is no need to steal one for a joyride.

The director feels the center could do much more to help youths in the area, if it had more money. Several unsuccessful attempts have been made to obtain a grant under the Safe Streets Act. The group wrote a proposal for $120,000, but has since scaled it down to $43,000. Except for his salary, Brulc operates solely on the goodwill of volunteers and on the contributions provided by various business enterprises.

Even though government money is tight, there is every hope that the private sector will continue to support the program. In the meantime Terry Brulc and The Associates have every intention of keeping the center and the cars running.

We're not here to train, we're here to motivate.
We want to develop the individual so he can grow
within the system—any system.

Urban Talent Development

Pittsburgh, Pennsylvania

A few years ago Jim Cleveland was a mailman going nowhere.
Today he's an operations supervisor for a major interstate bus company. He's a college graduate with a bachelor of arts degree in political science. And he's a man with a dream of someday perhaps starting a career in law.

At age 44, he has found that life has suddenly become a "heads-I-win-tails-I-lose" proposition.

"As long as I keep using my head and get off my tail, I can't lose," he says, reflecting the new self-confidence that has begun to dominate his philosophy of life.

Jim Cleveland is just one of hundreds of people who have suddenly become aware of themselves and their abilities because of an organization called Urban Talent Development, Inc. (UTD). Started in 1970, UTD has become known as the "Sesame Street" of manpower-training programs throughout the Pittsburgh area.

Cleveland minces no words when he tells someone about the fourteen days he spent at UTD in 1971.

"It was like a spiritual revival," he says unabashedly. "I came away baptized with a renewed faith in myself."

More than anything else, that's exactly what Urban Talent Development is all about.

UTD promises nothing, yet everything. It doesn't teach you how to be an auto mechanic, but it does teach you how to be a self-starter. It does not teach you how to be a carpenter; rather it teaches you how to build confidence in yourself and your abilities. It does not teach you a trade; rather it teaches you how to handle yourself under all job situations and opportunities.

In essence, UTD takes people—primarily people with under-developed talents who are wandering aimlessly in the world of work—and tries to instill in them self-motivation to go out and do what they want to do.

There are no stipends for attending UTD. That's one of the factors that separates the program from other manpower-training concepts. Urban Talent doesn't want the "program hoppers" who jump from one wage-paying program to the next and end up back on the street corners in between.

The basic ingredient demanded by Urban Talent Development is sincerity of purpose. Beyond that, applicants must be 18 years of age or older, in good health, graduates of high school or some equivalent, and with some demonstrated aptitude for the world of work. If these criteria can be met, the doors of UTD are open to everyone—free.

Many of UTD's students even have college degrees. But the college graduate of today—especially the black college graduate—is finding that unemployment plays no favorites, and that welfare rolls can be indiscriminate in their selections.

The dynamic leaders of UTD, Dick Barber and Len Burnett, like to say that perhaps Demosthenes, the ancient Greek philosopher, statesman, and orator, was thinking of them when he said more than 2,000 years ago:

"Small opportunities are often the beginning of great enterprises."

UTD seeks to supply the small opportunities in achieving its self-proclaimed goal of building careers. The statistics of the program over the last three years are proof that the approach is working.

Through the beginning of 1974, a total of 710 students have been enrolled in UTD training programs; of these, 614 have completed the two-to-three-week courses—and 544 have been placed in better jobs or in school for further education and training.

The average UTD student is between 20 and 30. He or she is unemployed, receiving unemployment benefits or welfare benefits, or no benefits at all, and he is groping through a lifestyle of hardship and poverty.

The student-body profile shows an average of $2,472 in yearly earnings before training, and an average of $5,271 after training (the after-training figure is deceptively low because it includes the earnings of those who have taken part-time jobs while they continue their schooling).

The bulk of the graduates are going into supervisory and management positions that give them unlimited opportunity for advancement.

Jim Cleveland is one example.

Cora Watley is another. From being an unhappy school teacher, frustrated by mandated teaching styles she didn't like and earning just $5,000 a year, she has moved on to an exciting, $9,700-a-year job as underwriter for an insurance company.

"UTD didn't teach me how to be an insurance underwriter," Cora Watley says frankly. "I didn't even know what an insurance underwriter was. But UTD did teach me about dealing with people. It taught me about the business world as a whole."

UTD had heard about a trainee position with the insurance company, gave her a crash description of what it was all about, and asked her if she was interested.

"I liked what I heard, applied for the position, and here I am," she says.

Like any successful program, UTD is a product of its leadership. From the very beginning, it looked like it was headed for success, at least in terms of improbability. After all, what else could result from the unlikely teaming of a former sharecropper, a pro football star, a pro football player who didn't make it, a vegetarian, and a Kelly girl?

Urban Talent now has a staff of nine dedicated people, headed by the ex-sharecropper—Richard Barber, nicknamed "Patches" because of his firsthand experience in poverty. But since his childhood as a plantation worker, Barber has managed to use his knack for self motivation to achieve success in practically everything he's done. Today he's working toward a PhD in business administration at the University of Pittsburgh.

More importantly, he's the president and co-founder of Urban Talent Development.

Dick Barber has a small wooden sign on his desk that says: "The Buck Stops Here." With Barber, it really does.

"We're not here to train, we're here to motivate," he says. "We want to develop the individual so he can grow within the system—any system. For any aspiration or goal to be achieved within the system, you've first got to understand the system. This is what we try to do in Urban Talent Development."

The need for UTD developed as a spin-off from lessons learned in a training program launched by All-Pro Enterprises, Inc., a food-service business organized by Brady Keys, a former football star for the Pittsburgh Steelers.

In developing All-Pro Enterprises, Keys had organized a special series of three-week programs to help train blacks and other minority-group people to be franchise operators. What he found, however, was that the trainees were going back to their home area, opening franchises—and failing as businessmen.

According to Len Burnett, the pro football player who didn't make it and UTD's current executive vice-president, "The lesson

A UTD student can receive personalized attention in a small class.

we learned was that merely teaching blacks and other minorities about franchises wasn't going to work, and that the real need was in understanding the whole aspect of the business world."

That's how Urban Talent Development was born—with Keys as chairman of the board, Barber as president, and Burnett and other dedicated people involved in operations. At first the program was structured to help minorities to go into business for themselves. After one year, though, it was found that the real need in the business world was for supervisory and management people—with the requisite business skills, of course.

"Civil rights groups were out banging on doors to get jobs," says Burnett, "but once they got them, we didn't have the properly trained people to fill them. Business executives were telling us, 'Okay, give us ten people here, twenty people there'—and we didn't have them."

With that as its challenge, UTD remolded its program and gradually it became what it is today—a concept combining the elements of supervisory management, business management, and career orientation into a series of three-week courses running six hours a day for five days a week.

Classes are small—around 15 to 20 students—and they tend to be informal and loosely structured. They are more like freewheeling discussion sessions than lectures.

Len Burnett, Les Misik, and Wellington Allen, the teachers, can be found straddling desks or perched on tables as they talk with their students. The language is the language of the student, not the business world. They may use "Peanuts" cartoon characters to demonstrate economics and the free enterprise system. But once the student has completed his studies, he will understand a profit-and-loss statement as well as any businessman.

Techniques of interviewing, personnel traits needed for supervisory positions, and even personal appearance are among the elements emphasized through imaginative methods devised by the instructors themselves.

"It's the little things that turned me on," says Beverly Gaskins, a 22-year-old high school graduate who eventually wants to open her own boutique. "Like interviewing, for example. They gave us some insight into the tricks interviewers are likely to pull in testing you out. What do you do, for example, when an interviewer offers you a cigarette knowing full well there's no ashtray around?

"They want to see how aggressive you are and whether you will ask for an ashtray or try to quietly sneak the ashes into the cuffs of your pants or somewhere else. These are the kind of things you'd never be aware of unless someone told you about them."

Role playing, public speaking in front of other members of the class on such topics as "what made me happy this week" or "something I really like to do" are all among the ways UTD seeks to build self-confidence.

"We don't want them talking about something they don't know anything about; we want them telling us things they want to talk about," says Barber. "We want them to convey feeling so we can share that feeling. If their experience is a happy one, we listeners should also be happy. And if they are sad, we too should be sad. We're more interested in how they say it than what they say."

Burnett is a living example to the students in terms of overcoming disappointment and hardship, and of turning their lives around through self-motivation.

A pro-football player with a lot of potential, Burnett injured a knee in his first year with the Steelers, and two years later completely washed out in an attempted comeback. Instead of disappearing, however, he emerged with a new all-star credential, this time in the field of education. His influence is seen dramatically in practically every educational aspect of the UTD program.

Urban Talent Development is presently a $165,000-a-year operation, completely funded through private foundations. There are no governmental or public subsidies. Barber likes it that way, because with no public subsidies there are no bureaucratic strings attached to the program.

"We look at manpower as a business, and so manpower training should be treated as a business," says Barber. "We don't want a program that perpetuates the welfare program. Our goal is to provide alternatives and remedies to welfare. A training program is not completely successful until it places all its trainees in jobs—jobs that are meaningful and offer a rewarding, satisfying career."

In some senses, UTD is ahead of its time, embracing the concept of career education that is only now beginning to infiltrate public education.

Perhaps Burnett captures the whole thing most effectively and dramatically in a poem he reads at some of the graduation exercises for UTD classes.

He calls it the "Penny Poem," and it goes like this:

> I bargained with Life for a Penny,
>   And Life would pay no more,
> However, I begged at evening
>   When I counted my scanty store.
>
> For Life is a just employer.
>   He gives you what you ask,
> But once you have set the wages
>   Why, you must bear the task.
>
> I worked for a menial's hire,
>   Only to learn dismayed,
> That any wage I had asked of Life,
>   Life would have willingly paid.

Maybe prison made me stronger in
what I'm trying to do now.

The Epicurean Kitchen

Seattle, Washington

The $1.25 price on the paperback book had been neatly obliter-
ated, because it was to be a gift. The book itself, *Prison to Praise*
by Chaplain Merlin R. Carothers, had been carefully chosen, as
had the words written on the flyleaf:

"To Anna Barnett. I praise God for your keeping after me to do
better. I am going to keep trying until you are proud of me. Love,
Mary."

Mary's eyes were shining and her cheeks were pink with emotion as she handed the book and three roses to Anna Barnett. "I
paid for it with my own money," she said.

A few months earlier, Mary had been a resident of an institution
for the retarded in Washington state, but counselors had decided
she was ready for referral to a unique, one-to-one, on-the-job
training program in Seattle called the Epicurean Kitchen.

Anna Barnett is the founder and executive director of the Epicurean Kitchen, a nonprofit corporation that takes the handicapped,
mentally retarded, those recovering from mental illness, and
prison parolees and trains them in various arts of food preparation so that they can find jobs and become self-sustaining.

"The day before," Anna Barnett recalls, "I'm afraid I had given
Mary a hard time. The main problem was to just get her moving,
not standing around and watching. I had to do something that
would get her started. Now she knew about my prison time. The
next morning she gave me the book and the roses, which broke
me up. I think she had decided overnight that if I could do it, she
could do it."

The choice of *Prison to Praise* was singularly appropriate for
Anna Barnett, a talented, determined woman in her mid-50s.

An occasional "cain't" in her conversation betrays her origin in
Wichita Falls, Texas, although this word is alien to Anna's personal philosophy. She had a pleasant childhood, but did not finish
high school—"I wanted to get myself a child, so I got married."
Later she attended colleges in the South, studying accounting.

Wherever she went she also studied with the best chefs to perfect her flair for preparing food. She learned food decorating and display in Boston from Henri-Paul Pellaprat, author of *Modern French Culinary Art*. And it was May Brennan of the renowned Brennan's restaurant in New Orleans who taught her how to use herbs and how to prepare sauces.

Anna Barnett adds her epicurean touch to a dish.

Anna Barnett's accounting career was uneventful until 1960, when she embezzled several thousand dollars from a firm in Colorado. She says: "That first robbery was very deliberate, but before long I felt the heat and left town. From then on, I ran scared." She embezzled as she ran, hitting six firms in six different cities. Although Federal Bureau of Investigation (FBI) records indicate her take was in the neighborhood of $300,000, she claims that a more likely figure of what she ended up with is about $100,000.

The FBI caught up with her in Hollywood two and a half years later. She was convicted of grand larceny and sentenced to a maximum of 20 years in prison. While serving her time at the California Institution for Women at Frontera, Anna Barnett was appalled by the number of women she saw returning to prison. "I couldn't understand why they went out so fast and came back even faster," she says. "I asked one girl if she didn't get tired of going out and coming back, and she just shrugged and said 'I guess it's an occupational hazard'.

"I got to thinking about it and decided the only answer was to work with people on a one-to-one basis, to teach them skills that would let them get jobs and get back their self-respect."

So she decided to use her own talent for cooking to start a commercial catering service that would serve as an on-the-job training ground, not only for parolees but for the handicapped generally.

When she was paroled in California, Anna Barnett was brought to Washington State to face charges of embezzling from a Seattle firm. Again she was convicted and sentenced to a maximum of 20 years. She appealed the conviction to the state supreme court.

While her appeal was pending, she tried to find work, but, as she says, "It was always a case of 'don't call us, we'll call you'. Only they didn't. I even tried to get building maintenance work, but there was no way I could get a bond."

Finally, through a domestic agency, she got a job as housekeeper for George and Pauline Vogel, an acting couple with the Seattle Repertory Theatre, whose friendship and support came to mean a great deal to her. She also worked as a cook for several prominent Seattle families. These jobs were valuable to her, not only for the friendship and restoration of her dignity but for contacts that would be helpful in establishing her catering service.

Her Washington conviction was upheld by the state supreme court in April 1967, and she was sent to the state penitentiary in Walla Walla. Although she served only six months there, she describes those months as "the worst of my life." However, she reflects, that "sometimes I think Walla Walla was the best thing that happened to me. Maybe prison made me stronger in what I'm trying to do now."

The years since Anna Barnett launched the Epicurean Kitchen in 1968 have called for plenty of strength on her part, but they have been rewarding years for her and for the seventy-six handicapped persons she has trained to be self-supporting. The kitchen began in her own small apartment with two pots and pans and a rented freezer. And she prepared herself by taking a brush-up course at Seattle Central Community College.

Armed with a list of potential customers, many of them people she had met while working as a cook, she designed an announcement of her catering service and mailed it out. "My first job was an order for thirty-five picnic lunches for the Junior League," she recalls. "I really thought I was somebody."

The Epicurean Kitchen has had a nomadic existence. When the catering business outgrew her apartment, she moved it to Mercer Inn, a halfway house. From there the Kitchen moved to facilities in Trinity Episcopal Church. But once again the Kitchen had to move on, when it appeared that the church would lose its property tax-exempt status if the Kitchen continued to occupy space there. Next stop was a location at the Seattle Center, site of the 1962 World's Fair. When the Kitchen had to move from those quarters, it settled in a cafeteria on the waterfront, under contract to the Port of Seattle.

All this time, referrals of people for training had been coming in from agencies such as the divisions of vocational rehabilitation and public assistance, the institution for the retarded at Buckley, the Washington Association for Retarded Children, Seattle-King County mental health, narcotic and drug-abuse programs, and federal, state, and county work release programs.

The training had been going on through all of the moving, and of the seventy-six handicapped trained under Anna's direction, 85 percent had been placed in competitive and continuous employment lasting more than a year. (Agencies have commented that placement of 25 percent would have been an excellent record.)

Trainees find work in every branch of the food-service business, as dishwashers, waitresses, bus boys, cook's helpers, waiters—at whatever level of attainment they have reached. People referred to Anna are on either social security or welfare when they are accepted, which means that they get $150 a month base pay. The kitchen pays an additional $40, for a total of $190 a month.

When they get a job and their pay reaches $268 a month, after a certain time period they go off welfare, a saving to the state of $5,000 a year for each person.

"Since the Epicurean Kitchen started, I have saved the taxpayers half a million dollars," says Anna Barnett.

"When these people are ready to go to work on jobs, on their own, they lose their institutional services, such as counseling, caseworker or perhaps a psychiatrist's care," she adds. "This is like Linus losing his security blanket, to them, so we have to be sure they are ready to go out on their own, and ease them into a job. Most of the Epicurean Kitchen's graduates make close to two dollars an hour when they go out and find themselves jobs."

Not only does the Kitchen save the taxpayers money but it also does without any government aid. Anna Barnett takes pride in the fact that "we have, fortunately, been able to meet our own operating expenses and overhead without benefit of state, county, or federal grants."

The Epicurean Kitchen, which was incorporated as a nonprofit enterprise late in 1971, has seized the imagination and heart of Seattle. Church groups, women's clubs, and business organizations have sent testimonials to Anna's tasty food and tasteful service. Media coverage has been consistent and friendly. Volunteers cut across social barriers, and range from Junior Leaguers to small groups of retired people. They have helped with everything from hairdressing and makeup to tutoring the retarded in reading, writing, and arithmetic and helping them cope with shopping and public transportation. Others have come in to help with the enormous amount of mail that the Epicurean Kitchen now receives from correspondents throughout the country.

In spite of its frequent moves, the Kitchen has kept going with its catering business. Anna has been a successful bidder on a contract to supply meals for day care centers, and she has bid on others to supply meals for the elderly. But the big handicap for the Kitchen has been the lack of a permanent home with adequate kitchen and dining space. A survey shows that in one eight-month period Anna Barnett had to turn away $64,829 in business that couldn't be handled for lack of facilities. In another four-month period, the Epicurean Kitchen was forced to turn down a total of $58,281-worth of business.

Anna's dream is to find a large enough place, and use the cafeteria as a sort of senior center to be run by trainees who have proven themselves. In 1973 she thought she had found the right space, and had launched a vigorous campaign for onetime capital funding to buy equipment. She lost the lease, though, because of failure to get a parking variance.

As long as there are handicapped people on the waiting list for rehabilitation, Anna Barnett will continue her search for a permanent home for the Epicurean Kitchen, in that she has clearly proved to be a beacon of hope for people who have slipped out of the mainstream of society. As William Ludwig, a former executive, says: "Anna continues to work her seven-day-week, twenty-hour day, and somehow, magically, things get done. This is a valid idea and it can work, with that kind of dedication and guts."

Anna Barnett herself has some brief words of advice for anyone considering a similar project: "Keep your chin up and pray."

*On Memorial Day 1972 my daughter committed
suicide. She was 20 years old and felt that there
was nothing to live for. A lot of the kids came
around and told me that they often felt the same
way. . . . I thought that someone was trying to tell
me something, that maybe I hadn't done enough
if some of the kids still felt that way.*

Young People of Watts

Los Angeles, California

Wilmington Avenue runs its dreary course through south-central Los Angeles, crossing dilapidated avenues and ancient railroad tracks as it winds into the heart of Watts. It runs past ramshackle storefront churches with their high-sounding names
painted unevenly across dirty windows, past small, dingy stores,
past homes with front yards that are littered with gutted refrigerators and the remnants of discarded automobiles.

At 10706 Wilmington Avenue stands an old building, once a
grocery store. Its wide doorway opens into a large, dark room,
where a young black man is earnestly mopping the stone floor.

Beyond him, through a narrow door, lies a second room that is
crowded with old schoolyard benches, a bookcase full of musty
old books and a battered soda pop dispenser. In this room a number of kids, most black, some Mexican American, are standing
around a middle-aged white man, five-foot-ten, about 230
pounds, dressed in a plaid shirt, T-shirt and Levi's.

The kids are members of a group called Young People of Watts
(YPOW). This old building is their headquarters. And the older
man is Laurence "Barney" Mull, their president.

How does a 50-year-old white man come to find himself deep in
Watts and the president of an organization dedicated to keeping
kids out of trouble and in school? "About fourteen years ago," explains Mull, "I had a wife, a family, and a $37,000 home in La Mi-
rada. One day my wife threw me out."

Mull doesn't like to say so in so many words, but he consequently suffered what could be called a nervous breakdown.
Dazed by the loss of his family, he wandered over into Watts.

"My work had brought me down here before so I knew the
area," he says. "The man next door [to what is now the YPOW

headquarters] gave me a room and I just sat on his front steps for eight or nine months. Didn't work, didn't do anything. Women in the neighborhood felt sorry for me, I guess, and they brought me food. Otherwise I would have starved.

"The kids would come around and see me not shaven, in the same clothes all the time and they'd say, 'Man, a white man shouldn't look like that'. Eventually, they were the ones that brought me out of my rut."

While talking to Mull, trying to make him feel better, the kids also started telling him about their own feelings, their own needs.

"I had wondered why these kids never seemed to be in school," Mull says. "Some of them said they just didn't see any sense in it, but a lot stayed away because they didn't have the right clothes to wear to school—and if they'd come in anything else they'd be punished. Like if they didn't have clean, untorn shorts to wear to gym and they went anyway, they'd get swatted. So they stayed away."

About the time the neighborhood children were beginning to pull Mull out of his stupor, a man showed up with a broken lawnmower. "The man wanted to know if I could fix it," Mull recalls. "I knew something about lawnmower motors, so I said, 'Why not?' Getting to fix that lawnmower also got me off my butt.

"There was this kid named Overton who used to hang around the place where I was staying, always tinkering with a bicycle. But he had never been too friendly and when I asked him to help me lift the mower, he said, 'F—— off white m——f——, I hate white m——f——s'. I said, 'Okay, so I hate black m——f——s, but I need help'. The man where I was staying told the kid he'd better help me, and I guess he was afraid of the man because he did. After that we became friends and fixed a lot of lawnmowers together."

Opening a modest little repair business was exactly what Mull needed. It not only gave him a little money to live on but more importantly it provided him with funds to fuel an informal organization he had formed with some of the kids who were hanging around. The organization was called Young People of Watts.

"Whatever money came in we would use to buy these kids clothes, such as underwear or socks or gym shorts," Mull says. "What money was left over or what we could scrape together we used for field trips. We'd put together our nickels and dimes and decide how far the gas we could buy could get us and how many hot dogs we could buy with what was left over. Of course we'd have to use our heads too when it came to going places where there was an admission charge. We'd all go and I'd go up to the gatekeeper or whatever he was and say, 'Look, I got all these kids from Watts, but they can't afford to pay their way in'. And he would usually say, 'Well okay, the little ones can go in free'. And then I'd say, 'Well, I need some of those bigger ones too to help me keep an eye on the little ones,' and we'd all get in."

Mulls' greatest concern, however, was—and still is—to make sure that the children who came under his influence stayed in school. He became a self-appointed truant officer, roaming the streets, looking out for those who played hookey, asking those who did go to school to tell him about those who were repeatedly absent, cornering the truants—and often their mothers—and talking their ears off about the importance of an education.

Over the years Mull has developed an informal organization that has become increasingly dependent upon itself to find ways of meeting its own needs. Helped by the boys who have been with him the longest, Mull teaches the younger boys who come to YPOW how to repair lawnmower motors. Then there is the neighborhood woman Mull found who comes every Saturday to teach the youngsters—mostly boys—to sew and mend their own clothes.

YPOW's independence of social welfare agencies, especially those that have the manpower and money to be of use to such a group, has not been determined solely by YPOW. Some of the more rigid agency heads whom Mull approached could not believe that this white man, who looked like the local garbage collector and kept track of the day's business by stuffing scrawled notes, invoices, and notices of meetings into his shirt pocket, could be very effective working among hardened, streetwise, ghetto youths. What is more, Mull admits, some of YPOW's long, earnest attempts to get some outside help have resulted in repeated disappointment and failure.

"We went to some of the unions and asked for help to fix up our building," Mull says. "We got promises from business agents who said that they would send volunteer labor. So we'd go out and scrounge up wood and cement and rent a cement mixer. The kids would come to work too, but those guys would never show up."

The only source of outside help that Mull has come to trust is the Earle M. Jorgensen Company, a firm specializing in steel and aluminum products that operates on the edge of Watts. Mull first met Earle Jorgensen in 1967 at a meeting of a community organization trying to reinvigorate housing in the Watts area. Jorgensen, who had already shown some interest in Watts youth by making scholarships available to senior high school students who wanted to further their education, offered Mull some financial help. From 1968 to 1972 Mull occasionally used to visit the Jorgensen corporate offices to ask for assistance with specific financial needs.

Until Memorial Day of 1972 a great deal of YPOW business was conducted with a by-the-seat-of-the-pants approach.

"On Memorial Day 1972 my daughter committed suicide," Mull says. "She was 20 years old and felt that there was nothing to live for. I just sat around in a chair and didn't move. A lot of the kids came around and told me that they often felt the same way, that they thought of killing themselves because there didn't seem to be any reason to live. I thought that someone was trying to tell me something, that maybe I hadn't done enough if some of the kids still felt that way. There should never be another kid that wants to kill himself, I said to myself, and we started to move."

From that time on, Mull became even more purposeful, and he started edging toward a more formalized approach to the business of running YPOW. Such a trend was already evident earlier in 1972, though, and was most likely a direct result of the influence of John Watkins, the Jorgensen vice-president. It was Watkins who had taken on the responsibility of serving as an advisor to YPOW and as a liaison between the group and the company. Early in 1972, for example, YPOW formed an ad hoc committee consisting of the few individuals in various social welfare agencies Mull had met and liked. And it was at about the same time that Mull incorporated YPOW as a nonprofit organization.

Since that sad Memorial Day, Mull has kept his promise to start moving. The group's endeavors now proceed on a more orderly basis, and its day-to-day workings are somewhat less dependent on the contents of his shirt pocket.

Mull's rededication, as well as the renewed efforts of others, has also improved the group's outside contacts.

Encouraged by his willingness to formalize YPOW's structure and by his own more determined ways, the Jorgensen company has significantly stepped up its financial support to YPOW. Jorgensen has provided funds to enable YPOW to buy the building in which it is headquartered and to purchase an empty lot next door for future expansion. Jorgensen has also purchased a van for YPOW and supplies gas for the vehicle. Because it has the van, YPOW has been able to land a contract with the state to transport mentally retarded children in Watts to and from special classes.

"More things will happen now," John Watkins says. "YPOW will have space soon to set up its own program where mentally retarded children will be getting specialized training. This is going to be a structured youth center prepared for action.

"Barney has even come in and asked for us to put money into the budget so he can buy himself a suit. He says it may be time to go to all those agency meetings now as Lawrence Mull."

An art that might have fallen victim to
the machine age is now assured of being passed
to still another generation.

Hispanic Rug Weaving

Hernandez, New Mexico

Audelia Martinez unfolded the handwoven rug on the counter of the small general store and said, "I learned how to make these as a little girl from my mother. The design is very old. Maybe other women would like to learn how to make them too."

The rug had been fashioned out of rags dyed brilliant colors and woven into geometric patterns. The designs resembled abstract medallions, or perhaps sunbursts—it was hard to be sure about the designs. But as he glanced from the rug to the elderly woman, Regino Salazar knew the rug was part of the region's Hispanic cultural tradition, which dates back to the 16th century.

It would be an excellent idea, he later thought, to start a rug-weaving school where local residents could learn this ancient art. Such an enterprise would not only revive a cultural tradition but would also provide the people with a new source of income—something that was greatly needed in this part of northern New Mexico, where the people were hard pressed to eke out a living from farming and from doing occasional part-time jobs.

At that time, 1964, Regino Salazar was a 25-year-old graduate of the University of Arizona who was very much interested in helping the people of the Española area to help themselves. He had already turned his store into a community center for them. Now he was intent upon interesting them in learning to weave.

Soon he secured an old adobe building and installed Señora Martinez, who was then in her 70s, as head of a school. The New Mexico Home Educational Livelihood Program (HELP) gave a $5,000 grant that went into the fabrication of hand looms. Both young and older women enrolled in the classes and in time they became proficient in recreating the historic rug patterns taught by Señora Martinez. This marked the start of the unique community project that has come to be known as Hispanic Rug Weaving.

During the past decade the project has continued to receive some financial assistance from HELP. And recently it has also been receiving aid from the Save the Children Federation (SCF).

Men and women from other villages in the Española district are presently being trained in the Hernandez school, which is now on a 20-hours-a-week schedule. The men take care of the looms and the women do the weaving. Although some wool is used, most of the rugs are made from rags, old stockings, pieces of denim, and other discarded materials—the use of such remnants rather than virgin wool being an authentic part of the New Mexico rug-weaving tradition. This also gives the older women of the community— those not able to weave—a chance to help by collecting the materials and tearing them into the right sizes for the weavers.

The handmade rugs, no two of which are alike, are offered for sale at Salazar's store, where they are eagerly bought by tourists. Meanwhile the weavers and Salazar hope to tap other markets and perhaps turn the enterprise into a cooperative.

Even if the co-op is set up, Salazar does not believe that the project can ever operate on a large scale. He considers it as much a social activity as a source of employment. "We experimented with letting the women weave or rip the rags at home, but the group is more effective when they meet at the project center," he says. "The classes are a chance to meet with friends and to escape the everyday hassles of life. And it also gives the people an opportunity to create fine rugs and nurture an age-old tradition."

Even the comparatively small amounts of money involved mean a great deal in the Española area, where so many live below the federally designated poverty line.

More important than the money, for the project backers, is the hope it will encourage the area's young people. They have been dropping out of school, with sixty percent leaving between the sixth and ninth grades, and migrating elsewhere. The rug project may help reverse that trend, or perhaps it would at least slow down the rate of departure.

"The students are hungry to learn more of their culture," according to Eduardo Atencio, a University of New Mexico consultant teaching cultural awareness in the Española district. "The rug program has very definitely created a new area of interest for many young people in this area."

One fairly certain outcome of the project is that an art that might have fallen victim to the machine age is now assured of being passed to still another generation. An economy has received a slight boost. The art, culture, and craftsmanship brought to and nurtured in America before the Pilgrims will not be totally submerged in the sea of plastic and neon that threatens to engulf the country and many of its fine old traditions.

Regino Salazar displays a traditional Hispanic rug crafted by a resident of the Española district of northern New Mexico.

I was the dreamer. Mary was the doer and
Jewel was the pusher.

Miracle Workers

Sparta, Tennessee

Veo Hardy doesn't give up easily even though life has dealt her one crushing setback after another. She has found a way of surmounting the disadvantages of being a widow with a disabled leg, with a very small income, and with no one to turn to in time of need. The way she has found is teaching others with physical and mental handicaps to make handicrafts and sell them.

She was at a low ebb in April 1971 when she sought out a member of her prayer group, Mary Agee, in Sparta's First United Methodist Church.

Veo Hardy had just recovered from a bout of mental depression, caused by a bad reaction to a prescription drug. A doctor had told her that, in his opinion, there was no job where she could "fit in." She was then in her mid-50s. Her leg, injured in an automobile accident, prevented her from standing for any period of time. She couldn't type very fast, and she had no other skills to qualify her for a job. What is more, she lacked one quarter of earned income to qualify for Social Security benefits and was getting along on $27 a month. Her late husband lacked three days of military service to qualify her for minimum veterans' benefits.

Talking to Mary Agee, Mrs. Hardy confided that, despite her hardships and bleak prospects, she had a dream—a plan—for leading a useful and productive life.

The next day Mary Agee, together with a friend named Jewel Sims, paid a visit to Veo Hardy. It was then that Mrs. Hardy revealed what her dream was all about. She showed her two visitors a great variety of handcrafted items—quilts, pot holders, strings of paper beads, toys, and dolls—that she had sewn or fashioned herself. There were nearly a hundred different items.

Mrs. Hardy explained that she was concerned about the handicapped people in the community. She had discovered there were several types of handicapped persons who were not being helped either by the high schools or the local rehabilitation clinic. (Some rehabilitation programs, for example, require the handicapped to have a high school education to make them eligible for training.)

"In many instances the handicapped are too old for one program, too young for another. Or they are physically handicapped and need to be mentally handicapped to receive help, or vice versa," she told her visitors. "I know how it feels to be told, 'You just don't fit in anywhere' and I think there is something we could do for these people."

She had in mind helping the young people in particular, and she told the other two of her idea of creating a workshop where young handicapped people could learn to make craft goods.

She had a sympathetic listener in Mary Agee, who had a son with both mental and physical handicaps. Jewel Sims also agreed that they should try to set up a program of their own. They estimated that there were about a hundred handicapped persons in the area who could benefit from it.

Five months of groundwork and exploring ideas followed before the project started in September 1971. Set up on a nonprofit basis, the project was named Miracle Workers—in recognition of the organizers' hopes for what the project would represent to the local community if it proved successful.

"I was the dreamer. Mary was the doer and Jewel was the pusher," Veo Hardy recalls.

Word of the project was spread throughout the neighborhood; donated materials soon began flowing in, along with offers from volunteers willing to act as trainers. Workshop sessions were held at the First United Methodist Church, with the volunteers to determine what each could do best in the handicrafts line.

A board of directors composed of the volunteer trainers was organized, and by December 1971 the board was ready to start raising some operating funds. Veo Hardy went to one of the local newspapers to place an advertisement about the formation of the organization and its first sale of products.

"When I explained to the people in charge," says Mrs. Hardy, "they wouldn't hear of me paying for the advertisement. They ran it free of charge and made arrangements for the sale to be held on tables set up on the sidewalk in front of their office."

Judy, a physically handicapped girl, was Miracle Workers' first trainee.

"She learned to write her name by using an artist's paintbrush in her mouth," says Mary Agee. "She really benefited from the workshop, and we learned a lot from her. She is currently in the process of learning to use a typewriter in Nashville."

"The first project was making paper beads and stringing them for necklaces," says Mollie Leonard, the organization's first treasurer. "They were then sold for $1.25 a string."

Success was slight in the first bazaar at Smithville, held in a neighboring county in December 1971. "But it was a good experience for everyone," says Veo Hardy.

E. G. Rogers, the only male board member, secured a rent-free building in Sparta for the project in May 1972. Miracle Workers had a relatively permanent home at last.

Factories in the county began donating fabrics and leather to the organization. And one factory outlet provided clothes racks for use at bazaars.

Slightly more than $3,000 was taken in during 1972, primarily from sales. Expenses during the same period totaled $2,700, so Miracle Workers entered 1973 with $300.

In June 1973, Miracle Workers obtained its charter as a tax-exempt, nonprofit enterprise.

The organization increased its production capabilities at the end of 1973, when it received an industrial sewing machine as a gift from a local merchant. Another citizen, the director of a workshop at the county high school, converted the machine to regular household current so the organization could use it.

The Miracle Workers work force now numbers about fifteen people, having grown as more handicapped trainees have been drawn into the organization.

Fay, for example, a cerebral palsy victim with a mental handicap, is one of the more productive trainees. She continues to attend workshop sessions, although her skill level is actually high enough for her to work at home.

According to Miracle Workers volunteers and board members, Fay never left the farm where she lived and very seldom did anything prior to attending the workshop. She now does cross-stitch embroidery on aprons; in her spare time at home she pieces quilts for gifts.

"We've gotten a lot of people out of their homes," says Mary Agee. "They wouldn't have considered moving about before."

Among the other trainees is Mary Agee's son, Sam Agee Jr., who has learned to string beads for necklaces.

The workshop entertainer during breaks is a 21-year-old youth who is blind in one eye, uncoordinated, and retarded. Between stringing beads and making seed flowers, he fills the place with music from his electric guitar.

Barbara, in her 30s, a mentally handicapped trainee, has been with the workshop program one year. She sews rick rack on cloth flower petals and produces pot holders at home for sale to the shop at a fixed price.

"She takes a great deal of pride in the products she makes," says Veo Hardy. "If one of the volunteers mentions buying a pot holder because Barbara made it, her face registers disapproval and disappointment. When a stranger happens into the shop and decides to buy one 'because it's beautiful' she really beams. She enjoys the work and looks forward to it."

Barbara saves her income from work on pot holders and items produced at the workshop until she has enough to purchase a suit. She has gained enough confidence in her decision making to select her suits and coordinate them herself.

Miracle Workers co-founders Mary Agee (left), Veo Hardy (center), and Jewel Sims. The three are elected members of the board of directors.

Approximately 25 quilts have been sold for Miracle Workers at prices ranging from $5 to $15. Some woodwork and handicraft items are sold occasionally to novelty and toy shops locally and in surrounding counties. These sales are a boost for the organization. But most requests from shops for 5 or 10 dozen dolls or shoulder bags are beyond the present production capabilities of Miracle Workers.

"We have had as much public support as we can handle," says Veo Hardy.

In 1974 the organization received its first grant—$600 from the United Givers Fund of Sparta, and it began to look confidently to the future.

With more funds, Miracle Workers plans to expand its activities and acquire more volunteer help from among skilled senior citizens. And instead of limiting training sessions to one day a week, Veo Hardy hopes to have a different activity going every day. Her dreams about miracles look like they will continue to come true.

We must move into the economic system of
this country through distribution of goods and
services. We've been primarily at the consuming
end of the system or at the retail service end.
We need to become suppliers in order to get a
meaningful part of the business dollar.

The Afro-Urban Institute

Milwaukee, Wisconsin

For years the only way most black residents of Milwaukee's North Side could get a taxi to come to their door was to call a bootleg telephone number and wait for the unlicensed and un-marked jitney called Apex Cab.

Today, for the first time in the city's history, there is a franchised taxi fleet owned by blacks. It employs a hundred people and has fifty brand-new cabs—all bearing the name, "Apex Cab."

There is also for the first time in Wisconsin's history a black-owned bank, the North Milwaukee State Bank. It opened its doors in February 1971 as only the twenty-seventh black-owned bank to be chartered in the nation.

These are but two of several flourishing minority-owned enter-prises that have sprung up in the city since the creation in 1969 of the Afro-Urban Institute (AUI), a nonprofit corporation that is dedicated to creating and expanding economic opportunities for Milwaukee's 105,000 black residents.

The corporation is the result of a three-day symposium held in the spring of 1968 by a small group of black professionals from business, social agencies, and activist groups.

Their meeting was a response to a disturbance that had oc-curred in July 1967, when several hundred teenagers roamed along North Third Street throwing rocks at store windows. The na-tional guard was called out, and the disturbance was labeled a "riot" although it could hardly be compared to the fiery rampages that struck the ghettos of other cities that summer. Nonetheless it did focus some long-overdue public attention on the plight of the inner city, as well as on the lack of student reading and math skills, deteriorating housing, and the sufferings of an economi-cally and mentally depressed segment of the population.

Ray Alexander, a community agency staff worker, chaired the 1968 symposium and set forth the challenge: "The time is now for Milwaukee's blacks as a community and a people to determine and utilize action necessary to help them gain economic and political power."

The Milwaukee-born Alexander was all too familiar with the city's segregated housing and schools, and with how the complaints about police conduct toward minorities had fallen on deaf ears for years.

"You are beautiful people," he told the group. "You are a credit to yourselves by the very fact that you are still around after so much effort has been made to snuff you out."

At the time of the Afro-Urban Institute's formation, the majority of black-owned businesses in the city were small "mom-and-pop" corner stores, small restaurants, barbershops, beauty parlors, and taverns. The largest black employers were a fast-food franchise store and a weekly newspaper, each with about thirty full-time and part-time employees. It was AUI's mission, with Alexander as its executive director, to change all that.

The first move was to establish the bank in the North Side community, where the service was urgently needed. Two branches of larger banks had closed their doors in the area. The North Milwaukee State Bank, funded by a group of black businessmen, opened in the former offices of one of those defunct branches.

AUI also quickly established the Center for Economic Development, now headed by Maurice Beckley. The center's purpose was to cultivate new minority business enterprises. It soon helped create the Center City Co-op which, in turn, opened The Sight Center, the first black-run optical cooperative in the nation. And it also aided in the creation of the Center City Supermarket later that same year, 1970.

Formation of Apex Cab was the special project of James Estes, the first director of the Center for Economic Development, and it proved a long and difficult battle. Ever since the late 1930s, blacks had been petitioning Milwaukee's city council for a taxi franchise. But they had always been turned down.

Estes tackled the council again in 1971, at the request of a black client who wanted to set up a cooperative. The two of them made out an application for a franchise—and were obliged to wait six months for a hearing. When the hearing finally was held, there were strong objections from the city's major taxi operators. They claimed their present service was adequate. The backers of Apex Cab had to produce thousands of signatures of inner-city residents to show that the service was not and never had been good.

And when Apex asked for a hundred cab permits, the competition said thirty was plenty. Eleven months and sixteen public hearings later, the city offered a compromise of fifty permits. The Apex people took it, and in 1973 they were able to put an effective taxi service on the streets—something previously unknown on the city's North Side.

Yet another important AUI creation was the Northside Community Design Center, an architectural-engineering consultant group consisting of ten volunteer architects and several students from the Milwaukee School of Architecture, which is part of the University of Wisconsin. The design center came into being as a direct result of a controversy over the planning of a new park named after the late Reverend Martin Luther King Jr.

The Milwaukee County Park Commission contracted with a suburban architectural firm for the park's design. This award was challenged by The Front Organization, headed by Al Flowers, who wanted blacks to plan the recreational area, the first to be located in the inner-city area in fifty years. Flowers eventually persuaded the commission that a design drawn up by a black architect from St. Paul, Minnesota, was better, and such a design was eventually accepted.

This incident highlighted the need for a AUI watchdog group to oversee community development and planning, and Flowers was placed in charge when the design center was established.

Since 1972 the design group under Al Flowers has waged several successful fights involving the location of a new high school and developing renewal plans for the North Side. It has also been encouraging local high school youths to take up professional careers in community development.

To Maurice Beckley, director of AUI's Center for Economic Development, the involvement of minority youth in the professions and in business is essential if blacks are to be more than wage earners and consumers. "We must move into the economic system of this country through distribution of goods and services," he says. "We've been primarily at the consuming end of the system or at the retail service end. We need to become suppliers in order to get a meaningful part of the business dollar."

AUI's director, Ray Alexander, is looking at this problem of establishing a broad economic foundation for the city's black community. He says his agency is thinking in terms of "a consortium of related projects—ideas that will provide jobs and a tax base, and not just another corner grocery."

In five years the Afro-Urban Institute has learned to think big.

The hammer is their symbol, not only of their
trade but of the impact they hope to make. . . .

United Community Construction Workers

Boston, Massachusetts/Philadelphia, Pennsylvania

"Build Baby Build!" is their battle cry. And how they wish they could build!

They are construction workers, or want to be. They are black and they live in Boston, where construction has been a billion-dollar industry for more than a decade. For these people, as well as their fellow blacks in other U.S. cities, finding work in the construction trades has never been easy. Doors to union hiring halls and apprenticeship programs have long been closed to them. That is why they united behind the slogan, "Build Baby Build!"

They are members of United Community Construction Workers, Inc., an organization of minorities formed in 1968 to fight—

and to train and to work—for equal employment opportunities in the building trades.

The hammer is their symbol, not only of their trade but of the impact they hope to make upon racial discrimination by labor unions, upon public apathy, and upon the complacency of government agencies that allow discriminatory violations against them to go unrecognized, unchallenged, and unpunished.

UCCW was organized in response to the threat of a layoff of all black workers employed on a Boston urban redevelopment project in November 1967. The reasons given by the contractor were a lack of technological skill and poor work habits.

The organizers of UCCW knew that training was a major deficiency, if not the fault of the blacks concerned. They embarked upon a strategy for both training blacks and then getting the trained workers hired. But the first priority was to correct what it regarded as unfair labor practices in the building trades within UCCW's own south Boston neighborhood.

In announcing its formation, UCCW issued a manifesto that declared the area "off limits to racist unions, nonfunctioning compliance officers, discriminatory contractors" and others. It demanded that minorities be given 50 percent of all the skilled jobs and all of the unskilled jobs on projects in the area. And it staged a series of demonstrations to back up its demands.

These militant actions produced an agreement from the redevelopment project contractor to train minority workers as sheetrockers, a trade then being performed in the area by imported Canadian workers. Twelve minority workers were chosen for the two-month program. "The trainees were paid subscale wages, put on the job with a journeyman on a one-to-one basis without any counseling or supervision," according to Errol S. Paige, one of the trainees who later became director of training for UCCW. A follow-up study showed that five of the men were still employed as sheetrockers two years later and that the rest of them had sought jobs in other areas of the country.

The training project was regarded as a step in the right direction, if not wholly satisfying. It at least gave UCCW and the building industry some experience in minority training programs. By the fall of 1972, Paige was able to note with some satisfaction that the UCCW program, originally planned to place twenty-four persons in training, had actually trained fifty. UCCW increased its placements by securing commitments for training slots from contractors *before* they signed contracts on government projects, instead of bargaining for such commitments later.

UCCW students meet in carpentry class for specialized training.

The organization also started its own on-the-job training program, putting men to work on various buildings it was renovating on the block near UCCW headquarters in a Roxbury storefront.

UCCW sent out a monthly newsletter, conducted job safety and health education programs, opened a bookstore, and a store that would sell arts and crafts made in the neighborhood. It also organized supplementary training programs in various trades.

Recently the group has been seeking support from neighborhood residents to help them achieve UCCW's goal of gaining a higher ratio of black workers on local construction projects.

Leo Fletcher, a carpenter who is executive secretary of UCCW, says that, since the campaign began, UCCW has directly placed 200 workers in building trade jobs. "And several hundred more blacks and other minorities have found it easier to get construction jobs as a result of our work," he adds.

The key to further progress, he says, is community organization to make UCCW stronger. "We need the brothers behind us to make the unions and the contractors give us more jobs and more training opportunities."

An offshoot of United Community Construction Workers has been launched in Philadelphia, but it has adopted a different approach. Rather than battling with unions and contractors, this project is devoted entirely to construction trades training.

UCCW-Philadelphia was started in 1972 by James W. Pitts, a successful black businessman who, as he says, was seeking a means of improving the lives of people in the ghetto. He embarked upon the training project after teaming up with Willie Rorie, who had been active in the Boston UCCW. They decided they wanted not only to develop job skills among the poor but, while they were doing it, to also improve housing in the ghetto.

They settled upon a decaying section of Philadelphia's lower north end that abounded in abandoned and delapidated buildings. "We deliberately looked for an area where what we wanted to do would really count," Pitts says. The neighborhood had been marked for renewal by the Philadelphia Redevelopment Authority, and the residents were objecting to being relocated.

A course was set up so that, in the process of remodeling and rehabilitating buildings, the trainees would become journeyman craftsmen. But the course also was constructed to give the men a general education, including basic English and mathematics. Pitts stressed the development of positive social attitudes in trainees embittered by their surroundings and lack of opportunity.

Pitts knocked on doors and spread the word when the course was ready. But at first he had no takers. "We recruited two men and discovered their attitudes were poor. That way wouldn't work for us," he said. "Now, we say, 'The program is here and when you're ready for us, you come in.' "

The course has three stages. For the first two months a candidate is given orientation toward work and is instructed in such essentials as being on time and present every day, and working a full day. For this stage he receives $6 a week.

The training stage follows and is divided into two phases. The first includes painting, general carpentry, light spackling, and plastering under the guidance of an instructor. In the second phase the trainee begins working with professional builders and tradesmen to improve his skills. For the first phase, the pay is $40 a week; for the second, $80. Both phases last two to three months.

Finally, the trainee is placed with a tradesman for six months and receives $100 a week. Then he is ready to work on his own.

The program has grown slowly to about a dozen trainees. There are two paid employes, the instructor and a secretary-bookkeeper who also prepares hot lunches for the crew. (Pitts found the trainees weren't able to put in a full day without enough to eat.)

UCCW expenses have been met by grants from various foundations and a loan. By early 1974 the trainees had rehabilitated two buildings. One was sold and the other rented. Several other buildings have been renovated. Income from the work goes toward the loan and training expenses. Three of the trainees have moved on to regular jobs in the construction field.

Pitts says he conceived the project as a small one and wants to keep it that way. However he would like to expand the idea to at least ten more areas in the city.

"My only regret," he says, "is that we have nothing to offer the young ladies."

*We can duplicate services from now until
doomsday and never meet the needs of all our
disadvantaged and disabled citizens.*

The Vocational Development Center
for the Handicapped

Akron, Ohio

The woman on the telephone had cancer—and a mentally retarded son. But there was a lilt in her voice when she said, "I want
to thank you for the most important Mother's Day gift that I have
ever received."

Her son, an 18-year-old, had just brought home his first paycheck and was proudly showing it around the neighborhood.

The person on the other end of the phone call was Joseph R.
Spoonster, whose Vocational Development Center for the Handicapped in Akron, Ohio, has provided the woman's son, and hundreds like him, with a chance to learn a trade and get a job. The
young man, like many others in Spoonster's center, had virtually
been written off by society and by the agencies that are supposed
to help the handicapped, the mentally retarded, and other
people with disabilities.

Like the people it serves, Spoonster's center had also been
written off by city and state agencies in its early days. Spoonster
and his wife had to cash in their insurance policies and retirement
funds to put together the money to start the project in 1964. They
had been hoping for loans from businessmen, but those fell
through when the community council refused to make a grant and
word spread that the project would fail.

Spoonster now sees the refusal by the community council of
health, education and welfare agencies as "the best thing that
could have happened to us."

"It was tough at the time, but it forced us away from the traditional conservative methods of meeting human needs," he adds.

Without government backing, Spoonster decided to set up the
vocational center as a free enterprise venture that would generate
enough revenue to cover its expenses. His formula was to hire the
best possible teachers and instructors. He then would obtain contracts with firms and government agencies to employ the center's

graduates. Trainees also would be given work on the center's premises, such as subcontract jobs with the major industrial companies based in Akron.

The odds were overwhelming, but those are the kind of odds Spoonster has been playing for many years. He started the nation's first school for the blind mentally retarded, and taught golf to thousands of amputees. And he set up the first communitywide program, in 1960, for early detection of phenylketonuria (PKU), a condition caused by malnutrition that produces mental retardation in newborn children (once detected, retardation can be arrested by the use of a proper diet).

Spoonster's inspiration to start the vocational center was a study that showed that by 1975 there would be 207,000 "slow learners" just in the three counties surrounding Akron. From the study, Spoonster concluded that 83,000 of them would need special vocational and educational services or else face an alternative lifetime of dependence. With the help of Dr. Herschel Nisonger of Ohio State University he developed the plan for the center.

Joseph Spoonster observes the progress of a vocational center student. The young man is blind and had never been to school until age 19. Today he reads and writes braille and attends the University of Akron.

The refusal of the city agencies to back the center spurred him to develop the free enterprise approach. His worst moments came after the businessmen turned down the loan.

The first year was a struggle, but by 1966 the center was developing results and a reputation. It was awarded a grant from the U.S. Department of Health, Education, and Welfare for a substantial expansion and was given a state award in 1967 as the "outstanding rehabilitation facility."

By 1970 the state vocational agency was busing clients from Cleveland to Akron. A Cleveland center was established later that year, and that project opened a new dimension in training. Not only were the clients handicapped, they also suffered special problems of the poor; consequently an advocacy function was added to the basic program at the Cleveland center.

In one typical case a 38-year-old black man had lost his government job on the basis of a civil service certification test. When he came to the center, experts there were able to prove to the civil service commission that the man performed poorly on the test because of vocabulary, not skill or job performance. The man eventually was restored to his job and later promoted.

The center computes its value in dollar as well as human terms. It has helped 357 welfare recipients obtain and hold jobs. Totaling their new money-earning and tax-paying ability, and deducting the welfare drain they used to be, Spoonster estimates the financial gain to the community at more than $5 million.

The program has met its goal of being entirely self-supporting, all costs being met by earned income. Spoonster is now taking it to other countries, and with it his free enterprise philosophy.

Special educators from the Brazilian city of Rio de Janeiro have studied the center's programs with hopes of starting a work orientation and evaluation program for adolescents and adults in urban poverty areas. The center is also working with a committee in Canada to establish the first private rehabilitation center in that country.

Despite his accomplishments, Spoonster feels the job facing his and similar centers is far from over. "Above all, don't get put off by the headlines that seem to say that the needs of all our handicapped citizens are being met," he urges.

As for those who contend the founding of more programs will lead to a duplication of services for the handicapped, Spoonster has a blunt retort:

"We can duplicate services from now until doomsday and never meet all the needs of all our disadvantaged and disabled citizens."

So many people think they have to get together,
have to agree first—politically, sexually,
religiously, everything—and then they might get
something done. I don't do that. I don't ask
anybody to agree with me or anyone else about
anything—just to work.

Home, Inc.

Atlanta, Georgia

Julia is a slim 17-year-old who ran away from home two years ago and became a groupie, trailing rock music stars around the country. Today she is learning how to become a business-woman—who can support herself by making and selling intricate pieces of wire jewelry.

Mike's specialty is making etched leather goods, which are a hit with the youth trade. He's quiet, and doesn't want to talk about the prison term he did for dealing dope.

Both are more concerned about their present work than their past escapades. Along with about 140 other former delinquents, spaced-out speed freaks, and homeless youngsters, they are concentrating on developing skills that will make them self-reliant. They are members of a commune-like self-help project known as Home, Inc., founded by a self-employed social worker named Samuel G. "Skinny" Watson.

"We have our share of fun, but we get most of it out of working," says Watson, who once led the somewhat rootless life of a well-heeled, fast-moving traveling salesman.

Skinny Watson says his life changed when he grew concerned about what was happening to youngsters caught up in the drug scene. One night he went with a friend to visit a home established to help kids on drugs. It shocked him when he saw it was merely a house, a place where the kids could sleep, eat—and do nothing else. He became convinced that this approach would never give young people a chance to learn what he had learned in his 36 years: self-reliance and self-confidence built from the work one has done oneself.

Watson bought an old, rambling house at the corner of Arizona and Indiana streets on the East Side of Atlanta in an area known as Little Five Points. He, his wife Susan and his mother, who is in her 70s, decided they would call the place Home, Inc.

That was in 1969. Since then Home, Inc. has not taken any federal or state funds—no major grants from any source—but has financed itself on its own wares, taking in over the years nearly 1,500 troubled young people who have been in need of help in reshaping and redirecting their lives.

Watson has only two rules:

1. "If you bring drugs into my place, I'll break your jaw."
2. "If you don't work, you don't stay."

He also has a philosophy: "So many people think they have to get together, have to agree first—politically, sexually, religiously, everything—and then they might get something done. I don't do that. I don't ask anybody to agree with me or anyone else about anything—just to work."

There were problems at the start. Money was a major one. Home, Inc. began as a hybrid commune, all income shared by all, with the central kitty paying the mortgage, buying the food, fixing whoever's car needed repairs. But the only major source of income was selling homemade candles—a business that Home, Inc. fell into pretty much by accident after a donor happened to drop off a case of candle wax.

Self-reliance and independence were the keys, Watson believed. So rather than look for outside help, he and the kids built their own street pushcarts and began selling candles and also flowers on the streets.

This activity, duly licensed by the city, of course, gave Home, Inc. some immediate income. The money earned was initially put to a good use other than needed purchases.

"First," Watson says with a grin, "we made enough money to show our records, the corporate records, to the bank." The steady and stable income was enough for one bank's high-risk loan department to take a chance on Home, Inc., and finance its purchase of an old, two-story office building in the center of Little Five Points. The members of Home, Inc. had decided that they would use the building as a shopping complex.

"That's what finally put us over, but it also almost did us in," Watson says. "We had our shops then, a whole first floor, half a block long, and we stocked it with secondhand furniture, refinished things, antiques, old junk, anything anyone could fix up, anything that might sell. And it sold.

"Upstairs there are twenty-seven little rooms, eleven of them right now turned into shops. Kids up there are making leather goods, quilts, jewelry, refinished furniture, and they pay the kitty $65 a month in return for daily encouragement and some practical business advice."

"What almost did us in back then was that old thing of every-body having to agree on everything else. We had a day care center then," Watson explains, "and the kids running it wanted to use it as a political class, sort of in socialism.

"I told them I had nothing for or against their socialism, but I didn't see how we could make a buck out of it, and all I did see was that it was going to alienate the community."

Rather than keep up an argument about it, Home, Inc. simply closed the day care center, letting another private community agency open one in its place.

"You've got to watch that kind of stuff," Watson insists. "That's one main thing people should remember when trying to set up something like Home, Inc. The other main thing is self-reliance. Sure, it's the point of our whole program, teaching these kids to do for themselves.

"But I'll tell you one other thing. All these little merchants around here, every hardware shop manager in Little Five Points, saw me and my kids out working every day, rain or shine, and that's what won them over to us—out there working, not asking for anything from anybody."

Fifteen of the youngsters live with the Watsons—all the room the old home has—and about 125 more work at the shopping complex.

Home, Inc. now grosses about $65,000 a year on sales through the shops. Mortgage payments on the store and living costs at the home take all of that, and although every week is a struggle financially, the project has convinced itself, to say nothing of downtown Atlanta banks, that it is financially stable. Economically the project remains very much a collective effort.

There are still no salaries, but no one complains. "Nobody's here to get rich. They're here to get themselves together, to stand on their own," Watson says. And a lot of the close to 1,500 youngsters who have made Home, Inc. part of their lives for a few months have learned to do just that.

Watson estimates that as many as half have stayed off drugs and are now self-employed as craftsmen. He hasn't made any follow-up studies to learn exactly what has happened to them. But he does know that many of the workers left him after earning the acceptance of the business community. His feelings are clearly not hurt by such desertions, though.

"There's a chance a lot of 'em might go on from here and get rich," he adds with his ex-salesman's grin. "Lot of money in sales, you know."

The checks were not large—averaging about $10 to $12 per worker—but it was "found" income to these people who were living on next to nothing. More important, it was "earned" income.

The SEMCAC Senior Services Program

Rushford, Minnesota

"When our people see old 'Roar' coming up the road," says Rollins Rasmussen, "they know they are in business."

"Roar," he says, stands for "rural older adult roadster," and it is the name that Rasmussen has jokingly given to the battered pickup truck he drives every workday through the fertile hills and valleys around Rushford, Minnesota.

The pickup carries parts made by an automotive switch manufacturer in Winona, and it is the lifeline of a thriving new cottage industry employing 10,000 retired farm people. They assemble the parts at home into various types of switches, which are eventually used to operate car lights, windshield wipers, power windows, and a variety of other automotive mechanisms.

The switch assemblers are all part of an enterprise known as the SEMCAC Senior Services Program, which was founded in 1972 to provide employment opportunities for the older residents of a rural, three-county area in southeastern Minnesota.

The program was started by the Southeastern Minnesota Citizens' Action Council (SEMCAC), a community action agency dedicated to eliminating poverty in Fillmore, Houston, and Winona counties.

Organized in 1965, SEMCAC already had a number of programs underway for young people when it began the SEMCAC Rural Older Adult Program in 1967. This program was aimed at providing recreation and fellowship for the older people faced with making the difficult transition from an active work life to retirement. The program involved setting up some twenty-one centers in local communities where older folk could meet once or twice a week.

These centers also enabled SEMCAC to reach the senior citizens with its health and nutrition programs as well. But all of these programs together could not alleviate one very real problem facing the area's older citizens—the lack of employment opportunities. Older people, like younger ones, need income and a means of occupying themselves in worthwhile activities.

The dimensions of the problem in the tri-county area were made evident by the 1970 U.S. census. The Minnesota reports revealed that, of 40,000 persons living in the rural areas of Winona, Fillmore, and Houston counties, more than half were 55 or older. Approximately 10,000 of these older persons were on the fringe of poverty and 5,000 of them were in even worse economic straits.

The statistics starkly reflected the flight to the cities by young people, leaving the elderly to their own devices.

In attempting to find a solution to the problem facing the area's older residents, SEMCAC looked in part to the activities of the SEMCAC Rural Older Adult Program. As a result of good administration and lively participation by local people, the centers developed two important services—one of which isolated the economic problem in scope, and the other of which suggested an approach to finding a possible solution.

The first was an income tax aid program in which young volunteers with accounting expertise aided the elders with their tax return forms. The forms clearly indicated the senior citizens' economic plight.

The second significant service was a craft-and-hobby program—culminating in a profitable senior citizens' bazaar—which demonstrated that the gnarled hands that had held the hoe and guided the plow were still skilled enough to take on other work.

No one at SEMCAC remembers the precise moment when the great idea struck. SEMCAC's executive director, Halvor Lacher, says, "All of us felt that, although these folks were generally too old for actual farm work, their manual skill should somehow have a market value that could be utilized."

The breakthrough came in early 1971, when it was noted that Asco Inc.—a promotional button producer located in nearby Winona—assembled button-clips on a piecework basis. A scouting team determined that Asco was willing to experiment with the idea, and the idea was accepted by SEMCAC's members.

"It was a great opportunity," says Lacher, "but it needed some seed money to get it going."

The best estimate of the SEMCAC planners was that it would take 13 weeks and $2,000 dollars to get their fledgling cottage industry out of the nest and, it was hoped, into the air.

Subsequent sessions led to a formal consultation with the Governor's Council on Aging.

It was agreed that the project idea contained the right elements envisioned in the concept of "self-help," and SEMCAC applied for a special project grant under Title III of the Older Americans Act. An application was endorsed by the governor's council and recommended to the Ober Charitable Foundation of St. Paul for private funding. Ober agreed to the $2,000 grant and, in February 1972, the new venture was on its way.

It was arranged that one full-time driver—Rasmussen—would transport materials from the factory to each of the older adult centers, as well as take the finished goods back to the factory. And part-time drivers based at each center would travel between the centers and the homes of the assemblers.

Rollins Rasmussen fashioned a do-it-yourself routing sheet. This, plus a lifetime of knowing the back roads and the people, enabled him and the others to establish a rural assembly line.

To handle the cash flow, SEMCAC opened a special bank account and billed the manufacturer against his production orders. On receipt of payment SEMCAC sent checks to the workers.

The checks were not large—averaging about $10 to $12 per worker—but it was "found" income to these people who were living on next-to-nothing. More important, it was "earned" income— far more valuable to them than any "in kind" dole.

Although the work of assembling a button clip is simple, the care, quality, and speed of the oldsters' efforts weren't lost on the small business community in the tri-county area.

The Lake Center Specialty Company in Winona was the next customer on the cottage assembly line—now known as the "ROAD Company" (ROAD = Rural Older Adult Dynamos).

Lake Center made an agreement calling for payment of $1.80 per box of 1,000 switches—picked up and delivered (assembled and inspected). Of this, the worker received $1.40, and 40¢ was retained in the special account to keep "Roar" on the road.

The arrangement fell far short of covering SEMCAC's running expenses on the project, but it was an important step ahead toward self-sufficiency—and few new businesses show a profit in their first year. SEMCAC estimates a flow of some $15,000 of "new" money into the hands of its ROAD Company.

The enterprise has made an enormous improvement in the lives of the workers. "We have something to look forward to when Rollie makes his stop off out here," says a 70-year-old retired farmer in Houston County. "We know we're going to be busy."

He adds, "It sort of restores your faith in the free enterprise system, because we're showing it bars no one on account of race, creed, color—or *age*."

This has resulted in earned extra income rather than mere do-good handouts, which only make poverty easier to bear and pride harder to hold onto.

Appalachian Craftsmen

Huntington, West Virginia

Most of southern West Virginia's poverty tends to be almost exclusively rural. The communities and settlements scattered across the countryside are characterized by poor housing (many houses are simply shacks), little or no indoor plumbing, and junked appliances and automobiles on front lawns, driveways, and along stream banks. As indicated by these outward signs, a hand-to-mouth existence is too often the way of life. In one four-county area (Cabell, Lincoln, Mason, and Wayne counties), up to 37 percent of the residents eke out a living below the federally defined poverty level. Yet within a distance of about 60 miles lie the comparatively wealthy metropolitan areas centered on Huntington and Charleston, the state capital. (Charleston, in fact, ranks among the ten leading U.S. cities in terms of per capita income.)

There are jobs in Huntington and Charleston, and good housing and a great variety of social amenities. Nevertheless long-range commuting is impractical, and moving permanently to the cities means giving up a cherished way of life.

But there is another possibility: instead of getting the people to go to the jobs, create the jobs for the people in their own mountain communities. This possibility is currently being tried, with considerable success, by Appalachian Craftsmen, Inc.

Appalachian Craftsmen is a self-help organization, headquartered in Huntington, that is dedicated to helping poor families in the four-county area supplement their incomes by working at traditional crafts in their own communities. This has resulted in earned extra income rather than mere do-good handouts, which only make poverty easier to bear and pride harder to hold onto.

Appalachian Craftsmen has capitalized on patchwork sewing, a craft that is as old as the region itself and one that remains a source of regional pride. Through training, a carefully chosen product line, and a variety of marketing efforts, the organization has been successful in turning this traditional craft into a real moneymaking job for the women of some 110 mountain families.

The Appalachian Craftsmen plan is simple. Women gather at a number of local community centers in towns such as Upper Mud, Dunlow, Henderson, Leon, Hamlin, and Hubball to produce carefully designed products—quilts, hostess skirts, slacks, vests, and home decorator items. All of these products are considered to be of high quality, formal, and comparatively expensive. The completed items are taken to Huntington, where the organization's director and several volunteers from the Junior League of Huntington find a market for them through style shows, holiday shops, and regional buyers' shows. In addition, Appalachian Craftsmen products are retailed at several gift and clothing shops around the United States. In fact about three-quarters of all Appalachian Craftsmen products are sold outside of the producing region.

Producing quilts at home means extra money to this Appalachian woman.

Appalachian Craftsmen, Inc., is a project sponsored by the Southwestern Community Action Council (SWCAC) in Huntington. Chartered in June 1971, the project has a paid director and a board of directors who generally supervise the project's activities without SWCAC intervention.

The project has depended heavily on volunteer help. According to Carter Seaton, the project's paid director and herself a former Junior League volunteer, "Ours is a project with a continuing need for a great deal of volunteer help. We're not strictly free enterprise—we would have failed if we had been, quite frankly. Rather, our success had depended heavily on the thousands of hours of clerical help, sales trips, talks, letters, training, instruction, and pickup and delivery that the volunteers have provided for the project. It's this kind of enthusiasm and these donations that make the difference in an undertaking of this nature."

Carter Seaton also cites the expertise represented by the board of directors and especially the work of SWCAC's community organizers in the four-county area as primary reasons the project has been as successful as it has.

"These community organizers have been our contacts and most active instructors from the very beginning," she says. "They're not outsiders. The people know them, live with them, and trust them. I think this has been a most important element in the fact that we have been able to provide this kind of service at all."

In its less-than-four years' existence, Appalachian Craftsmen has been able to generate $27,000 in supplementary income for its participants.

"We pay our workers through a piecework system," Carter Seaton explains. "The worker chooses an item from the product line that she wants to make during the current season, and the organization provides her with the materials and any special training that may be required. From that point, she's on her own. Her earnings are governed only by the amount of time she is willing to devote to manufacturing the item. Our average yearly income for each worker has been about $240, but that has varied from $10 in one case to about $800 in another."

Appalachian Craftsmen has markedly improved the quality of life for many of its participants. In a community where the lack of a pair of good shoes sometimes keeps youngsters out of school, supplementary income earned through Appalachian Craftsmen can make an appreciable difference to how people live. The craftmakers tend to use their extra money carefully—using it, for example, to buy better clothing for themselves and their families, as well as to pay for improvements on their homes and property.

The skills and output of the project's participants have in a few instances led to more than just a supplementary source of income. A number of women, for example, have moved on to jobs at a local clothing factory.

Appalachian Craftsmen, Inc., has brought a lot of hope to the communities it serves in the four-county area. And just as important as the hope it has brought is the fact that the organization has not brought about unwelcome intrusions on the lifestyle of the participants. The people of the mountain communities of southern West Virginia have had to give up nothing of their traditional way of life—other than a still all-too-small portion of its poverty.

It is something that has been created out of nothing but the easy discards of our country—discarded telephone poles, discarded tires—by discarded people who wouldn't settle for being discarded.

SWEAT Associates

Milwaukee, Wisconsin

Two men pounded a sign into the earth of a city-owned vacant lot strewn with broken glass and rubbish. The sign read "Future Site of SWEAT Park." It was a put-on—of sorts.

But the forty men and women who immediately started work there perspired in earnest as they cleared the small lot of its large accumulation of trash. They hand-dug five-foot holes to anchor lengths of telephone poles for some monkey bars. They made a sandbox, positioned some scrap sewer pipe as play equipment, planted a tree, and put a fence around the lot.

The "tot lot" was shaping up very well the next day when officials of the Milwaukee Department of Public Works appeared on the scene and ordered the work to stop. What's more, they told the group to dismantle the equipment and restore the site to its former condition.

But the workers, all unemployed residents of the South Side neighborhood, ignored the order and toiled on into the August night until the playground was completed. The next day the city attorney issued a formal cease and desist order. A legal battle ensued. But the little playground opened anyway, to the enjoyment of neighborhood children.

Then the workers, who called themselves SWEAT Associates, billed the city for a total of $670.50 for labor. The city countered by threatening to bill them for the cost of restoring the lot to its former condition.

The city's newspapers gave running accounts of these curious happenings in the late summer of 1971, and the publicity couldn't have better suited the designs of SWEAT Associates. (The letters in the word "SWEAT" do not "stand" for anything; the word means what is says.) Their work and wit got across the point that many of the unemployed are eager for any kind of job, and there are many sensible low-cost tasks they could perform if given the chance.

"We wanted to show that the job market is the problem," says SWEAT organizer Jack R. Gleason. "We wanted to get people to stop blaming the unemployed for being unemployed. We wanted to show public officials, neighbors, the media, that the unemployed are not lazy and unwilling to work."

The unemployed on the South Side of Milwaukee are mostly poor whites, together with some poor Spanish Americans. They have been out of work for days, weeks, even years—and when they do manage to find work from time to time, it usually involves only unskilled jobs.

Chuck Miller

SWEAT workers apply a fresh coat of paint to the house of an elderly widow. A bill for the repairs will be sent to city housing officials.

SWEAT Park gave them a chance to be part of a group intent upon finding jobs. It also gave some of them a job, if only for a day or two. But as one three-year veteran of unemployment said, "I did it so I didn't have to sit around."

And a 20-year-old jobless ex-medic added, "I did it because I couldn't find a job. I like to help people and I hope I get paid, but if I don't I'll still keep working."

That was SWEAT's hope, too. But the publicity generated by the SWEAT Park project failed to produce either money from the city or job offers from anywhere. So SWEAT turned to creating other projects.

The new activities displayed perhaps even more imagination than the tot lot. They included:

• *SWEAT Farm.* Fourteen volunteers spent an hour planting wheat on a portion of a city-owned lot. Then SWEAT sent the U.S. Department of Agriculture a bill for $294 for not planting more wheat during the remaining seven hours of the workday. It requested the money under federal provisions for crop controls. Comments Gleason: "We noted that people like John Wayne and Senator James Eastland [D-Miss.] got this type of welfare and decided this was a more preferable type to receive."

• *SWEAT Model Alleys Program.* The group selected a slum alley, cleaned it up, and decorated it with Christmas tree lights—a counterpart of Model Cities street lighting program that was underway on Milwaukee's North Side. Then they billed Model Cities for $144.

• *SWEAT State University* (S.S.U.). This institution was created (on paper) after SWEAT members found that to be eligible for Emergency Employment Act jobs they had to have a college degree for such positions as housing inspector assistant. "We sure knew more about slums than some cat out of college," says Gleason. So S.S.U. issued degrees to a dozen people in such disciplines as "slum housing" and "water pollution fighting," and they reported for work as housing inspector aides. The city didn't give them the jobs. So they went to work anyway, inspecting twenty houses on their own and then billing the city for their work.

• *SWEAT Redevelopment Authority.* A house owned by an absentee landlord was repaired and painted. He was invoiced for $59.32. Much to SWEAT's collective surprise, though, the man paid the bill, saying it was reasonable and the work was good. The authority also fixed up the house of an elderly South Side widow who could not afford repairs. The bill was sent to the city development department, which customarily provided funds for this type of work on the city's North Side, but not on the South Side.

• *SWEAT Image Builders.* A vacant county-owned lot was turned into a project dubbed Civic Center West. It consisted of a duck pond (a small plastic swimming pool with a rubber duck), a fountain (made from a pail of water), and a rock garden decorated with plastic flowers. The center was created in response to charges that SWEAT had damaged the image of Milwaukee. A bill for the work was sent to the county.

Chuck Miller

SWEAT's Tiretoys enterprise markets playground equipment made from abandoned tires. As Mary Anne McNulty says, "The neatest thing about SWEAT is that it is always moving to do something more."

SWEAT Associates embarked on several projects that similarly made serious points in a lighthearted way. They found, though, that, with the exception of the absentee landlord, no one was paying the bills being submitted by SWEAT (the disappointment being compounded with irony when SWEAT received a $537.25 bill from the city for demolishing the SWEAT Park four months after its construction!).

More importantly, most members of SWEAT were still unemployed, despite all of their efforts.

In May 1972 the SWEAT group decided to drop its program of "public improvement projects" and embark on a self-help enterprise of creating playground equipment made from used car and truck tires. The so-called Tiretoys are bolted-together tires arranged in pyramids and odd shapes so that children crawl through, climb around, and bounce on them.

This venture began in the backyard of one of the workers, making use of borrowed tools and retail hardware. When the city building inspector discovered what was underway, he promptly issued a cease and desist order. So SWEAT moved to someone else's backyard. Three more backyards and three more cease and desist orders later, the operation finally moved into a small, and legal, manufacturing facility.

Borrowed tools were replaced with new ones purchased with a cash grant from Milwaukee's Hunger Hike. The Wisconsin Independent Tire Dealers and Retread Association helped with developing advertising and marketing materials and printing. The state assisted with some funds to pay for a designer and a part-time business advisor. And soon SWEAT Associates' Tiretoys began to sell to churches, schools, and parents.

By 1974 the Tiretoys enterprise had grown to the point where SWEAT was ready to market the toys in five Midwestern states and to offer them nationally through the Community Market Catalogue. Money was coming in—not enough to cover all expenses but enough to show that SWEAT was now on the road to financial independence.

Mary Anne McNulty, the group's president, doesn't expect SWEAT to stop at Tiretoys.

"The neatest thing about SWEAT is that it is always moving to be something more," she says. "It is something that has been created out of nothing but the easy discards of our country—discarded telephone poles, discarded tires—by discarded people who wouldn't settle for being discarded."

Even beyond immediate solutions, the program
had demonstrated to at least one segment of the
Lower East Side community that the media could
be used as a constructive force for change.
Community-Action-Newsreel had scored
its first big success.

Community-Action-Newsreel

New York, New York

At one point in the hour-long video tape, the superintendent of a Lower East Side school says, "The police are here to listen. It's up to us to tell them what our problems are. All cops aren't pigs. Some of us are pigs."

The tape is an edited version of five days of discussions held in the summer of 1973 between members of the New York police force and residents of the Lower East Side, including gang leaders. The project, called "No More Words," is the work of the Community-Action-Newsreel. It is one of several productions aimed at helping bring about social change through broadcasting the frank discussion of mutual problems. (The "No More Words" tape is now being shown at the city's Police Academy as an aid in training police cadets in community relations.)

The tape brings out the growing fears of area shopkeepers, the frustrations of police officers searching for better ways of preventing crime, and the surprise of tough youngsters demanding a straighter lifestyle (says one, "We don't look for trouble, we look for jobs").

At the end of the tape one gangleader sums up the five days of talk, saying: "I've met some cops here who I can juggle with. Now when I walk down the street, I don't want to spit in their eye. I want to shake their hand."

Community-Action-Newsreel (C.A.N.) is a project of the Young Filmmakers Foundation, which also runs a film club, a media equipment resource center, and a teacher-training project.

The foundation, currently supported by both public and private grants, was started in 1968 by Rodger Larson and Lynne Hofer, both former teachers, and Jaime Barrios, a filmmaker from Chile.

Larson had begun making films with a group of teenagers in a summer theater arts program that was conducted in the Bronx in 1963. "A few of the students pounced on this idea and ran away with it," he recalls. They produced a number of films, and Larson became so enthusiastic about continuing that he quit his job as an art teacher a year later to try and "convince various organizations that filmmaking meant more to many teenagers than any of the creative arts."

Lynne Hofer got involved in film when she was a remedial-reading teacher and was experimenting in how it could be used to help in the learning process. She heard about Larson's work, and they teamed up. "We decided," Ms. Hofer says, "the best way to convince people that you could get kids to do very effective things in film—particularly those who were not doing very well in school—would be to set up a demonstration project."

They arranged with the city's parks department to let them take a moviebus around to parks and playgrounds in order to show kids films made by Larson's group about growing up and about neighborhood experiences. Subsequently the two filmmakers established a 16mm production unit in the kitchen pantry of the University Settlement House on the Lower East Side. After Barrios joined them in 1967, they established the foundation and moved a short distance to a storefront on Rivington Street.

C.A.N. volunteers Santiago Nieves (left) and José Colon.

In the fall of 1971 the foundation considered the possibility of starting a local news network.

"We felt," explains Lynne Hofer, "that the neighborhood had a need for a community media information center, and we had the resources and experience to build such a service."

"At the same time," adds Barrios, "some of the kids in the film club were growing up. They had been making highly personal films about their own lives and problems. Now they were becoming concerned with problems beyond themselves, problems of the community around them."

Less than a year later New York City's public television station, Channel 13, aired a 10-minute documentary called "Baruch Housing Project: A Community in Fear." It was the first big effort of Barrios and the rest of the group that was to become C.A.N.

The film dealt with the concerns of residents of a Lower East Side public housing project following a rash of burglaries and muggings and two deaths.

"When someone sets out to do a documentary, they usually have a specific idea they want to express," says Barrios. "Then they go out and look for people to interview to support their idea. Our approach was different. We wanted to present the point of view of the tenants. We wanted it to be their show."

This attitude, coupled with the fact that the newsreel crew consisted mostly of Lower East Side youths (some of whom actually lived in the Baruch project), made the tenants more willing to voice their fears and grievances than they had been with the professional news media.

"There had been lots of television coverage," Barrios says. "But just 30-second spots on the nightly news which were quite inadequate. The people were beginning to get very hostile to these uptown camera crews descending on them."

The young news crew worked overtime with the tenants, inviting representatives to their storefront studio to help edit the film.

Was this one-sided reporting? "Of course," replies Barrios. "The housing authority always has access to the media—the people don't. We were only concerned with expressing the people's point of view, and we kept asking them, 'Is this the way you want it said?' "

When the film was finally completed, Channel 13 liked it and thought it was suitable for its controversial current affairs program that was known as "51st State."

"The evening the film was to be shown there was a tremendous air of expectation at the project," Barrios remembers. "We had flooded the area with leaflets telling all about the program and had

A C.A.N. film crew takes to a New York street to film documentary on the Hell's Angels motorcycle gang. C.A.N. is "involving teenagers and adults from local community groups in using the media as a constructive force for change."

set up TVs in lobbies of the buildings. When the show came on, you could sense the almost festive atmosphere amongst the people. They were really together."

A studio interview followed the film with some of the tenants meeting face-to-face with an official from the New York City Housing Authority. Commitments were made for better police protection, stronger locks, brighter lighting. But even beyond immediate solutions, the program had demonstrated to at least one segment of the Lower East Side community that the media could be used as a constructive force for change. Community-Action-Newsreel and its members had scored their first big success.

Others followed. A year later a second "51st State" television program detailed the lack of surgical and obstetrical facilities at a new and much-heralded hospital on the Lower East Side. Like the first show, this program attracted the attention of city officials and triggered at least the beginnings of necessary action.

Community-Action-Newsreel also turned its attention to the schools and to police-community relations. "School District No. 1: A Community In Change" focused on problems of community control and a controversial local school superintendent. It was monitored at local showings as well as being aired on cable television. "No More Words," the videotaped dialogue between police and local youth gangs, also was shown at C.A.N. headquarters to police and city and community officials.

While these achievements obviously stand out, C.A.N. crews, which use both videotape and film, have also prepared short news features in English, Spanish, and Chinese on such subjects as programs for the aged, birth control, drug treatment centers, and street festivals. A number of videotapes have also been produced on performing arts groups such as the Urban Arts Corps, the Negro Ensemble Company, and the Teatro Campesino. C.A.N. shows these tapes at community centers, schools, housing projects, churches, hospitals, and libraries. And informal screenings are held at markets, laundromats, social clubs, and on the streets using the old moviebus.

The Community-Action-Newsreel has clearly succeeded, as Barrios says, "in involving teenagers and adults from local community groups in using the media as a constructive force for change."

The center's outreach program, for example, instructs community leaders in the "how to" of successful video projects, and has itself been so successful that it has been adopted by various civic, religious, and neighborhood organizations.

The changes resulting from C.A.N.'s activities have not only affected the community and the public's perception of local issues, but also the filmmakers themselves. Thirty of C.A.N.'s neighborhood trainees, for example, have found positions in the world of professional filmmaking.

As to the future of the Community-Action-Newsreel, Barrios and the other members of the group are optimistic. As one young man said, with a confident smile, "C.A.N. can."

*We have finally won the confidence and trust of
the people. And in Watts that's about the hardest
currency you can earn.*

The Watts Job Clearing House

Los Angeles, California

Emmett Brown has been trying to get the word around Watts.

His message is simple: "There are some jobs in town, and I can get you in touch with the bosses that have them."

Emmett Brown, president of the Watts Job Clearing House (WJCH) has not solved the employment problems in the Los Angeles neighborhood where more than two-thirds of the potential labor force is looking for work. He does not make those kinds of big promises or claims. What he does claim is that the job clearinghouse has put approximately 25,000 Watts residents in touch with prospective employers during the past eight years.

Getting workers together with available jobs has, unfortunately, been only one of the obstacles confronting the all-volunteer clearinghouse since it was established in 1966. The WJCH has spent much of its time running interference among city agencies, state and local employment boards, as well as contending with a private employment agency in Watts that doesn't like the competition.

Typical of these time-consuming conflicts is one between the WJCH and the Los Angeles Human Resources and Development Agency. The city agency had provided the clearinghouse with an office, desks, telephones, and the WJCH's one paid staff member. Now the agency claims the clearinghouse is competing with a private employment agency, and it is threatening to withdraw even that limited support from the WJCH.

Brown is used to this kind of thing, and attributes the city agency's welching to its bureaucratic struggles elsewhere.

Even if Emmett Brown and the clearinghouse cannot avoid bureaucratic struggles, they do feel they can at least fulfill their fundamental obligation: to get workers and bosses together.

Simple as that sounds, it is an objective that has for many years eluded employment and social service agencies in the poverty areas of Los Angeles. The pattern has traditionally been one of agencies with jobs but not enough applicants and agencies with applicants but not enough jobs. When the clearinghouse concept was unveiled in the fall of 1966, it was greeted with a skeptical here-we-go-again attitude among the jobless of Watts.

According to Brown, statistics are by no means the sole measure of community response to the clearinghouse. Only the city's free clinics have had more widespread community acceptance.

Such trust is hard to come by in the Watts area, which is 91 percent black, united only in its poverty, its blackness—and its long-time distrust of outside agencies.

Trust, according to Brown and other clearinghouse backers, is based on results and communication with the community.

Brown and the board members feel they have now achieved such acceptance. "We have finally won the confidence and trust of the people," says Brown. "And in Watts that's about the hardest currency you can earn."

They also feel they have stimulated community awareness, if not pride, in Watts. And even more importantly, perhaps, the WJCH may have paved the way for other local self-help efforts.

The WJCH is currently running four programs: (1) job consulting with unemployed and underemployed people, (2) job placement, (3) encouragement and placement of students in higher education programs, and (4) stimulation of business and employment in Watts.

The backbone of the clearinghouse is its board, which includes representatives of local agencies, service organizations, and businessmen. The businessmen, with assistance from the AFL–CIO and the United Auto Workers and Teamsters unions, are the principal source of information about jobs and job-training programs.

The board meets biweekly, often with prospective employers in attendance. These meetings are also usually open to local residents. Volunteers staffing the WJCH offices spread the word about employment prospects as well as the center's activities, and they try to make full use of the local grapevine in doing so.

In 1966 the President's Commission on Manpower met in Los Angeles, hoping to stimulate some action on the massive unemployment problems in Watts. One of the group's principal recommendations was for coordination of the many manpower programs already in operation.

The idea of a clearinghouse was developed at a subsequent meeting of state and local employment officials. These people, though, had very limited objectives; they merely wanted an organization that would exchange information on available jobs.

The clearinghouse had barely started operations before it ran into its first bureaucratic obstacle. The California State Employment Service, for reasons it never spelled out clearly, threatened to dismiss several of its employment security officers who were helping the WJCH start in business. The state agency, though, later backed down.

During its early days the WJCH profited from the leadership of Larry Higginbotham, a member of the faculty of the School of Architecture and Urban Planning at the University of California at Los Angeles. For more than two years, Higginbotham and a secretary, Yvonne Townsend—with help from the WJCH board—kept the WJCH functioning.

Some of the clearinghouse's troubles were monumental in their pettiness. Once, for example, the WJCH applied for a United Way grant for housekeeping expenses, but it was turned down because it would not change its name. And then there were the frequent squabbles with the city's human resources and development agency.

Despite the obstacles, Higginbotham managed to establish a key link with businesses and employers—the people who could supply the jobs so desperately needed by Watts residents. It was largely a personal selling job, meeting constantly with businessmen and manpower and job experts. Higginbotham also established the basic pattern for the WJCH—an information center about jobs combined with a placement and job-training center.

Emmett Brown succeeded Higginbotham in 1972, and inherited some of his problems, especially those having to do with local government agencies. Brown is convinced, however, that the clearinghouse has survived the major problems. More than that, red tape may never be eliminated, but the WJCH has avoided being strangled in it while helping thousands of residents of Watts find decent jobs.

Since 1966 the clearinghouse has had to struggle against heavy odds to stay in business. Although it has won that battle for survival, it needs continued assistance to make its financial position more secure. Therefore it could use more funding from either government or foundation sources, as well as a professional and paid staff. And its acceptance in the community needs to be matched at city hall.

Brown acknowledges the tasks ahead, especially that of maintaining the clearinghouse as a vital, active community force on a shoestring budget. Despite bureaucratic and financial problems, though, Brown insists—and the Watts community agrees—that the WJCH is a permanent feature of the Los Angeles scene.

The Urban Youth Action program in the Hill district . . . is urban renewal . . . in its purest and most direct role.

Urban Youth Action

Pittsburgh, Pennsylvania

Down the street from the Duquesne Club, where Pittsburgh's corporate leaders meet, young black people are striving to get their cut of the free enterprise system's employment pie.

They are participants in Urban Youth Action (UYA), a program established in 1967 and overseen by a group of mostly young black businessmen. UYA is primarily in the business of teaching the young people of Pittsburgh about the business world and developing their employment potential.

Much of UYA's work involves finding jobs and providing training for young people in the low-income Hill and Homewood-Brushton districts of the city. Bernard H. Jones, the man behind the idea and now the chairman of the UYA board, sees the program as having a far more profound influence on young lives than simply an economic one. "Coming out of UYA," he says, "are a cadre of revolutionaries. They will revolt against the dismal futures their brothers and sisters have faced in the black ghettos. They are building self-esteem."

More than 4,000 youngsters have participated in the program since its inception. The current "class" numbers 450—nearly all elementary and high school students. There is also an active "alumni" group that promotes UYA projects in its dealings with local businesses and the community.

UYA adheres to the principle of "learning by doing," and that includes the staff, which is composed for the most part of high school volunteers. There is a full-time director, C. Richard Gillcrese, who began with UYA when he was 19 years old and it was just beginning. He has three full-time adult assistants, a secretary, and a controller, all of whom were in the program as students.

UYA headquarters is a busy place, as can be seen by a glance at the various department activities. It has departments for employment, and also for education, community service, and economic development.

● *Employment.* Urban Youth Action is an organization run much like a business. Gillcrese says the older youths who work there in managerial positions are constantly grooming younger workers to assume their jobs when they graduate from school.

There is an incentive system for trainees. When a student first applies to join the program, he must fill out an application form, be interviewed, and discuss his salary and hours of work, as if he were applying for a job.

"We do this so they will know what they will be facing when they try to get a job after they leave high school," the director says.

The staff of the Urban Youth Action employment relations department stays in touch with major companies in the area to learn of employment opportunities. They also work with placement agencies and try to guide UYA members into particular jobs that are available.

A key part of this placement program is a summer job program that has found employment for more than 500 youngsters over the past seven years or so. Many of the youths have stayed on as permanent employees after graduating from school.

● *Education.* Several volunteers are engaged in educational projects. Part of the young staff is keeping abreast of opportunities offered by colleges and technical and vocational schools. Information is gathered from these institutions on a regular basis and made available to UYA members and other students interested in continuing their education.

The UYA staff members of the organization's board of directors also provide counseling as to what institutions UYA members should apply to and how to go about it.

One of the UYA's most successful education programs—for elementary school students—is also its oldest. Bernard Jones relates how it got started:

"We went to a school and told the principal we would like to hire the entire fifth- and sixth-grade classes for three weeks and pay them a dollar an hour for three hours of work." The students worked in the school office and with teachers and custodians, and also did a variety of odd jobs.

"In that three-week period," says Jones, recounting the experience, "it helped youngsters get interested in English. It helped the math teacher get some new courses up."

"For example the students got some catalogues from the stores. They figured out what presents they wanted to buy for their parents. They had to read the catalogues, so the English teacher got them involved in reading. They figured how much money they were going to make, how much their gifts came to. So that got them involved in math.

"One parent said she had always had trouble getting her son to go to school but during that three weeks, he was getting her up in the morning! There were kids waiting outside of school for the teachers to arrive to get in there so they could go to work.

"This project was so successful that after the three-week period the parents and teachers and all met with us and said, 'You've got to continue it'."

Jones says that UYA, which exists primarily on donations, has managed to come up with enough money to pay about twenty-five of the school's students 75 cents an hour for three hours a week. UYA has also extended the program to other elementary schools.

"One of the best letters I ever received," Jones says, "was from a girl who had returned to school from pregnancy. She was able to work [in the junior high school program], and she thanked me because she was able to buy clothes and things for her daughter.

"By working she relieved the pressure she had of supporting her kid at home. Although her kid lives at home with her parents like she does, she still wanted to do something to support her."

• *Community Services.* Work aspects of the community services program are also administered by the employment relations office. Service workers must be high school students and must attend a weekly UYA training session conducted by a business professional. These young workers perform a number of tasks designed to help needy individuals or the entire community. They may do housework for the handicapped, shop for the elderly, paint houses, and weed lots.

Sometimes workers are employed on jobs that have been contracted for with UYA by a major company or a government agency. The entire program is intended to provide the youths with valuable work experience, as well as money.

• *Economic Development.* Director Gillcrese administers the organization's economic development program for new ventures. This program is financed partly by contributions deducted from the paychecks of the UYA staff and student workers. Donations from businesses, foundations, and other sources also go into a fund to support the program, which includes assistance for students who are going on to college and other schools. Another source of revenue consists of the UYA alumni members, each of whom contributes $6 a year.

Bernard Jones got the idea for starting UYA when he was a community worker for the city's urban redevelopment authority. He saw the need for assisting young people to make the transition from school to the world of work and, at the same time, to imbue them with pride in themselves.

Over the years, UYA has launched hundreds of youngsters on successful careers. How many are carrying on the revolutionary spirit isn't known. But Robert B. Pease, the former executive director of the urban redevelopment agency, thinks they will create a different city in the future.

"If I were asked to name the most significant urban redevelopment contribution to the Pittsburgh community over the past twenty years," he says, "my vote without hesitancy would go to the Urban Youth Action program in the Hill district. For this is urban renewal, as I view it, in its purest and most direct role."

*I wanted to capture the potential of the graffiti
movement before it becomes self-destructive.*

United Graffiti Artists

New York, New York

Works of all the great "masters" are on exhibit.

The name "Snake-1" done in large, bold letters leaps out of a bonfire and is encircled by a string of tiny hearts. The technique used in the painting is known as "Manhattan style."

Complex swirls and ornamentation characteristic of "Brooklyn style" make the name "Nova" all but indecipherable. But it commands the eye.

"Phase 2" looks like a bubbly snake writhing in a cloud of flames. It is executed in "Bronx style."

There are many more embellished signatures—"Co-Co 144," "Stitch-1," "C.A.T. 87"—all done in vivid reds, greens, purples, orange, and shocking pink. They are a wild fantasia of super-doodles mixed with shooting stars and sunbursts and arrows.

The surprise for most visitors on this September day in 1973 is that the artwork on display seems out of place. Graffiti are customarily the decorative art of public places—billboards, subway cars, subway station walls, and just about any other vertical surface. The strange thing is to see graffiti painted on canvas and hung on the walls of an art gallery.

The strangeness soon wears off, though. Five minutes after the exhibit opens a woman pays $200 for one painting. Other works are snapped up at prices ranging up to $3,000 paid for a 30-foot canvas bearing more than a dozen of the ornate signatures. The show ends sixteen days later, having netted $12,000.

The 1973 gallery show was quite a change in fortune for the dozen young graffiti writers, half of them black and most of the rest Puerto Rican. They were being paid for what they had been doing for free, if illegally. It also was a great change in status; their midnight scrawls with cans of spray paint markers were being recognized as "art." What's more, they had been launched on legitimate careers in art.

All of this had come about because a 22-year-old sociology student at the City College of New York, Hugo E. Martinez, had done some work with street gangs in the summer of 1972 and he had

gained appreciative insights into the graffiti world. "I wanted to capture the potential of the graffiti movement before it became self-destructive," he says.

Martinez, a Puerto Rican, used his street connections to round up a dozen of the city's best graffiti "writers" (there are hundreds of them) and organize them into the United Graffiti Artists, Inc. (UGA). After getting them to swear off decorating subway cars and stealing cans of spray paint, he enrolled them in art schools.

"Graffiti had been approached only as a form of vandalism, not as a social problem," he explains. "I set out to rechannel the writers' artistic energy into more constructive areas, especially education, to give them an alternative."

The first months of the organization were lean. But after a television news show displayed some of their work, UGA writers were offered $800 to paint onstage during a production of the Joffrey Ballet at City Center. The onstage painters won as many plaudits as the dancers.

"But what really turned our fortunes around," says Martinez, "was the art exhibit." The city's newspapers and a national newsmagazine gave the exhibit wide display. Art critics began to see what Martinez had perceived in graffiti. As he said at the time of the show:

Graffiti artist Bama has been drawing cartoons since he was 9.

Michael Lawrence

Michael Lawrence

The paint-spattered director of UGA, Hugo Martinez

"These kids have no one to identify with. The schools don't relate to their problems, so they turn to the streets for stimulation, which they usually find in either drugs or gangs. Until graffiti the kids had never based themselves on a nondestructive, non-annihilating lifestyle. Here for the first time is a lifestyle which permits them to face anonymity creatively."

Co-Co, one of his young graffiti masters, puts it another way: "I saw my friends doing it and it was an adventure. Going into the subway yards was exciting, like entering a haunted house. It was eerie and dark, and you would get scared.

"We wanted to put a little fame in our lives," he adds. "People in slum areas really want to make themselves known, but we don't know how to do it."

Martinez feels it is significant that many of the writers picked property that was also a mobile medium for giving their work high visibility—the subway cars.

"This society looks down on a lack of property," he said. "You're not of consequence unless you have it. By signing their names to the subway cars, it's as if they were acquiring possessions: 'I own the number 6 line'."

The graffiti explosion started in 1970, when a young boy from 183rd Street began documenting his presence all over New York with a felt-tipped pen that traced an unadorned "Taki 183." His followers, though, have gone on to more elaborate designs.

As the graffiti styles of the various boroughs have evolved, so has a certain code among the writers. It is against the code, for example, for anyone to write over the signature of a WAR (Writer Already Respected)—a recognized master.

Martinez says there is one major criterion for a masterpiece—"it can't drip." By way of illustration, he says, "Super Kool 223 does beautiful pieces, but his paint drips. He doesn't use the spray can well."

Martinez has arranged for all twelve writers to enroll, tuition-free, in the Universidad Boricua, a "university without walls" which has asked Martinez to find instructors to teach subjects that UGA members want to learn. The writers, all of whom had been on the verge of dropping out of high school, have also been given scholarships for four credit hours in the City College of New York High School Enrichment Program.

An abandoned doll factory in Washington Heights was made available to UGA in June 1973 by the mayor's chief of staff at an annual rental rate of $12. The 5,000-square-foot studio hums with the sounds of hammers, power sanders, and the latest soul music. And an occasional welcoming whoop signals the arrival of another member to do a specific chore he himself chooses from a long list of things to be done to make the building usable. Young neighborhood kids, low on the membership waiting list of some 200 aspiring artists, hang around the studio in hopes that one of the masters will take a look at their work.

Guided by a two-page list of bylaws and legitimatized by an advisory board that includes college professors and a transit authority representative, United Graffiti Artists holds weekly meetings at the studio.

The group still looks for leadership and advice to Hugo Martinez. Their leader is a strange mixture of insecurity ("I write lousy proposals") and cocky self-assurance ("I can channel violence or ambition, but not apathy"). He labors twelve hours a day for UGA and swears his allegiance to and affinity for the working class. Yet, occasionally, he spouts—and gets away with—curiously middle-class platitudes, such as, "In unity there is strength" and "Through work there is freedom."

Martinez' scenario for UGA's future includes painting murals in the city's Washington Heights section, and doing silk-screen works to exhibit at Chicago's Museum of Science and Industry and in Puerto Rico. And after that? "I would also like to go to Japan, because of its tradition of calligraphy," he says. "Japan buys a lot of paintings—it's second only to West Germany."

The graffiti movement itself may well be the tail of a brilliant but nevertheless a dying comet. As "T-Rex" says, "The city paints the cars every two years, man. By the time they paint them again, I'll be too old to write."

But Hugo Martinez succeeded in capturing the comet's zenith, putting it on display in the establishment's galleries—and turning around a dozen lives in the bargain.

Michael Lawrence

CHAPTER 4

Housing

A decade has passed since the United States first announced an assault on inadequate and unsafe housing. The war is ten years older now, but the enemy is still entrenched.

There are still at least 11 million substandard and overcrowded dwelling units in the country, and they account for about 16 percent of all the units available.

Blighted clusters of inner-city tenements represent just a fraction of the overall problem. About 60 percent of all substandard housing is found in rural areas.

Self-help housing programs will never be able to provide enough low-income dwellings to appreciably reduce the country's overall demand for better housing. But they can help to meet that need on a local basis.

The self-help housing project can be the agent for creating community pride, the organizer of a neighborhood clean-up campaign, the advocate for better tenant treatment, or even the initiator of a private corporation to build and renovate low-income houses and finance disadvantaged families so they can buy their own homes.

Such housing programs can also play a valuable role in helping focus public opinion on the need for making sure that all Americans have adequate housing.

When a massive urban renewal project displaces a low-income neighborhood, for example, the self-help housing program can organize and influence government and corporate decisions that will create alternative construction programs. And if municipal services do not extend to rural poverty areas, the self-help project can either lobby for better public services or seek private funding.

The self-help housing movement can't rebuild cities or renovate all the ramshackle houses in rural America. But the efforts of local communities to at least tackle the problem of substandard housing mean that a number of people do obtain better housing and that government and business are given the opportunity to recognize what really needs to be done on a national scale.

Black people can do best the things that are
needed to alleviate black people's problems.

The Roxbury Action Program

Boston, Massachusetts

In 1689 the colonists in Boston rose up against the royal governor, seized him, threw him into prison, and forced him to resign. Today the place where the governor was seized, Fort Hill, is the home of a group of people involved in another kind of revolution—a nonviolent revolution aimed at ridding the area of the urban blight that began at the turn of the century and has continued almost unimpeded until the present day.

The contemporary counterparts of the 1689 colonists are members of the Roxbury Action Program, Inc., a community-based, nonprofit, tax-exempt organization that, since 1968, has been revitalizing a one-square mile area of Fort Hill and turning it into what some day will be a model neighborhood.

The aims of the Roxbury Action Program (RAP) are to seek better housing, increased local home ownership, and community-based economic action. The force behind this is a philosophy that goals can be best achieved by permitting, encouraging, and assisting residents of an area to help themselves.

"We decided to concentrate on housing so we could control the land," says George Morrison, one of the two people who have done the most to organize RAP and help it succeed. "But housing isn't our only forte," he quickly points out.

Morrison and Lloyd King, the other key man in the venture from its start, conceived the idea of such an organization in the late 1960s, when there were many projects and programs in Boston, especially in the predominately black sections such as Roxbury. Morrison and King were actively involved at the time in attempts by the American Friends Service Committee (AFSC) to improve living conditions for the residents of Roxbury.

RAP began in 1964 as a component of the AFSC's metropolitan housing program, which had offices in the Blue Hill Avenue section of Roxbury—a district where twenty-four other service organizations had sprung up with varying degrees of success.

RAP's staff meets frequently to plan a model community for blacks.

"There were a lot of failures," says Morrison of those other organizations, "but from them we learned what not to do."

The AFSC was primarily a service organization that focused on
working for the rights of low-income residents, improving tenants'
relationships with their landlords, and forcing, through court action, stricter enforcement of the housing safety code. In 1968 the
AFSC turned over control of its Roxbury office and its programs to
RAP, whose membership comprised Morrison and King and other
black men and women who had been AFSC staff members, along
with an executive board composed of Roxbury residents.

Formation of RAP as a separate entity constituted what King
describes as a "political" move.

"In the 1960s there was racial strife throughout the country, and Boston was no exception," notes King. Blacks, in other words, were weary of waiting for the full fruits of citizenship, which so many others had said should be theirs. Through RAP and similar organizations throughout the country, blacks took the initiative.

"We decided to do something that would be more lasting, and to develop something that would be more tangible than what the other organizations were doing," says Morrison.

In retrospect it is difficult to understand why Boston, so proud of its historical heritage, so famous for its Bunker Hill Monument and its Freedom Trail, had done so little to restore Roxbury and Highland Park—especially the historic area, Fort Hill (which played a role in the Revolution as well as the earlier 1689 incident). Far from being restored, in fact, the area adjacent to Highland Park had been virtually denuded by bulldozers preparing a swath for an expressway that, as of 1974, had still not been built and seemed to have been permanently rejected by the city and state as impractical.

RAP began in 1968 to establish in Highland Park what it calls a "model black community." To do it, Morrison, King, and the others felt, the people who are to be helped should be helped to help themselves. Says George Morrison, RAP's president: "Black people can do best the things that are needed to alleviate black people's problems."

And he has long felt that, if the people who are to benefit become involved in producing the benefits, they develop an understanding of both the problems and the solutions, and they don't have to depend on organizations, even RAP, for what Morrison describes as "the long-range answers and solutions to their social, personal, and economic problems."

Some agencies that try to help minority groups independent of RAP and other organizations firmly based in the community, says Morrison, "have not solved any of the problems. They have compounded them."

"Organizations like RAP," he adds, "are the last hope for solving the problems of the urban ill and poor people. At the root of this achievement has to be getting black and poor people to understand their problems, and hence to work at eliminating them with organizations like RAP."

Beginning in August 1969 the Roxbury Action Program began to sell itself to the residents of Highland Park, many of whom were skeptical about the help new organizations promised to provide. RAP divided Highland Park into four areas and sent a community organizer from its staff into each area to talk to the people and get their views of what role they felt RAP should play, on what RAP could do to help them the most.

"During the first two weeks we were in our new office in Highland Park," declares Morrison, "we invited people from the community in to meet us, to talk with us and tell us what they wanted."

While developing rapport with the residents of Highland Park, RAP encouraged involvement by people and institutions outside the community. Many responded. The Boston Architectural Center, for example, helped RAP obtain funds for an overall physical planning study of the neighborhood. Some students from Harvard's graduate school of design conducted extensive planning surveys. And from metropolitan Boston's academic, cultural, and business communities came volunteers to help with legal work, financing, designing, and planning and other specialties needed for successful development of the area.

"Today, we can measure significant tangible progress towards our goal of a model black community," says Morrison with justifiable pride.

RAP has acquired, completely rehabilitated, and now manages twenty-six buildings containing a total of ninety-seven low-income and moderate-income housing units. It owns Marcus Garvey House, a five-story, 33,000-square-foot office and community service building. It operates a community pharmacy, which is only the fifth black-owned drugstore in Massachusetts. It also operates the Continuing Education Drop-In Center, which caters to young people, and Roxbury Rent-a-Kid, which provides summer jobs for neighborhood teenagers.

Financing for RAP's diverse programs comes from a successful mix of public and private resources. The Roxbury group is the first U.S. community organization allowed to serve as the only active partner in a limited-dividend approach to housing development. The program has been made possible by federal legislation allowing for tax-shelter incentives for private individuals wanting to invest in low-income housing development. RAP receives $10,000 annually for administering this program.

Future projects will include the rehabilitation or construction of hundreds of more housing units and development of new commercial space. Although the Roxbury Action Program may tap federal sources for much of this money, responsibility for the planning and implementation of the projects will be RAP's.

"It's a revolution alright," quips George Morrison. "And believe me, it's just begun."

You can give all the grass seed in the world, all
the paint, all the peat moss, but if you don't work
with the people inside the houses, you
have wasted your time.

Operation Better Block

Pittsburgh, Pennsylvania

Pittsburgh's Homewood-Brushton section is a neighborhood in transition.

On block after block the people are out repairing and painting their houses. Lots have been cleaned up, grass seed planted, and new lawns kept neatly mowed. Hedges and bushes are trimmed. Sidewalks have been repaired, holes in the street filled in, and the trash is gone.

This transformation of a once-decaying neighborhood is the doing of Operation Better Block—an idea that never caught on in the place it originated, New York City, but has flourished since being transplanted to Pittsburgh. Carrie Washington, assistant director of Better Block, feels the project failed in New York's slum neighborhoods because it was sponsored by the city.

"Here, the people themselves are doing it—they are doing it because they want to take more pride in their community," she says. "And they are making more than just physical improvements—they are bringing about change in their lives."

Better Block was put together in 1970 by a coalition of Homewood-Brushton community organizations known as Forever Action Together (FAT). The housing committee of FAT spent eighteen months designing the project, then went from block to block trying to organize the residents. These efforts eventually resulted in the creation of some thirty block associations or clubs involving a total of about 6,500 people.

The effect of these associations has been widespread. The city has been pressured into fixing sewers and streets, improving street lighting, and removing trash. Absentee landlords have been forced to repair and maintain their buildings. And the people of Homewood-Brushton, as well as of other areas of the city, have become much more concerned about their physical environment than they used to be.

But Better Block emphasizes much more than just cleaning, fixing, and repairing. It is concerned about the entire community and
all of its problems. Consequently any list of Better Block's accomplishments must be extended to include the fostering of community pride and neighborliness, persuading families not to leave the
area, providing part-time work for neighborhood youngsters, organizing sports and other recreational activities, and giving local
people a chance to find out what they all have in common.

"What people have discovered in the clubs is that they can sit
down and discuss common problems and help one another," says

Ron Ryriuk

*Newly planted bushes symbolize both the success and hope of Operation
Better Block, which is headed by James Givner.*

Carrie Washington. "They are generating a whole different spirit than was here before, when nobody cared about anything."

What Better Block itself has learned is the importance of caring for and dealing with the people. As Carrie Washington says, pointedly, "You can give all the grass seed in the world, all the paint, all the peat moss, but if you don't work with the people inside the houses, you have wasted your time."

Organizing a new block association begins with Better Block's five staff members undertaking a study of the problems and characteristics of the prospective new member block. Is it, for example, primarily a block of elderly people? Are there a lot of children? How many people are home owners? Is there a high percentage of absentee landlords?

One of Better Block's two field representatives then assists the group during its first shaky days as it sets up priorities and begins organizing a block association.

Better Block initially provides $25 to the new association, and it will subsequently contribute additional seed money of up to $500 as the association requires it. Better Block staff members maintain a close watch over expenditures to see that policy is carried out.

Residents are given grass seed, shrubbery, and other items, along with donated clippers and mowers. Project leaders buy paint, gas lamps, and fencing materials at cost and sell them to the residents at the same price. Better Block keeps on file a list of contractors who will do reliable work at reasonable cost for those who can afford it.

From the beginning the project has maintained close contacts with the city, although its financing has come from the Allegheny Conference on Community Development United Fund and several large Pittsburgh companies.

"Consequently," says Carrie Washington, "people have been amazed at the fast action we get. It runs all the way from sewer cleanups to better street lighting—whatever you can think of. The city fixed a hole in the middle of Monticello Street that could have swallowed a compact car. They sent in the Neighborhood Youth Corps to help in the cleanup."

The project has ways of dealing with absentee landlords. It first makes residents fulfill their obligations as tenants. Then, if necessary, they bring legal action against obstinate landlords.

The Better Block clubs serve as a forum where one person can take a complaint against his neighbor without generating personal friction.

"When we tell Mrs. Smith her garbage is attracting rats, she gets mad at *us*, not her neighbor, Mrs. Jones, who wants it cleaned up," says Carrie Washington.

Representatives of different blocks meet once a month to discuss their programs and exchange ideas. Most of the ideas concern how to keep the club going after the funds from Better Block have been used.

FAT's president, James Givner, the owner of a beauty-products store, has been fostering the participation of youth in Better Block. Individual clubs are urged to include young people in their meetings and solicit their ideas for improvements. High school students have been paid to make and install new house numbers and to build trash receptacles, with some local companies providing the necessary money.

Efforts are also made to provide recreational facilities and activities for the neighborhood youngsters, partly to involve them in Better Block, partly to provide them with leisure-time activites, and partly to expand their horizons.

In 1973, for example, Operation Better Block sent a team of Little League all-stars to play in Madison, Ohio. The excitement of the game was compounded by the fact that most of the Pittsburgh youngsters had never been out of their home city before.

"The coaches selected those kids who were able to get along with other players, those with a positive attitude, and those who showed evidences of leadership," Carrie Washington explains. "All we heard from the others when the all-stars came back was, 'Boy, next year I'm going to be like one of them so I can make the team'."

Carrie Washington says that numerous donors have attempted to influence the direction of the project. "We have had more spin-offs suggested than you can imagine, and we have had to say our goal is here.

"We went to a donor who suggested certain changes . . . and made this a condition of his donation. He was told, 'No, we will not accept any funds from anyone on the basis of change of this program. It has already been designed and we will not let anyone build in failures.' Now this was a $10,000 grant, and we didn't have a penny. It jolted him."

Nevertheless the organization received the grant that year—and each year thereafter.

"Obviously if there were more money, more blocks could be helped," Givner says. "But the response from the residents has been tremendous."

And that's the real name of the game.

The repairs were started one week later—the
week Angelique died. The landlord came
to the building—to collect the rent—the
day of Angelique's funeral.

The Ocean Hill-Brownsville
Tenants Association

New York, New York

On a cold morning in January 1974 an eleven-month-old baby girl died in her crib of bronchial infection. For two and a half weeks before her death there had been no heat in the tenement where her parents lived in the Ocean Hill-Brownsville section of Brooklyn.

The death of Angelique Saninocencia symbolizes in human terms the waste and disintegration that has turned Ocean Hill-Brownsville into one of New York City's worst slums. The circumstances surrounding her death exemplify the indifference that the city government and property owners seem to demonstrate for the people of Ocean Hill-Brownsville.

Angered by the misery and squalor in which they are forced to live—and pay for—residents of Ocean Hill-Brownsville have organized to combat official indifference. They are using the courts to force landlords to keep up their properties, and to make their community a better place in which to live. They work on the assumption that only when the people of Ocean Hill-Brownsville have warm and safe apartments and homes can the community begin to tackle its many other problems.

In four years the Ocean Hill-Brownsville Tenants Association has begun making some headway against the official and landlord indifference. As a result of its efforts, some people are living in better apartments. Yet, as Angelique's death demonstrated anew, their problems are overwhelming. In their eyes, the death was no mischance but could be laid at the doorstep of city hall.

In April 1973 the association proposed to the city's commissioner of rent and housing maintenance a plan for forty unemployed construction trades men in the area to make emergency repairs in dilapidated buildings. The city would only have to pay the bills it would normally pay under its own emergency repairs program. The work would be professionally supervised, and the association would manage the project.

The tenants were told to wait, because it was an election year and the timing was "politically inopportune." They were kept waiting through summer and fall. After the election the association wrote Mayor-elect Abraham Beame, urging his support for the program. The letter cited thirty-one buildings, housing more than 300 families, that had no heat or hot water.

"There is no reason in the world that a community which agrees to help itself by providing its own force of workers and mechanics should have many, many buildings with hazardous violations and lack of heat," the letter continued.

It added, prophetically: "We are calling upon you . . . to see to it that children do not die here again this winter because of the ineffectiveness of the city's Emergency Repair Program."

Other appeals were made. The landlord of the building where Angelique's parents lived had been informed but did nothing. Four times the city housing and development agency sent inspectors. Three times they reported "sufficient heat." On the fourth trip the inspector found the heating system badly in need of repairs and fuel.

The repairs were started one week later—the week Angelique died. The landlord came to the building—to collect the rent—the day of Angelique's funeral.

Angelique's death was not an isolated incident. The infant mortality and malnutrition rates in Ocean Hill–Brownsville are four times higher than the rest of the city. Half the residents are on some kind of public assistance. All the ghetto landmarks are there—boarded-up stores, gutted buildings, and streets littered with rusting cars and broken bottles. In the previous decades, millions of dollars were spent on low-income housing, but according to many experts those programs only "institutionalized" poverty. The building programs were not accompanied by proper planning for schools, health and recreation facilities and job training.

Whites, and those blacks who could afford to, left. Decay and disintegration spread. Landlords waited for the city to take over the buildings. Vacated apartment buildings that had been slated for demolition refilled, becoming permanent way stations for the poor.

The tenants association was formed in November 1970, an indirect offshoot of another neighborhood program, the community-controlled school board. Two of the association's principal backers were Father John Powis of Our Lady of Presentation Church and Dolores Torres. Both had been on the governing board of the experimental community-controlled schools. The association was established on the principle that bad housing was at the core of the area's troubles and that tenants needed to be unified and organized to approach the city housing authority.

Tenants were organized in buildings, and a general meeting followed. Delegates were selected to present the neighborhood's problems to the city agency and to request that housing code violations be remedied.

The city officials listened, but nothing happened. The association took direct and dramatic action, and called a rent strike.

"With no outside help and no funds, the going wasn't easy," recalled Frank Torres, one of the organizers. "Over eighty percent of the buildings had no heat or hot water, but people were still afraid that they'd be kicked out of their homes if they struck, afraid that they'd be left alone."

Neighborhood unity was threatened in other ways. "Some blacks didn't trust Puerto Ricans, and some Puerto Ricans didn't trust blacks. But we just kept at it, explaining to the people why they shouldn't pay rent, telling them their rights. They [Father Powis and Dolores Torres] weren't afraid of waging a struggle, but still had a way of making people trust them and want to cooperate."

The strike was organized so effectively that only eleven tenants out of more than 1,000 paid their rent that month. The strike was

Why tenants strike. The scarred hallways and peeling walls of a tenement are grim evidence of years of neglect.

James M. Fesler

ended through the intervention of then Housing Commissioner Simon Golar. He met with tenants and promised to make repairs.

Starting with a victory, the association has since grown to an active membership of more than 700 tenants in the area. It has lobbied and pleaded for new federally-funded housing. On one new project residents worked with architects, stressing the necessity of large apartments suitable for people in the neighborhood with big families. For another project, tenants persuaded architects to draw up plans for duplexes.

When building on the seven sites started, residents demanded a black contractor who would employ and train men from the community, all unemployed and many recently out of prison. The contractor was willing but feared union problems. Residents picketed the site. Eventually ninety percent of the laborers were hired from the community, and half a dozen have since joined unions.

The tenants association has also taken over part of the city agency's function of clearing tenants for moving into projects. It feared the city criteria would bar, as they had in the past, families with too many children or children born out of wedlock, families entirely on welfare, or families with a single parent. The association set up a screening committee to consider applications and make recommendations to the housing authority on the basis of need.

"I think this is one of the most important things we do," says Gloria Ford, a member of the association's board of directors. "We're very interested in getting good tenants in the projects. But just because a woman has a large family doesn't mean she won't be a good tenant."

The association has become increasingly active in the courts and on the legal front.

Working with lawyers from Brownsville Legal Services, the association is blunting the force of eviction notices in court. Landlords who bring actions against tenants find they are backfiring.

With the aid of the group, Johnnie Mae Bell has been successfully fighting eviction notices as she refuses to pay the $300-a-month rent on a six-room walk-up until repairs are made. She is waiting to move into a new project, but meanwhile her plumbing is shot, the bathroom walls are crawling with insects even in winter, the ceiling is caving in where the roof leaks, and huge rats scurry across the floor. And there is no heat. Her family lives in the living room, relying on the oven and gas burners for warmth.

Before a court fight, tenants collect specific information on housing code violations throughout the entire building. Pictures are taken for evidence. On the day of the court proceeding, all tenants and staff members go to court to show the judge their unity and to show the landlord they mean business.

Recently thirty-six tenants went to court complaining the boiler of their building was under ten feet of frozen sewage that had poured into the basement from backed-up pipes. The ceiling in the main hall, caving in at one place, was laced with icicles stretching to the floor. The landlord insisted in court the tenants were lying. The judge went to look for himself and was so horrified he used a special court procedure and "gave" the building to the tenants.

The tenants have since spent what used to be rent money on building repairs. The heating works, the plumbing is repaired, the hallways are clean. The basement has been made into a playroom for the children. Under a city program the building will soon become a cooperative. Tenant owners will pay off the city-held mortgage with rent money.

The association hopes to expand its cooperative program and is now negotiating with the city for 300 buildings seized for failure to pay taxes. The association has suggested the buildings be rehabilitated by men from the community, employed by the association's new nonprofit construction corporation. After repairs, ownership of the buildings would revert to tenants who would pay off a 30-year mortgage.

The association's expanded activity has been developed through a democratic system. Board members are elected by tenants. Decisions are made at monthly meetings. Staff salaries are set on the basis of need, not seniority.

Outsiders are impressed by the way the organization functions. "I've worked with other tenant groups, but I've never seen a group quite like this," says Ron Parker, a lawyer from Brownsville Legal Services. "There's virtually none of the inhouse bickering or power plays you see elsewhere. What the group lacks in polish, it makes up for in dedication and willingness to work together for a common goal."

The association works despite many frustrations and the feeling that city and other agencies have little faith in the community and are more interested in talking than action. It's impatient with red tape, delays, and endless negotiations, such as those involving the 300 apartment buildings. It sees the chance to create a thriving neighborhood, more employment, less welfare, good housing instead of slums.

Much remains to be accomplished, and the association intends to stay impatient until no more Angeliques die in their cribs.

A decaying part of a great city can be revived—
not by an act of benevolence from the outside but
by an act of will from within.

Jeff-Vander-Lou, Inc.

St. Louis, Missouri

The crowd of poor blacks from the Near North Side of St. Louis jammed the meeting with the city's building commissioner, Kenneth O. Brown.

They were protesting the city's lack of concern for flagrant building-code violations in properties owned by absentee landlords—the decaying buildings located in the slum area bounded by Jefferson Street, Vanderventer Avenue, and St. Louis Avenue: the Jeff-Vander-Lou district.

Brown had heard all the complaints many times before, and along with other St. Louis political leaders, he had tacitly shrugged off the area as hopeless. But he had never said so. This day in 1966, he did. He gave the group the "message" that seventy-five percent of their Jeff-Vander-Lou district "was not worth saving."

The comment had a stunning effect.

"We suddenly realized we were in a crisis situation," recalls Macler C. Shepard. "They said the area wasn't worth saving, but we knew if we couldn't live there we couldn't live *anywhere*. They had destroyed part of Pruitt-Igoe [a public housing project later almost completely abandoned by its residents]; they had torn up Millcreek area for urban renewal.

"That meant about the only place left for us was the Mississippi River. We had to do something ourselves or we weren't going to survive."

The next few months were hectic as Macler Shepard assumed the leadership of a small group of residents who decided they should buy the decaying properties and fix them up themselves. But the absentee landlords refused to sell.

Reaching out for help in dozens of directions, Shepard's group organized Jeff-Vander-Lou, Inc. to serve as a focus of community action. The organization's efforts led to many more complaints being leveled at the landlords—who finally agreed to sell.

"We went to the churches for the money," says Shepard. "And through the churches of St. Louis we reached concerned individuals and other organizations." They made an appeal based on "neighbors caring for neighbors." And it worked. Recalls Shepard, "The money—enough for those buildings—came in and we got the property."

For the next year the residents of the area pitched in to help clear the land, carry out demolition, and begin the long job of

Macler Shepard (left) and workers on a JVL Housing project

rehabilitating the properties that remained. And in 1968, Jeff-Vander-Lou, Inc. achieved its first benchmark of success: fifteen rehabilitated housing units were opened to local families.

The corporation subsequently decided to create a new enterprise to handle the housing work. This was duly accomplished, and the poor people of St. Louis had another corporate tool at their disposal—JVL Housing Development, Inc.

JVL Housing was among the first groups in the country to mount a successful building and rehabilitation program under the terms of section 236 of the National Housing Act of 1967, which provides low-cost mortgage financing for multi-unit housing if at least ten percent of the units will be rented to low-income poverty families; federal "rent supplements" cover the difference between what these families can afford and what a fair rental would be.

In the summer of 1972, JVL Housing opened 74 units in multi-unit buildings. A year later the corporation opened the first of another 56 town house units. Rents averaged $108 to $170 a month for two-bedroom houses, and $149 to $230 a month for five-bedroom town houses.

The first group of seven houses consisted of rehabilitated buildings—stripped and reconstructed from the foundations up—that had formerly been occupied by as many as fourteen families simultaneously. Here seven families would benefit from more space, better lighting and plumbing, and the personal dignity that comes with giving each person enough space in which to live. When these town houses began to open up, JVL Housing already had an inventory of 326 units—either condemned and waiting for rehabilitation or already reconstructed and inhabited.

At the time it was facing down the city's building commissioner and thirteen absentee slumlords, Jeff-Vander-Lou, Inc. was also concerned about the lack of employment opportunities for the people of the area. A very high percentage of the 50,000 residents of the black ghetto were jobless most of the year. If the housing situation was improved for area families, would they be able to afford it for very long?

Jeff-Vander-Lou, Inc. applied to the federal government for help. Nothing happened. "Our application and proposal went to the Office of Economic Opportunity," Shepard remembers of those days in 1967, when a war on poverty was supposedly being waged from Washington. "Somehow our papers went over to the Department of Health, Education, and Welfare. And they never came back."

The Jeff-Vander-Lou papers may still be drifting about HEW, but Shepard couldn't care less. Thrown back on their own resources, the Jeff-Vander-Lou residents scraped together the necessary funds from the Greater St. Louis area to try to create their own source of employment. Financial self-reliance is imperative, they believe. In the words of Macler Shepard:

"The reason so many nonprofit organizations have failed is because they have a crutch. That crutch is government money. But the thing that's wrong about that is when the Man puts you on a crutch, he doesn't come around to see if you can ever walk again. Chances are, you can't."

The opportunity to establish an economic base for the community came as a result of some contacts Shepard and his group had made with the Brown Shoe Company of St. Louis. They were able to tell their story to the company's board of directors, and a period of talks led to an arrangement that suited both parties.

Jeff-Vander-Lou, Inc. had acquired a large tract of condemned slum property for a small amount of money. It now agreed to sell the tract to Brown at cost, if the company would use the land for its proposed new plant. To further cement the deal, Jeff-Vander-Lou,

Inc. would screen and send to the Brown plant employable residents of the area for training and steady work—and Brown would put them on the payroll.

In 1968 the Brown Shoe Company opened its new facility on the Near North Side. Jeff-Vander-Lou, Inc. gathered together a cadre of instructors and formed a manpower training corporation and employment service, with Brown as its prime client.

The partnership between corporation and community had its effect on the St. Louis community at large. A group of downtown businessmen formed the Arrowhead Foundation to provide ready money for the JVL Housing effort. And additional funds came in to underwrite a nursery school (the JVL Learning Center) and a community health facility (the Sheridan Medical Group).

All these activities of the Jeff-Vander-Lou organization affect the lives of at least 10,000 residents of a once condemned community. Only seven years ago the area was written off as not worth saving, and the citizens as little more than a collective nuisance.

City hall now listens to Jeff-Vander-Lou, Inc. The city planning commission consults with the group before making a move in the area, and local officials and at least one congressman are now among those who recognize that a decaying part of a great city can be revived—not by an act of benevolence from the outside but by an act of will from within. That is the "message" that has come back from Jeff-Vander-Lou—fortunately for St. Louis.

Macler Shepard (rear) checks records of JVL Housing with staff members

*The tenants we have worked with have
proved that the only way to save the tenements in
the city is by their involvement.*

Interfaith Adopt-a-Building

New York, New York

At a ceremony in New York's City Hall late in 1973, the titles to four run-down tenement buildings were transferred from the city, which had become their reluctant owner, to some tenants who thought they could make the structures habitable again.

It was, as the mayor noted, a historic occasion. Never before had such a thing happened in the metropolis. Officials were hopeful. Now, perhaps, self-help housing endeavors would flourish throughout the city.

The title transfer making the tenants the owners of the buildings—and responsible for the upkeep of their new homes—was the work of a little-known project called Interfaith Adopt-a-Building, Inc. It was a remarkable feat for an organization that had started off only three years before in the slums of East Harlem under the guidance of a young ministerial student named Bill Eddy.

Adopt-a-Building was founded on the principle that people would rather help themselves than be helped.

"This is strictly a tenants' program," is the way Eddy characterizes it. "They've got to do it. All we do is provide some assistance, assurance, and advice."

The assistance provided includes organizing tenants of individual buildings to conduct rent strikes, as well as teaching the tenants their rights in dealing with the absentee landlords who refuse to maintain their buildings. The organization also puts out a bilingual (Spanish and English) newsletter, which informs tenants about various aspects of the law that have to do with housing and which follows a number of Adopt-a-Building cases. It is through the newsletter, for example, that the people have been taught that they can gain legal control of a building if the landlord fails to pay his real estate taxes for three years; the city takes over the building and the tenants have a right, before it is auctioned, to obtain a loan and to buy the property and renovate it.

"For the past three years," Eddy says, "the tenants we have worked with have proved that the only way to save the tenements in the city is by their involvement. The struggle has been hard and will continue to be that way. But the people have the willpower and initiative to see the projects for their buildings through."

Adopt-a-Building works in four different parts of New York—the Bronx, the West Side, East Harlem, and the Lower East Side. These are all areas where poor people—Puerto Ricans and blacks and whites—live out their lives amid unemployment and poverty and drug addiction and dogs foraging through garbage in the streets. They are areas where fire engines wail as often as babies and where crime is so commonplace that people don't even bother to call the police ("Ours is the kind of building where people don't report muggings to the cops," says Penny Hunts-berger, who lives in an Adopt-a-Building tenement on the Lower East Side). And they are areas where almost the only housing available consists of aging structures that are too hot in summer and too cold in winter, and many of which are in the process of being either ignored or abandoned by the landlords.

Why did city officials choose Adopt-a-Building tenant groups as recipients of those first, historic building deeds?

"Because they're economically and socially feasible," says Robert Hamilton, a housing specialist in the city's budget bureau. "Adopt-a-Building impressed a lot of people downtown because they didn't move in and bust up a neighborhood, like urban renewal often does. And they're a buffer between the city and the tenants. Eddy and the others understand tenants' problems, but they're sophisticated enough to deal with us."

Bill Eddy first came to understand such problems while living in East Harlem, where he had moved in part to learn Spanish. He joined the 100 Worst Buildings Committee in 1968—a volunteer effort to improve ghetto housing conditions in East Harlem. It was from this experience that the idea for Adopt-a-Building emerged. Putting his idea into action, Eddy committed himself to the project and became its first director.

Under his leadership the project worked out the basic tactics needed to save the tenements—and the tenants—and give low-income people a chance to obtain decent housing.

On the Lower East Side, for example, the project has a four-member full-time staff that works out of a storefront neighborhood services office in the heart of the run-down area.

Adopt-a-Building usually gets its foot in the door of a tenement when it learns that the building is without heat, hot water, or other basic services. The staff contacts the city's emergency repair office, with which it maintains good relations, and assists repairmen and tenants in restoring those services. Sometimes that means finding a used boiler, or a friendly plumber who is willing to help out for free. Then Adopt-a-Building canvasses the building, learning of the tenants' other needs and teaching them about some of the alternatives available to them—alternatives such as insistence on legal contracts with uncooperative landlords, rent strikes, tenant management of the building, or even eventual cooperative ownership. Interested tenants are encouraged to get together, test the general feeling and response within the building, and, if it seems suitable, then form a tenants' association.

Should an association try without success to win the needed improvements from the building's owner, then Adopt-a-Building

James M. Fesler

Tenants have taken over this dilapidated building and are renovating it.

staffers will aid tenants plan and carry out the next steps. If a rent strike is called, the organization will secure legal aid for the tenants, as well as assist in opening a bank account where rents can be held out of reach of the landlord and eventually put toward payment of repairs and renovation.

At times the necessary reliance on people inexperienced in such complex efforts as tenant-landlord showdowns has led to frustration for a number of Adopt-a-Building workers, particularly when they see tenants making costly mistakes. Yet the staff knows that true self-help is the only way to lasting success. The tenants have to become involved in making the effort themselves, in dealing with all of the physical and bureaucratic complexities related to maintaining good housing in New York City. If that involvement produces mistakes, then that is the way it has to be—in the hope that the tenants will do better next time. The tenants must aim at both self-help and self-reliance. And Adopt-a-Building knows that it must, during the formative period, remain patient with—and especially accessible to—the tenants.

"Being close to the people is one reason it's worked so well," believes Richard Merrick, executive vice-president of the Bronx Chamber of Commerce.

It was while he was with the Manhattan Chamber of Commerce that Merrick got that group to sponsor annual luncheons to which dozens of corporate representatives were invited to hear Eddy outline the housing experiment. Partly as a result of such efforts, Adopt-a-Building has been successful in winning financial backing. At first, local churches and synagogues were the project's source of income. Then a few small foundations gave. Larger contributions followed, in part because of the preceding support. Gradually the seemingly impenetrable wall around establishment sources was breached. Money came in from several banks, among them Chase Manhattan, First National City Bank, Bankers Trust, and Morgan Guaranty. Not only were these institutions interested in the project as an expression of community self-help, but they responded to the caliber and success of the organization. In 1973, for example, Chase Manhattan gave Adopt-a-Building its annual $35,000 award as the most worthy housing effort in the city. Now Bill Eddy and the group's board of directors (such a board was thought unnecessary until recently) are looking to the prestigious national foundations for continuing funds to keep the Adopt-a-Building program going on a sound financial basis.

Adopt-a-Building's skeleton staff, unencumbered by titles and bureaucratic overlays, has proven itself extraordinarily cost-effective. "Their budget was terrific, very low," remarked an officer of

Morgan Guaranty. The proposed 1974 budget is $81,000, a sum that includes for the first time a salary for a construction supervisor who will work with tenants in buildings being renovated.

Bankers Trust, which in addition to dispensing yearly stipends has picked up the printing bills for Adopt-a-Building how-to manuals for tenants, sees the program as being relevant for its own people. "On behalf of our employees we ought to take steps to up-

Masked against dust, workmen begin cleaning up an Adopt-a-Building tenement being rehabilitated on the Lower East Side of Manhattan.

grade housing," says the bank's urban affairs officer Eileen Fox. "We've stayed with Adopt-a-Building because we agree that we ought to improve what we've got."

It is not that Interfaith Adopt-a-Building has met with universal acclaim. It has met with some resistance from real estate brokers or agents for landlords who suddenly find their properties in jeopardy. But even some real estate people see the advantages and benefits of the program. Says one realtor, "Where people have a bit of their own money involved, they're less destructive."

An employee of Helmsley-Spear, Inc., a giant New York realty firm, concurred. "There's nothing like people's equity," he said. "It's the strength of our country."

*Blighted urban areas will become attractive
again only as individual families are able to own
their own homes and experience the satisfaction
of living in well-kept houses in communities of
which they can be proud.*

Menno Housing/Tabor
Community Services

Lancaster, Pennsylvania

Grace Wenger, a college English professor, was on the telephone to a landlord. Yes, the apartment was available. Would she care to see it?

"Well, actually," she said, "I'm looking for some friends. They're black—does it make any difference?"

"All of a sudden he became hard of hearing," she recalls. "It was such a transparent thing, it was almost funny. But when I thought how this man was treating people, I became furious."

What angered Grace Wenger even more was that this racial slight should occur in Lancaster, in the heart of a region with a Mennonite religious tradition based upon love and compassion for one's neighbor. Her reaction was to assemble a dozen friends to see what could be done to improve housing conditions for the low-income people—whites, blacks, and Spanish-speaking individuals—who, for the most part, were crowded into one neglected corner of the city.

The people who attended that meeting in 1967 had almost nothing in common with the people they decided to help, but together, in the next six years, the two sets of people were to bring about startling changes in the living conditions of hundreds of families.

The group at Grace Wenger's house included a math teacher, an industrialist, the president of a shoe company, a lawyer, a nurse, the manager of a poultry-processing firm—all of them Mennonites. The group wanted to do something not only about discrimination but the blight that was overtaking housing in the city's core. They decided that they would form a corporation to buy good housing and rent it at reasonable rates to poor families in need of shelter.

During that first meeting the members of the group took their first step. Each of them wrote down on a slip of paper how much

money he or she was willing to commit at once to bringing about better housing opportunities. The slips added up to $4,650—enough, they reasoned, to organize.

Menno Housing was incorporated in June of 1967. Five months later the first group of stockholders was approved—eighteen people with a total investment of $6,880.

That was the beginning.

By selling over 500 shares of stock, mostly through church appeals, and by borrowing from banks, businesses, and individuals, Menno Housing has managed to create a total investment that exceeds $300,000. Technically the enterprise is a for-profit corporation, but its purpose has never been to make money. As set forth in the corporation's own statement of purpose, Menno is committed to the principle that "our aim is service rather than a high rate of dividends." So it was that Menno tended to operate at a loss until 1972, and it has yet to pay its stockholders a dividend.

In the years since 1967, Menno Housing has bought more than forty houses in Lancaster, paying an average price of $6,000 for each building.

Half of the houses are in the southeast quadrant of the city, where Lancaster's poor and the minorities are clustered. The other half are elsewhere in town, providing homes in previously all-white middle-class neighborhoods for poor whites, blacks, and Spanish-speaking people.

After being given cosmetic retouches and minor repairs as needed, the houses are rented to low-income families at rates ranging from $80 to $110 a month.

While Menno does all it can to assist the tenants in meeting their financial obligations, it does not tolerate any extended non-payment of rent. If a tenant fails repeatedly to pay his rent, he is evicted from the house, for, as Menno has learned, low-income tenants rarely catch up if they fall far behind in making payment.

Although this is a tough line to take, it has helped improve the corporation's ability to sustain itself and grow; the failure of a few tenants to pay their rent was a major factor in Menno's being in the red during the early years.

Menno's executive committee and volunteer staff (there is only one full-time employee), in addition to keeping rents as low as is practically possible, make an effort to keep all of the properties in good repair. Tenants' complaints, as well as their suggestions for improvements, are given prompt attention and careful consideration.

The poorest families in Lancaster cannot afford even the modest rents charged on Menno's housing units. In an effort to help find a solution to this problem, Menno has leased four of its houses to the Lancaster Housing Authority, which in turn rents the houses to needy families on public welfare.

The organizers of Menno came to realize that many people were interested in owning their own homes rather than renting other people's houses. Consequently Menno's executive committee decided in August 1968 to set up a sister corporation that would be geared to home ownership and related problems. It would be chartered as a nonprofit enterprise so as to qualify for assistance from the federal government, as well as to be in a better position to seek volunteer help from the community.

The new enterprise was officially incorporated early in 1969 under the name, Tabor Community Services. (Tabor is the mountain in Palestine where, in biblical times, the Israelites won their freedom from the Canaanites.) Basic to Tabor's total program, says Grace Wenger, has been "the belief that, while public housing projects, multi-family apartment complexes, and low-cost houses for rent may meet immediate needs, blighted urban areas will become attractive again only as individual families are able to own their own homes and experience the satisfaction of living in well-kept houses in communities of which they can be proud."

Operating under the wing of the Model Cities program, Tabor has initiated and maintained three major programs: a home rehabilitation program, a credit and home-buying counseling program, and a maintenance training program.

Under its home rehabilitation program, Tabor has, at last count, rehabilitated twenty-three buildings. Most of the buildings were bought at a minimal cost (around $1,000) from the Lancaster Redevelopment Authority; some in fact had already been condemned for demolition.

The money for renovating—and that usually includes installing a floor, new roof, heating system, plumbing fixtures, and electricity—has come from Model Cities and from a $150,000 line of credit extended in equal parts to Tabor by the city's three major banks. The only security Tabor has put up in return is its word.

Tabor went into debt for nearly the full amount as homes were bought and redone; it whittled down the obligation as they were sold again. Eight of the houses have been sold to the Lancaster Housing Authority for a scattered-site public housing program. The rest have been sold directly to low-income families at prices averaging $14,000–$16,000. One reason why these prices are low is that Tabor draws heavily on volunteer labor in the rehabilitation of rundown houses.

The houses Tabor sells its clients are in good condition. One

A volunteer worker cleans up inside an old house that will eventually be fixed up to match the other residences in Lancaster that have been rehabilitated by Tabor Community Services for sale to low-income families.

of the corporation's principal concerns is to make really sure that each house will be relatively free of serious problems for at least ten years, so that a low-income family won't be faced with sudden and overwhelming repair bills.

Tabor's credit and home-buying counseling service screens potential home owners and helps arrange Federal Housing Administration (FHA) mortgages, a must since local financers will not write conventional mortgages in the low-income section of the city.

In fact, people wishing to become home owners through FHA programs must seek credit counseling and budget training from a licensed agency. Tabor Community Services is the only agency in the Lancaster area licensed by the U.S. Department of Housing and Urban Development to perform this service.

At last count, Tabor had screened some 500 applications, and had made it possible for more than eighty-five families to buy low-cost homes.

Once a home has been purchased, Tabor offers the family continuing advice on budget management, encouraging the residents to put small amounts of money aside for needed repairs. A "compassion fund" of $3,000 has been established to help out in emergencies in which a family may be threatened with foreclosure. The family obtains a loan from a local bank, but Tabor then secures it by buying certificates of deposit equal to or greater than the amount of the loan.

Tabor's maintenance training program, the youngest of the three programs, began when the corporation signed a contract with Model Cities in January 1973 to establish a program for instructing first-time home owners in the fundamentals of routine maintenance and repair. A person skilled in the construction trades visits each family twice a year. The object is to teach the new home owner how to take care of small household problems so that major fix-ups are not necessary. Tabor also gives courses in wall and floor covering, floor care, interior decorating, electricity, window repairs, pest control, and lawn care.

Tabor Community Services has about ten full-time staff members. Like Menno, though, it relies on volunteer and part-time help. Neighborhood residents are recruited to serve as counseling aides, clerical help, and unofficial advance publicity people for their bosses.

"We hired people as much for what they can say to friends and neighbors in their off-hours as for what they can do during the day," says Tabor Community Services' executive secretary. "We have to develop credibility and confidence."

The executive secretary of Tabor (and also of Menno) is Paul A. Leatherman, who once worked in Puerto Rico for the Mennonite Central Committee (MCC), the church's relief agency, before spending thirteen years selling shoes. After coordinating refugee efforts in Vietnam during the mid-60s, he rejoined the MCC and now directs volunteer work throughout the United States and Canada, in addition to taking care of his Menno/Tabor responsibilities.

Tabor's director is the Reverend Daniel Sensenig, who gave up a refrigerator dealership for the Mennonite ministry some thirty years ago. Following twenty-three years of mission duties in Ethiopia, he returned to the United States to join Tabor.

A single executive committee oversees the activities of both Menno and Tabor. It consists of Leatherman, Sensenig, Wenger, and other Mennonite leaders, all dedicated to giving as much time as possible to this venture.

Whatever their interest in seeing the two corporations expand, the leaders of Menno and Tabor are careful about being able to keep all activities on a practical scale. "We tried to do things in a small way, on a manageable basis," Leatherman explains. "It's 40 homes we're renting, and not 400; 20 homes we've rehabbed, and not 200. In retrospect we feel good about that."

Menno Housing and Tabor Community Services have together undertaken an unusual project in a poverty pocket in the Welsh Mountains in eastern Lancaster County. In 1971, Menno Housing formed a special Welsh Mountains committee. The first step was to find better housing for two families—fourteen children and three adults—who were living together in an old restaurant, which had no plumbing and a leaky roof. A decision was made to build two new three-bedroom homes on separate lots and rent them to the families.

The New Holland Mennonite Church adopted the construction of the two homes as a project and mustered over 1,400 hours in volunteer labor and $7,500 in contributions. Over 30 area businesses gave a total of more than $4,000 in materials, appliances, and furniture. The families moved in during November 1971.

In 1972, Menno Housing was approached by the Community Action Program (CAP) of Lancaster County to build a new medical clinic in the Welsh Mountains. A 12,000-square-foot building was constructed in a wooded area by July of 1972. The cost was $27,750. Menno Housing is not involved in the operation of the clinic, staffed by a registered nurse and local doctors, but it is the landlord and as such it leases the building to the CAP.

Despite its accomplishments, the tandem of Menno and Tabor has seen a number of dark days over the past six years.

One plan failed, for example. That was a training program for apprentices in the building trades, organized by Tabor through Model Cities. More than thirty young men from the impoverished southeastern part of the city went through the four-month course in 1972 and early 1973, but those later placed in permanent jobs soon quit.

"We had conflicting priorities," says Paul Leatherman. "We were under pressure to rehabilitate houses faster" (as many as twenty-five a year, although Tabor never finished more than twelve in as many months). "We also weren't satisfied that we had enough administrative ability to carry out the training."

Another difficulty for Menno/Tabor has been that volunteer labor, as enthusiastic as it can be, has certain drawbacks. The unpredictable availability of free help has made it difficult to schedule work with any degree of regularity. So it has been hard at times to find a group with several months' time to devote to the total restoration of a house.

Recently, since 1973, Tabor has been confronted with a number of funding difficulties. Tabor's leaders were never totally comfortable with a dependence on yearly refunding of Model Cities projects. One-year budgets, they decided, were an impediment to thoughtful, long-range planning. "We held our breath when contracts expired," says Daniel Sensenig.

As 1974 began, Tabor's funding had run out. Tabor is now seeking support from local business and industry. And if Tabor's history means anything, the help will materialize. The nonprofit corporation, for example, has the support of the city's redevelopment authority, which remains eager to enlist private business in the rehabilitation of Lancaster's slums.

More important, perhaps, is the fact that the attitude of the low-income people of Lancaster is not the same as it was before the advent of Menno and Tabor. If they are listened to, then Tabor won't be allowed to wither away.

"Before this, if people went to buy a home they felt they were being taken," asserts one staff member. "The people trust us. They think they need us."

"The main benefit," Paul Leatherman feels, "is the growth in [the people's] self-worth. Their credit gets straightened out, they can go to the bank and borrow. They are home owners for the first time. They get the feeling that they are somebody. And that someone cares about them."

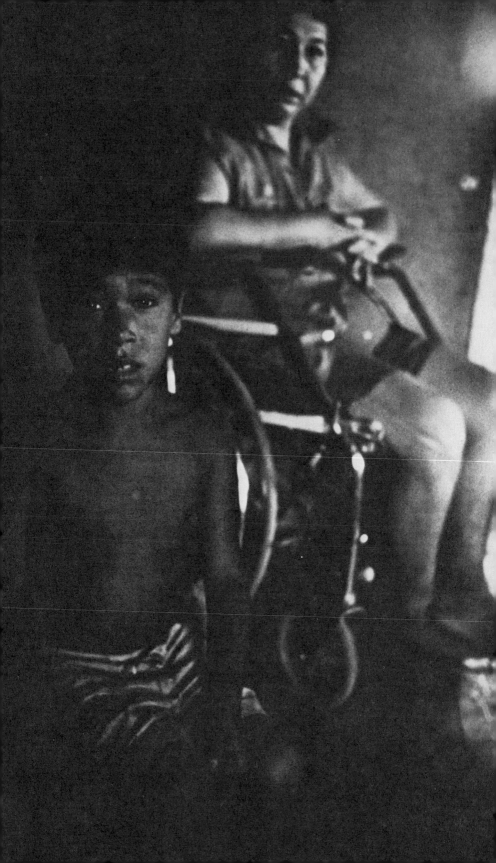

CHAPTER 5

Social Services

There is no less of a need for social services in the low-income communities of America than there is in the middle- and upper-income areas. But whereas affluent America is served by a great variety of public and private social service organizations, disadvantaged America is saddled with social institutions that often reinforce rather than reduce its condition of need, and that offer services generally limited in both quality and scope.

Alternatives to government social services are now being developed throughout the country, as communities and neighborhoods initiate their own self-help programs to meet local needs.

Some of these projects are broad-based enterprises designed to deal with the entire spectrum of community problems, while others concentrate on providing assistance in a particular category or to a specific subgroup. The multi-service program operated by a neighborhood church, for instance, stands ready to assist any resident who needs immediate emergency help. Other programs feed a hungry family or give aid and comfort to people stranded in a strange city. And there are various projects aimed principally in aiding the elderly, children under 18 years of age, households headed by women, and individuals who are not part of family units.

All of these self-help projects take their strength from being community enterprises determining community needs and working out acceptable solutions. They are flexible enough to dispense social services as they are needed, without forcing the recipients to meet rigid rules of eligibility that tend to exclude rather than include people in need. And they use their resources to not only assist local residents directly but also to assist them in finding their way through the maze of government agencies and regulations to the point where they can reap the benefits of public assistance.

Community social services projects represent an effort to humanize the business of helping others and being helped by others, and they offer disadvantaged people a chance to lead lives of dignity and self-fulfillment.

*We just want to change the system that throws . . .
[handicapped] people on the junk heap. Our people
are now learning to use community resources in
solving their problems and to help others with
common problems. But the real reason why this
thing has worked is that people are willing to try.*

People United for Self-Help

Phoenix, Arizona

The hot Arizona sun is taking its customary toll of men and machinery, as the secondhand tractor strains to pull its load and the workers bend tired backs to their work. Like the battered, grinding tractor, the people themselves are secondhand. They are all handicapped—cast-offs from society. The usual condition of such people is unemployment, despair, and hopelessness. But the condition of these particular fieldworkers is different. Not only are they employed but they work with a willingness that belies the tedium and hardship of harvesting turnips.

The difference stems from the fact that this is a project of PUSH.

The people laboring in the nine-acre turnip field are all members of PUSH (People United for Self Help), and, as with the rest of their projects, they are determined to make this one work.

PUSH is the creation of Barbara Norton, who, as a Salvation Army worker, made the painful discovery one fall day in 1970 that even charity discriminates. She found out that various government agencies were turning away partially disabled people who were willing and determined to work. "Many of the agencies," she recalls, "ostensibly were structured to help handicapped people. Instead, they screened them out. What they didn't understand—or at least deal with—was that a 50-year-old man still has fifteen good years ahead of him, if you can just help him."

Working at the Salvation Army, she began to take an active interest in the welfare of disabled people. Yet she quickly discovered she had no means of helping them beyond offering understanding and politeness.

But, as she says, "I never could say, 'better luck next time'."

So, on December 20, 1970, Barbara Norton left the Salvation

The turnip harvest provides PUSH with both food and a cash crop.

Army and founded the Norton "brigade"—PUSH.

"As I got more and more involved," she explains, "I discovered that handicapped people live in a state of prolonged emergency every day." She learned that the disabled are the unlucky possessors of a combination of poor diet, poor money management, poor education—and very poor employment potential. What is more, in Barbara Norton's words:

"They have problems getting medical attention. Many are weeded out of rehabilitation programs by lack of education or poor health.

"When the head of the household is disabled, the family suffers from tension between the man and his hard-pressed wife. They may lose their house or get behind in rent. The car may break down, the kids may eventually drop out of school. The father himself, often used to hard labor, may now be restricted to light work.

"But what if he is undereducated, as many of these people are? What kind of 'light work' is open to him?"

The fathers and their families undergo physical and psychological deterioration, and in many cases the father finally leaves his family.

Barbara Norton believes that the rejection of the pleas for help of disabled people are a result of the "belief of Congress and many agencies that people would rather sit at home and draw checks than work."

"This is a myth," she says. "All these men have good, substantial work records. Chances are one thousand to one they would rather work than draw welfare."

Consequently the first priority of PUSH was jobs. Because of the difficulty in finding suitable jobs, PUSH began by creating its own—baking, selling donated fruit and vegetables, home repair, just about anything. Next, with a $1,350 donation from the Lutheran Social Ministry of Arizona, PUSH bought a freezer, stove, pots, pans, and dishes, and used them to start a catering service in an abandoned farmhouse.

After that, PUSH ventured into the field of consumer education. The women learned how to balance a grocery store cash register. During the summer a full-time nutritionist lectured the women on proper diet and food-buying techniques. (Many of the women are obese and/or have diabetes—the nutritionist got them started on diets that were sound and that served their medical needs as well.)

Adult education followed consumer education. Since many handicapped people did not have a formal education, Barbara Norton started an intensive English and mathematics program in the donated back room of a doctor's office.

Lack of fluency in English had been a major obstacle for many people. When Santiago, for example, had first applied for welfare after suffering a serious back injury that kept him out of work, no one at the welfare agency spoke Spanish. Consequently, in a tragic bureaucratic bungle, they referred him for mental counseling. Instead he came to PUSH. He enrolled in school and is now reading English on the fifth-grade level. He is also working again, and during his spare hours he helps to till the PUSH acreage.

The school is successful. Consider the case of Willie, a 35-year-old disabled worker with a perforated ulcer, who looks twenty years older than he actually is. He was illiterate before PUSH. Now he is reading on the sixth-grade level after only four months!

School is taught by Roger Rohrbach, a 28-year-old graduate of the University of Wisconsin. "They are not just a bunch of cripples here," says Rohrbach. "They are eager to learn and to work. And they learn well from each other."

With the assistance of Legal Aid attorneys, PUSH was incorporated in January of 1971. Soon after that, the organization began expanding its programs to include up to fifty families. By April of 1971 the group was ready to work on the city-donated land. With only a few hoes and some donated seeds, they planted turnips, black-eyed peas, tomatoes—and a few surprises. When it was time to harvest their crops, what they didn't need they donated to other poor people.

When local government agencies saw the work PUSH was doing, there was some jealousy. "We were upset at first," says one Phoenix poverty worker, "that they were able to do things we were not. But as we watched them grow, we began to learn that perhaps we had been playing an adversary role with the disabled."

As PUSH continued to expand, Barbara Norton continued to discover lingering problems that served to further handicap the disabled. Many of the people were on welfare, and they had serious difficulty budgeting money that was insufficient to begin with. And the power company had a questionable policy of turning off the electricity first and asking questions later. Consequently Barbara Norton established a $2,500 revolving fund. Now, families late in paying their electricity bills can obtain one-month extensions.

The $2,500 represents part of a number of grants the project has received—most of the money being allocated for continuing education programs. (The U.S. Catholic Conference's Campaign for Human Development, for example, awarded the project a $16,300 grant in December 1972. In 1973 the United Way fund gave 2 percent of its total budget to PUSH; the following year it raised the amount to 4 percent.

In June 1973 the youth groups of the Phoenix Church of Jesus Christ of Latter-Day Saints donated a $5,000 International tractor to PUSH. And thanks to PUSHcarts (metal carts built from an $850 grant from IBM—the carts are used for selling the fruits and vegetables grown in the PUSH field), Barbara Norton's idea has now become virtually self-sustaining.

"We just want to change the system" she says, "that throws these people on the junk heap. Our people are now learning to use community resources in solving their problems and to help others with common problems. But the real reason why this thing has worked is that people are willing to try."

When you can't get what you need, you make do
with what you can get. . . . Only never stop
bugging the power structure for more.

Action House

Detroit, Michigan

The passerby's impression says it's an abandoned store. Except for a decorative paint job and a sign over the front door, it could be just another vacant shell in Detroit's inner city.

But to many of the 16,000 Detroiters who live in the one-square-mile area known as the Gartiot-Van Dyke neighborhood, this vacant shell is a vital reminder that someone still cares. It's called Action House, and it's one of the few places that people in this part of Detroit can come for recreation, education, or advice in meeting personal problems.

The area served by Action House is a textbook example of the challenges faced by those working to prevent America's large industrial cities from deteriorating.

Twenty-five years ago the Gratiot-Van Dyke area of Detroit was a residential neighborhood where most families lived on steady, middle-class incomes derived from blue-collar jobs, office work, or shopkeeping. A majority of its residents were whites (both native Detroiters and European immigrants), with some blacks up from the South.

A quarter-century has brought substantial change. The population is now predominately poor and predominately black. It is also disproportionately young, with close to half of all the residents of the area being under 21 years of age.

Urban blight and all of its attendant problems have settled on the Gratiot-Van Dyke neighborhood, as they have on other inner-city areas around the country. But Gratiot-Van Dyke also suffers from being physically isolated from the rest of its parent city. The combination of Detroit City Airport, a belt of light industrial plants, and major thoroughfares form an almost triangular wall that shuts off the area from what would otherwise be adjoining neighborhoods.

Like many of the community service projects in Detroit, Action House has its roots in the concern for neighborhood preservation that developed in the city following the 1967 civil disturbances.

It was during the 1967 tragedy that Lizz Haskell, a black woman, was asked by some white friends if she could help bring together people from the neighborhood for some meetings to discuss what could be done to protect Gratiot-Van Dyke from the vandalism that was hitting other areas. Mrs. Haskell responded by setting up several such meetings, which were attended by people from the suburbs as well as the neighborhood itself, together with staff aides from the mayor's office and representatives of other political leaders. The informal program, known as Operation Friendship, Understanding, and Peace, was instrumental in maintaining neighborhood stability.

One concern repeatedly voiced at those meetings was the neighborhood's almost total lack of places where residents could get together. This was especially true for the young people, for in the entire one-square-mile that constitutes Gratiot-Van Dyke there is only one playfield, a stamp-sized lot for small children.

Lizz Haskell and others who had initiated the program decided to mobilize this newly awakened community spirit behind a campaign to get a community center for the neighborhood.

This meant trying to raise funds from any and all possible sources—community renewal agencies, social service organizations, and so forth. For more than six months, the neighborhood leaders labored to write a formal proposal that would document the problems, define the objectives, and detail the programs they wanted to initiate, and that would identify the kinds of support these would require. Undertaking this proposal was a big step for its authors, in that most of them had had only minimal formal education. Developing and setting down their ideas and suggestions in a concise, orderly fashion was a challenge—one on which they spent many long days and nights. By the fall of 1968 they had completed a 45-page document, complete with letters of endorsement and support from clergymen, political figures, and others who were familiar with the needs of the Gratiot-Van Dyke area.

Then came the agonizing wait while various potential sources of funds considered their proposal. In the meantime, though, they had the satisfaction of formally incorporating as Action House and of being designated as a tax-free organization.

The financial response to Action House's proposal was disappointingly limited, so the organizers redoubled their efforts. But after weeks of meetings, appeals, and presentations to a variety of organizations, it became apparent that funding was not available for the program the people of Action House wanted to start.

It was then that Lizz Haskell and her fellow organizers decided to change tactics and make do financially with whatever they could get.

Among the sites suggested for the center was a boarded-up grocery store. But it was estimated that $67,500 would be needed to purchase the building and to renovate it if Action House was to have a truly suitable community center. Such an outlay seemed impossible, in that all of Action House's appeals to date had produced barely a tenth of that sum.

So Lizz Haskell and her husband decided to take action on their own. They bought the building and told the other Action House leaders that it was available as a community center if enough people would volunteer to help fix it up, equip it, and assist in running the programs.

Since that time, the little grocery store has truly become a focal point for residents of the entire neighborhood. In the words of a song by Lizz Haskell, Action House is "where the Action is."

Bill Peronneau

Many of the Action House programs are aimed at keeping young people off the streets and involved in constructive, personality-developing activities. Most of these programs take place in summer, when youngsters have ample free time.

Trips are among the most popular youth activities. Whenever the Action House volunteers can get city buses or other donated transportation, they arrange an excursion. Trips have been made to the zoo, to museums, to the beaches, to ball games—to places that many Detroit-area youngsters routinely visit but that few from the Action House neighborhood usually have a chance to go to.

While trips away are a treat, Action House itself is the scene of many popular programs geared to the young people. Parties are frequent. Sometimes they are just a spontaneous idea—the roping-off of a street for a summer frolic, for example. Others are special occasions, like the Christmas parties where gifts collected by Action House are distributed to the needy.

There's educational activity, too. Lizz Haskell (who studied under one of America's greatest dancers and choreographers, Martha Graham) has set up several dance classes for preteenagers and teenagers. Neighborhood people have been recruited to teach sewing, arts and crafts, and other subjects. And from time to time, speakers are brought in from government and social service agencies to discuss current problems and programs with both young and older residents of the neighborhood.

Above all, perhaps, Action House is a place where anyone in the community can come for help. The files hold numerous letters from people who have found Action House invaluable in times of trouble—it may be an elderly lady who needs transportation to the hospital for an eye operation, a concerned mother calling to ask help in finding a lost child, a teenager wanting advice about a job, or a group of homeowners needing assistance to oppose substandard construction proposed for their block.

They are all welcome at Action House.

Some of the most important events, say residents, have been just plain rap sessions. These encounters provide an opportunity for blacks and whites, young and old, to get together on neutral ground and discuss problems, air their complaints, and start to move toward, instead of away from, each other.

This reputation as a force for building community "friendship, understanding, and peace" is, perhaps, the finest achievement of Action House. And there are many people who believe that without Action House the Gratiot-Van Dyke area would have much worse problems of crime, delinquency, racial disharmony, and general deterioration than admittedly it has.

An abandoned store? Maybe it is. But as in other aspects of modern life, surfaces can be deceiving. The facade of Action House is humble, but its patrons have created something worthwhile in their community, and they have no intention of letting it die.

"Sure, we've got problems," says Lizz Haskell. "Who doesn't? When you can't get what you need, you make do with what you can get." A short pause produces a laugh.

"Only never stop bugging the power structure for more."

The speeding car missed George. But Pedro was not as fortunate. The impact flung him to the pavement, fracturing his right leg. Wasn't there a better place for them to play after school?

Centro Mater

Miami, Florida

An elevated overpass arching high overhead casts a morning shadow on a small frame house in Little Havana. A nun walks swiftly to the door, peering through trifocals. She is in a hurry. She is always in a hurry.

A sign on the house says "Centro Mater," and in Spanish there is an explanation: "Al Servicio De La Juventud."

Five years ago there was another sign on the house: "Condemned." The building had been abandoned. The roof leaked. Someone had yanked out the floorboards for lumber.

This was a poor neighborhood in Little Havana, where living conditions were going from bad to worse—where prostitutes walked the streets, muggers made a good living, and drugs and pushers weren't hard to find.

It was no place to raise children. Yet, then as now, children lived there—children mostly of Cuban heritage and mostly from low-income families.

Conditions in the neighborhood have improved somewhat since then, at least for the local children. They now have Centro Mater. And they have Sister Margarita A. Miranda, more affectionately known as Mother Miranda.

Centro Mater is an after-school community center for the children of working parents. From 2 p.m. to 6:30 p.m. each afternoon Centro Mater vibrates, as scores of Cuban youngsters aged 6 to 17 descend upon it in high spirits and youthful enthusiasm. Two adjacent portable schoolhouses and the nearby Meyers Senior Center also vibrate, in that they take the community center's overflow; one small frame house, the staff has learned, cannot hold 300 young people.

Under the firm but friendly guidance of some twenty-five adult volunteers, the youngsters spend their time playing games, reading, socializing, and learning. They learn arts and crafts, guitar, typing, sewing and other skills. Instruction is given in both Spanish and English, for Centro Mater is truly bilingual—a heritage preserved, yet an adopted language accepted.

Not all of Centro Mater's activities take place inside. Yellow school buses rumble off for tours of the Crandon Park Zoo, the Planetarium-Museum of Science, the Vizcaya estate, the Monkey Jungle, the Parrot Jungle, a bottling plant, newspaper offices, and the ocean beaches.

The buses come free, for Mother Miranda has spoken to the gentlemen who own the bus company. She speaks to everyone and she does indeed get things done—for God, as she says, and for the youngsters of Centro Mater.

Mother Miranda was born in Havana some sixty-odd years ago, the daughter of the president of the Havana Tobacco Company. After earning a doctorate in education at the University of Havana in 1948, she entered a convent in France. Four years later she returned to Cuba, where she taught art, history, philosophy, religion, and French in various well-to-do private schools.

In 1959, the year that Fidel Castro seized power, Mother Miranda left Cuba—moving first to Puerto Rico and then to Mexico, where she taught philosophy and literature at the junior college level. Six years later she was transferred to Maryville College, in St. Louis, where she served as chairwoman of the department of Spanish.

But the academic life eventually took its toll. By 1968 she had begun to question herself. Couldn't she do something more useful than teach earnest American college girls the skills of a foreign language?

She asked her superiors for permission to transfer to Miami. They consented, assigning her to the Carrolton School for Girls in Miami. She taught there on a part-time basis, while exploring social conditions in Miami and other parts of Florida. She inspected the migrant labor camps on the land-rich winter farms in south Florida. She investigated the hospitals. She visited Miami's Little Havana.

As much as she was moved by the plight of other disadvantaged groups, she felt her conscience touched most by the sad condition of Miami's Cuban community. Tens of thousands of people—her people—had fled from Castro's Cuba to take refuge in the United States, and many of them had arrived with little or nothing in the way of money, material possessions, knowledge of English, or skills for which there was a ready market in a foreign land. It was these people, Mother Miranda believed, who were

Centro Mater's playground keeps kids busy after school.

confronted with the greatest problems and who were receiving the least amount of outside assistance.

But what could she do?

She was particularly interested in the welfare of the community's young people. She noticed that in many cases both parents in Little Havana families held jobs, which meant that a lot of school-aged children were left unsupervised after school hours. Not surprisingly the kids took to the streets—but plainly the streets were not a proper place for them.

As she did not have any resources that would enable her to get the youngsters off the streets, Mother Miranda began her project by simply playing with the children herself—in the streets.

In the meantime she also began looking for assistance that would enable her to conduct the program in some other, less public location. She turned to the people of Miami's Cuban refugee population, including some of her former students from Havana. She spoke to parent-teachers' associations, and she interviewed a great many parents by going from door to door.

Before long she had a squad of volunteers to help her. Subsequently she requested and received permission from the principal of Ada Merritt Junior High School to use a classroom and the school grounds after school hours. And she also found space available at the Meyers Senior Center, where she started classes in typing and sewing.

By the end of 1969 the Miami archdiocese's Catholic Service Bureau had begun a system of matching funds with Mother Miranda's project. The volunteers raised their portion by holding rummage sales and soliciting donations from people and businesses throughout the city.

But they still did not have a place of their own. And the need became increasingly apparent.

There was, for example, the day a car sped west on S.W. Fifth Street. A ball rolled into the street, closely followed by two boys, George Perez, 7, and Pedro Gonzalez, 8.

The speeding car missed George. Put Pedro was not as fortunate. The impact flung him to the pavement, fracturing his right leg.

Wasn't there a better place for them to play after school?

It was late in 1969 that Mother Miranda found the condemned house at 345 S.W. Fourth Street, windows out, surrounded by weeds among the palms and pines. She traced the ownership to Plato Cox, president of Auto Marine Engineers. He had grown up there, close to the south bank of the Miami River.

Mother Miranda visited him and put her proposal to, as she later put it, "this very nice Protestant gentleman."

"Sister," he responded, "If you can keep one child off the streets you can use my property." He leased the house to her for $1 a year.

Now it was a question of putting the house in good condition. Undaunted, Mother Miranda went out and found plumbers, electricians, carpenters, and painters—both amateurs and professionals—who were willing to labor for love of the church; more precisely, perhaps, they were willing to labor for the good of a community when confronted by a persuasive, arm-twisting nun. And it was the same energetic person who convinced local service clubs and businesses to contribute equipment and supplies for the center.

The archdiocese then decided it would buy an adjacent lot and donate it to the center. Subsequently the Dade County school board trucked in two portable schoolhouses to be erected there on foundations supplied by a local industrial firm.

Over the years since it was founded, Centro Mater has become more than an after-school center. During the summer, for example, the center is turned into an all-day summer camp. Centro

Mater also has a choir that sings at local nursing homes. It runs a thrift shop for the convenience of the neighborhood. And it provides informal counseling for just about anyone who comes there in need.

But finding enough money to keep itself going is a recurrent problem at Centro Mater.

For those who can afford it, the cost of participating in the center's programs is a dollar a month. But no one says anything about the dollar when it isn't offered.

Mother Miranda has prevailed upon various service clubs, churches, and charitable organizations in the Miami Latin community to help meet expenses.

The center's major source of funds comes from the staging of an annual spring celebration called Gran Fiesta Guajira del Centro Mater.

The fiesta's attractions include an art auction, with Cuban artists donating their works for sale. And there is a fine selection of Latin food. Seven booths representing the six provinces of Cuba and the Isle of Pines sell such culinary delights as *tortica de moron* (a sugar cookie), *pan con lechon* (pork sandwich), and *guarapo* (sugarcane juice). (In 1973 there was also a booth selling certain non-Cuban foods: ice cream and hot dogs.)

In April 1973, Mother Miranda and a group of neighborhood children attended a meeting of the city commission. It pleased them greatly when the commissioners voted unanimously to buy a five-acre tract of land along the south bank of the Miami River in order to create a community park—the first—for Miami's Latin areas.

Although the park included the present site of Centro Mater, it seemed very likely that the center would be allowed to stay there. There was even said to be a chance that the center would be given a new home within the park so it could serve as a full-fledged community center for all of Little Havana.

Subsequently the people of Miami took sides on the park and center issue, some opposing and some supporting the idea. As a result the issue was still unresolved a year later.

On the same day that the city commissioners finally voted for the park, a formal luncheon was held at a downtown Miami hotel to honor Dade County's outstanding personalities of 1972.

And when the woman of the year came forward to accept her award, the chairman spoke in glowing terms of "the little nun who gets things done"—"the woman who saved 2,000 children from the dangers of the streets."

*Within a year it became apparent that it was up to
the residents of the neighborhood to ensure that
there would be continuity of the project.*

The Organization of People
Engaged in the Neighborhood

Philadelphia, Pennsylvania

They planned a big rock music festival to chase the fund-raising blues. They rented a car, increased the staff, spent money on advertising. They were certain they'd make $200,000.

But the heralded event never came off. Instead, this organization which provided essential services to a neighborhood of 45,000 people in a bleak section of north Philadelphia was plunged into bankruptcy.

For a time it looked like the end of the Organization of People Engaged in the Neighborhood (OPEN). It seemed that all the hard work in building up OPEN's services over a six-year period since 1966 would be swept away—the learning center, the social services program, the summer camp, the food-buying cooperative, the job-training program, and the credit union.

By the end of June 1972 there was no money for wages, so the staff was laid off. OPEN's programs were curtailed. The board of directors even decided to cancel the annual contributions it had been receiving.

"We wanted to be honest with our donors," says Edward J. McNichol, who has since taken over as executive director. "It was the only thing to do while we tried to straighten out the mess."

This policy has paid off, for OPEN has made a complete recovery from the catastrophe of two years ago. In the process it has learned two lessons valuable to all self-help enterprises: (1) never leap into big-time fund-raising promotions without the proper preparation and know-how, and (2) never give up if there's even a slight chance to recover.

OPEN had its beginnings in a remedial-reading program for neighborhood children started by Father Thomas Craven of St. Edward's Church. He had checked the records of youngsters in the parish situated a few miles north of Philadelphia's city hall and found that most of the students were well below the reading norms for all students in the city and the county.

He interested an ex-nun, Toni Tracey, in setting up a remedial-reading program. Soon, through friends asking friends, a small corps of teachers and volunteers, many of them suburbanites, came regularly to teach at the church.

Within a year it became apparent that it was up to the residents of the neighborhood to ensure that there would be continuity of the project. So it was that the idea of a community organization was born.

The idea became fact when Toni Tracey and several residents established the Organization of People Engaged in the Neighborhood, which was duly incorporated as a nonprofit enterprise.

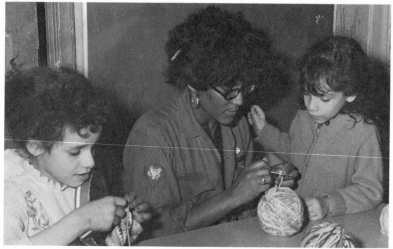

Crochet lessons intrigue youngsters at OPEN's learning center.

"The neighborhood didn't have a name then," says Toni Tracey. "Now it's called the OPEN neighborhood."

Half of the 45,000 residents of the 80-block area that makes up the OPEN neighborhood are black, and most of the rest are Puerto Rican. At least 70 percent of the people are on welfare, and nearly 50 percent are under 20 years of age. Like most urban low-income areas, the neighborhood has long lacked adequate municipal services and facilities in the fields of education, recreation, housing, employment, and so forth.

In the years between 1967 and 1971, OPEN initiated a broad array of programs, all geared to the OPEN neighborhood's needs.

Using a building donated to it by St. Joseph's College and

renovated by volunteers, OPEN started a learning center. In addition to the remedial-reading program, OPEN began to offer preschool training for 4- and 5-year-olds (similar to the Head Start program), as well as a high school diploma program for adults.

The following year, 1969, OPEN added another educational program—after-school tutoring, which was aimed at students aged 6 to 12 who were not doing well in school but who clearly had the potential to succeed.

One of OPEN's first programs was its summer day camp, which was intended to give neighborhood children a week-long summer vacation out of the area. The program, for youngsters aged 6 to 12, made use of facilities at such places as Villanova University, Rosemont College, Immaculata College, Waldron Academy, Cabrini College, and School of the Holy Child, all of them located in the suburbs, with extensive lawns, creeks, woods, and swimming facilities. Children attended the camps five days a week, from 9 a.m. to 3:30 p.m. Buses from the school district and private sources provided the needed transportation.

The agency also set up a recreation program for youngsters aged 6 to 16, under which the children were taken to parades, live theater (when free tickets were available), pools for swimming, movies, dances, and so forth.

Operating in an area where most residents are tenants rather than home owners, OPEN decided in 1969 to set up the North Tenant Council. The council was intended to handle issues involving landlords, including the local public housing authority.

Tenants also received assistance from OPEN's separate casework program, which was established to provide such services as consumer education, family counseling, legal aid, and English-Spanish translation for Spanish-speaking people trying to deal with public agencies and officials.

Concerned about nutrition in the OPEN neighborhood, the organization mounted a food program in 1968 to ensure the distribution of staples to individuals or families faced with emergencies, such as loss or theft of welfare check, robbery, fire, and eviction. By 1971 a number of local families were ready to form a food-buying cooperative to deal directly with wholesalers and distributors for better prices.

OPEN also became active in the employment field. For several years it maintained a very successful job-training program in the computer career field. The course was six months long, given two nights a week, and held at various locations in the Philadelphia area. It produced forty-five graduates, of whom thirty-four were placed in jobs that paid starting salaries of $95 per week.

At the other end of the job ladder, OPEN joined with Concilio, a Puerto Rican self-help group in the neighborhood, to train and place youngsters in various summer jobs, usually positions involving school maintenance.

One of OPEN's most successful programs was the credit union it took over from St. Edward's Church. Despite fluctuations in the level of deposits, the credit union helped bring the savings habit—and the skills of family budgeting—to the OPEN neighborhood. It proved to be so successful a project that OPEN spun it off as a separate activity with its own board of directors.

By early 1971 the organization had fifteen full- and part-time employees, including its first executive director, and an annual budget of $25,000. Local businessmen and members of VISTA (Volunteers in Service to America) were contributing heavily to the growing enterprise.

But as the organization grew, so did the difficulty of obtaining sufficient funds. It was hard work to keep conducting raffles, dinners, contests, and an annual Christmas toy sale. And approaching large private donors was time-consuming and not always fruitful. Assessing the funding situation in 1971, the OPEN board of directors decided to gamble on the rock music festival to achieve financial independence.

It proved to be a terrible error, born of inexperience. Promotional expenses for the project wiped out OPEN. OPEN's other liabilities mounted rapidly, and liens were placed against OPEN's properties.

OPEN's board of directors decided to seek an executive director, and approached Edward McNichol, who had become involved in OPEN's computer training program in 1968 and was now director of the data division of the Delaware Valley Regional Planning Commission. McNichol accepted (although he also arranged to continue his commission job on a part-time basis), and he moved his family into a house in the OPEN neighborhood.

The road back for OPEN wasn't easy. A repayment schedule was negotiated with OPEN's creditors. McNichol and other members of the board launched a series of personal meetings with past major donors. Gradually they reestablished the trust and confidence of the community of givers. By 1974, OPEN was debt-free and even had $24,000 in the bank. What is more, a continuing source of revenue was assured, and OPEN's programs were flourishing again.

Not all of the programs were retained, though, for the organization had wisely decided not to revive its marginal programs (such

Jerry Miller

OPEN volunteers weigh produce for members of the food co-op.

as a thrift store), but to concentrate on the learning center, summer camp, food distribution, and social services.

If anything, the 1972 crisis and its aftermath have brought the neighborhood people closer together. OPEN's president, Jerry C. Dean Sr., for example, notes that the blacks and Puerto Ricans, once indifferent or hostile to one another, have given up their occasional gang wars. They are now beginning to work out fair arrangements regarding representation on OPEN's board of directors, as well as means of sharing the organization's services. He adds, "I like to believe that people prefer seeking solutions to problems this way."

They come to town looking for work and have only a limited amount of money. It lasts them maybe two or three weeks. If they don't find employment in this time, they don't know where to turn.

The Portland
American Indian Center

Portland, Oregon

Roast bobcat, stewed beaver, and stewed salmon eyes are on the menu, along with wapatos, bitterroot, bannock bread, and huckleberry jello. And there is usually a turnaway crowd at $10 a plate.

This is the annual All Indian Dinner held each March in Portland's town hall. The diners not only sample the great variety of Indian delicacies but also learn about the sacramental lore of sharing food together and the meaning of the traditional ways of Indian dress and handicrafts, and watch ancient dances performed by members of one or more of the fifty tribes in the area.

The annual dinner is the chief event held by the Portland American Indian Center (PAIC) to finance a proposed $400,000 multipurpose center that would enable the PAIC to expand its current programs for helping Indians coming to live in the Portland area.

Edward "Bud" Butcher, president of the PAIC, is particularly concerned about assisting the Indians who have recently left the reservations. These are the people who need the most help in making a smooth transition to the stepped-up pace of urban life.

"This is a lost group of people," says Butcher, a non-reservation Indian of Cheyenne heritage and president of the Triangle Milling Company. "They have nowhere to turn for counseling and help once they leave the reservation. They cannot go back for aid from the federal government.

"They come to town looking for work and have only a limited amount of money. It lasts them maybe two or three weeks. If they don't find employment in this time, they don't know where to turn. And it hurts their pride to ask for help."

One of the younger dancers at the Rose Festival Pow Wow and Encampment, which is held each June in Portland's Delta Park ▶

As Butcher points out, "There are so many ways in which a center could help them—a place where they could go for emergency food supplies, counseling, medical advice, and to find someone who knows and understands their problems."

Several Indians are employed by Butcher's company, and he is aware of the difficulties they have in adjusting to business work schedules.

"They run at a relaxed speed on the reservation, where their work habits are very different," he explains. "We kid about 'Indian time,' but its true. If it doesn't get done today, it will get done tomorrow. But when they come to town, the pace is changed."

Once the Indians adjust to city life, though, they prove to have, as Butcher says, "a very high learning curve and the ability to out-work others."

The problems facing reservation-reared Indians in urban Portland are more complicated than simply adjusting to a new work environment. The new arrivals have to contend with having stepped into another world and another century.

Consequently the PAIC tries to provide a full range of programs and services dealing with all aspects of city life. There are, for example, tutorial programs for elementary, secondary, and college-level students, as well as remedial classes for adults.

The PAIC operates a number of basic referral services aimed at assisting people in finding jobs, housing, and medical care. It also runs its own emergency medical program and day care program, as well as classes in family health education. (There is also a separate facility for the treatment and rehabilitation of alcoholics.)

Skill-oriented programs at the center include classes in arts and crafts, cooking, and homemaking. The PAIC also works with young people, providing them with a variety of programs and recreational opportunities.

The Portland American Indian Center was founded in 1959 by a group of Indians who, having made the adjustment to modern urban life, felt it was important to do something for their fellow Indians. Their initial aim was to provide counseling and guidance, in that they felt a preventive approach could help many Indians steer clear of the pitfalls of city life. Later they added educational, vocational, and recreational programs, and so forth.

The center was incorporated as a nonprofit organization in 1970, in the hope that, as Butcher says, "it would be run a little more like a business."

The PAIC currently has 1,000 members, out of the estimated 4,500–7,000 Indians living in the Portland metropolitan area.

The center is presently located in a section of Bud Butcher's factory, where the available space is somewhat limited. Nevertheless the PAIC makes do, just as it does with an all-volunteer staff and a $15,000-a-year budget.

To meet its expenses the PAIC engages in a variety of fund-raising activities. The most important of these is the Rose Festival Pow Wow and Encampment, which is held over a three-day period in June during Portland's annual civic celebration.

This is as much an occasion for Indians from around the Pacific Northwest to get together as it is for the PAIC to raise funds from the general public. Between four hundred and five hundred Indians—many of them from reservations—converge on Portland's Delta Park, where they live in teepees for the duration of the celebration. The chief attractions for non-Indians are the ceremonial dances and songfests, plus crafts and foods for sale.

The June powwow is a popular event. "Depending on the weather," says Butcher, "we have 7,000—10,000 admissions."

At $1.50 a person, that provides the PAIC with a considerable portion of its annual budget, even after expenses.

The PAIC also stages a "mini-powwow" in April in order to raise additional funds. "We have bingo games and stick games to raise money," says Butcher. "One member teaches beading classes, and the small fee goes to the center. Booths are set up at flea markets to sell artifacts the ladies make."

The PAIC is also doing what it can to raise money for what Butcher hopes will be the Portland Indian Urban Center. A total of $400,000 is needed, and Butcher estimates that they have to have a minimum of $200,000 before construction can start. There is currently $10,000 in the building fund.

Aside from the proceeds from the All Indian Dinner, the building fund receives small donations from a variety of sources. For example, there is a group of young Indians that demonstrates Indian dances and handicrafts at schools. "There's hardly a school in the Portland area that hasn't had one," says Butcher. "We don't charge for the show. We ask for a donation for our building fund."

Although the PAIC has never received government aid, it once applied for a $40,000 Office of Economic Opportunity grant. "They said we weren't grass roots enough," Butcher recalls. "I don't know what they meant. Maybe we weren't militant enough. Anyway, the money went to another Indian group."

Militant or not, the Portland American Indian Center has become an integral part of the Indian community in the Portland area, and it has done so without being either helped or hampered by government. As Bud Butcher says, "Our desire is to make the center a stable, enduring organization which stands on its own."

Women in Distress

Miami, Florida

Helga had her purse and passport stolen at a bus station. A schoolteacher, she was enroute to Bogotá, Columbia, to take a position at the German embassy. When neither German nor Columbian officials in Miami could help her, Helga was directed to an agency called Women in Distress (WID).

In a matter of hours the agency had paid Helga's way to Atlanta, where it had located German officals who could issue her a new passport and traveling funds. She was soon on a plane to Bogotá.

Elsa, a 20-year-old wanderer, was cut up when she was attacked on Miami Beach. She came to WID after her release from a hospital and stayed three months, serving as house manager. She saved her weekly $25 salary and eventually returned to school to resume nurse's training.

"I really believe in this place," Elsa says. "They helped me when I was down, and its good that I had a chance to help other women."

Mary was broke and homeless when she came to the WID home, which has a motto over the front steps reading "To Care Is To Share." When her confidence returned, WID sent her off to a job interview. Mary is still giving WID a dollar or two a week out of her pay as an office worker.

More than 3,000 women have been fed and housed temporarily by WID since February 1971, when the agency was created by Roxcy Bolton, one of Florida's leading women's rights advocates. Not all the women in distress have had their problems solved, but in one way or another all have benefited from WID's hospitality, its financial and legal services, and its job-finding assistance.

It was a phone call in the night, Roxcy Bolton says, that "got me into this thing." She had been aware for a long while that there was no place for down-and-out women to go in Miami except jail or, if they were lucky, to one of the few beds for women at the Salvation Army, which permitted them to stay only one night.

"You don't know me, but I'm a woman in distress. You're my last

Living together at WID House means living with house rules.

resort," said the young voice on the telephone that February night in 1971. "Can you help me?"

Mrs. Bolton learned the woman and her child had been evicted. She found them a place to stay, gave them clothes from her own children's wardrobes, and paid a $40 back bill at the pharmacy to get more medicine that had been prescribed for the child.

After that episode she told her attorney husband, David Bolton, "We simply must do something for these women." And they did, by calling together a group of friends involved in her women's activities and his work in the Urban League and the Greater Miami Coalition. They set up a campaign to acquaint city officials, educators, businessmen, and people in the cultural world with the need for an agency to assist women.

"I became the chief beggarwoman of Dade County," Roxcy Bolton says of her many speaking engagements. Some clubs took up collections on the spot. Others responded by mailing their contributions some time later. It was not until August 1971 that WID received its first large donation—all of $50.

Entreaties to the United Fund, the Community Relations Board, city and county commissions, among others, didn't bring any monetary action. One public official was so frustrated with his stubborn bosses that he managed to shift $600 from another budget to WID.

By January of 1972 the future looked bleak for WID. Even the Salvation Army was proving uncooperative—it turned down WID's request to keep its doors open 24 hours a day to women.

But then the group's luck changed. Good fortune arrived in the person of Maurice Ferre (now the mayor of Miami), who had business holdings in Dade County, including The McAllister, one of Miami's principal downtown hotels. "Maurice Ferre had faith in what we were trying to do," recalls Roxcy Bolton. He made hotel rooms available at far-below-cost—$4 per night—to shelter WID "clients."

During the spring and early summer of 1972 the Ferre generosity provided many women with a temporary haven. But there had to be a place more suitable than a dressy downtown hotel.

And at last there was. A rental house was found at 122 N. E. 24th Street, within walking distance of the heart of Miami and its public services and stores. Insurance man Frank Gabor, who had seen Roxcy Bolton pleading for WID on television, contributed $600 for the first month's rent for the old frame structure.

"It was the filthiest house I ever saw," shudders Mrs. Bolton. They had to shovel out junk and rubble and get busy with paint, hammer, and nails. People pitched in with soap, time, and a great deal of enthusiasm.

WID House opened on August 1, 1972, with four beds and a couch. Department stores and individuals, reached by personal contact and the media, contributed more beds, another couch, an electric sweeper, a dining table and chairs, small appliances, and sheets and blankets.

Then came a generous gift from Robert Pentland Jr., retired businessman and philanthropist. Approached by friends, he made a large donation and then went all the way, purchasing the house for $19,742. Subsequently he turned over some stock to support the house maintenance fund.

The resident acting as manager of the house has $26 a week to buy the groceries, never knowing how many people will be there for dinner. A produce market owner donates a bushel or a peck when WID sends out one of its frequent crisis calls; other friends help restock the larder from time to time. There are no federal food stamps for WID. "We are a hand-to-mouth operation," says Roxcy Bolton.

WID means a great deal to the people who run it, as well as those aided by it.

Georgia Ayers, 45, social service coordinator for the Dade County Community Action Agency and a 20-year insurance agent, is a charter officer of WID. "I came from a meager beginning," she says. "Though I've made it I keep my sympathy for the women who haven't, because they are sisters. WID isn't a dumping ground. When we take institutional cases on their way out, family castoffs, robbed or poor women, our only aim is to get them the care they need. When there are personality conflicts, I tell them, 'The pot can't talk about the kettle when they're both cooking on the same smoky stove'."

The current president of WID is Delores Turner, 43, a WID charter member and a public school teacher. "I felt other agencies were not meeting the needs of these distressed women," she says. "When Roxcy called us together, this was an opportunity. A woman with a broken wing can't get it all together by herself." She adds, "I wish there was funding enough for continuing counseling for the many marginal cases."

Outsiders are also concerned. According to Janet McCardel, a clinical psychologist and the supervisor of the Dade County Women's Detention Center, "WID is the only place that we have to send released women to stay. It is a blessing to us. My only criticism is that we need more professional aides there."

Shortness of money and of trained personnel have necessarily and unfortunately limited WID's scope. The group has submitted a proposal to a Dade County agency for funding to retain such needed assistance, but it does not seek to become the bureaucratic structure with the kinds of restrictions and requirements that caused the need for WID in the first place. At WID there are no limitations as to citizenship or nationality, length of state or county residence, or reason for need. "Distress" is enough.

The assistant county manager, Dewey Knight, says, "I know they are attempting to meet a need that is not being met. There is no question WID is an asset."

Looking back, Roxcy Bolton says. "The funding should come first, if at all possible. The drain and strain on the WID volunteers has been immeasurable."

Then the founder of WID smiles. "But we had to pioneer. There was no choice, the need was so great."

*We've tried to work it so people will do things
for themselves, to help each other so there
won't be so many personal crises. And there
haven't been as many.*

The B.O.N.D. Community
Crisis Center

Atlanta, Georgia

At the age of 40, Juanita Borden has seen, as she says, "just about every kind of trouble and problem folks can get into and just about every government-type program to help them out."

Juanita Borden is director of a private community project, the B.O.N.D. Community Crisis Center. The center is a privately financed office serving residents in an Atlanta neighborhood that wanted to show that neighbors can still help one another.

The office operates as a kind of clearinghouse, accepting phone calls and visits from people of all ages with all types of problems. The center tries to help them deal with the immediate crisis, and to then teach them how to help themselves.

The center's services encompass day care, temporary food and shelter, emergency household moving, finding the right clerk in the downtown social security office, and helping get an errant child out of trouble. In less than four years the center has given aid and comfort to more than 500 people in the community.

The B.O.N.D. center was begun in July 1971, when a similar crisis center funded by federal programs was closed in a federal budget cut. The local people fought the closing. As Juanita Borden recalls, "We went to the government, to the press, everything we could think of, but to no avail. They closed the old office and that was going to be that. Until this great neighborhood just decided to do it itself."

The neighborhood is actually composed of five small neighborhoods ranging in income level from poor to wealthy. The neighborhoods, all in east Atlanta, are Inman Park, Little Five Points, Candler Park, Lake Claire, and Ponce-Highland.

In the late 1960s, people from these areas formed a private group calling itself the Bass Organization for Neighborhood Development (B.O.N.D.)—Bass being the name of the local high school. B.O.N.D. was set up to fight the construction of an expressway that would have cut through five neighborhoods. The complete success of that effort, and the community unity the campaign produced, subsequently led B.O.N.D. to undertake a variety of programs for the people in the community—such programs as a summer camp, day care, legal aid, a community credit union, and a campaign to restore old homes through individual private ownership. What began as an anti-expressway campaign developed to become a return to small-town, old-time community identity and neighborliness, in the heart of a major American city.

One of the later programs to be started by B.O.N.D. was a community crisis center.

B.O.N.D. was not in a position to launch the crisis center with much in the way of equipment and personnel. But the center's needs became known to the community, which responded with all kinds of donations—for example, a truck for moving, office supplies, and volunteers to staff the office (in fact, the staff is still an all-volunteer force, with the exception of two part-time people.).

But the center needed about $300 a month to pay its phone bills, keep the lights on, and so forth.

Any major metropolitan center has scores of worthwhile projects always looking for money from banks, businesses, civic clubs, and residents. Rather than compete with them, the B.O.N.D. organizers devised a completely different approach.

A community project, reasoned B.O.N.D., not only needs money to function but also needs the community—needs its residents' involvement and support, both in terms of man-hours and money. So the B.O.N.D. organizers proposed a system of having local people make small monthly payments—a dollar or two—specifically for the crisis center (like a church tithing system).

The proposal was printed in B.O.N.D.'s newsletter, which is distributed throughout the community. The public response was excellent. Hundreds of residents responded, agreeing to participate in the plan. This marked the beginning of the crisis center's financial stability, giving it the opportunity to operate on a permanent and stable financial footing.

But the center has received more than money from the community. It has been swamped with volunteer staffers, and a number of local lawyers have offered to provide free legal aid during the evening hours. Even the young architect down the street has offered to help with building plans for the day care center.

"We've tried to work it so people will do things for themselves, to help each other so there won't be so many personal crises," says Juanita Borden. "And there haven't been as many."

Morris has come a long way since spending his teen years as a gang leader and his early 20s as a drug addict.

The Southwest Community Enrichment Center

Philadelphia, Pennsylvania

Al Morris speaks softly, his Borsálino hat cocked slightly to the right, and fingers a pencil as he describes what the Southwest Community Enrichment Center in Philadelphia has accomplished in the past few years.

Morris has come a long way since spending his teen years as a gang leader and his early 20s as a drug addict. Now, as the center's associate director, he tries to prevent gang warfare, which is a serious problem in the area.

Much of his effort has gone into redirecting the attention of the youngsters. Which is why Morris has established four rock groups, a football team, and a boxing team, and why he's on call when tensions are ready to erupt in the schoolyards.

The multi-purpose center, Morris explains, has been a most useful tool for working with youth and for providing such services as tutoring, distributing emergency food, dealing with housing complaints, running senior citizen programs, setting up a special prison program, and operating a medical clinic and learning center for the residents of the neighborhood.

Back in 1969, the center was only a dream shared by three Catholic priests and a nun. Having conducted the first of many surveys of southwest Philadelphia, they had quickly determined that this was a forgotten part of the city, an area that desperately needed the services that other, more well-to-do areas take for granted.

After four months of door-knocking, holding neighborhood meetings, and careful planning, the nun, Sister Anne Boniface, opened the first center in a dank, dark cellar that lacked a number of necessities, including toilet facilities.

Six weeks later the local residents succeeded in helping to find the center permanent quarters in a two-story row house at 1341

Bill Peronneau

Volunteers pack an emergency supply of food for a needy family.

South 46th Street. The owner of the vacant house was tracked down, and arrangements were made with him to pay the necessary taxes and fix up the place in exchange for two years of rent-free occupancy. Four years later, in 1974, the center was only paying $25 a month rent and was thinking of buying the building.

Being white Catholics in a predominately black Baptist community, the center's founders discovered, had a two-edged effect. On the one hand it created a neighborhood fear that the newcomers were really missionaries trying to convert the people.

"We did all but wave a flag that we weren't missionaries, but we couldn't do anything about being white," Sister Anne recalls. But in time the local residents overcame their suspicions and gave their full support and approval to the center.

On the other hand the situation enabled the founders to raise money, for here was a community clearly in need. In response to an initial appeal for funds, the center received $6,000 a year, mainly from Catholics, during 1970 and 1971. And after obtaining offical tax-exempt status in 1971, the center was successful in tapping primarily nonsectarian foundations for assistance.

But it was not until 1972 that the center had enough money to start paying its staff minimal salaries of $100 a month. During 1973–74, though, it was able to up the pay to $300 a month.

In view of the center's limited financial resources, it is fortunate that the center can and does depend heavily on volunteers. Not only do the volunteers conduct various ongoing programs, but some of them have taken the initiative in starting new projects. Volunteers, for example, are responsible for having set up the girls' and boys' clubs, the medical clinic, and the prison program.

Both despite and because of their importance, volunteers are allowed to join the center only after careful scrutiny and assessment by the organizers.

"We're slow to take on people," Sister Anne says. "A community center has to be more than a job. There must be a sense of liking the center and liking the people who come to the center. If you bring in people too quickly, you make mistakes."

The Southwest Community Enrichment Center's tutoring program is aimed at helping children who are currently attending local public schools. It is not a large-scale program, and it averages only about twenty-four students a year. But it is effective, thanks in part to the foresight of Brother Hugh Maguire, its founder and director. To make sure there would be real progress in school, Brother Hugh made the parents enroll their children through the school counselors. Each counselor then contacts the teacher to find out what each student's difficulties are in class, and then he notifies the center's tutoring program. In this way the school, the center, the parents, and the student all participate in the program. The tutors, most of whom are nuns, are all volunteers and are all teachers from the area.

The center's emergency-food program is aimed at both finding and aiding the local families who are most in need of such assistance. This program has particular value in the neighborhood in that, owing to legislative difficulties in the state capital, the delivery of state welfare checks is sometimes seriously delayed. And it is the Southwest Community Enrichment Center that helps the poor people bridge the food gap caused by the delay.

The center's medical clinic opened in December 1972 as a result of the efforts of Sister Anne Marie, a student in Temple University's community nursing program. After being assigned to nearby Misericordia Hospital, she became convinced of the need for a free medical clinic in the neighborhood, and began a one-woman effort to bring her idea to fruition. Overcoming hospital red tape, enlisting legal advice, and finding a volunteer doctor, Sister Anne Marie was successful in adding to the center's range of community services.

The center's prison program, which is known as Helping Everyone at All Levels (HEAL), was set up after Ted Williams, an inmate on furlough from Graterford State Prison, suggested that the center do something for prisoners from southwest Philadelphia.

Two groups were formed, one inside and one outside the prison, and contact was established between them—contact that consists of letter-writing and weekly visits.

The program has had good results. In addition to helping to meet some of the emotional and social needs of the men in confinement, it gives them some sense of direction and belonging. In the words of Steve Ransom, 23, a former Graterford inmate who now directs HEAL, "Instead of old dudes up there teaching the young dudes to break into a car when they get out, the dudes look to the center to see if they can help the community."

The needs of prisoners returning to society are also part of HEAL. A recent grant from the Law Enforcement Assistance Administration is enabling HEAL to find jobs for released prisoners.

What of the future? The center's main thrust will continue to be in the field of education. A soon-to-open learning center will give the Southwest Community Enrichment Center the facilities to coordinate and reorganize its tutoring program for junior high and high school students. It will also offer basic adult education for school dropouts who want to earn their high school diploma. And it will also serve as an extension center for Philadelphia Community College, which is scheduled to offer college courses to community residents.

Community enthusiasm for the Southwest Community Enrichment Center is still going strong.

"The center was the turning point for getting people together," says Anna Mae Arnold, a 32-year-old mother of two. "It's really made a difference."

"The difference," adds Al Morris, "is our people."

*You have to do something for a man before you
can do something with him. I can't preach about
heaven far off when they have no comforts here.
The prayer says, "In earth as it is in heaven".*

St. James Baptist Church

Greensboro, North Carolina

As a boy the Reverend Prince Graves wanted to be a preacher, but he happened to grow up to become a brick mason instead. And yet in 1953, at the age of 31, he did become a clergyman, accepting the pastorate of St. James Baptist Church. But despite his change of vocation, he never stopped building.

"I was not strong in rhetoric," he recalls, "so I went where my strength was—in building and helping others."

Putting that strength to good use over the past two decades has turned Graves and his congregation (which has grown in strength to over 1,100 members) into architects of a great variety of projects to assist the disadvantaged. These projects include:

● An apartment complex, St. James Homes, of 90 units, later expanded to 114 units. Built with the aid of a loan of over $1 million, the complex is limited to families whose low incomes qualify them for federal rent subsidies.

● A day care center for the children of working mothers.

● A program to provide emergency furniture and food supplies to the needy.

● A secondhand clothing store in a low-income neighborhood.

● A social services department, with a full-time caseworker and a secretary to lend people a helping hand in finding jobs and in solving personal and family problems.

Prince Graves' reasons for launching these services go back to his childhood. "I fight poverty because I know what it is," he says. He remembers what it was like not to have enough heat in his family's small house, not to have a lunch to take to school or the money to buy one—and the temptation to steal when he was hungry and cold.

"But I was never poor," he says. "My family was temporarily broke, but there's a difference between being poor and being broke. Being poor is a state of mind. My mother raised rich children, rich in love and togetherness."

As a minister, Graves wants to infuse that same sense of richness in the people around him—and he does. He started by "pawning" the house that he and his wife owned in order to buy the materials for a new church building, which he and the congregation erected in 1958.

Graves holds his religious convictions deeply. He believes that you have to feed a hungry man before you can feed his soul. "You have to do something for a man before you can do something with him," he says. "I can't preach about heaven far off when they have no comforts here. The prayer says, 'In earth as it is in heaven'."

"Doing something for a man" is what Prince Graves and St. James Church are all about. They work to provide food and clothing where it is needed, to provide decent housing that meets the needs of the individual family ("We don't want a family with nine kids in a two-room shack; that just causes problems."), to find employment for those needing jobs, to give advice to those with problems they cannot handle, and to counsel youngsters who may be on their way to serious trouble with the law.

The church's earlier programs—clothing, food, housing, financial assistance, day care and the like—were all designed to meet very real, immediate needs in the community, ones that involved tangible, material assistance.

The more recent programs, specifically those undertaken since the church established its social services department in 1971, go one step further. These programs bring together the earlier efforts to better meet specific needs. And beyond that, the new programs move the church closer to dealing with the problems that are less easily identifiable—the fears and needs and desires that an individual may keep bottled up inside himself until they force him into desperate action.

"We found," Graves says, "that there were a lot of problems because people did not know what was available to them, or how to present their case to people in agencies that can help. A lot of people in these agencies talk down to these people, so they refuse to go and feel mistreated. The people don't know how to fill out the forms or cut through red tape. So we go with them and act in their stead. We stand in for them.

"Why, there are cases where people had to stand for an hour or more out in the cold to take a bus across town to stand in line to get food. Then before they got the food, they were told the office was closed for the day, and they had to wait in the cold and catch a bus to ride back across town, and then do the same thing the next day."

So, in addition to offering direct help and providing shelter and food and clothing and counseling, the St. James social services department is serving as a bridge between low-income people and existing public and private agencies that can help them.

There are a lot of specific ways in which the church helps meet the community needs. In the general field of education, for example, it provides transportation so that local school children can participate in extracurricular school activities, as well as in free public programs and events that they could not otherwise get to, and it pays some school and activity fees for children whose families can't afford them. And during the summer months it helps local youngsters who want to go away to camp.

The church also steps in to help people who have financial difficulties. It works directly with businesses and loan firms to iron out problems with people who have not kept up scheduled installment payments. Sometimes this assistance is in the form of providing funds to bring an account up to date, then counseling with the individuals on how to keep the account current. Sometimes it involves working out a refinancing arrangement that is satisfactory to the business or lending agency, and sometimes it is a combination of the two methods.

In housing, in addition to operating St. James Homes, the church sometimes takes over mortgage payments for individuals to help them through a rough period. The church also leases individual dwellings and then subleases them to individual families. This way, Graves says, the church is able to see that the housing suits the requirements of families, and is thereby able to help prevent overcrowding. Another aspect of the church's housing program is the use of church influence to persuade landlords to fix up substandard housing.

It is clear that in dealing with people the church does much more than just talk or lecture to people in need. In addition to its activist programs, it has also made efforts to meet the specific and often demanding needs of individuals. So it has, on occasion, paid for medical services, taken over outstanding bills, helped families organize and maximize their financial resources, and provided furniture or appliances—all on a current annual budget of only $60,000, which is financed by the congregation and outside donations.

To understand the church's impact on individual lives it is useful to look briefly at the story of Hazel.

Hazel is a young woman who found herself at the crisis point in March 1973. Her marriage of more than eleven years had broken up; she had, as she says, "gotten involved" with her boss; and an unmarried sister who was pregnant had come to live with her. The emotional problems became so heavy that Hazel quit her job and "closed myself up."

Although she did not seek help, her condition did not escape the attention of the people at her church—St. James Baptist Church. Prince Graves personally offered his assistance. The church arranged for private psychiatric treatment for two weeks in a local hospital, and when this did not dispel her depression, the church helped to have her admitted to a state mental institution.

When she was released four months later, Graves brought her back home. The church then arranged for her to go to her family's home in Texas for six weeks. During all this time the church paid her bills and kept up the mortgage payments on her house, and when she returned to Greensboro it was the church that helped her to get back her old job as a seamstress for an interior decorating firm.

Today, Hazel seems well-adjusted, poised, and happy. In addition to having come to terms with herself, she is now more aware of the problems of other people and is helping them when she can.

"There is no telling what would have happened to me without the church's help," Hazel says. "I would have lost everything. They worked with me all of the time. That was the only thing I felt I could hold on to. I knew they would be there to take care of me and give me advice. Often I just called and talked."

Graves doesn't really worry about money or facilities to do the job his church is trying to do. He thinks that somehow they'll find a way. "It's never a question as to whether to keep going," he says, "but how. It has never entered our minds as to whether to go on."

And he feels that the job will never end.

"We're all dirty until the last one takes a bath," he says. 'We're all rogues until the last one quits stealing."

And Graves doesn't have much patience with churches that pride themselves on their fine buildings or on how fast they can pay off a mortgage. "Any church in a poor community that can brag about burning a twenty-year mortgage after five years and hasn't done anything in the community has burned the wrong thing," he says.

"They ought to have burned the church and raised chickens on the land, so at least somebody could have something to eat."

*You've got to be willing to take gambles or you
get nothing worth having.*

Youth for Service

San Francisco, California

Bloodletting among rival street gangs had turned to open warfare in 1958, when Carl May, a quietly persuasive Quaker, managed to arrange a peace parley. One night he brought together
leaders of the Marquees, the Titans, the Outlaws, the Sultans, and
some other ethnic gangs and talked them into forming a council.

This marked the beginning of what has become a major peace-
keeping force on the streets of San Francisco, as well as the citywide launching of Youth for Service (YFS)—an organization that
channels the energies of some 2,000 disadvantaged youths a year
into more constructive pursuits.

YFS can trace its origins back to November 1952, when the San
Francisco Friends, a Quaker group, began organizing under-
privileged boys into volunteer crews to undertake "free" work
projects in their own inner-city communities. Their first project
was a modest one—cleaning, repairing, and painting the fence
around a local church.

The work idea caught on quickly.

Carl May was one of the organizers of those mini-work battal-
ions that sallied forth each Saturday to build playgrounds, repair
houses, cut lawns, and undertake other tasks intended to improve
the appearance of their neighborhoods. He was the one who persuaded the gang leaders, after they had formed the Youth Council, that, besides mediating territorial disputes among their multi-
ethnic constituents, they should get into the Saturday work program. Soon he had them recruiting their members to pick up
shovels and hammers, and the integration of the gangs back into
community life was underway.

May eventually accepted an out-of-town assignment with the
Friends, but before he left the city he found an excellent replace-
ment in Orville Luster, a teacher and youth worker. At that time,
1958, Luster was counseling delinquents at Log Cabin Ranch, a

A youth thinking about dropping out of school raps with a YFS volunteer. ▶

camp-like detention home. He was making good money, working a 40-hour week, and doing something he enjoyed. But the persuasive May convinced him he should take a cut in salary and accept the round-the-clock, seven-day-a-week responsibility of running the newly created agency.

Luster says that he took the position because "you've got to be willing to take gambles, or you get nothing worth having." It turned out to be more than a quick gamble; Orville Luster stayed with YFS for the next fifteen years, becoming the chief architect of its many programs.

He has a philosophy for dealing with youths who have been bent on violence. "When you approach street kids," he says, "you've got to let them know you can be useful to them—go to court for them, but don't lie for them; talk to their parents, their school teachers, the district attorney, their probation officer; get them job training, educational opportunities, and counsel them on how to stay out of trouble."

It was in 1959 that Orville Luster became executive director of YFS. Then, as now, lack of money was a recurrent problem. The American Friends Service Committee (AFSC) had provided the initial seed money—just a few hundred dollars, and in 1958 the Rosenberg Foundation provided a grant to carry on the experiment under the condition that the AFSC assume administrative responsibility for the new program. This agreement enabled Youth for Service to draw up articles of incorporation as a nonprofit, tax-exempt organization that would be eligible to receive foundation support.

In 1960, Orville Luster was able to secure a Ford Foundation grant that carried the organization until 1962, when it emerged as an independent agency participating in the United Community Fund.

Youth for Service was no child of the war on poverty; rather, it was a forerunner. However, when federal programs were launched in the 1960s to help the disadvantaged, YFS was ready to adapt.

"You have to run with the traffic and flow of the money," Luster says, explaining how YFS displayed great skill in identifying funding trends and tailoring its program proposals accordingly.

So it was that in 1965 the agency began moving in another direction, as a series of manpower projects were added to the crisis-oriented streetwork program. The first of these was the massive Neighborhood Youth Corps program, funded by the Department of Labor. This was followed by the Job Development Program, also in 1965; then the Job Corps screening program in

Michelle Vignes

"Want to help on this project?" asks a YFS streetworker. "We need you."

1967; and then the highly successful Neighborhood Beautification Program, which, with the help of the Building Trades Union, resulted in many construction jobs and nine miniparks in the Western Addition section of San Francisco.

Public gratitude for the YFS street worker program was never greater than during the summer of 1968. Rioting had exploded in Hunters Point and was threatening to spread to other locations. YFS workers under the direction of a former gang leader, Percy Pinkney, played a critical role in cooling the crisis. They called it "Operation Freeze, Baby," and it succeeded.

Early in the 1970s one of the agency's main benefactors was John R. Cahill, a wealthy builder, who raised $530,000 for the purchase of a warehouse, which was subsequently remodeled to become YFS's new headquarters and community center.

The community center houses YFS's carpentry shop, plumbing shop, and welder's shop, as well as the project's school. The school is currently offering a broad-based education program that is aimed primarily at 16- and 17-year-old high school dropouts. YFS's priorities are to get the dropout to reenter high school, earn a high school diploma or its equivalent, the General Education Development (GED) Certificate, and subsequently enter the City College of San Francisco.

San Francisco Community College provides the education program with three teachers to conduct academic, commercial, and vocational courses, and it has plans to add three more teachers. The program includes reading, to upgrade reading skills ranging from nonreaders to high school-level readers; mathematics, both basic and advanced; and advanced general education, which covers the five academic areas required on the GED test—mathematics, English, literature, social sciences, and natural science. YFS members can move into advanced general education only after completing the reading and math courses or after passing a special battery of tests.

For those who choose not to go the college route, the education program offers vocational skills training, work preparation, and referral to entry-level job opportunities.

YFS's adult work program (AWP) is designed to find employment for people over 18 years of age, especially those with families or dependents, as well as those handicapped by poor labor skills and by little or no work experience.

AWP arranges with prospective employers to hire and train enrollees on a trial basis from two to four weeks at the program's expense. Satisfactory performance means going on the permanent company payroll at the prevailing rate of pay. Under AWP placement, wages generally increase anywhere from $.50 to $2.50 an hour above what YFS youths had earned before.

YFS is currently flourishing in San Francisco, despite a recent change in leadership—long-time leader Orville Luster resigned in 1973. Al Herrick, the acting executive director, is conducting an aggressive search for new funding and new permanent leadership. Education program director Paul Schmidt enthusiastically describes his students' progress both in qualifying for high school diplomas and finding good jobs. "Lefty" Gordon and Dawson Leong, both ex-street gang leaders, are hard at work on their streetwork and Neighborhood Youth Corps programs.

The creation of Carl May and Orville Luster goes on. Youth for Service is alive and well in San Francisco.

I almost cried when I drove down that street for the first time after so many years and saw what had happened. There was garbage strewn everywhere. Old furniture was rusting on the sidewalk, and most of the houses had their windows broken out. It was then that I decided that my mission was right here in Cleveland.

Our Lady of Fatima Mission Center

Cleveland, Ohio

They call themselves the Famicos, and they build and repair housing in the Hough—a Cleveland neighborhood that was once called "the worst slum in the country."

The Hough is still a slum outwardly, but it has changed in spirit. Where the people used to live in sullen misery, unknown and uncaring, there is now a new spirit of neighborliness, of helping one another, of hope.

The change is apparent in the way people greet each other on the street, and especially in the pride with which they take care of their homes. And it can be seen in the work of the Famicos.

The Famicos, who are all formerly unemployed district residents with some training in building and repairing, have renovated scores of apartments and houses in the Hough, including one apartment house that has been converted into a condominium. In addition they have constructed the first new house built in the district in forty years. And they are now clearing new sites on which to build low-cost housing when the money becomes available.

These changes overtaking the Hough are largely the doing of one tiny, 67-year-old nun, Sister Henrietta of the Sisters of Charity of St. Augustine. Now the driving force of the Our Lady of Fatima Mission Center, Sister Henrietta came to the Hough in 1965. This was actually a return to her childhood neighborhood. She had lived in a grandparent's house just down Quimby Avenue from where the mission center is now located, back when this section of Cleveland had been a fashionable suburb.

"I almost cried when I drove down that street for the first time after so many years and saw what had happened," she recalls.

"There was garbage strewn everywhere. Old furniture was rusting on the sidewalk, and most of the houses had their windows broken out. It was then that I decided that my mission was right here in Cleveland."

The white-robed nun had long wanted to be sent overseas as a missionary, but she had wound up instead as an administrator of Catholic hospitals in northeastern Ohio. Her return to Cleveland was prompted by a request from the "slum priest" of Hough, Father Albert Koklowski. He had appealed to the bishop of the diocese for a nun to help him in his work at Our Lady of Fatima Mission Center.

"I don't care if she does nothing more than come down here and sit on the porch," he had said at the time. "This place needs a woman's touch."

Peter Renerts

That is precisely what Sister Henrietta has supplied. She began by getting a letter of introduction from the district's state representative and calling on all the neighbors. She asked the people about their problems and invited them to the mission center.

"I was concerned about the awful conditions the homes were in," she says. "They weren't cared for. They weren't clean. The same held true for the children. They were all so thin and dirty. The mothers just didn't know how to take care of them or their houses. Living like that was obviously unhealthy. But just as importantly it destroyed whatever chance they might have of having any pride in themselves. It was terribly demoralizing, terribly destructive of the people who lived like that."

Along with the bags of food and the clothing that Father Albert had been distributing, Sister Henrietta began bringing soap, detergent, and cleaning equipment. She also arranged for courses to be taught at the center in child care and homemaking.

In time Sister Henrietta devised a plan that involved organizing a so-called credentials committee of neighborhood women. The women visited homes, giving advice on how to clean and other kinds of assistance, after which they started a program of grading housekeeping.

Many of the local women became involved in the program, which soon acquired the name "Caridad" ("Charity"). As it continued over the years, an incentive was added. Those who adhered to certain housekeeping standards for a full year became eligible for improved housing, which was being provided through the mission center and later, in greater quantity, by the Famicos. It was Sister Henrietta's way of "making every house into a home."

In July 1966 there was a riot in the Hough—six days and nights of burning and fighting in the streets, which left four people dead and many injured. The riot not only caused death and destruction; it left many residents in a state of shock and despair, uncertain about the future.

At the center, during the post-riot period, Sister Henrietta began holding nondenominational prayer meetings at the mission center, and she encouraged neighborhood women to come and talk of themselves, their problems, and their hopes. "This was a very important step," Sister Henrietta explains, "in rebuilding these people's sense of their own value as human beings, and it met a deep spiritual need for many of them."

By this time, word of the nun's work had begun to spread throughout the rather sizable Catholic community in the Cleveland area. Consequently several suburban churches arranged collections of food, clothing, and household goods for distribution

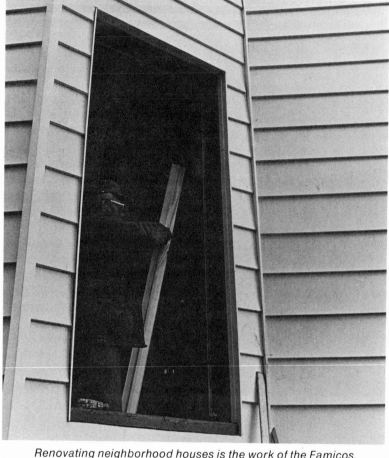

Peter Renerts

Renovating neighborhood houses is the work of the Famicos.

through the mission center in the Hough. And along with all of the supplies came an increasing number of volunteers, both men and women, to help out at the mission center.

It was during this post-riot period that some of the neighborhood men started coming to the center. They began attending classes teaching home repairs and elementary building skills. And in time they began doing repair work in houses and apartments throughout the neighborhood.

The repair-work project flourished, and in 1968 the group of men involved formed the Famicos Foundation, which was officially incorporated as a nonprofit enterprise. This was set up to acquire property, rehabilitate buildings, and build new ones, as well as to sell or rent housing to neighborhood people. (Famicos stands for Family Cooperatives.)

Since 1968 the Famicos have acquired control of approximately $120,000-worth of property in the neighborhood, property that they have fixed up and rented or sold to area residents. The money for these projects has come primarily from small donations of less than $100 apiece. One individual donor, however, has given the center about $60,000 since 1970, and a local business firm has given a $10,000 no-interest loan. The mission center itself is housed in a neighborhood building that was bought by the Catholic diocese shortly after the 1966 riot. The center occupies the first floor, while Sister Henrietta and another nun use the second floor as their living quarters.

As a result of the mission center's work so far, the population of the Hough neighborhood is showing signs of becoming stabilized. Turnover in housing has been reduced from about 80 percent a year to about 35 percent. And the average length of residence in a housing unit has increased from six months to two years.

The value of such gains is that they have helped to develop a sense of community in the Hough, and that sense of community has in turn provided the base from which the people of the neighborhood can move on to better and more productive lives.

Peter Renerts

*The strength of America lies in people across the
country who are giving of themselves and their
resources in human development and self-help
projects aimed at preserving the dignity of man,
so essential to the preservation
of a democratic society.*

The Help One Another Club

Birmingham, Alabama

Downtown Birmingham has its share of major corporations, financial institutions, department stores, and other enterprises engaged in the world of business. But it also has an unusual social services organization called the Help One Another Club, which is engaged in the business of helping people.

The club, which currently aids some 5,000 people a year, provides direct assistance to people facing emergencies with regard to their living expenses; collects food, clothing, and household goods for distribution to the needy; sponsors cleanup campaigns and other projects aimed at general community improvement; runs recreational centers for senior citizens; helps find jobs and job training for the unemployed; and produces weekly radio programs featuring consumer news and inspirational material.

Offering both help and hope to the disadvantaged people of Birmingham, the Help One Another Club is run on a limited supply of money and a vast amount of human willingness. As its originator and president, Geraldine H. Moore, says, "The Help One Another Club was founded on the premise that there are always in our midst people needing assistance of some kind, and that, through others who are willing to get involved, the help needed by some can be provided by others."

Geraldine Moore was one of the earliest voices of black self-awareness in the Birmingham area. In 1961 she authored a book, *Behind the Ebony Mask*, in which she described the rising aspirations of blacks in Birmingham, their hopes, their pride, and their devotion to family, church, and neighborhood.

The book reflected her own upbringing and experience.

"I grew up among people who showed concern for each other," she says. "There was always someone wanting to give a neighbor what he needed—food, clothing, rent money, or money to pay the utilities. If sickness or death occurred in your family, someone was soon knocking on the door and offering help. People thought nothing of washing, ironing, cooking, or bringing in stove wood and coal for their neighbors. And in time of real crisis, a family was never left alone, day or night."

Geraldine Moore believes deeply in the principles of neighborliness, and in 1965 she took her first tentative steps toward translating personal belief into the beginning of community action.

The daughter of a close family friend, a young woman qualified as a secretary but unable to find work, had asked Mrs. Moore for help.

"I just made a job for her," Mrs. Moore recalls. "I rented a small office, paid for the use of lights and water, and moved in my own typewriter and a mimeograph machine. I paid the young lady a small amount to do my personal correspondence. And then others began bringing in work. Her happiness was the inspiration for wanting to help more people with their personal needs."

Mrs. Moore decided to involve others in her efforts. She placed a sign on the office door. It read: "Help One Another Club."

"When the sign went up," Mrs. Moore says, "people thought we were already in operation and began calling us for help. I'll never forget that first case that started us on a social welfare program.

"Someone told us about a family in Roebuck [a low-income suburb]. The parents and their six children were living in a two-room house with no running water. They had very little food. It was just three days before Christmas, but there were no toys for the children. A bare Christmas tree had been put up in one room.

So two friends and I got together food, clothes, toys, fruit, candy, and nuts and carried them to the family."

It was about this same time that Mrs. Moore was hired as the first black reporter on the *Birmingham News*.

"They weren't too sure at the paper how I'd be received around here, so I had plenty of spare time to get out of the office and work on some of these things," she says. "In 1965 things were supposed to have changed, but even then young blacks were running into job discrimination. They would answer interviews, but when the employer saw they were black, it was to no avail. I thought I would see if I could devise a scheme for creating a few jobs. I personally called friends and business acquaintances and asked them if they had work—anything for blacks who needed jobs."

However, when this approach did not prove altogether successful, Mrs. Moore devised another strategy. Together with the many volunteers that had joined her club, she launched two thrift stores in 1967 to serve as collection and distribution points for goods to be dispensed to the poor. The goods were either given away or sold at a small charge. At the same time the stores became places of employment for a number of low-income people living in the neighborhoods served by the stores.

Hundreds of volunteers now contribute time to collecting clothing, food, furniture, and household items to stock the stores. They also help support the club financially. Over the years thousands of low-income people have benefited from the stores. The club also had another reason for opening them. "We wanted to show we could operate even if we were not accepted by the whole community," says Mrs. Moore.

Another major project was a "rescue house," started in the fall of 1968. But this soon became one of the more sobering experiences of the organization.

The rescue house was intended to provide lodging for those needing temporary help due to fires, evictions, and other emergencies. The project got off to a good start, but then lost its footing when the first house was acquired by urban renewal for expansion of a medical center. The club found another home for the rescue house but, unfortunately it was in a neighborhood in which the city's housing codes were being strictly enforced and in which an ethnic transition from predominately white to predominately black was taking place.

They bought a four-unit apartment house already occupied by four white families. This caused some difficulties between the local residents and the Help One Another Club's members.

"The worst part was that, as soon as we acquired the property the city department of health officials brought pressure on us to make improvements," says Mrs. Moore. "They threatened to declare the house unfit for habitation unless we made $6,000-worth of improvements within thirty days. The insurance company which had the policy on the house was white-owned and it dropped our insurance. We went to a black agent and had it reinstated, only to find out later he was an agent for the same white-owned company—and it was dropped again.

"All this stemmed from the unreadiness of people to accept the project at face value. But we still have the house and recently we found a way to rehabilitate it."

In 1971 the club took a step in another direction. "We started two radio programs," says Mrs. Moore. "At first they were for the purpose of providing spiritual help. One program interprets the international Sunday school lesson. The other one is a weekly inspirational program that also involves discussions of some of the more pressing social problems within the community."

Mrs. Moore produces the programs herself and injects her own opinions into their messages.

"There was one faction in the community which wanted to replace a black man on the city council. I took the position on the radio that the contributions he had made were worthy. I don't tell people how to vote, however. We've gone a long way in building race relations here. White people have a different understanding of problems relating to black people. We keep saying on the air that love is the key; we keep saying that we cannot afford hatred on either side."

In April 1973 a recreation center for senior citizens was established by the Help One Another Club. A second such center for older people was organized in 1974.

Help for the projects has come from many quarters, including the Jefferson County Committee for Economic Opportunity, the Christian Service Mission, the Downtown Jimmy Hale Mission, the Red Cross, the Salvation Army, the state department of pensions and securities (the welfare department), and the Birmingham Crisis Center. Most of all, though, it has come directly from the people of Birmingham. In 1972, for example, most of the $10,000 received came from poor blacks in the city. As Mrs. Moore says, "This could mean that these people are still grasping for identity with something which holds out hope for them."

One of the things Mrs. Moore thinks was "done right" was to integrate the club.

"Projects have the greatest hope of success when they are integrated," she says. "Whites will support black programs, but black folks, in my experience, don't as often have the cohesiveness and racial understanding that will enable them to work with whites.

"If the club were not integrated, it probably wouldn't be alive today. Some say the lack of cohesiveness is not a problem confined to blacks, but throughout my life I have found it does affect blacks more than whites. We can't keep businesses or charities going because of personality clashes. Blacks should not organize strictly black social welfare projects.

"The strength of America lies in people across the country who are giving of themselves and their resources in human development and self-help projects aimed at preserving the dignity of man, so essential to the preservation of a democratic society."

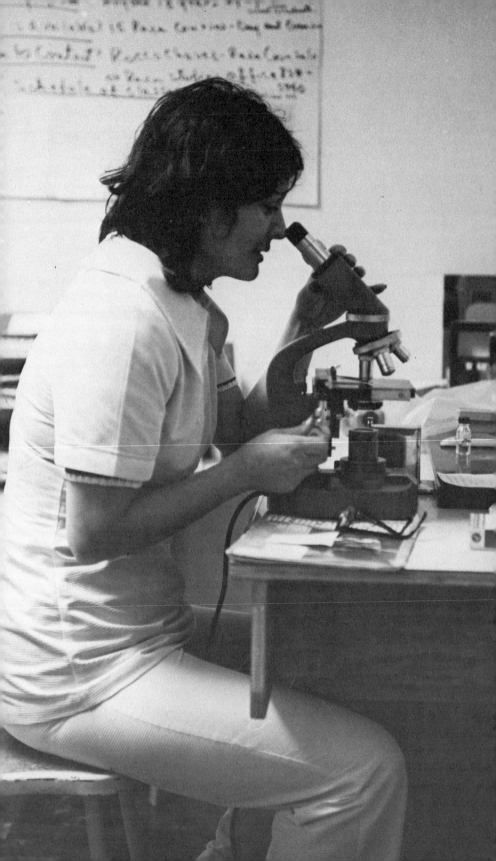

CHAPTER 6

Health Services

T he spiraling costs of medical care in America cause even middle-income families to say, "We can't afford to be ill."

But what about the disadvantaged? Not only can't they pay for necessary health services, but they live in areas that generally lack even the most basic of health care facilities. And the health services that are available to the disadvantaged are limited—by the medical establishment's disinterest in poverty areas, by government's indifference, and by the people's own fears about seeking medical aid and their inability to afford to travel far to doctors.

While government and the medical establishment continue to debate various solutions to the problem, self-help health care projects are springing up throughout the country to serve disadvantaged people within their own communities.

Some of these projects concentrate on dealing with drug addiction and alcoholism, two of the most serious health problems confronting urban America. A converted mansion, for example, provides a peer-group environment and counseling for teenagers trying to kick the drug habit. And a halfway house for alcoholics gives food, shelter, and redirection to men and women who have lost their way in life.

The effectiveness of such treatment centers derives largely from their being located within the communities and from their being manned mostly by local people—some of them ex-patients. In view of their concern for all aspects of the patients' lives, these places, in effect, are community rehabilitation centers.

Other self-help health projects provide outpatient treatment and counseling and referral services for disadvantaged people.

Many health care projects are aimed at combatting malnutrition and poor diets in low-income areas. They provide both food and sound advice to people who have long lacked both.

The small-scale neighborhood health project is not a hospital, but it does bring medical treatment and advice to people who are stranded by high medical costs or alienated from a health care system that often seems distant and removed.

*There is not much room for self-pity. It is one
drunk helping another drunk. This is why
we have been successful.*

Hope House

Boston, Massachusetts

The cartoon character on the screen has a big red nose like
W.C. Fields'. A pointed hat with a yellow band covers the rest of
his face. He wears a tattered blue dinner jacket and he goes by the
name Ike N'Schtop.

A dozen men are gathered in the basement classroom to watch
Ike's antics. Most of them are between 30 and 50 years of age, and
the few younger ones look older than their years. There is a quiet
sadness in their faces as the slide projector clicks new scenes on
the screen: Ike getting into a fight with his boss, Ike arguing with
his neighbors, Ike stealing money from his wife's purse, Ike getting beaten up in a barroom brawl, Ike telling lies to a priest.

Ike N'Schtop's name is bewildering at first. Each man has to say
it over to himself several times, pronouncing it as though he had a
drink-thickened tongue: "Ike N'Schtop . . . I can schtop . . . I can
stop."

How many times had each man said that until some member of
his family or a friend had demanded he "do something" about his
drinking? Each man remembers, because each is an alcoholic.

The slides are shown in Hope House, which is one of the country's first halfway houses designed exclusively for alcoholics. It is also a place where each year hundreds of alcoholics are rehabilitated, and are encouraged, assisted, and given the means to restore their lives.

Ike N'Schtop is the creation of Jack Burns, a man in his middle thirties who has been the manager of Hope House since 1965. An accomplished artist and a recovered alcoholic, Burns draws sketches of Ike, colors them, and has them made into slides. The slides—Burns has produced hundreds—are used to explain both alcoholism and Hope House to men accepted as residents, as well as to outsiders.

"Ike is a kind of roguish fellow we use to point out to the guys some of the myths about alcoholics, how Hope House is run, what we expect of them, how alcoholism affects both the alcoholic and people around him," explains Burns. "We use Ike to show them that the old saying by alcoholics that 'the only one I'm hurting is myself' is not true because all alcoholics, like Ike, get involved with a lot of people, such as their employers, their wives, guys in bars, the clergy."

Ike's hat hides all his features except his nose, so the alcoholic watching him can get no clear idea of what he looks like. This, his creator says, enables the alcoholic to quickly get the chief message that Ike delivers: Ike represents every alcoholic.

"We use Ike to help the guys open up about themselves and their alcoholism, so we can have a common base on which to help them," adds Burns. "Most alcoholics go through all the scenarios played out on the screen by Ike. They easily relate even to the tattered dinner jacket which alludes to the respectability which Ike once enjoyed. When the slides are shown to the guys, they talk about Ike's alcoholism, and this makes it easier for them to talk about theirs later."

Hope House wants its residents to talk about alcoholism among themselves and with the staff. Discussion is part of the learning process that the staff members of Hope House have found to be essential in the rehabilitation of alcoholics.

Hope House plays it straight. It displays warmth, empathy, understanding, and a sincere desire to help. But from the first moment a man accepted for residency arrives, Hope House lays it on the line: he's an alcoholic. His drinking is wrecking his life and the lives of people around him. He cannot drink as long as he lives there; if he does he must move out. He must not drink the remainder of his life; if he does he must then be prepared to pay for it, quite possibly with his health if not his life.

Alcoholism is a disease, he is told. But with his cooperation and trust, Hope House will help him lick it. Hope House will get him the medical, psychological, and economic assistance he needs to rebuild his life.

And in turn the alcoholic must be willing to work.

Jack Donahue, a rehabilitated alcoholic and Hope House's initiator

Hope House founder Jack Donahue says: "About 98 percent of the men have no jobs when we take them in. We get a man a job as soon as possible, usually within the first two weeks, because employment provides the nucleus of self-respect to those very much in need of it. We also have learned that if a man does not want to work he will not stay long—he is merely getting himself physically ready for the next binge."

For the man who cooperates, there are other benefits. Hope House offers to obtain family and marital counseling, and also psychiatric help for him. It will help him get back his driver's license after he has been sober for a year and has demonstrated his intention to remain that way. If possible it will obtain a pardon to wipe out armed service or court records pertaining to his alcoholism. And it will seek to restore his civil service rating if he has lost it.

"The most important structure in a halfway house is not the building but the relationship which the human beings in it have to one another," observes Donahue. "Because of their mutual problems, there is not much room for self-pity. It is one drunk helping another drunk. This is why we have been successful."

The "one drunk helping another drunk" relationship starts the minute an alcoholic walks up to the registration desk to ask if he can be admitted. Within fifteen minutes six residents offer to help him, to give him the personal attention which he probably has not seen for years. One offers a package of cigarettes, another a cup of coffee. There is someone to make a telephone call or write a letter for him. Another hands him a dollar, explaining, "You might be able to find some use for it," so he won't offend the newcomer. And one offers a poker chip.

The poker chip is a psychological prop that Donahue has found extremely effective in helping residents of Hope House maintain sobriety. They keep a poker chip in their change pockets. "When they get a temptation to have a drink, they reach into their change pocket and feel the poker chip," he explains, "and it reminds them that they are alcoholic and cannot drink. This little reminder often is enough to convince them to forget about the drink."

Jack Donahue is a gracious man, middle-aged, with a calm manner that is just as effective for consoling a wino as for pacifying a roomful of legislators arguing the merits of a bill to help alcoholics.

A rehabilitated alcoholic, he has been helping others recover from the disease since 1956, when he first took another alcoholic into his home. It was New Year's Day, cold and snowy, and he and others with drinking problems had just come from a community meeting at which the problems of alcoholism were discussed. One of the men said the welfare department wouldn't help him because he had no permanent address and he had no money and no place to stay that night. Donahue invited him into his apartment to live.

In those days there was little help available to alcoholics, particularly the skid row types who, according to popular opinion, lay in gutters and slumped on doorsteps either by choice or because of a moral weakness. But then as now, in Boston as in every city, there were thousands of alcoholics who needed help. So the word spread faster and faster that a guy in need of a place to "flop" and an understanding friend should go to the South End to Jack Donahue's place. "My place filled up rapidly," he recalls. "Soon I had seven men living with me."

His apartment became so overcrowded that Donahue moved to a house in south Boston in 1958. There he took in four more men. The word continued to spread along the skid row grapevine, and more men arrived. In November 1961 he rented an apartment building in a once-prestigious section of the South End. Later he purchased the building with the scant savings he had managed to accumulate. The savings consisted of what little money he could collect from his residents after they found work, plus money he saved by working round-the-clock every day himself to save hiring help.

"Although we still had room for only eleven men, the guys kept coming. So from 1961 to 1966 we were handling between three hundred and four hundred men a year," says Donahue. "Most of the men were about 45 years old. They came to us from the state hospital at Bridgewater, from skid row or jail." So, in the spring of 1966, he bought another building, a five-story brownstone, in which Ike N'Schtop is currently shown.

To benefit from tax exemptions, Donahue and his wife, Marion, have formed a corporation with a group of friends, including a rabbi, a lawyer, a priest, a banker, a general contractor and a doctor. Hope House, Inc., has been chartered as a nonprofit charitable organization.

During the past few years Hope House has expanded into four buildings, three of them contiguous, the fourth a three-minute walk away, with accommodations for ninety men. Hundreds of men reside at Hope House each year for varying periods, depending on the capability of adjusting to a way of life without alcohol.

Donahue and Burns have developed Hope House, meantime, into an effective educational facility. Burns' slides of Ike N'Schtop, for example, are shown to medical personnel and others from the community seeking information on alcoholism. And Donahue was an important guiding hand and becalming voice in convincing the state legislature to pass in 1971 a law that abolished public drunkenness as a crime, recognized alcoholism as a disease, and established a system of detoxification centers throughout Massachusetts.

Wherever he can, Donahue carries the message of what proper treatment can do for the alcoholic. And he also carries the desire to put a poker chip in the pocket of every drunk in the land.

*We had nothing, so we went ahead
and built on that.*

La Clinica de la Raza

Oakland, California

Most of the people who attended the community center meeting were poor and knew only a little about the topic of health maintenance. But they did know one thing: their fellow Chicano residents of the Fruitvale section of Oakland were not receiving adequate health care and treatment.

When they needed medical help they found the fees prohibitive, transportation difficult, appointment hours inconvenient for those with jobs or households or children. And the medical personnel they did encounter didn't understand their language or their lives.

"Well then," said someone at the meeting, "why don't we open our own clinic?"

The fifteen people at that meeting in 1970 had no idea then how to answer such a question. But eventually they found a way.

They were laborers, housewives, a couple of students from the University of California at Berkeley (UCB). They had no money, no professional mentors to consult, no housing for a clinic, and no

The receptionist's desk at La Clinica de la Raza

idea of how to find such basic necessities as medical instruments and materials. They weren't even sure that their neighbors in the barrio would come to such a clinic if they could start it.

The students suggested that they get in touch with David E. Hayes-Bautista, who was interested in Chicano problems and was about to receive a degree in sociology from UCB. Hayes-Bautista came to the next meeting, which lasted for three hours.

"We gave the plan a name," recalls the indefatigable Hayes-Bautista. "La Clinica de la Raza. Then we got twenty young people in the barrio to conduct a survey. Would the clinic be used if we opened it? The people said yes. Next we went door-to-door asking for money, and with the $300 we raised we rented a little four-room storefront. We talked to every person and place we could think of as being possibly helpful.

"Things began to happen. A doctor and two medical students promised to donate some time. The Oakland Tuberculosis Association said they'd lend a mobile TB unit. Medical supply firms and doctors gave us some basic medical equipment, otoscopes, and first aid kits. Rudimentary, but a start."

By the spring of 1971 the clinic's founders had lined up an all-volunteer staff consisting of seven community members with no health-care training, five university students, and one doctor (who lasted for only a week). La Clinica was officially opened on May 5, 1971, less than a year from the night the idea was born. A priest held mass in the reception room and the place was crammed, mostly with people who had come out of curiosity. But before that first month was up, almost 200 people had visited the clinic.

Many people had to be turned away that first summer, as would-be patients came from the entire Oakland area, from 50–60 miles away, swelling the already large numbers of local people who flocked to a clinic "of their own."

In June the clinic's members elected a board of directors and a chairman, Juan Cochran. Hayes-Bautista was appointed clinic director. And the two students who had been active in founding the clinic, Joel Garcia and Alec Velasquez, were named as the clinic's coordinators.

The patients were asked to donate whatever they could afford as a fee. On the third visit they were invited to become clinic members; as members they would attend monthly meetings to voice their needs and to vote on clinic matters.

There was an evident shortage of staff, of supplies, of cash for the simplest operating expenses—a shortage of everything but patients. The greatest threat to continued existence was the shortage of medicos. Doctors came for a few days or weeks, and then they suddenly withdrew. To be effective the clinic had to have physicians, at least on a part-time basis.

"So we faced the fact that to keep them we'd have to pay them—something, at least. But we had no money," says Hayes-Bautista. "We had to get funds to keep going."

Chairman Cochran, Director Hayes-Bautista, and coordinators Velasquez and Garcia worked on funding proposals and submitted them to possible sources—the state public health department and the UCB student body. Both were successful. The UCB student organization gave the first of three annual grants of $7,000 each that first summer; in November the health department approved a $30,000 grant.

Three part-time physicians, two nurses, and three office workers were hired. And when the involved and voluble membership stressed the need for dental care, one full-time and one part-time dentist were added to the paid staff.

The clinic quadrupled its size, taking over two adjoining storefronts. More medical equipment arrived, as doctors retiring from practice donated the contents of their offices to La Clinica. The unpaid staff was enlarged when the San Francisco Medical Center and some UCB medical departments agreed to give academic credit to students working part-time at the clinic.

The leadership never ceased its efforts to find funds "with the fewest strings attached."

In 1972 the clinic received private and state agency grants totaling $100,000; in 1973 the figure climbed to $288,000 (two-thirds of it being from county revenue sharing).

A long-felt need for mental care and attention to those dealing with bicultural problems has been met with the help of a $27,000 grant from the state department of mental health. El Centro de Salud Mental ("the Center of Mental Health") opened in January 1973, in a former barbershop across the street from La Clinica; later it was moved to a two-story building a block away.

The little storefronts now house the clinic's administrative office; a 20-room building near the mental health facility provides space for the medical and dental programs.

The principal purpose of the clinic's medical programs is to provide basic diagnostic care and treatment for most illnesses. And if a case happens to be beyond the scope of the clinic, the doctor arranges to have an outside specialist examine the patient. Other, more specialized medical services at the clinic include preventive medicine, immunization, pediatrics, and gynecology.

In addition the mental health center provides bilingual therapy and counseling, and the dental department provides general dental treatment and also orthodontics.

The clinic does not make money through charging fees. Most patients pay a maximum fee of $2 a visit; those in financial difficulties are not asked to pay anything.

The clinic's staff numbers fifty-three, of whom forty-two are paid. The constantly changing, disappearing, tired and volunteer medico has become six dentists, six general practitioners, four psychiatrists, an optometrist, six graduate mental health students, six medical students, five nurses, and three social workers. And there are two administrators, an accountant, three secretaries, and ten community members (five of them dental assistants in on-the-job training, and two of them administrative trainees).

The average staff member is 28 years old, completely bilingual, and paid only one-third the wages of a person holding the same position in a regular clinic.

What is it that impels skilled people to work for only a third of the money they could command elsewhere? It is clear that much more than money is involved in their decisions:

● Dr. David Teegarden, 31, general practitioner, graduate of the Stanford Medical School: "I wanted to work in a community. I've learned as much during my year and a half here as I learned in medical school. I've learned to be a doctor here. . . . Why do I work here? To help it progress."

● Julie Olguin, 30, a former doctor's secretary, and La Clinica's internal coordinator for the past two years: "I could get a better paying job but I wouldn't be as happy. I enjoy my job. Here we run our own clinic, nobody runs it for us."

● Ynocensio Alcoser, 26, program coordinator: "The people here, paid or unpaid, want to help the community. But without community support and participation, we would be nothing."

Looking back on the clinic's short history, David Hayes-Bautista observes:

"The clinic was needed. We had nothing, so we went ahead and built on that. I stepped down as director in the third year because people kept coming to me for decisions they didn't want to make themselves. It would have been easy for me to become a dictator. Now they're finding out they really don't need even a director."

These thoughts of Hayes-Bautista's express most clearly an essential function and result of a community effort such as La Clinica—the discovery in people, particularly in poor people, of purpose, strength, and ability in themselves.

*Their front porch at times looked like a stall on
Portland's Produce Row, overflowing with
cartons of cherries, pumpkins, apples, collard
greens, carrots, potatoes, and brussels sprouts.*

The Community Care Association

Portland, Oregon

The idea came to Clara Peoples on a Sunday drive through the
lush Columbia River bottomlands.

She had her husband stop the car by a farm. "I had noticed,"
she says, "several of the fields that had been harvested still had
food rotting in the rows. Before my courage deserted me, I asked
the farmer if we could harvest this usable food. I promised that we
would honor his land, and use the food for the greatest good of
the community."

The permission was granted by the white farmer to the black
family on that Sunday in 1968. This marked the beginning of what
has become Community Care Association, Inc., which, under the
direction of Clara Peoples, dispenses free food to thousands of
poor persons in the Model Cities area of Portland.

The organization serves hot meals at its headquarters in a
former store. It also provides prepared meals and packages of
groceries to take home. Often an unemployed father will eat his fill
and leave with both hot meals and groceries for his family.

Many of the food items being served are frozen or canned fruit
and vegetables—that are either salvaged by volunteers from
farmers' "second crops" or given outright to Community Care by
the producers.

"It is," says Irvin Mann, director of the Oregon Department of
Agriculture, "one of the most remarkable programs going. It's a
bootstrap operation that teaches self-reliance. And it makes a lot
of sense because it utilizes our oversupply of agricultural products for those who need them."

The need is a very real one for the poor people of Portland, in
that, like the residents of other poverty areas, they have long suffered the ill effects of an inadequate diet and malnutrition. Consequently the food program conducted by Community Care represents a preventive medicine approach to health care for the
people who live out their lives in the inner city.

Carrying out her promise to that first farmer she approached, Clara Peoples shared her harvest of cabbage and squash with poor neighbors who had an inadequate diet or who were downright hungry. Then she proceeded to enlist friends—particularly teenagers—to go with the Peoples family to the fields, hauling the produce back "in my husband's raggedy old truck."

The volunteer harvesters kept part of what they collected and donated the rest to the needy members of the community who were unable to go to the fields.

The clearinghouse for the produce was the Peoples' home. Their front porch at times looked like a stall on Portland's Produce Row, overflowing with cartons of cherries, pumpkins, apples, collard greens, carrots, potatoes, and brussels sprouts.

Most of the food had to be processed quickly to preserve it. The Peoples' kitchen became a busy scene of canning and preparation of meals for the hungry who dropped by. As word spread of the bounty, "our house became one big soup kitchen," she smiles.

It became apparent to Mrs. Peoples that her little project, undertaken on impulse, had awakened a great need in the community. She was determined to meet that need, and so she set about finding both support and funding for her plan.

To begin with, it seemed a good idea to establish a formal organization. Consequently, the Community Care Association was officially incorporated as a nonprofit enterprise in December 1969.

News of the project spread throughout the community. So it was that, as Clara Peoples remembers, "businesses in the area, such as dairies and bakeries, were soon volunteering some of their vehicles, and donating items such as ice cream, bread, and pastry. And churches, community groups, and individuals became interested enough in this work to begin volunteering their time and money."

The crop of 1970 proved to be a good one, for both Oregon and Community Care. But arrangements had to be made to ensure the organization's full gain from a bumper harvest. As Mrs. Peoples recalls, "We enlisted the aid of several of our volunteers, and they began canning jams and jellies in their homes, and began freezing many of the vegetables that we harvested. Because we had no funds to cover processing costs, we again enlisted the aid of church and civic groups for donations of sugar, jars, lids, freezer bags, and other food-processing equipment.

"Because food-processing regulations do not allow home-

◄ *Clara Peoples assists Lewis Martin in the preparation of a meal. Community Care serves breakfast and lunch to needy people in the inner city of Portland in the hope that better nutrition will lead to better health.*

canned vegetables to be distributed outside your home, we decided that we would have to educate the families that we gave fresh produce to in the fundamentals of home canning and preserving. Therefore, locally grown crops would be available to these families through the winter."

Funding was now imperative. So Clara Peoples immersed herself in the technicalities of writing a funding proposal to be presented to the local Model Cities planning board. The proposal was duly submitted—and eventually approved. Community Care received its first major funds, $67,000, in 1971. In the following years this sum was increased to $105,000 per year.

"With funding assured," Clara Peoples explains, "it became imperative that we find permanent quarters for our program, and after searching throughout the area we found a landlord willing and enthusiastic about renting his building to us.

"This building required extensive renovation to bring it up to the standards set by city and county codes. We enlisted the help of an interested architect who planned for best utilization of space, and worked closely with the plumbers, carpenters, and electricians to see that his plans were carried out.

"We installed a large walk-in freezer, and several large stainless steel sinks, so vital to food processing. This, of course, necessitated a larger hot-water tank, and subsequently more wiring and plumbing. We were donated a few refrigerators and stoves, and found that this also meant rewiring to bring our old building up to code.

"Gradually the building began to take shape. A donation of carpeting for the small reception area, some used desks and cabinets, the purchase of office machines, and we all really felt that we had arrived, and could lean back a little and rest from our labors. Not so. We found that we had only begun to grow."

In 1971, Community Care workers became farmers themselves. They were given vacant lots in the city and the use of 11 acres of land west of Portland.

"We were able, that first year," recalls Clara Peoples, "to raise potatoes, tomatoes, greens, peppers, green beans, cabbages, and other produce on these lots, and the fruit trees growing here also yielded a fine crop.

"We also found a good source of vegetables and fruits came from backyard gardens and fruit trees. Picking and harvesting these residential gardens also gave us an opportunity to visit with family people, and explain our program."

That "raggedy" family truck used in the first harvestings soon was augmented by the use of rented trailers pulled behind the cars of neighbors joining in the project. But more transportation was needed.

Clara Peoples' characteristically direct solution was to ask the manager of the local Carnation Company branch for the loan of a truck. He agreed—and also gave her 10,000 gallons of ice cream for the children in her neighborhood.

It was a survey of its neighborhood clientele that prompted Community Care to begin serving hot meals on its premises. The poor people of Portland did not eat well. As Clara Peoples said, when she testified at length before a U.S. Senate subcommittee in March of 1973, "46,000 people in our city are suffering from malnutrition. A concentrated consumer-education thrust is of exceptional importance."

A typical breakfast served at Community Care offers pancakes, eggs, bacon, and sausage.

"For lunch," says Mrs. Peoples, "there could be liver, brown rice, cabbage, gravy, and apple pie. Supper could be fish or ox tails, green beans, and peanut butter cookies."

Community Care's chief sources of food are, of course, the farms where the volunteers gather produce. Other food sources are bakeries, creameries, seafood processors, and other businesses. The organization also obtains such items as lentils, oatmeal, flour, lard, peanut butter, and dried peas from the U.S. Department of Agriculture's Abundant Food program.

Once 10,000 pounds of crab arrived "in an unmarked truck, from an anonymous donor," Mrs. Peoples recalls. And over the years, several tons of fresh salmon have been donated. Although the Community Care kitchen "home cans," such products as fresh fish are put in tin cans at a Portland custom cannery.

"Some of the things we've canned that will help us this winter," says the agency's report for September 1973, "are mixed pickles, different kinds of relish, peaches, beets, pepper sauces. Some of the things canned at the cannery are mixed vegetable soup, applesauce, lentil soup, pickled beets and grape juice."

Volunteers used in running the harvesting, processing, and meal-dispensing operations number about fifty, augmented by a full-time staff of nine (including the director, Clara Peoples) whose salaries are covered by the Model Cities grant.

"They were unemployed persons I gave jobs to," the director says of her eight staffers. "They all have to be able to do anything —cook, can, pick, drive a truck."

Community Care continues to draw heavily upon all segments of the community for support. All of the contributions, in cash and in kind, add up to a significant proportion of the project's support.

A bookkeeper who contributes assistance to the project, Allan Z. Bowen, has estimated that the Community Care Association's total annual income in terms of donated goods, money, and volunteered time and services amounts to as much as "three times the $105,000 Model Cities grant."

Individuals, of course, also play a major role in funding Community Care. One of the chief donors, in fact, is Clara Peoples. Bowen has recounted that when he went over her personal income tax returns, her records showed she was contributing more to Community Care than the disposable income from her $12,000-a-year salary as director. "She actually puts back more than she takes out," is Bowen's considered opinion. Of course her contribution to the association has to be reckoned in terms that go beyond any dollars-and-cents figure or value.

Clara Peoples is clearly the driving force behind Community Care and its success, and yet she herself has had hardly any training in the difficult art of creating and maintaining a community self-help project. She is the mother of three children and the wife of a laundry foreman at a U.S. Veterans Administration hospital. Now in her late 40s, she was born and reared on an Oklahoma farm. She attended business college in Portland and worked 16 years as a nurse's aide and receptionist at the county hospital in Portland. In addition she served as a volunteer counselor at a local high school, where she first became aware of how poor people—in this case teenagers from low-income homes—suffered from the lack of good, nutritious food.

All of this sprung from a Sunday family outing. But Clara Peoples says there is yet another unforeseen bonus—"A greater degree of rapport between farmers and the urban residents that we feel is unique to our city. Through our harvesting we have gotten to know one another, and the clichés and prejudices common to each group are beginning to pass. It is not uncommon for city residents to worry with the farmer over the weather and its effect on the crops, and the rural growers now realize that poverty often cannot be avoided, and that many people without jobs are more than willing to work, but lack the opportunity."

Mrs. Peoples sums up: "The reason for Community Care can be put into one sentence. Poverty is what happens when people quit caring."

Speaking for the Community Care Association, she says with great conviction: "*We* care." And she goes on to express her feeling that this caring "will eventually make real inroads into the overwhelmingly depressing problem that is poverty."

*If what the medical community says is true—that
anyone can go to a doctor and receive charity
treatment—then this clinic should ultimately
close for lack of patients.*

The Green Bay Area Free Clinic

Green Bay, Wisconsin

To most Green Bay residents the free clinic on East Mason
Street looked like just one more hippy hangout. It was located
above a drug abuse center and seemed to attract the same young,
long-haired, strung-out crowd.

Even the poor of the neighborhood had trouble taking the clinic
seriously. They had little use for hippies. They felt mocked by the
rich young middle-class students who seemed to adopt poverty
as a lifestyle.

Area residents and merchants complained that the clinic was
giving the neighborhood a bad look, if not name. And local doctors did not wish to become involved with such a disreputable
project.

After suffering through some eight months of community disapproval, the clinic finally found new quarters on South Chestnut
Street—and a new lease on life. It has since gained both the acceptance and patronage of thousands of patients who need free
or low-cost medical care in the Green Bay area. It has gained increased support from the medical profession. It has gained a reputation for being seriously committed to the health care needs of
the poor people in and around Green Bay.

The free clinic was the idea of Linda Pratsch, a social services
student at the University of Wisconsin–Green Bay. Having learned
of such free clinics elsewhere, she believed that one was clearly
needed in Green Bay. And she backed up her belief by collecting
information showing that few of Brown County's poor families
were receiving medicaid or other benefits.

Her aim was to set up a free clinic that would provide a wide
range of medical care, referral services, and counseling services
for low-income people.

Collaborating with a young internist named John Randall, she
set up a clinic—formally a tax-exempt, nonprofit corporation—on

East Mason Street, on the second floor of a building used by the People's Drug Abuse Center. The arrangement with the drug center was that the clinic would not have to pay rent.

Equipment, furnishings, and small amounts of money were donated to the two organizers by local physicians and other individuals. And two doctors promised to volunteer their time and services, along with a number of medical support personnel.

The clinic opened in July 1971. Initially it was open just one day a week, from 11 a.m. to 7 p.m. In September, though, with a larger staff, the clinic changed its schedule to three mornings a week.

Although the clinic quickly began to attract patients, its association with the drug abuse center hampered its efforts.

"In the eyes of the public and many doctors, the free clinic was merely an extension of the drug abuse center," one doctor recalls. "They thought the only reason the clinic was established was to deal with drug abusers and give abortions. Of course, nothing could have been further from the truth."

Despite the controversy the clinic continued to attract more and more patients. In fact it provided medical and counseling services to some five hundred people during its first six months of operation.

The clinic began overcoming its basic public relations problem in March 1972, when it moved its quarters into a building provided by a local Lutheran church. There it began expanding its operations, increasing its volunteer staff, and lengthening its hours—to two full days a week.

It was also in early 1972 that a local pharmacy began making drug samples available to the free clinic, thereby giving the center a much-needed boost in being able to supply free drugs to needy patients.

Early the next year the clinic entered into an agreement with the Northeast Wisconsin Technical Institute, under which local poor people would receive free dental care at the clinic, with advanced work being performed elsewhere through an arrangement with the institute and its staff members.

The clinic is currently treating more than a hundred people a month. They come in with a variety of medical problems and requests, ranging from respiratory disease to venereal disease, from pregnancy testing to prenatal care advice, from dental work to physicals.

The clinic's staff undertakes a broad range of diagnosis and treatment—including some laboratory work, although much of that, plus x-ray work, is done on a rotational basis by three local hospitals. Where necessary, the staff counsels the patient about the availability of other medical services in the Green Bay area, and sometimes makes the specific arrangements for such treatment as well.

The clinic also serves as a general counseling service for the community. People come in with a great variety of nonmedical problems and questions; they want information or advice on employment, housing, family counseling, and local governmental agencies. The clinic does what it can to help, for it operates on the principle that it needs to assist the client in finding other sources of help for problems outside the medical field.

This counseling service serves to strengthen the clinic's ties with the community, as well as to develop good relations between the clinic and social services agencies in the Green Bay area.

The clinic cooperates closely with government on both the local and federal level in order to provide better medical services for

Father Michael Bent, a volunteer, interviews a clinic client.

the poor. The clinic, for example, is part of Green Bay's venereal disease screening program. Its participation has been very successful, in large part because young people seem willing to come to the clinic for testing and treatment, whereas they are reluctant to trust the family physician.

Although the clinic offers its services at no cost to the community, some patients try to pay whatever they can afford. They feel too proud to take something for free, to be subject to criticism as freeloaders. This response, together with the public's general response to campaign drives, results in most of the clinic's $5,000-a-year budget being covered by individual donations. Another principal factor in meeting financial obligations is the use of an all-volunteer staff. There are no paid staff members—only volunteers.

But therein lies one of the clinic's weaknesses—its necessary reliance on the voluntary participation of physicians and other medical personnel. It is estimated that about 12 of the area's 120 doctors participate regularly, donating between two and four hours of their time a month to the clinic. And about 45 doctors take clinic patients at their offices at reduced fees.

If there were more doctors, or if the doctors presently participating could give more time to the clinic, then the clinic would not be so hampered in the services it offers and the hours it can remain open. As Anneliese Waggoner, current director of the clinic says, "People don't get sick just on Tuesdays and Fridays."

The Green Bay clinic does not claim to have answered all the controversies involved in health care for the poor. Despite its expanding role, the clinic thinks there are still hundreds more people it could and should reach, for it is the only free clinic in the Green Bay metropolitan area, and it also knows that about 20 percent of its clients come from outside the area.

Simply on the grounds of its continued existence and expanded services, the clinic feels it has proved to be meeting a genuine need in the low-income community.

"It's easy to say anyone can go to a doctor and be treated. But people who have come to the clinic say that's not true," says Dr. Jeremy Green, one of the clinic volunteer physicians. "If what the medical community says is true—that anyone can go to a doctor and receive charity treatment—then this clinic should ultimately close for lack of patients."

The Green Bay Area Free Clinic shows no signs of being threatened by the possibility of closing any time soon.

When you take the bottle away, you have to fill
that void with something. . . . The religious life
and hard work do it here.

Hope Harbor

•Greensboro, North Carolina

John Stephenson awoke the day after Christmas too sick to even lift his head.

He had run out of liquor and at this point, as he says, "I had drunk away not only my material possessions but all my friends. There was no one to bring me another drink, even if it would save my life. Everytime I breathed, I thought it would be my last. I knew I was going to die that night. And I really didn't want to."

John Stephenson was 27 years old when he hit rock bottom as an alcoholic in 1949.

Today he is known as Brother John and is executive director of Hope Harbor—an alcoholic treatment program that he started in 1966. The program now enjoys a widespread reputation in North Carolina for success in taking washed-up people and making them productive members of society again.

Hope Harbor describes itself as a "Christian home for alcoholics." In a period of eight years it has evolved from a one-man counseling service into a highly successful business operation and mission-type ministry. It's annual budget has expanded to $380,000—nearly all financed out of business ventures run by patients—which is used to maintain homes for alcoholics in three cities and one rural area.

In eight years Hope Harbor has treated approximately 5,200 patients in its resident rehabilitation facilities and has worked with 28,000 more people in its mission for transients. The program for salvaging alcoholics leans heavily on religious teaching, adherence to a rigid set of rules, and a steady diet of hard work—not unlike the demanding lifestyle that Brother John Stephenson himself has adhered to for the past quarter-century.

After that miserable awakening in 1949, Stephenson went to a Presbyterian minister in Raleigh for help. That, he says, was the beginning of his recovery. He was ordained as a Presbyterian minister in July 1954, and subsequently held pastorates in southeastern Virginia as well as in two North Carolina communities, Fayetteville and Greensboro.

His own experience, he says, taught him that God, an ordered life, and hard work are "the cures" for alcoholism.

He also feels his experience gives him something that many who deal with alcoholic rehabilitation do not have—identification with the alcoholic: "It is difficult for an alcoholic to relate to a sociologist who has been trained from a book."

Stephenson had been at Glenwood Presbyterian Church in Greensboro for four years when he resigned and opened his one-man alcoholic counseling service in January 1966. It is here that the Hope Harbor story begins.

"I felt that God was calling me to work with alcoholics," he says, with great conviction. "The need was there. There were the men sleeping out in alleys, in parked automobiles, on railroad tracks—men dying from exposure. And there was absolutely no place in Greensboro they could go for help."

Stephenson opened his counseling service in an office rented from a local nondenominational businessmen's religious group, the Fishers of Men. During the first six months, Stephenson talked with many alcoholics. But he soon saw that more than counseling was needed. Consequently, on August 9, 1966, the first Hope Harbor home was opened, in rented quarters, with a capacity for twenty patients.

Late in 1967, Stephenson arranged for Hope Harbor to purchase an old church building. This not only gave the project some much-needed office space but it also provided a place to set up a rescue mission program for transient men.

John Stephenson's ability to help alcoholics was matched in those early days by his success in dealing with the community at large—and by his self-confidence. Although he plunged into the task of organizing the project and arranging for quarters *before* he found the necessary backing, he was eventually able to obtain sufficient support from the community to put Hope Harbor on a reasonably firm financial footing.

Since 1967, Hope Harbor has continued to expand its facilities and services. Facilities for men have been opened in a number of localities outside Greensboro. These include a farm at Snow Hill, North Carolina, where the patients not only reside but actively share in what is now a productive enterprise. Most of the men's residences are small, being able to accommodate between 15 and 40 patients. The largest, a former YMCA building in downtown Greensboro, has space for one hundred and four residents, including 50 transients. This building is also used now to house a number of Hope Harbor's programs and activities.

The old church building currently houses the organization's women's division, called Peace Haven, which had been originally started in a rented house in 1968. It has room for twenty-five residents. The building is also used to house the rescue mission for transient women, which can handle up to ten people at a time.

Transients in the rescue programs are given food and lodging for one night or for several nights. They pay $1 for a bed, an evening meal, and breakfast—if they can afford it; otherwise it's free.

A Peace Haven resident working in Hope Harbor's furniture shop

Knowing that an overnight stay is just an emergency measure, Hope Harbor encourages transients to "go upstairs" and join the program as full-time residents.

People in the resident program must agree to stay for a minimum of two months. Once there they go through a "drying-out" period, then are worked into the regular program. The program involves required religious services, required work, and stringent regulations on leaving the premises and on life in general in the dormitory-like living quarters.

Residents are required to work at jobs in the Hope Harbor business enterprises. Or they are asked to staff the living quarters, to cook for the residents, or to work on the farm or in some outside job arranged by Hope Harbor.

They pay for their room and board with the wages they earn. And throughout their stay, they receive counseling and job training and exposure to religious activities.

There are neither doctors nor medical facilities at Hope Harbor. If patients need medical or psychiatric attention, it is arranged for them. They pay for it themselves if able, or they can obtain it through donations or through public assistance programs.

Stephenson estimates that approximately 50 percent of those who are in the program for at least two months are rehabilitated.

A resident at Hope Harbor's farm heads for the barn to begin the day's chores. The farm is located about 125 miles southeast of Greensboro.

About 30 percent of those who enter the full program, with the time requirement, drop out before the two months are over. They are welcome to return, though, and many of them do.

Hope Harbor's chief business activities are the restoring and reselling of used furniture, appliances, and clothing, plus running a service station; these provide most of its income.

Perhaps the story of Hope Harbor is best told in the lives of the men and women who are there or have been there.

Bill, for example, spent ten months at Hope Harbor. He recently moved back home with his wife, and now operates his own delivery service in Greensboro. He had been a laboratory technician with a textile firm, earning more than $12,000 a year, until alcohol caused him to lose his job in 1970. He didn't come to Hope Harbor voluntarily. He was sent by the courts after he had been arrested for drunken driving.

At first Bill resented the regimen at Hope Harbor, and he thought it silly. He went to the religious services only because that was required. But gradually, through counseling and other experiences, he overcame his problem. He also had a profound religious awakening.

"I'm not just an alcoholic who stopped drinking," he says. "I'm a sinner who stopped sinning."

Marie was the first resident patient in Peace Haven, the women's unit. After a month and a half, she became supervisor of the women's program. She still is. Her problem with alcohol began with so-called social drinking—sipping cocktails. Then she began to need the cocktails "because I liked the effects."

What is it about Hope Harbor and Peace Haven that helps? Marie says: "When you take the bottle away, you have to fill that void with something. You can't just take people in and sober them up and leave them sitting around. Unless you have something to give people once you sober them up, they are going right back down. The religious life and the hard work do it here."

Johnny has been at Hope Harbor for five years. He now manages the appliance store. He had worked in appliance and furniture stores, and as a timekeeper for a large construction firm, before he developed his "problem" at about age 40. He lost his wife, his job, his friends, and his self-confidence. He came to Hope Harbor voluntarily.

Now, he says, "I feel like I've got the problem licked. I feel like it'll never be a problem again."

Johnny adds, "Hope Harbor can help anybody. I found it through the Lord and the Reverend Stephenson."

These people are helping to restore faith in the providers of medical care.

The People's Free Medical Clinic

Baltimore, Maryland

"Medical Care is a Right, Not a Privilege."

This is the slogan of a medical clinic that, on an annual budget amounting to only about half of what a successful doctor earns, provides free or low-cost health care to an entire neighborhood of Baltimore. It is a slogan that has been carried into reality by the People's Free Medical Clinic.

The clinic is intent upon making this medical "right" available to every one of the 25,000 residents of the Waverly section of the city—an area where many people are not poor enough to qualify for public assistance but are too poor to be able to pay for either good health care or adequate medical insurance.

Operating in a pair of storefronts on Greenmount Avenue, the clinic has provided treatment and counseling to some 10,000 people since it was founded in 1970.

The clinic came into being as a result of the antiwar and social radicalism of the 1960s. In 1969 a group of political activists, feeling that public protests and demonstrations were not succeeding as methods of bringing about social change, began to look for alternative courses of action.

"We were looking for a social issue which touched the bulk of the community—an issue upon which we could exert a positive force. We settled on medical care," said James C. Keck, one of the clinic's organizers.

Deciding what to do turned out to be far easier than doing it.

"We did a whole lot of talking," says Keck, "but we weren't really getting anywhere. I don't think many people believed it was going anywhere, and there were some pretty lonely times."

The lonely times ended in the spring of 1970, about the same time that the group formally chartered itself as a tax-exempt, non-profit corporation called the People's Free Medical Clinic, Inc. The organizers found an available storefront for rent.

"That was the turning point," Keck recalls. "It was something tangible. It showed people we had more than just an idea."

With four doctors, two nurses, and a laboratory technician—all of whom had volunteered their services—the clinic opened its doors in May 1970.

During its first year of operation it managed to increase its staff considerably. As Keck says, "We were flooded with volunteers." In its second year, 1971, the clinic purchased the adjoining store-front, and thereby it greatly enlarged its available space—a necessary step in that more and more neighborhood people were seeking out the clinic. Between 1972 and 1974 the clinic expanded its services, developed new approaches to health care, and began to give literally thousands of people what they had never had before—good, personalized, inexpensive health care.

Primary health care of the type provided by a family doctor is the most popular service of the clinic. Also offered are counseling for women in birth control, abortion, and tests for pregnancy. There is individual and group therapy, couple therapy, and family counseling, emergency and diagnostic dental service, and referral service for patients requiring the attention of specialists. The clinic is also equipped to provide dental care—principally emergency care and diagnosis of dental problems.

In its overall concern for the general health of the community, the clinic also undertakes large-scale screening programs to test for sickle cell anemia, tuberculosis, and venereal disease—diseases that are all too common in the inner city.

People can come to the clinic for advice, counseling, and referral five days a week. Medical diagnosis and treatment, though, are available only in the evenings, 6 p.m. to 10 p.m., four days a week—principally because of the limited availability of medical personnel.

The clinic is virtually an all-volunteer operation. The nine paid staff members receive only $35 per week. All the medical professionals are nonpaid volunteers, with most coming from the large Johns Hopkins and University of Maryland teaching hospitals in Baltimore. Backing them up are a staff of almost 150 nonprofessional volunteers.

The volunteer system is the key to the way the clinic is managed. All policy decisions are made by a majority vote at staff-community meetings, with all attending having an equal vote. Keck says the system may not be the most efficient, but adds, "You have to remember that the people working in the clinic are a very independent group. They're not willing to put up with someone telling them what to do. If we lose our volunteers we lose everything."

The nonprofessional volunteers are also the backbone of the clinic's pioneering innovation of "health advocates." Health advocates stay with a patient throughout treatment, explain what is happening, inform him of all available aid programs, and make sure physicians explain all treatment and prescribed medicines. The clinic's efforts to take some of the mystery out of medicine and to resolve the fears of patients have been successful largely as a result of the use of health advocates.

These services are offered on an operating expense budget that came to slightly more than $30,000 in 1973, very little money by general standards in the medical profession. More than $22,000 came from contributions of $25 or less. The money is raised through use of a donation box in the clinic and by mail appeals. There are some larger private, foundation and school grants, used for capital outlays. The only government aid is in free drugs and laboratory tests. The clinic has so far adamantly refused outright government funding.

"By depending on a large number of small contributions," according to Keck, "we have been able to maintain our independence. If we had to depend on one or two large sources, it wouldn't be long before they started telling us what to do."

The clinic also has gained acceptance in the community. One convert is Dallas Weigel, community relations director for Union Memorial Hospital, which is the only hospital located in the Waverly neighborhood.

"The people who are involved are doing a wonderful job," says Weigel, who acknowledges having reservations about the clinic when it started. "It is amazing that with their lack of funding they are able to do what they do."

Before the clinic was established, Weigel says, many people in the area received medical care only on a crisis or emergency basis. People without health insurance would think twice before going to the hospital, where even one treatment in the emergency room costs close to $30.

Now there is more emphasis on health maintenance and people are getting treatment earlier, Weigel says. Attitudes are changing within the community, he notes. "These people [at the clinic] are helping to restore faith in the providers of medical care."

Keck and his colleagues at the clinic had never intended it to be a cure-all for medical problems in the area. They feel, nevertheless, that they have not only provided a community service but have put pressure on regular doctors and hospitals to do a better job. And they have demonstrated that, as Keck says, "Medical problems can't be divorced from social and economic ones."

I saw people I was helping change from human
wrecks into persons contributing to the
community and helping to save themselves.

St. Jude Home

Boston, Massachusetts

When Tom Dineen decided to quit the life of a policeman he never thought he would wind up operating a halfway house for skid row derelicts.

Twenty-eight years old, ambitious, energetic, idealistic, and still restless after leaving a Catholic seminary two years before, Dineen was bored by the monotony of police work in the suburban town of Stoughton, Massachusetts.

What he really wanted to do was work with young people. He was already involved in part-time youth work, helping a group of local teenagers put on Christmas parties for every nursing home in Stoughton. The success of these parties was leading to even grander ideas—proposed by both the policeman and the teenagers—about how to help others. As the young people looked to their future, so did he, and he decided to leave police work and get into a field in which he could become involved on a full-time basis helping youth.

An ideal job, Tom Dineen thought, would be operating a halfway house for young people who needed advice, an encouraging word, a warm handshake, a pat on the back. He couldn't find any openings of this sort, though, so he looked for alternatives. Subsequently he accepted a job as director of a halfway house for alcoholics that was to be set up in Boston.

"I took it for the experience," he explains. "I wanted to work with kids, not alcoholics. But I figured if I had some experience I could get a job later working with young people."

He was asked to establish a halfway house in a dilapidated building near the city's skid row section. The house turned out to be so run down that three of its six apartments could not be inhabited. And the only alcoholics who had stayed there were winos who had crawled into its cellar or collapsed in its hallways until rousted out by the tenants or police.

Turning to friends he had made in the seminary and others he had acquired while a policeman, Dineen cleaned up the garbage in the hallways, scrubbed and sanded the floors, painted the walls, replaced sagging ceilings, papered the bedrooms, and renovated all eighteen rooms. The people he invited to live there were men discharged from an alcoholism ward at the state hospital for the criminally insane in Bridgewater. Many of them gladly accepted his invitation.

As the months went by, Dineen discovered that he enjoyed working with alcoholics as much as he liked working with young people. As he says:

"I found by helping these men my life was becoming more meaningful. I began to get more out of life myself. I saw people I was helping change from human wrecks into persons contributing to the community and helping to save themselves."

After eight months, though, Dineen decided to leave. While he got on well with the patients there, he was finding himself more and more in disagreement with the policies and practices of the organizers of the project.

So, again calling on the friends who had helped him renovate the broken-down building, he formed a corporation to set up a halfway house that he would run more fully in accord with his own philosophy about how unfortunates should be treated.

In August 1970 the corporation rented a building while Tom Dineen and his friends looked for a permanent location. On January 1, 1971, making use of Dineen's $2,700 in savings, the corporation opened at 13 Woodside Avenue in Boston's Jamaica Plain section, the first of what has since become three houses that together make up St. Jude Home.

St. Jude Home has had no opposition from the neighborhood people. Fears that the community would oppose a facility for alcoholics were dispelled when the Reverend Robert Gale, assistant pastor of Our Lady of Lourdes Roman Catholic church, which serves the area, went to the homes of Jamaica Plain residents to explain St. Jude Home, and its goals, and the community's need for such a place. He emphasized that alcoholics are sick and need help, that they should not be left on the sidewalks—or in anyone's private home—to suffer and shift for themselves.

Jack Doherty, a reporter on the local weekly newspaper, took the same message to leaders of the community personally. Tom Dineen and Elliot Lee, his chief assistant, explained the home and its purpose at school assemblies, meetings of church organizations and civic groups, and on radio talk shows. The cordiality between St. Jude Home and the community has thrived as the people of the area have seen for themselves that St. Jude Home really does help individuals in dire need of assistance.

Tom Dineen, the founder and director of St. Jude Home

St. Jude Home is located in what Tom Dineen considers a very suitable environment, one far removed from the defeatism and decay of skid row. The halfway house's location is a lower-middle-class neighborhood of three- and four-story apartment buildings, which are predominately the homes of families rather than single people. Children pass by every day going to and from the school, which is so close that the schoolbells can be heard at St. Jude Home on a clear day. Women stroll by with bags of shopping, and people of all ages go by on their way to the metropolitan transit system's ugly but handy elevated railroad stop, which provides convenient access to other parts of the city. In many ways the area around St. Jude Home is a typical urban neighborhood.

Although the halfway house began as a treatment center for men only (it was known initially as the St. Jude Foundation for Homeless Men), it has since expanded its facilities to accommodate women as well.

St. Jude Home accepts people referred to it by hospitals, detoxification centers, and police and other agencies. To be accepted the men must demonstrate an ability to get along with others in a group-sharing environment and a desire to maintain sobriety. The physically able are expected to find employment, if necessary with help from the staff. And all residents are expected to pay $35 weekly to the house (the state welfare division pays the fee for the unemployed).

In return the residents receive free medical care from a community health agency, individual and group therapy, vocational counseling, and encouragement in their efforts to restructure the lives that they had almost destroyed by drinking. All are required to attend regular meetings within the home and elsewhere in the community. Alcoholism is discussed at the meetings, and the men are forbidden to drink alcoholic mixtures of any kind. Residents who are found to have been drinking must leave St. Jude Home until they are sober again.

In addition to the main building on Woodside Avenue, St. Jude Home includes two nearby apartment houses—one of them for men and the other for women. Both of these buildings are scheduled to be used as cooperative apartments for people who have achieved advanced periods of sobriety. These people will be able to come and go as they please, as they would if they were living in their own homes, although food and supportive programs will come from the main house. Income from the apartments is expected to broaden the financial base for the entire operation.

St. Jude Home is a successful operation. Each year hundreds of adults are given a guiding hand, the friendly yet disciplined atmosphere, and the motivation to climb out of the hellhole of alcoholism and to restore themselves as productive members of society.

Tom Dineen works long hours at St. Jude Home, rarely taking a complete day off. He works harder, probably, than he would have if he had remained with the police department. But he loves his work. Ask him why and he responds by saying that "it's the people, the involvement, knowing you are helping others, the friendships you make with the people you do help."

Everybody thinks what you need is publicity. . . .
But it's much better to work with professionals
and talk to people on the street. Besides, our
clients don't read newspapers.

Walden House

San Francisco, California

It had only been two years since 1967 and the "summer of love" that transformed San Francisco's Haight-Ashbury into the mecca of the counter culture. But as the first summer fog drifted past the tattered Victorian tenements in June of 1969, the dreams of the flower-children were disappearing in the haze of drugs and violence that was enveloping the Bay Area.

It was a time when much of urban America was in the grip of a heroin epidemic, and nowhere was the plague more evident than along the narrow streets bordering San Francisco's Golden Gate Park.

While Haight-Ashbury was busy shooting up, a number of people in San Francisco (and elsewhere, of course) were trying to find a solution to the drug problem.

Among them was Walter Littrell, a 29-year-old pharmaceutical salesman, who made a comfortable living selling tranquilizers to psychiatrists. He knew that a variety of approaches to the problem were being considered. The one that interested him the most was the concept that drug abuse can be treated effectively by placing the individual in a surrogate family.

Littrell had experienced the surrogate-family way of life when living in a college commune. He had learned that the surrogate, or substitute, family produces a certain degree of conformity among the people living together, as well as a close-knit peer group that stresses "togetherness" as a means of solving problems.

Littrell knew that Haight-Ashbury had spawned numerous communal living groups, many of which were centered around the use of drugs. If a surrogate family could, in effect, keep drug users on drugs, he reasoned, then surely a drug-free surrogate family could wean users away from drugs.

It was early in June 1969 that Littrell met Hosea Blye, a ex-junkie who had kicked the heroin habit and had become a counselor at Daytop Village, an experimental drug rehabilitation project in New York. Littrell found that Blye shared his view that a small therapeutic community based roughly on the Daytop experience could be effective in filling the void left by other groups that had tried to deal with the drug problem.

Consequently Littrell and Blye decided to start such a therapeutic community, based on the surrogate-family approach to treatment. This marked the beginning of Walden House.

"There was nothing like Walden House when we started," recalls the tall, bearded Littrell. "We were flying by the seat of our pants most of the time. At lot of what we did was experimental."

While Blye set about developing a clinical strategy, Littrell began to promote the program with all the enthusiasm he had used to sell pharmaceuticals.

As an expression of his faith, Littrell sold his suburban home and used the $10,000 as a downpayment on an aging Victorian mansion in Haight-Ashbury. This was christened Walden House.

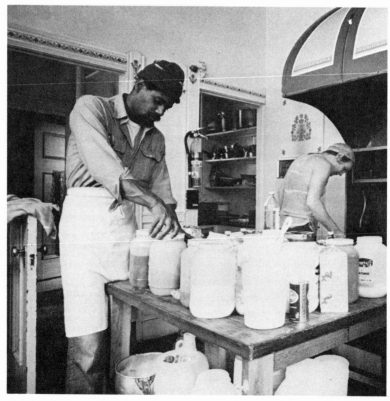

Walden House residents work in the kitchen as part of their daily routine.

Gigi Carroll

Initially the Walden House staff consisted of Littrell, his wife, and Blye. While they worked with a handful of young addicts, Littrell continued to seek financial and legal support for the program. He assembled a board of directors, secured a charter for Walden House as a nonprofit corporation, and found funds where he could. There is some truth to the observation of Keith Matthews, the ex-U.S. Air Force officer who currently serves as the project's administrative director: "In reality, Walden House exists because of a monumental string of lucky occurrences, most of which weren't planned." Through a chance meeting at his church, for example, Littrell secured the program's first grant, a $10,000 capital assistance grant from the San Francisco Foundation—which proved to be the first of several grants from that foundation in the next few years.

By 1971 the program had been expanded, the staff doubled to six people, and a total of 75 clients were being served. Littrell had, by this time, convinced authorities in several Bay Area counties to give youthful first offenders a choice of going to Walden House or of being thrust into the never-ending labyrinth of the criminal justice system. The willing cooperation of Bay Area judges, coupled with the youngsters' common sense, provided Walden House with a steady supply of clients—as well as allowing it to tap public funds to support their work with young offenders.

The clinical structure of Walden House has been evolving since the basic system was devised by Hosea Blye. Current practice calls for the client to be introduced into the surrogate family, which enables him or her to rebuild self-confidence and establish trusting relations. Group and individual therapy are supplemented by household duties, which make everyone responsible for the functioning of the unit.

Walden House's basic objectives are elimination of what society identifies as criminal behavior (the consumption or distribution of illegal drugs), the development of a positive personal image, and the eventual reintegration into society of stable, competent individuals capable of living with, if not within, the system.

The organization will consider accepting anyone, male or female, between the ages of 15 and 30. After an initial screening, the person begins a four-part "reentry" program that usually lasts six months.

The first phase of a resident's treatment is called "community enclave." He becomes one of the residents living together and involving themselves in informal rap sessions to discuss mutual problems. Next, he is introduced to individuals who are all still in reentry but are out living on their own. The former residents return to discuss problems of mutual concern. The third phase of treatment schedules adjustment sessions for the family of the resident. This action is designed to help his relatives fully understand the problems of adjusting to life without drugs. The final step attempts to place the resident in a job, employment training, or educational institution.

A resident enjoys a quiet moment alone in one of Walden's private rooms.

Throughout its existence, Walden House has maintained a low public profile. "Everybody thinks what you need is publicity—a good newspaper article," says a Walden House staff member. "But it's much better to work with professionals and talk to people on the street. Besides, our clients don't read newspapers."

In fact Walden House gets most of the good news it needs in the series of follow-up studies with which it assesses its work annually. These studies indicate a steady reduction in postresidential use and abuse of drugs, in involvement in criminal activity, and also in antisocial behavior.

The staff seems to have a fairly objective view of its strengths and weaknesses. And while the project has recently expanded to include an adult residential house and a storefront outpatient program, its staff members do not seem to have overreached their abilities.

But then, Walden House does not look upon itself as an institution. It sees itself as a family in which the members help and draw strength from one another.

Before 1972 the area . . . relied chiefly on two
local doctors to attend to the medical needs of its
10,000 residents. Since then . . . there has also
been the Chicano Community Center, and
with it has come free medical care
and compassion and understanding.

The Chicano Community Center

San Diego, California

Every Tuesday and Thursday evening they file slowly into the old building on National Avenue in San Diego. Once inside the building they make their way to the receptionist's desk. There they explain their problems and fears, in rapid, soft-flowing Spanish or in halting English.

Then they wait. The children quickly adapt themselves to their new surroundings, playing gleefully in whatever open space they can find. The parents smile shyly at one another, exchange small talk or watch television. They still seem somewhat anxious, but their nervousness has clearly subsided. The people who have come for help are among friends. They are at the Chicano Community Center, a medical clinic that serves the poor people who live in the Logan Heights section of San Diego.

Ten thousand people live in the city blocks sprawling around the Chicano Community Center, in the shadow of the San Diego–Coronado Bay Bridge. About 98 percent of them are of Mexican descent, 70 percent are Spanish-speaking people who know at least some English, and close to 25 percent speak only Spanish.

The neighborhood residents cling to their Mexican heritage, and they treasure the ways and values of their people. They greatly respect family ties, and place great store by such qualities as loyalty and dignity and pride. Their life is not easy, but they meet tragedy with the age-old credo of "God wills it so."

What God wills, apparently, is a neighborhood where housing conditions are poor and job opportunities are limited. Most of the people have very low incomes, being dependent on public assistance and/or low-paying jobs that are often only part-time ones.

Many of the neighborhood people are immigrants from Mexico. Although most of them are legal U.S. residents, a considerable number are not; they've smuggled themselves into the country, determined to have a chance at a decent life whatever the danger. And they do live in danger—of being caught and sent back by the U.S. authorities, of being preyed on by unscrupulous individuals who know that illegal aliens won't seek help from the law.

Legal and illegal aliens alike tend to be community-bound. The bewildering complexities of a strange large city make them hesitant to venture beyond the boundaries of their neighborhood.

And even within those boundaries, they are fearful of doctors and hospitals and medical care. To many of them, such facilities have traditionally been the exclusive domain of the Anglos. And if they, the Chicanos, sought treatment, there were all the fears of the unknown, not to mention the threat of high fees.

Before 1972 the area in the shadow of the bridge relied chiefly on two local doctors to attend to the medical needs of its 10,000 residents. Since then, though, there has also been the Chicano Community Center, and with it has come free medical care and compassion and understanding.

Back in the late 1960s a group of local people had been upset that construction of a nearby freeway had forced the demolition of the building that housed the area's only medical clinic.

Concerned about the future of medical care in the Chicano community, the group decided it would be best to start a new clinic. One possibility was a certain building on National Avenue. It was owned by a social service organization, but for several years had been relegated to serving only as an administrative office.

"It provided no services for the people," recalls Dick Weiss, a member of the group and also a city employee at the time. "We formed a committee of people to talk to the agency about using their facilities. We talked with them for six months, but nothing happened."

Finally a group of college kids who had grown up in the community approached Weiss and the others and asked if the community would back them up if they simply took over the building.

On October 6, 1969, while hundreds of community residents marched outside, three college students barricaded themselves inside the old building. They were there for three months.

"It was an abrasive thing to do," says Weiss, "but necessary. We successfully demonstrated the public's interest in having a clinic in the neighborhood. After the fact, however, nobody really cared."

The student occupation in effect gave the community the building it needed for a clinic. But it took a lot more time and effort before the community had a full-fledged clinic in operation. In fact it took close to two years, together with the cooperation of various groups of people inside and outside the neighborhood.

Restoration of the building itself was made possible in part by the volunteer efforts of a group of Seabees from the naval air station on North Island, as well as the labor and materials donated by a local carpenters' union. And gangs of neighborhood people worked their way through the building, mopping and scrubbing, wiping and cleaning.

Even before work on the building was completed, the clinic was already serving the people of the community. Like the restoration program, the medical program was largely dependent on volunteers. Doctors from San Diego's Mercy Hospital, for example, volunteered their services. And even a number of U.S. Army Reserve doctors and pharmacists helped out at the clinic in their spare time.

In March 1973 the center was formally incorporated as a nonprofit enterprise called the Family Health Services Center, Inc.—a name chosen principally to reflect the center's goals. Nevertheless it continued to be known popularly as the Chicano Community Center—or simply as the Chicano Clinic.

The center fills a major community need. "People love the clinic," says Laura Rodriguez, one of Weiss' fellow founders and a woman who has lived in the neighborhood ever since she was born there some sixty-five years ago.

"The people depend on the center," she says. "When the old clinic was torn down, they simply had no place to go. They needed a clinic that was close to them—and one they could trust."

Trust gives the center both credibility and clients. Not only does it attract people from the neighborhood, but it now draws people from Chula Vista, San Ysidro, and National City as well.

And it has special meaning for one particular group. In the words of one woman staffer: "Consider the people who have never seen a doctor. If it weren't for the clinic, they would die. And they won't go anywhere else unless they feel at home."

Perhaps the best statement of the clinic's impact comes from Irma Barreto, the administrator of the center.

"It takes about all the courage we have some days just to face the problems of keeping the center open and the programs in force," she says. "But someone always seems to come along at the right time."

"To everyone," she says, "the center is home."

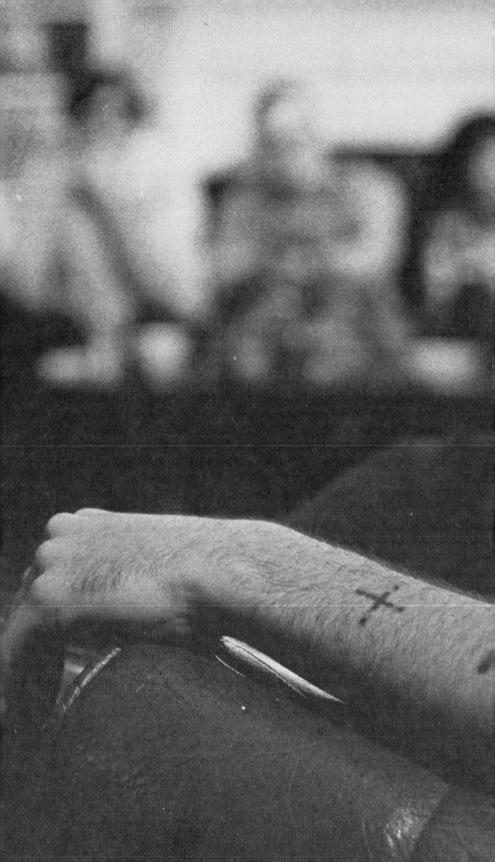

7

Offender Rehabilitation

Although officials like to refer to them as "correctional institutions," most prisons are places where offenders are held in confinement, without rights, without training, without hope.

There are currently some 500,000 prison inmates in this country, but they account for only about 35 percent of the total offender population; the rest—some 950,000—are actually on the outside, on parole or probation. Whether they have served out their sentences or have been released conditionally, nearly 50 percent of all offenders wind up being convicted of another crime and sent back to prison.

If prisons are supposed to rehabilitate criminals, why is the return-to-prison rate so high?

Clearly most offenders are unprepared for life on the outside when they are released. Either they lack the skills and training to compete in the job market, or they suffer the fate of being almost universally discriminated against as "ex-cons."

Self-help projects for offenders are currently active in America's prisons helping prepare inmates for life on the outside. And they are working with ex-offenders on the outside, helping them find their way back into society. They get jobs for the unemployed, teach skills to the unprepared, and try to provide the opportunities and encouragement needed to prevent a return to prison.

There are other, related self-help projects aimed at helping people avoid the world of prisons altogether. There are, for example, projects aimed at educating adults about the dangers of child abuse and other forms of antisocial behavior. And there are projects that work with young people who seem likely to drift into a life of crime unless given some guidance and redirection.

Self-help rehabilitation projects and related programs are of national importance in that they point the way—at least one way—to conserve America's human resources. More than that, they help the offender and potential offender to steer clear of the revolving doors of crime and punishment and to take a productive role in society.

Lifelong "takers" who are learning to be "givers."
For their own sake—and for the sake of
society. In that order.

The New Directions Club

Houston/Galveston, Texas

At first glance there seems to be no social pattern to the group of people lounging on the couches and chairs scattered about the large, old-fashioned, and comfortable room. At first glance, it could be a scene in a boarding house. But common sense rules out even that impression. After all, blacks and whites and Chicanos just don't board together. And the age differences are too great; some of the people are in their late 40s and 50s, a few are in their 60s; others are obviously much younger—barely out of their teens. Cultural differences show through in dress, too, with some of the people wearing boots and Western-cut shirts; others are modishly dressed, hung with beads and draped in fashionable tie-dyes. As they speak the room is filled with the babble of soft-edged Southern accents, clipped Northern syllables, and the rumbling echos of deep black voices.

In this old, ivy-covered, red-brick house the routine interpersonal conflicts of the outside world seem forgotten.

"Everybody is loved here," murmurs a black woman to visiting outsiders. "When one person hurts, every one of us hurts."

"We gather strength from each other," twangs a man in a striped Western shirt. "If one of us in trouble, everybody is in trouble."

A 47-year-old electronics technician speculates that "ever since I've been here I've been trying to find out why this place is so special. I've tried to intellectualize it, but it's really just a feeling we have, and it can't be explained in an intellectual way. You get a feeling that you want to do something for somebody. Not because you have to—but because you want to."

He pauses. "It's kind of what a lot of religions have, I guess."

But this is not a religious organization. In fact it's a group of thieves and thugs and dope-fiend whores, plus a smattering of hot-check artists, pickpockets, narcotics addicts and pushers, pimps, armed robbers, killers, burglars, and other assorted varieties of lawbreaker. At least they used to be. Now they work as cab drivers, technicians, construction workers, housekeepers, typists, clerks, counselors, and so on.

And this is the pattern to the gathering. It is a pattern of lifelong "takers" who are learning to be "givers." For their own sake—and for the sake of society. In that order.

This is one of the five halfway houses operated by the New Directions Club in the Houston-Galveston metropolitan area—halfway, that is, between prison and the mainstream of society. In a little over three years of operations, starting on the thinnest of shoestrings and only now beginning to splice together the supporting cables of an all-encompassing rehabilitative effort, New

Directions has taken in and sent out more than 800 people. Of those 800-plus ex-convicts, only a fraction over 3 percent have subsequently gone back to prison—an incredible achievement when it is considered that the national rate of return-to-prison averages more than 50 percent.

New Directions offers not only a haven but a number of services to the ex-convict (and on rare occasion to the socially troubled individual who has not been to prison). First, as its name implies, New Directions offers a place of readjustment between one world and another—between the world of self-satisfying criminal activity plus its prison penalty and the world of the squares. It provides the basic necessities of food, clothing, and shelter to those who would otherwise be tempted to take them by force. It finds employment for the ex-convict—and it includes training if necessary.

But of far more worth than this material assistance is the help that New Directions gives the takers to readjust to the straight world in which they will now have to live.

"Man, before I came to this place all I did was scheme against them dumb squares," reflects a former pimp and narcotics addict. "They were so easy. All I had to do to live cool was to outsmart them. But I was really outsmarting myself. Sooner or later I'd always end up in prison."

The mental readjustment of ex-convicts is done so simply that many psychologists might not believe the method could possibly work. It is accomplished through an insistence on total reality. And that brings with it a demand for total self-honesty. Reality, reasons the ex-con, can't be disputed successfully by anyone with good street sense. And if there is anything the underworld character has in abundance, it's good street sense.

At first glance this emphasis on total reality may seem brutal—as it often does to new arrivals.

"When I first came here they told me like it was," says Peggy in a husky voice. "They told me I was nothing but a dope-fiend whore and that I was going to die that way unless I did something about it. And nobody would give a damn. Sure, I'd been told that before, but not by people who had been through everything I'd been through. And not by people who were standing by to help me change, to really work at it, if I would give them half a chance. They weren't trying to be mean or shocking. They were just telling me like it was."

Peggy is now totally straightened out and serves as part of the administrative staff of New Directions. "It wasn't easy," she says with a toss of her blonde hair, "but everybody here understood—really understood—and helped me over the rough spots.

"And for the first time I saw that people could care about people simply because they were human beings. No angles. No games. Now I go to sleep at night with a clear conscience, and when I wake up in the morning I'm not sick. That may not sound like

The New Directions Club's prime mover, "Papa" Sonny Wells

much to a lot of people. But to thousands of people like me, it can be a kind of heaven that they never thought they'd get to."

The founder and executive director of New Directions is Sonny Wells, often called "Papa" by the ex-offenders. Wells is a black man, 50 years old, who has been in the penitentiary five times. He formed New Directions almost by accident while working as a reporter for a Houston newspaper (where he worked his way up to news editor before resigning recently in order to be able to give the New Directions program his undivided attention).

Wells began the project by taking aimless dischargees from the prison system into his home. In the beginning they were mostly old prison buddies who had written to him in desperation. With the help of his wife, Selma, Wells began to invite the ex-cons to stay in his home while they got on their feet. In time, though, it got to be too much of a crowd. So Wells borrowed some money from his publisher and opened a halfway house. He paid the rent the first month, and he helped the convicts find jobs with the idea they could keep the rent going by chipping in. The idea evolved and matured from that point. One night, while making an appearance on public television with George Bush, a former U.S. ambassador to the United Nations, Wells fired a few verbal blasts at do-gooder operations that defied the reality of human existence with ever-present and mind-boggling bureaucracy. Bush wanted to know more about the halfway house, and he subsequently sent out letters to his friends telling them of the Wells effort. So New Directions was born.

At first, Wells held New Directions together almost unnoticed by the community. But the financial pressures mounted until, in desperation, he took his problem to the mayor of Houston. After having New Directions investigated, the mayor helped Wells prepare a grant application for seed money. In the meantime, the letters sent out by George Bush on behalf of the project began to bear financial fruit. Wells started to receive invitations to speak at various community gatherings. He was astounded by the reaction to his appearances. Churches, civic organizations, and private individuals began to pitch in with money, labor, and gifts (such as free rent and furniture). The police and sheriff's departments, seeing the changes being brought about by the program, voiced support for New Directions when inquiries came in.

Wells modestly gives the community the majority of the credit for making New Directions work. "A lot of people wouldn't believe it could happen as simply as it has," he says. "And a lot of people wouldn't think it could happen here. But it did, by God. This is a fantastic community."

"Furthermore," adds Wells, "we've been practically adopted by various groups. The Exchange and Rotary clubs help us build job banks of our own. There are churches and private individuals who are in constant contact with us to see if there's anything we need and to find out what they can do to help us."

New Directions members agree with their founder's assessment of outside response. Pat McCoy, for example, remembers that, on his first day at a New Directions house, fresh out of the penitentiary, Wells sent him to appear before a church group that had requested a speaker. "I was scared to death of these squares," recalls McCoy. "I thought, 'there ain't no way these people want to hear what I've got to say'. Sonny just sent me out, though, and told me to say whatever I wanted and to answer any questions I could. I don't even remember what I said, I was so scared. But after it was over some of these people asked me if I'd like to stay around and have a bite to eat while they took care of some business. They had their committee meeting right there with me in the room. And they voted to help New Directions with some money. Man, I can't tell you how that shocked me. Here were a bunch of squares just pitching in. I didn't think things like that really happened. I thought money and stuff came from the government, or some philanthropist, or something like that. I didn't know until then that it was just people who really made things work. And that's a lesson that hits all ex-cons that come here."

One primary requirement for making a halfway house operation successful, Wells firmly believes, is having to deal with as little bureaucracy as possible—and therein lies one of the reasons for the success of New Directions. The organization operates as a buffer between human needs and bureaucratic rules. An ex-convict seeking a job through accepted channels, for instance, must ride strange buses along strange streets, stand in line at an employment commission, wonder whether to confess his past, fidget over both lack of training and (depending on how long he has been locked up) a strange world, be interviewed by a hurried and often harried civil servant—then be told to wait until he is called. New Directions does the interviewing in the home and sends out the word through the businessman's grapevine, using interested civic groups as connectors. Within a short time a call is received back that a job is open. The employer knows the background. And the ex-convict is on his way.

Naturally there are various official agencies to take care of the readjustment needs of ex-convicts. They can provide training, special tools, medical care, and so forth. But their wheels grind agonizingly slowly, especially for a man who has patiently served out his prison term, and it is New Directions that is able to take up the slack.

"When a man comes out of prison with $50 in his hand," says Wells, "and it takes him two weeks to get a job, he's going to run

Ex-convicts listen during a therapy rap session. The woman (right) is a "facilitator" from the University of Houston who encourages everyone to speak frankly and to really communicate with one another.

out of money. That means he's going to go to people he knows for help. And those he knows are going to get him in trouble again."

"We give him a different way."

In the formative years it seemed that New Directions was destined to focus only on ex-convicts who had been freed from prison. Government rules and regulations forbade the gathering of parolees on the basis that they were required to stay away from known criminal elements. Nevertheless Wells managed to get the board of pardons and paroles to relax that restriction. Consequently many people who formerly could not be paroled because they had no home or job waiting can now be released to New Directions.

Another important factor in the project's success is the use and enforcement of a number of operating principles and loose rules. For example, no squares are allowed to make policy or operating decisions. The ex-convicts run the houses, under firm directions from the more experienced members, as well as the therapy sessions, and the job-finding services, and everything else.

Most of the rules are bendable, as long as permission is granted in advance by the executive director. But some are firm. For instance, there are no exceptions made to the midnight curfew; the curfew is intended to make sure those with jobs establish a life pattern that enables them to give a full day's work for a full day's pay. Another unbendable rule is that there is to be no use of narcotics or alcohol in any of the halfway houses. By and large, though, the rules and regulations at New Directions follow the dictates of common sense.

New Directions operates four houses for men and one for women. Although there are separate living quarters for each sex, coeducational activities are conducted in all of the houses, the principal exceptions being the biweekly therapy sessions.

The average stay in a New Directions halfway house is 90 days. Some people leave sooner, some stay longer. It is Sonny Wells who makes the decision—and it is a decision based on his common sense and deep understanding of the individual involved. All members, once they have a job, contribute $25 a week toward New Directions efforts. They also save one-fourth of their paychecks in order to give them a financial pad to fall back on should they find themselves unemployed for some reason.

Only rarely has anyone been kicked out of New Directions (although once or twice members have been turned in to the police for criminal offenses committed while living at a halfway house). Moving-out time, whenever it comes, is emotionally painful. But it's like the separation of a grown child from the family. If the child is really grown, the necessity is realized by all concerned. And the doors are always open for those who want to return for a visit.

New Directions currently operates on a total budget of less than $120,000 a year, and that modest figure covers all five houses and their roughly 175 residents (148 males and 27 females at last count). It is financed in equal thirds by government grants, private donations, and the resident ex-cons themselves.

One of the key tools used at New Directions is the therapy session. Twice each week the members of each house get together for therapy (frequently being joined by long-discharged members of New Directions). This takes the form of a rap session. Usually the sessions are guided by an ex-convict staff member who not only has undergone the traumas himself but has been especially prepared by completing a long and arduous counseling course at the University of Houston. Once in a while they are guided by squares invited from the university classes.

"In some ways we operate like Alcoholics Anonymous," says Wells. "In fact, since alcohol is one of the main problems of a lot of these people, we often have speakers from Alcoholics Anonymous."

Adds a New Directions veteran: "Everything we do is eventually aimed at helping the people here to not cut off the rest of society.

You've got to remember that we come out of that joint ready to cut society off. We figure they look at us as ex-convicts with long records, and don't want anything to do with us. Really, we're sub-consciously looking for some little excuse to go back to a con-niving life of self-satisfaction.

"But the longer we stay with this program, and the more we are around other people in our jobs, the more we begin to realize what we've done to ourselves. Things like self-confidence and self-worth begin to develop. And we see that society won't really cut us off if we're honest about our problem. Hell, it works the other way around. And that really shakes us up the first time we find it out."

New Directions has found these ex-con-controlled rap/therapy sessions to be so therapeutic that outside professionals, no mat-ter how officially qualified, have been banned. The ex-offenders' faint but real resentment toward authority is thus respected dur-ing their readjustment.

As one woman put it succinctly, "I don't need no psychiatrists or doctors or Indian chiefs. I need somebody who has been there—and back. You can read all the books in the world, but unless you've been there you don't really know what you're talking about."

This ex-convict attends therapy sessions at a New Directions house, but he lives outside the house and works regularly as a cab driver.

It takes more than just being honest with oneself and others to make it at New Directions. The ex-con has to really work at redirecting his life and outlook.

As one member says, "The main thing about New Directions is that nobody jacks with you here. We ain't got no probation officers or social workers or police officers to tell us what to do. We tell each other. And there's no hassling. A dude is welcome in the program if he really wants to make it. We'll help him. And there are lots of examples around here that show it works, so a dude can say to himself, 'Man, I'm just as stout as they are', and bear down on himself. If the dude won't work at it on top of everything—including lots of sincere caring on the part of everybody here—then out he goes. And we can make room for somebody else. That's the way it is. That's the way of the world. He's welcome back. But somewhere along the line he's got to start pulling up. And he can't game around with us because we know when it's happening."

Thus it is that a common aspect of people used to a life of crime is made to work for New Directions family members: vanity is turned into a pride of self-worth. And it is done by example.

Consider the case of Pat McCoy, now 46. Once a heroin addict who committed assorted crimes to support his habit, he was one of Wells' first converts, and is now an assistant director of the New Directions program.

McCoy learned from Wells. "Once you set the example and stick by it," says Wells, "it has a snowballing effect. All those people look at me and the other examples. Of course they just wait for the slightest hint of a failing. We insist on total self-honesty. I do it, and everybody else does it. We pull our own weight in every way. I know that every person who first comes in here looks us over and thinks we've got something going—that this thing can't really be true. They think, like I used to think, that anybody this dedicated has got to be ripping something off on the side. Once they find out differently—and believe me they'd find out if we were—then they can start to get their thinking straight. They see that if we can do it, they can, too. Their pride makes them do it."

The remarkable new world of New Directions probably wouldn't have come about if it hadn't been for the dedication of Papa Sonny. And it's kept moving by his personal example as he prowls bearlike through the rooms, hallways, and kitchens of his creation, grumping at things undone—sometimes with fatherly affection and sometimes with rage—but always seeming to have time for a personal talk with a troubled member.

Papa Sonny knows how it is.

When you're in the joint . . . you do things for one
main reason. That's to get out.

Job Therapy

Seattle, Washington

The Camerons give an outward impression of being a fairly average suburban family. Gordon is vice-president and branch
manager of a Seattle area savings and loan association. Jean
takes care of running the Cameron household. And both of them
spend much of their leisure time with their two young sons.

For three months, though, the Camerons housed another person. His name was Frank. He was an ex-convict, but he wasn't a
guest. For the three months Frank Smith lived with the Camerons
he was part of the family.

The circumstances that placed an ex-convict in a comfortable
suburban home in Seattle were brought about by a project called
Job Therapy. Since its beginning in 1965, Job Therapy has spread
to 20 states and has made 2,500 "matches" similar to that between Frank Smith and the Cameron family.

Job Therapy's inventor is a slim, dynamic, and compassionate
United Presbyterian minister named Richard Simmons. He had
worked for two years as a missionary in the slums of New York,
and his experiences convinced him that the title of "Reverend"
was a barrier rather than an entree into the world of people he encountered. So he became a layman while remaining a Christian
and a Presbyterian. Simmons is a frequent quoter of scriptures.
His favorite (Matthew 25:40): "As you did it to one of the least of
my brethren, you did it to me." Simmons remarks: "And those
people in prison are the least of these. They're society's rejects,
outcasts. There's no one lower on the scale." His interests are the
high-risk convicts, the ones least likely to make it when they leave
prison.

Simmons had done a great deal of research and traveling before he hit on the idea of Job Therapy. He was especially impressed with the results obtained in the Netherlands, where 90
percent of all ex-offenders succeed on probation, compared to
the United States' figure of 50 percent.

Simmons remarked to his wife that "Holland has twelve million people but only 1,500 inmates in maximum security. Our

own State of Washington, with three million people, has more than 3,000. If our ratio were equal to Holland's, we'd have only 375 prisoners in maximum security. That would mean an annual saving in manpower of 2,625 lives, and a savings in wasted taxes of at least eight million dollars."

Simmons likes to say: "I'm not a zealot. I'm just an angry taxpayer who wants to see the money we pay in taxes being used to the best advantage."

Simmons told some friends in Snohomish County, Washington: "This is a tremendous problem all over the country, and somebody has to make a start. We've got to get to the prisoners before they're released and help them build some positive attitudes. I'm convinced this can only be done on a man-to-man basis, with the free man going to visit the imprisoned man for one reason only—because he cares. I'd like to start such a program and I'd call it "M-2"—meaning "Man-to-Man.""

It was the M-2 program of Job Therapy that brought the Cameron family together with Frank Smith.

Gordon Cameron (right) still considers ex-convict Frank Smith (left) "part of his family" and also one of his closest friends.

Six years ago, Gordon Cameron was sitting in the suburban church he attends and listening to an attorney talk about his experiences in a new program aimed at prisoners and parolees. As the attorney talked about his experiences, his voice became choked. "When I saw this man, an attorney who is accustomed to appearing before an entire courtroom, having trouble communicating his emotion, it made me think that this could be a very meaningful experience," recalls Cameron.

Cameron's intuition was right. Since that time, Cameron and his family have become friends with three men serving time in Washington prisons. Frank Smith was the first.

Smith, 26, was doing time for a drug charge and burglary when he was released on parole. The five years he's been out of prison have been spent working as a draftsman for a construction company, a skill he learned in 1,200 hours of work in prison.

During Smith's last year in prison, the Camerons visited him every two weeks. "I think the big difference in coming out was that I had somebody to care," says Smith. "And most of all I had a place and someone to spend my leisure time with. We went to the beach for picnics, or to swim in somebody's pool—things like that. The leisure time is the hard time when you're broke, and I was broke."

Cameron helped Smith find employment when he finally got out. "Gordie did the talking when I applied for the job," Smith remembers, "and I showed my drawings."

Smith met his wife, Anna, three weeks after he got out on parole, and their son, Simon, is now three years old. The Smiths have their own home in Seattle, and Frank, who grew up in the rootless existence of military life, is busily making friends. "I just bulldog them until they realize we're their friends," he grins.

With a home, family, and job, Frank Smith can look back on his years in prison and recall the motivations that made him piece his life back together.

"When you're in the joint, and I'll call it the joint because that's what it is, you do things for one main reason. That's to get out. If you want out, you impress the parole board and even though I thought I might want to be a draftsman, I didn't study for that reason.

"Chances are, I wouldn't have finished that drafting course, but I had somebody who cared whether I was doing well, and somebody who cared whether I finished. You can go out in the prison yard, and if you tell someone 'oh, I got an A in history' they'll say, 'Drop dead, who cares? Who do you think you are?' If you go to the visiting room and there's somebody there that cares, that's different. You can't let somebody down who cares."

In the five years that Smith has been out, he and Gordon Cameron have made many talks before groups, telling about their experiences and trying to recruit sponsors. "Usually, you have to talk to about two hundred people before you get a sponsor," Cameron says.

The two men have an extremely strong friendship. Cameron says: "I think that Frank and I have discussed more things together as friends than any other friend I have. One of the things that has helped me was Frank asking me questions. I had to sort out what I really thought, what I believed. I don't think that people are inclined to get together and talk about serious things. I've gained a lot from this relationship."

Frank Smith and Gordon Cameron represent just a fraction of the Job Therapy success story. Since 1965 there have been 1,525 cooperating employers nationwide; businessmen who are willing to offer employment to men on parole. In community education and involvement there have been audiences totaling more than 300,000 people. Of the 1,500 clients seeking employment in 1973, there were 1,100 job placements.

Dick Simmons says: "Job Therapy is a good title. It's job-work alternatives to traditional incarceration. We believe that ex-offenders should be incarcerated in a work situation. Of course this brings up a lot of questions, because people are not as committed to the work ethic now as they used to be.

"We're saying that if a person wants to work, he should have every chance to do it."

The M-2 program of Job Therapy has now been joined by the W-2 program for women, and both of these programs are about to be joined by the Y-2 program for youths. Although headquartered in Seattle, Job Therapy has reached beyond that location.

"We've come to feel," Simmons explains, "that we're moving toward a franchise concept. We're in every major institution on the West Coast now—California, Oregon, Washington, and British Columbia. We're also in Ohio, New York, and Oklahoma. I started projects all over.

"We've struggled with the problem of how you put together a project quickly, effectively and get it adequately staffed and moving. We decided the only way you can do it is to build a good, strong model and develop a franchise system and then develop a leadership training institute."

One of the most astute—and complimentary—assessments of Job Therapy has come from Dan Evans, the governor of Washington State:

"It pays off in three ways: the ex-offender is helped to become a useful citizen, the taxpayer is saved a great deal of money, and the volunteer himself becomes a useful person."

The handshakes and the expressions on the
faces of these men when we were about to leave
was enough to change the mind and heart
of the worst dude.

Awareness

Buffalo, New York

The young man peered out the bus window and craned his neck for a better view of the medieval-looking turret on the prison wall. A stern guard stared back.

"Did you see the dude up in the tower with all that artillery?" the teenager asked his companion.

The seatmate responded, "I don't want to ever be in this place."

The "place" was Attica prison. The busload of teenagers that pulled into the fortress that day was made up of gang leaders who, until recently, had roamed various neighborhoods of Buffalo.

The youths were visiting Attica, the scene of the bloody riot of 1971, as part of a program called Awareness. The project was put together by Buffalo businessmen to show gang members there were both good and bad alternatives to street battles. The trip to Attica was meant to persuade them—and it seemed to—that prison is one of the worst alternatives.

The presence of the youths on a field trip sponsored by businessmen was testimony that a community and neighborhood can change. In the summer of 1971 there were few people, white or black, who felt that way in the North Fillmore district.

The North Fillmore district, part of Buffalo's East Side, is an area of substandard housing, limited job prospects, and an abundant supply of street crime and drugs. It is close to 65 percent black, with youth unemployment running above 7 percent. About 14 percent of the families are on welfare, 16 percent of the families have incomes below the federally designated poverty line, and only 35 percent of the adults have high school diplomas.

North Fillmore's restless youths roamed freely during the summer of 1971. Gang wars flared at night; gang members were killed and wounded. Other residents lived in fear. Storeowners expected to begin their mornings sweeping up broken glass and then taking inventory of all the missing merchandise.

The people of the neighborhood felt something had to be done.

Contestants in Awareness Unity Day beauty pageant

"We had to get the kids off the streets somehow," one businessman said. "Security was the first thing on most persons' minds."

The vehicle for doing something, residents and businessmen decided, was the North Fillmore Avenue Businessmen's Association. The organization had been inactive for years. Its original purpose of being a business association for a German and Polish ethnic district no longer seemed applicable to North Fillmore.

The association was rechartered, it launched door-to-door campaigns for funds and community participation, and it expanded its membership so that it was transformed from a business group into a community group.

Once the organization had been re-formed, ideas started pouring in. To put the ideas into practice, the association had to win over community youths and push projects to completion with little help from the officials at city hall or others in local government.

The existence of street gangs turned out to be an asset in getting the Awareness program started.

"The young people had more consciousness of neighborhoods. That's what gangs are all about. The kids have a stronger instinct for territorial imperative," says the Reverend Joseph Davis, an early backer of Awareness.

Awareness' objective was to channel the energy and activity of gang members into more productive and less violent pursuits.

The Attica trips were only part of a series of programs developed by the association.

The association president, Randolph Jordan Jr., arranged the Attica trips with the help of a local bank loan. The youths, male and female, talked with and questioned prison inmates. Descriptions of prison life and confinement, of being allowed to watch television only at certain times—these were things the youngsters could relate to. The knowledge clearly jarred them. Some inmates tried to encourage them to stay in school, a "square" message that suddenly took on new meaning. Others stressed black pride and economic power, urging the youngsters to make it within the system and within the law.

As Jordan later wrote, "The handshakes and the expressions on the faces of these men when we were about to leave was enough to change the mind and heart of the worst dude."

One of Awareness' principal projects consists of its various sports programs. These involve supporting eight football teams, twelve basketball teams, and eleven baseball teams, as well as organizing track meets and tennis matches. The Awareness teams play in parks around the city and in the suburbs. (It used to be that the Buffalo city government refused to allow the teams to use the city's parks and playgrounds for their organized activities; it took Awareness' members a 5,000-signature petition to city hall plus the support of a Catholic church program to get the city to permit them to use public facilities.)

Another of Awareness' principal projects is its job program for teenagers. Awareness contacts local businesses to see if they will hire neighborhood teenagers. It maintains a storefront job-referral center. And it has coordinated its efforts with those of the local Model Cities office. The results have been that hundreds of North Fillmore teenagers have been given the opportunity to work—often at what are their first jobs.

Awareness is a nonprofit organization that makes do on a budget of between $20,000 and $30,000 a year. Expenses are held to a minimum, of course, in large part because all of the staff members are nonpaid volunteers. Awareness raises the funds it does need from dues, dinners, the sale of bumper stickers, and personal and business donations.

Although directed primarily toward the young people of the neighborhood, Awareness has gradually come to expand its area of concern to encompass the entire community. Consequently, in August 1972, the organization staged what it called Unity Day. This was designed to focus the entire city's attention on North Fillmore and its achievements, as well as to help instill a sense of pride and accomplishment among the neighborhood people.

The event featured an elaborate parade, complete with floats and football star O. J. Simpson. And there were art shows, beauty contests, dances, and stage shows. And booths were set up along the sidewalks. The celebration was a great success, attracting some 20,000 enthusiastic spectators and participants.

There were no disruptive incidents during Unity Day, for an effective security force was on duty the whole time. Law and order were maintained by none other than former gang members—who also cleaned the streets after the festivities were over.

The following year Awareness organized an even more elaborate celebration. Called Open House Awareness, this lasted four days and featured even more events than 1972. Thousands of people thronged North Fillmore for the event.

Not surprisingly, Awareness scheduled a third festival for the summer of 1974.

Gang wars and gang raids are a thing of the past in North Fillmore—as are the days when the neighborhood youngsters had almost nothing else to occupy them and no one to guide them.

A key factor in the development of the neighborhood's peaceful productivity is that the businessmen of the community have come to know and understand the teenagers, just as the teenagers have come to terms with the businessmen.

"I suppose our motives were a bit selfish at first," remembers an association officer. "Our stores were constantly being looted and besieged by the gangs. We started Awareness to combat that problem. We soon found out that gang members were really nice kids with a lot of energy but no place to channel their enthusiasm."

"I used to think all businessmen were squares," remarks one gang member, "but now I see I'm wrong. Besides, I'd like to have a shop someday, and I sure hope something like Awareness is around so I can maybe get to help some kids in life."

Everybody volunteers for something.
Some men coach football and Little League
baseball. The women of SCAN are dedicated.
They've got their own thing.

SCAN Volunteer Services

Little Rock, Arkansas

Her earliest recollection of life is an event that happened when she was two years old, says Linda, the third of twelve children in a family that traveled the country during the harvest seasons.

"Mama hit me in the head with an iron skillet."

Instead of parental love Linda got what she remembers as "whippings with a coffeepot cord that beat the blood out of us."

Two and a half years ago, with a child 13 months old, Linda was on the run from officials in two states who wanted to take her baby. Though she didn't know why at the time, Linda too had become an abusive parent.

But Linda was lucky. By chance she met someone who cared, someone who wanted to help her and her child. It was in a drugstore in Little Rock, Arkansas, that Linda first got to know Sharon Pallone, a psychology major and mother of two children. And that chance meeting had far-reaching effects, for it eventually brought about the birth of SCAN Volunteer Services, Inc., a volunteer organization that since August 1972 has provided immediate service to more than 550 children in over 200 families.

Supplied with funds by the Arkansas Social Services Division and private contributions, SCAN has trained a staff of more than 50 people and has begun expanding its services from its highly urbanized home base in Pulaski County to four regional centers in other parts of the state.

SCAN (which stands for Suspected Child Abuse and Neglect) began by making the community at large aware of a serious problem that exists in its midst. Subsequently, through cooperation with public and private agencies and professionals in the fields of health, social work, and law, SCAN proved that its highly motivated volunteers can achieve professional results in treating and reducing the abuse and neglect of children.

When she set out to help Linda and her abused child, Sharon

Pallone was frustrated to find that all the assistance available was badly fragmented, slow in coming, and woefully inadequate as far as lasting results were concerned.

"This was a crisis situation," she now says. "One woman was going to take Linda's baby to the state line and turn her over to authorities."

Financing Linda's welfare out of her husband's pocket, Mrs. Pallone set out to find some agency, public or private, that could tend to the needs of people who shared the young mother's predicament. She could not find even one.

Since 1939 the legal responsibility for the protection of children has rested with the Arkansas Social Services Division (formerly the Arkansas Department of Public Welfare). The agency, although dedicated to its task, is like most comparable public agencies throughout the country—badly understaffed and underfunded. In 1967 the Arkansas General Assembly noted and corrected through legislation one particular major problem—namely, the reluctance on the part of the general public to report cases of abuse and serious neglect of children. The scope of the new legislation was so broad that it even required lay persons to report all suspected cases of child abuse and neglect to the authorities. Furthermore it directed the state welfare department to keep a central registry of all such reports.

After the legislature acted, a child protection committee was formed at the University of Arkansas Medical Center (UAMC) at Little Rock. The membership was made as broad as possible, encompassing health professionals as well as welfare and social service agencies. The committee became the nucleus of the Pulaski County Task Force on Child Protection, which was formed in October 1971. The task force membership was even more broadly based, being set up to include twenty agencies, as well as laymen and professionals interested in child protection.

With the task force (now officially the Arkansas Council for Child Protection) operating as a facilitator or coordinator of service, Dr. Lloyd Young, a UAMC staff member, suggested to Sharon Pallone that some kind of agency or organization was needed "to deliver the services."

Already involved with Linda and her problems, Sharon Pallone seized the opportunity to found SCAN in the spring of 1972.

Seeking help, advice, and cooperation from doctors, nurses, welfare workers, and hospitals, Mrs. Pallone trained the first six volunteers and set out to talk about the program to anybody who would listen.

From April to July of that year (1972), SCAN operated on a

"The volunteer is the key to the success of SCAN," says Sharon Pallone.

shoestring budget funded by private donations. "I realized we were broke," Sharon Pallone now says. "We had two choices: get some permanent funding or fold."

One fund-raising technique failed miserably, she recalls. "My approach was to go up to an individual or a group and say, 'I need $20,000—today'—and with that they would gag and faint."

"It is better," she says, "to get a little from more people."

And that, as it turned out, is exactly what she managed to accomplish.

By August 1972, SCAN had convinced the community that it was a workable organization staffed entirely by volunteers. Its success so impressed the Arkansas Social Services Division that the state agency provided the first contract funding for SCAN and began to refer cases involving child abuse and neglect to it.

The Arkansas Children's Hospital, where the social work director sees about four suspected cases of child abuse a month, maintained a close working relationship in referring cases to SCAN. The University of Arkansas Medical Center and its staff, including Dr. Lois Malkemes of the School of Nursing, also moved into high gear, expanding its already extensive cooperation with the volunteer organization.

SCAN was really going to work, and Sharon Pallone was able to breathe a sigh of relief about its prospects for the future.

The volunteer is the key to the success of SCAN, Sharon Pallone says. Most of the volunteers are college graduates, some of them with advanced degrees. And most of them are women with children of their own. They tend to be people who have tried club work and are now seeking more of a challenge in dealing with the problems of their community. Each volunteer is carefully selected and trained by SCAN. Drawing upon experts in health, social work, and other professions, SCAN conducts an extensive three-day training session with lecture topics ranging from "What is Mothering?" to "Transactional Analysis" and "Intercultural Communication."

Each volunteer is trained in how to deal with parents in a home where there is a possible case of child neglect or child abuse. It is important to be able to enlist the support and cooperation of the parents while at the same time taking care of the child's needs. So the volunteer is taught to approach the parents in a supportive and helpful way without being openly critical of them. The volunteer also learns how and when to advise the family about the vast array of services provided by state and private agencies in the general fields of health care, employment, housing, and so on.

The volunteer learns to probe deeper if necessary, to be able to identify the crisis that set off the abuse. She must also make decisions about getting care for the child (foster care if that is necessary). And most important of all, perhaps, she must be able to "parent the parent," for about 99 percent of abusive parents were themselves abused as children. When Sharon Pallone first began training volunteers in 1972, Dr. Lloyd Young's advice to her was succinct and most valuable: "Be sure they can parent."

The volunteer is faced with situations that range from relatively simple to considerably complex. As Sharon Pallone observes, "It might be as simple as convincing the mother who beat her child because she didn't mop the floor that 2-year-olds can't be expected to mop floors. It may be much tougher—improving housing, getting food stamps and money for the needy, getting health care. We work with every agency to solve the thing that spawned the crisis situation."

About half of SCAN's more than 55 volunteers are based in Pulaski County, the Little Rock area. Each of them receives $50 a month from SCAN. Even so, as longtime volunteer Wanda Hamilton says, "The money doesn't mean anything. SCAN is not like other agencies that are bogged down in bureaucratic red tape. We deal on a person-to-person basis. Sometimes some other agencies aren't as human as they ought to be."

The humanity of SCAN is evident, though, for each volunteer is a dedicated individual who is willing to work hard without pay (the $50 is intended simply to help cover expenses) and to give at least 80 hours of time a month to the project.

Experts figure that for every million persons there are 160 cases of child abuse and neglect each year. But Sharon Pallone, pointing to Arkansas's rate, which is rising rapidly as the community becomes aware of the problem, says that the estimate certainly now must be revised. There were 10 reported cases of child abuse in Arkansas in 1967. In 1972, with SCAN in operation only since April, 92 cases were recorded. In 1973 the number of cases reported that involved serious physical injury to children rose to 360, with the prospect of an even higher total for 1974.

It is clear that SCAN's existence is essential.

SCAN's role in both identifying the problem and dealing with it has received widespread acceptance and praise from various segments of the community at large.

To the Arkansas Social Services Division, which cooperates with SCAN and sends it cases, the private organization means over 50 volunteers working principally at their own expense; it is, in effect, an effective specialized agency that operates without needing to obtain large amounts of public funds.

To Judge Mary B. Nash of the juvenile court, SCAN is filling a void by teaching the community about the problem and helping to alleviate it through education and volunteer service.

To Detective Jim Green, SCAN is a valuable agency because it "acts immediately and takes over from the police" when no charges are filed. And thanks to SCAN, a person is not jailed in a child abuse case unless it involves criminal charges.

Green concedes that he sometimes wonders what motivates the volunteers to "take on the problems of somebody else. I guess everybody volunteers for something. Some men coach football and Little League baseball. The women of SCAN are dedicated. They've got their own thing."

And the people of Arkansas have SCAN.

Jim is streetwise and stirwise, and he talks their
talk. They can't con him—they know they can't.

We Care

Detroit, Michigan

An organization backed by a suburban white minister and run
by a black ex-convict is helping hundreds of young people in Detroit avoid a return trip to jail.

Operating out of a tiny office, We Care, Inc. is trying to cope
with one of the most difficult and intractable problems of law enforcement—the high percentage of ex-convicts sent back to
prison for committing another crime. We Care, in business since
1972, seems to have reversed the usual return-to-prison rate. Of
the 825 ex-offenders it has tried to help, only 27 of them—a phe-
nomenally low 3.2 percent—have returned to prison.

The program has even received the grudging respect of the city
probation office, whose experience makes it notably cynical about
such self-help ventures. "They're doing a reasonably good job
with what they've got, as good a job as could be done," says probation officer Donald Tippman.

More importantly, Tippman himself is now one of the people
referring ex-offenders to We Care.

We Care operates on a very small scale. Its annual budget is
only $14,500. It is run with a small staff of volunteers working out
of an office donated by a suburban church.

For all practical purposes the We Care seen by ex-convicts
looking for help is James Spivey, himself only four years out of
prison after serving a 36-year sentence for murder.

Spivey, a Catholic, came to We Care in 1972 after working in a
halfway house operated by the Capuchins, a Franciscan order of
monks. He speaks the language of the men and women who come
from prison seeking a job and other help. He says it is important
to reach the ex-offenders and parolees as soon as possible after
their release. If an ex-con is going to violate his parole, he usually
does so within ninety days after his release.

Most of the people Spivey sees come to the We Care center a
day or two after their release. They are usually young and black,
most coming from the state penitentiary in Jackson, eighty-five
miles west of Detroit. The majority were in prison for minor

crimes, such as attempted breaking and entering—not for murder, rape, or other major crimes.

"When the guy walks in," Spivey says, "he sits down and we rap. I'm concerned with his living conditions. How uptight is he? Is he living with relatives?"

Spivey or his wife, Darlene, have the person fill out a brief form listing education, work experience, address, and phone number. That is about the only piece of paper to be filled out in an organization that dislikes paperwork and bureaucracy.

We Care's original emphasis was on job placement. It has now shifted to training and education, especially with the job slump in the auto industry caused by the energy crisis. Spivey would still prefer to place ex-offenders in high-paying auto jobs, but he must take what is available. That often means lining up the man as a day laborer, working at least three days a week.

"Even though I don't agree with it, it [laboring] beats doing nothing, and keeps him out here," Spivey says. "Here" means on the outside.

Spivey tries with his staff of volunteers to line up other self-help programs. He worked out one deal with a bus company to transport families to see their relatives in jail. It is currently out of operation because of insurance problems with the bus company.

Behind Spivey and the We Care operation is the Reverend Louis Gerhardt, of the North Congregational Church in the affluent suburb of Southfield. Gerhardt grew interested in prison work fifteen years ago when a friend was convicted of murder. He became familiar with the self-help approach through his experience with Alcoholics Anonymous, Gamblers Anonymous, and even Weight Watchers. Deciding to apply the approach to ex-convicts, he persuaded members of his congregation and a reluctant board of deacons to put up $13,500 to start a program in crime-plagued Detroit. Gerhardt made the decision to hire Spivey.

Gerhardt and other church members have made a point of staying in the background, despite the obvious temptations to become more involved.

"If you're really going to take the risk, you've got to let him [Spivey] do his thing," Gerhardt says, describing his relationship with Spivey and We Care. He notes, realistically, that ex-convicts have "met 100 guys like me," but "Jim is streetwise and stirwise, and he talks their talk. They can't con him—they know they can't."

Gerhardt also appreciates We Care's disdain for paperwork. "We're not in the numbers game of statistics," he says. "We would rather Jim helped a few people in depth with jobs and families and stay with that person than something superficial. It's strictly a

We Care's James Spivey served 36 years for murder. He now helps ex-convicts get the training they need to "make it" on the outside.

quality program. We simply have got to cut down this terrible recidivism [return-to-prison] rate."

Based on the success so far with We Care, Gerhardt says his church wants to raise another $50,000 to start three more programs in other areas.

If they can find more Jim Spiveys, they hope to offer the chance for hundreds of young men to break free from the relentless cycle that takes a man from crime to court to conviction to prison to crime to court to conviction to prison, and so on.

We sat the parolees down and explained to them
that this was their chance to make good, and that
if we blew it, we were blowing it for a
lot of other guys. . . .

H.I.R.E.

Minneapolis, Minnesota

Dick Mitchell was in the middle of issuing a challenge:
"There are large numbers of skilled, talented, and able-bodied men waiting to get back into the mainstream of society. They could make it, if companies like your's would give them a chance."

Together with sixteen other ex-offenders, Mitchell was presenting a case to Lee Madden, an executive of Minneapolis Honeywell.

"It's a vicious circle," one of Mitchell's companions interjected. "You have to have a job waiting for you before you can be paroled, but you can't find a job until you are paroled."

"That's right," said Mitchell. "And it's costing taxpayers over $14,000 per year per man to keep us in penal institutions."

Madden listened, but he was dubious. It was 1968, and business just wasn't getting involved with ex-offenders; most companies had a strictly hands-off policy. Nevertheless he decided to take up the matter with other company executives. A short while later Minneapolis Honeywell offered the ex-offenders a deal.

The company would pay Madden and four more of its personnel executives to find jobs for ex-offenders throughout the business community. There was one major condition: Dick Mitchell and his group had to provide the counseling necessary to keep the parolees on the job once the openings were obtained. "I told them," Madden recalls, "if these first men did not make good in their jobs, it was all over as far as future efforts were concerned."

Mitchell and ten members of the group at the time were employed by New Careers, a Minneapolis anti-poverty program. They were elated. This was the break they had been working for. Madden made good on his promise, speaking to the business community and the state employment agency, and in particular urging Honeywell division managers to find some jobs.

"Business was willing to take a step," Madden recalls. "But it was a cautious step. They wanted to test it out."

The job openings began to come in, and now it was up to Mitchell's group to live up to its part of the bargain.

Mitchell minced no words when he addressed the first group of parolees to receive job assignments. "We sat the parolees down," he recalls, "and explained to them that this was our chance to make good, and that if we blew it, we were blowing it for a lot of other guys who might otherwise have had a chance."

The ex-offenders from New Careers worked constantly with men coming into the program. They located housing and transportation, and they went with the parolees to meet their new employers. They found counseling help for men with alcohol, drug, or marital problems. Where specialized job skills were required, they got the parolees enrolled in a six-week training program (sponsored by the federal government) called Passport.

Within a year nearly 400 ex-offenders had entered the job market—with an 80-percent retention rate. What was the secret?

"We were on the same level as they were," Mitchell explains. "We had done time too, we understood the gripes and complaints, and could help them over the rough spots. That's what they needed—someone to relate to."

With nothing but success on the horizon, New Careers asked Dick Mitchell to seek funding for a separate organization to be called H.I.R.E. (Helping Industry Recruit Ex-offenders). Minneapolis Honeywell paid for and helped arrange its incorporation. An application for funding was made to the U.S. Department of Labor. A board of directors was formed, mostly of ex-offenders.

By late 1969, though, not only had dark clouds appeared on the horizon but the sky had fallen down. First, the federally funded New Careers program was phased out. Then the Department of Labor turned down H.I.R.E.'s funding proposal.

By early 1970 the New Careers men were scrambling for jobs for themselves. Dick Mitchell was holding down three part-time jobs while helping parolees find employers and employers find parolees. He never gave up the search for money, but each H.I.R.E. application was turned down in quick succession. For over a year and a half, ex-offenders still counseled new parolees on a voluntary basis, but the number of volunteers was dwindling.

"They had to make a living too," Mitchell says. "We were all pretty discouraged."

In mid-1971, though, Mitchell's persistence paid off. The Minnesota Department of Education provided H.I.R.E. with the funds to employ a full-time director-coordinator, who was to reconstruct the program and seek additional funding.

When H.I.R.E. board met, though, it was faced with having to make two major decisions. Should H.I.R.E. employ a man who was not an ex-offender but had a background in fund-raising and administration? And should H.I.R.E. expand beyond a strictly volunteer organization? The decisions were both "yes."

In the summer of 1971 Stan Kano was hired as director-coordinator and a new era quickly began. Kano immediately asked for the organization of a new board, to include a much larger representation from the whole community. "I felt," Kano says "that we needed more views represented by the business, industry, and labor groups, as well as the public and private agencies. Each of these components represented part of the problem, and each had to be involved if there was to be a solution."

When the board asked Kano about the objectives and methods he saw for H.I.R.E., he replied: "Don't set any without the involvement of ex-offenders, businessmen, labor, criminal justice agencies, and other social agencies as a group. Each have unique and significant input and concerns. If the project goals and objectives do not find a way to assimilate those concerns, the ex-offender can't be expected to assimilate himself into a community that is disjointed and unwilling to deal with the critical issues affecting *everyone* in the community."

A new board was formed and, within two months, H.I.R.E. had received an additional grant from the governor's crime commission. But if H.I.R.E. was to find employment for more than a thousand parolees, as the new board wanted, Kano felt he needed two things: (1) a full-time staff of ex-offenders (as had been the case in 1968-69 through New Careers), and (2) a multi-source budget.

With his new staff dividing time between counseling and fundraising, Kano gave them the following advice:

"Never go by yourself. Get someone else to go with you who is respected by the business community. Do your homework before making any appeals."

This advice proved to be sound. H.I.R.E. is now funded by fifteen companies and four government agencies. In 1972 the organization helped find employment for over 800 ex-offenders, and in 1973 its efforts resulted in over 1,000 jobs.

H.I.R.E.'s board members feel that employment is the principal factor in parolee rehabilitation. But they also feel that three other factors make it possible for H.I.R.E.'s success story to be duplicated anywhere in the United States:

1. The National Alliance of Businessmen has been a major resource in finding job openings and orienting the business community, and it has chapters across the country.

2. There are helpful federal and state agencies in each state.

3. The credo, "Ex-offenders helping Ex-offenders," works.

Their intention was simply to entertain,
to make life in the institution a happier
experience. They quickly found their captive
audiences not only wanting to be entertained
but also to perform themselves.

Mother Goose

San Francisco, California

Many nursery rhymes are a strange combination of fantasy and common sense. But in San Francisco's juvenile halls and halfway houses the wisdom of a Mother Goose means something else. Rather than being the imaginary narrator of children's verses, San Francisco's Mother Goose is an alternative to the boredom and alienation experienced by young people who have been separated from the mainstream of society by confinement. Mother Goose, Inc. is an arts program for institutionalized juveniles.

"Institutionalized juveniles," states Mother Goose's director, James Cavanaugh, "have their schedules crammed with movies, gym, church groups, and cleanup. Before Mother Goose there was nothing to give them a sense of involvement, participation, and self-productivity."

That "sense" is achieved in phases. Initially Mother Goose staff members and volunteers put on stage performances—simply to entertain the residents of a juvenile hall, a home for unwed mothers, a halfway house, or similar institutions. Then, as the youths' interest is awakened, they become students in Mother Goose workshops. They are taught drama, music, dance, puppetry, and other art forms. And in acquiring specific knowledge of the various arts, they are also learning the more subtle lessons of how people live together—of cooperation, interaction, and trust.

The workshops are run on an improvisational basis, thereby providing an atmosphere in which the students can use their imagination and learn to relate to one another and their teachers.

"All of us were embarrassed at first," says one resident of a home for unwed mothers. "I guess we were afraid to act and let ourselves go, in front of other people. Living in an institution makes everyone suspicious."

Living together harmoniously within the institution is only one stage of the Mother Goose program. Beyond that lies the difficult task of preparing institutionalized youngsters for their return to the community. In this too, the arts help bridge the gap. The kids are taken out of the institution to temporarily become both performers and spectators at a variety of outside cultural activities.

"I had never been to a stage play in my life," notes one teenager, "until the staff of Mother Goose took me. I always thought going to the theater was something only grown-ups did."

Mother Goose began in the summer of 1969, when Phillip Pare and Stan Vincent, fresh out of veterinary school in the East, came to San Francisco. Having both decided against setting up practice as vets, they began playing guitar and singing at the Fred Finch Center, a home for emotionally disturbed children. Their intention was simply to entertain, to make life in the institution a happier experience. They quickly found their captive audiences not only wanting to be entertained but also to perform themselves.

Pare and Vincent recognized a real human need, and they set out to fill it. They talked to their friends, many of whom were performers, and got them interested in setting up workshops in which kids could participate.

The early success of Mother Goose owed much to the fact that Pare and Vincent lived in the Haight-Ashbury section of San Francisco. The low rents and flower-child atmosphere of the mid-60s had drawn many artists and other creative people to the area—people who were used to living on little income. Dick Gibson, former director, recalls the project's early years: "The people who originated Mother Goose lived communally. They were young and unattached. As older people got involved in our workshops, we saw the need to provide minimum salaries for their work."

Providing those salaries, as well as meeting the increasing costs of running workshops and of traveling to and from the institutions forced the project members to seek outside financial aid. Fortunately public attention in the early 1970s was focused on the issues of prison reform and government rehabilitation programs. So the response was good when Mother Goose, Inc. (by now an incorporated nonprofit organization) submitted grant proposals to several foundations. Explaining the financing of the program, Dick Gibson says, "We operated, for the most part, on foundation grants. We got a little bit of money from various institutions and

A dance workshop gives troubled youth a window on the arts. "We had to turn the kids on," remarks Dick Gibson. "They had to have some understanding of what art and entertainment was before we could spark them to become involved." ▶

outside performances, but not enough to cover the costs of doing the programs."

In the early days a typical Mother Goose workshop was a simple affair. A volunteer would visit an institution, bring along some records, and everyone would dance. In time, of course, the workshop program was expanded to encompass a variety of art forms, but it remained a program set firmly within the institution. In 1973 the project staff began to expand its services to focus on getting the youngsters out of the institution. Trips were arranged to theaters, concert halls, and other public arts places.

"We had to turn the kids on," remarks Gibson. "They had to have some understanding of what art and entertainment was before we could spark them to become involved."

Full involvement came when Mother Goose set up a coffee-house for the juveniles in its programs. The coffeehouse was a place the youngsters could call their own—a place *outside* the institution, a sort of arts halfway house. The kids responded enthusiastically, and began to devote as much time as possible to attending performances at the coffeehouse, as well as staging their own productions there.

Mother Goose reached full flower in the period between October 1972 and March 1973. During this period the project took more than 180 groups to outside performances and ran over 270 workshops. This, however, represents only the measurable side of the program. Most of the benefits accruing to the participants cannot be quantified. In the words of Joe Brocko, co-director of one of San Francisco's institutions for girls, "Any program that provides a girl an opportunity to develop a skill or to learn something new ties in with the idea of bettering one's image of oneself and developing a little more self-confidence. The girl comes to feel a little better about herself for having done it. That's really at the core of what rehabilitative work is about, because the lack of self-confidence and the lack of a good self-concept highly correlates with delinquency, poor school performance, and any other type of adjustment problem."

The performing arts have long been a tool for bringing about social change in the community. The Mother Goose project in San Francisco, though, is using art both to entertain and teach an almost forgotten segment of society—the institutionalized youngsters. Whatever the success of such a project, it must be recognized that social change comes slowly to such kids—but never as slowly as would have been the case if the modern-day troubadors of Mother Goose hadn't come their way.

Somewhere between his going in and his getting out there is a need for a process that prepares the prisoner for his eventual return to society.

Project Inmate Human Rights

Canon City, Colorado

Once the doors slam shut on a man in prison he needs a lot of help and guidance. Somewhere between his going in and his getting out there is a need for a process that prepares the prisoner for his eventual return to society.

One way to meet this need is to establish self-help groups within prisons and supportive institutions on the outside.

This is being done at Colorado State Penitentiary, at Canon City. The prisoners set up their own self-help groups to assist themselves in the struggle to achieve a successful end to their prison terms, as well as a new and better life after their release.

The self-help groups at Canon City exist under the umbrella of a committee called Project Inmate Human Rights (PIHR). This is an unofficial, ad hoc organization that actively assists the self-help groups within the prison and also works with assistance groups on the outside. The committee operates in conjunction with prison officials, state corrections committees, other elements of the criminal justice system, friends and families, and the inmates.

The self-help groups at Canon City were originally established to help inmates adjust to the prison experience. The basis on which each was organized varied considerably, ranging from cultural identity to length of sentence, from an interest in self-improvement to a concern for civic endeavor. Each was founded on the general principle that rehabilitation is a cooperative process requiring the assistance of everyone involved.

Each group was officially recognized by the penitentiary, and functioned under a formal system of bylaws. And each gained the confidence of the inmates, the prison officials, and the public.

By 1970 there were eighteen self-help groups within the penitentiary at Canon City, some having as many as 400 members. But in 1971, when an inmate strike effectively closed the prison, the self-help groups were shut down completely.

The prison administration had been under the leadership of

acting wardens since 1969, and the temporary administration that was established during the strike was primarily interested in "keeping the lid on" until a permanent administration was appointed. Deputy Warden Alex Wilson reestablished the self-help groups in 1972, but with new restrictions.

According to Wilson, "There is some controversy about self-help in prisons."

"The groups," wrote Wilson back in 1968, "have been recognized as an activity that keeps inmates out of plots against the discipline of the institution. At the same time they have been considered conspiracies against discipline and manipulation movements. They, no doubt, can be either of these."

The 1972 effort at self-help in the Canon City prison was based on self-improvement and discipline maintenance. Strict rules inhibited the growth of large groups, with membership in each being limited to 60. The number of outside resource people allowed at each meeting was restricted to 30. And inmates were subjected to a total strip-search after meetings involving outside people, in order to avoid the passing of contraband. Nevertheless a new effort was being made to increase the activities and effectiveness of self-help groups within the prison. It was this new effort that gave birth to PIHR, which began reestablishing the outside support the groups had enjoyed before the 1971 strike.

PIHR is an offshoot of an older organization, the Latin American Development Society Supportive Organization (LADSSO). Unlike its predecessor, though, PIHR is directed at supporting all self-help programs at Canon City. The group is currently composed of many of the people previously involved in LADSSO prior to the strike in 1971—legislators, businessmen, welfare workers, and other volunteers. They work almost exclusively on a volunteer basis. Although PIHR occasionally receives funds from Action Centers and the Colorado Pinto Project, it often operates on a budget of close to zero dollars.

The prison self-help groups are established to help inmates deal with the four key factors in their lives as prisoners and then ex-prisoners: (1) adjusting to prison life, (2) self-improvement and growth in prison, (3) getting out, and (4) staying out.

1. *Adjusting to Prison Life.* Sammy Morrison, president of the Black Culture Development Society, discusses adjustment:

"When we first started our self-help group in 1968, they were sending guys in here [maximum security] who didn't know anyone and didn't know what to expect. They sometimes got into trouble, and maybe would get hurt or something. Our group is interested in this fellow. We want to find them so they don't get into trouble."

Morrison adds that it took a while to work: "Some of the brothers would end up in Cell House 3 [solitary] because they really couldn't get along with the other guys. So we tried to give them something to identify with."

"Inmate" Gift, past president of the Progressors self-help group, tells of the personal problems of adjustment to prison life:

"Most of us [the Progressors] are the little people. Basically what we have to offer is ourselves. It is a sense of saying simply 'I care'. As a whole we are basically antisocial, and that's why some of us are here. All of a sudden you are somewhat forced to mingle with absolute strangers. This can be very difficult."

He adds, "Whether a person ever really gets involved or not, something is bound to rub off on him."

Another problem of adjustment is trying to keep families together. This is where outside help is very necessary. Julius Martinez, chairman of PIHR and a long-time worker with prison inmates, discusses the problems of families left on the outside:

"Some of the families can't get down to Canon to see their men, and the relationships run thin. It is very important to keep the families together, both for the families and so the men have something to come back to. Our group has been setting up buses to take families down here. And we counsel them, and get them together to share common problems."

2. *Self-Improvement and Growth in Prison.* The self-help groups assist prisoners in attempting to make their prison experience productive. Even the process of organizing and managing their own groups provides most inmates with a useful social exercise previously unknown to them.

Several groups that focus on self-improvement include the Progressors, the Dale Carnegie course, Alcoholics Anonymous, and Narconom. Royal O'Connor, current president of the Progressors, talks about his group's program:

"We participate in a 17-week course with an outside instructor. Basically we examine who we are, why we are here, and try to establish some way of assuring that we stay out. It's based on a concept of 'positive mental attitude'."

3. *Getting Out.* It is here that the assistance of outside resource people is of primary importance. As Julius Martinez says, "We have a strong education program both for families and inmates. Often a man is convicted, and say he is sentenced to twenty years. His family may not even know he is eligible for parole in seven

years or whatever. There is a lot of ignorance in this area, and the families and the men are entitled to know what is expected of them for release."

PIHR groups at Canon have educational programs to help prepare inmates for parole. Often an inmate will go before a parole board and discover he needs a job and a "plan" in order to get parole. This would often be impossible without the assistance of PIHR's resource people on the outside.

One group particularly involved with prisoner release and the law is the Life Term Prisoners' Union, an organization of "lifers." The union meets with attorneys, judges, and legislators to try to establish an enlightened approach to the laws and to the specific laws that affect those serving life terms, as well as those facing the death penalty.

4. *Staying Out.* Once prisoners have been released, they need help staying out. They must have employment, and generally have a good understanding of what is expected of them. This is where the self-help supportive organizations such as PIHR are so valuable.

PIHR has established training and hiring programs. It also sets up meetings in urban action centers and community centers. The meetings involve construction companies and other potential employers, as well as apartment owners and people who can provide housing. PIHR also sets up counseling programs and on-call counseling to assist the ex-offenders when they need help.

Drug addiction is a particular problem for many ex-inmates. As Martinez states, "Drugs are the one thing we want to help the men stay away from. For many of them that's why they were sent up. But it is like an illness, and we can treat it. We have methadone programs and other programs for treating drug illness. We can help them if they pick up a needle; but we can't do a thing for them if they pick up a gun. We want to make sure that doesn't happen."

The assistance that PIHR and the individual self-help group can offer to the released prisoner is essential if the man is going to have a chance to make it on the outside. As Martinez explains:

"You don't just throw a guy out into the streets and say 'you're free'. Especially if he has been institutionalized for a long time. The prisons themselves don't do that. They ease them out with preparations, medium security, pre-parole centers, and parole.

"But once they are out, we can help them the most. We just let them know we are here. They have someone to turn to; and a job, hopefully a family that is still intact, and friends. We just don't give them a chance for desperation."

*The key to rehabilitating a youth
is to present him with a challenge, get
him involved and committed.*

Operation SHARE

Phoenix, Arizona

An Indian woman carrying a bundle of firewood paused at the home-construction site and surveyed the gang of white teenagers hammering and sawing away. Along with other Pima Indians at Sacaton, on the Gila River Indian Reservation just south of Phoenix, she was a little mystified by the activity of these strangers.

The previous year, 1970, another group of teenagers had built one house and started two more. Now this group was erecting wooden frameworks on the foundations of those two.

They had arrived one day in a truck loaded with materials, set up sleeping bags and tents, and, under the casual supervision of an older man, had started working. Although it wasn't obvious to an outsider, for several members of the crew it was the first time they had ever built anything.

The woman also had no way of knowing that many of the youths had police records for drug charges and juvenile delinquency, that some were school dropouts and others were kids with emotional problems who had been pushed out by their families. But here they all were, working hard to help someone else.

Erecting housing is one of many projects to assist American Indians undertaken by the teenage group that is called Join Hands. Based in Phoenix, Arizona, Join Hands is an offshoot of another work-oriented organization, called Operation SHARE (Student Help and Resource Effort), which was started in 1966 by Robert Rihr. The 50-year-old Rihr, a greenhouse contractor, believes strongly the best way to help troubled teenagers is to give them plenty of hard work and the responsibility for doing it properly.

"Operation SHARE is operated on the two-way-street principle," says Rihr. "Those who give, get. Nothing is given without sharing. Nothing is gotten without sharing."

Robert Rihr is the father of four children, the youngest a three-year-old and the oldest a law student. He was in his car one day in October 1965 waiting for his daughter Kathy to leave a Catholic

Youth Organization meeting.

"I got tired of waiting, so I went in. I was appalled at what I heard. Here were all these kids, supposedly doing charitable deeds, and all they were doing was talking about dances and parties and things for themselves."

Rihr says he got mad. "I said to them, 'Let's do what What's-His-Name did and help some poverty people'."

The next summer, on June 15, 1966, Robert Rihr led 21 teenagers armed with $2,000 of donated money, picks, shovels, and goodwill down to Corbaca, Mexico. There they renovated a burned-out nursery school and helped rebuild an industrial trade school. Within two weeks they had helped a whole town recover.

Several more building projects followed—the roofing of houses and barns, laying the foundation for a new church, and in 1968 and 1969 construction of a medical clinic and a house for the doctor in a small community in Mexico.

Because Rihr would occasionally ask a friend for donations, he had to incorporate as a nonprofit group if he was to comply with the law. And that's how Operation SHARE was born.

When the group came back from Corbaca, Rihr began working with delinquents. Through informal contacts with juvenile authorities, he became a kind of one-man halfway house for kids in trouble, out of trouble, or looking for trouble.

In 1972 SHARE worked on Phoenix-area housing projects for a variety of ethnic minorities. The next year about 35 members of SHARE spent the summer at Roberts Mesa, 76 miles north of Phoenix, planting 10,000 ponderosa pine tree seedlings in an area that had been destroyed by a forest fire several years before. The seedlings were purchased with money the youngsters raised.

Join Hands started out in 1970 at Sacaton. Later that year, the youngsters built a room addition for the house of an ill Navajo woman, and then moved on to the Apache reservation at White Rock, where they laid the foundation and floor for a library. After that came the completion of the two houses at Sacaton in 1971.

Rihr says his group doesn't just walk in and start building on Indian reservations. They first obtain the consent of the tribal elders, as well as the U.S. Bureau of Indian Affairs.

They have encountered some initial hostility on reservations. But by the time they are finished, the Join Hands members invariably have established good relations with the Indians, who appreciate the improvement in their living quarters.

Rihr is straightforward and tough, but he is also capable of as many affectionate bearhugs as the youngsters can stand.

"Love 'em, understand 'em, give 'em a kick in the pants—whatever they need," Rihr says. "I want to deal with all of the child. The child is the product of his parents. No matter how you slice it, he learned it at home. Society didn't do it to him."

It is Rihr's philosophy that troubled teenagers can find their way if they are removed from the scene of past failures, and they can establish interdependent working relationships with their peers. "The key to rehabilitating a youth is to present him with a challenge, get him involved and committed," says Rihr. "This is the way he will develop leadership qualities." (Anyone involved in a Rihr-led project who complains about how something is being done is urged to take command of the work.)

Rihr's daughter, Kathy, who is now a counselor of the group, says that it is "amazing how much kids can figure out on their own. They take complete charge of a project and solve their own construction problems. We've built some good, sound buildings."

Robert Rihr concedes his workers make many mistakes, and he has to restrain himself from moving in and showing them how to do something correctly. "But that's the only way they learn—straightening it out themselves."

For several years Rihr has been developing a center "where transient kids can get their heads cleared out for a while." It is being built on an 80-acre ranch donated by a middle-class couple out of gratitude for Rihr's helping their son when he needed it. A young architect has drawn up plans to make the ranch self-sufficient, employing windmills to produce electricity. It will have a vegetable garden, a dozen or so small cabins for private living quarters, and a central dining area and hall. It is being built by the SHARE youngsters, including some Indian youths on probation.

Of the several hundred youths who have participated in SHARE, many have gone on to professional careers. Among the project's "graduates" there are currently eleven nurses, four social workers, three teachers, one doctor, one lawyer and one PhD.

Some of these professionals may return for another Join Hands project—to attack alcoholism on Indian reservations. For this new interest, Join Hands plans for the first time to seek financial help from foundations and government agencies. No one who knows Rihr is surprised about his initiating such an ambitious undertaking. It is only natural in his formula for working with teenagers.

"The way to set up a project like ours," he says, "is to get a leader—someone over 35 who understands kids. Then get a sharp teen, an extrovert, who knows the teen scene and can act as liaison between the teens and the leader. Then get a popular

Operation SHARE matches troubled youth with hard work. When completed, this house will be shelter for a large family of Pima Indians.

cause, such as ecology, Indians, mental retardation.

"Put all the responsibility of the program on the teens' backs. Use the adult only as a resource person—not someone who gives them all the answers, but whose experience is greater than theirs. Treat teens as adults and expect them to accomplish all things."

"Then," Rihr adds, "let it happen."

*When you hear a volunteer talk about a youngster
who had deliberately planned a criminal career
for himself because he saw no other way,
but who then turned away from it, you know
you really have something.*

Social Advocates for Youth

Seattle, Washington/Trinidad, Colorado

*Reason for referral: Mike is 11 years old. Mike's parents
are divorced, and he lives with his mother and younger sister.
Mother is on welfare, father has drinking problem. Counselor
at school became concerned about Mike because he didn't
seem to have any friends at school, seemed isolated from
other kids. His grades were bad, far lower than he is able to
achieve. Referred to SAY.*

SAY is Social Advocates for Youth, a one-to-one program
aimed at preventing juvenile delinquency by carefully matching
young volunteers, many of them college students, with troubled
youngsters such as Mike who may be drifting into serious difficulty with the law. The advocate agrees to spend at least three-to-
five hours once a week with his match over a nine-month period.
The advocate becomes a friend, tries to broaden the youngster's
horizons and to increase his self-esteem.

A year after Mike was matched with Bill, who is a forestry major
in his junior year of college, he seemed a different youngster. He
is now attending a parochial school and getting good grades.

"If I went to another school, I don't think I could learn as much,"
says Mike. "I'm learning more, and it's easier. Besides, I have no
excuse for being absent, because I live just around the corner
from school. I have lots of friends at school now."

Bill has also noticed the change in Mike's life: "I almost have to
make an appointment to see him now."

It has been a year packed with good times, new experiences,
and good memories for Mike—as well as for Bill. And the advocate has found time to be a good friend in spite of his own 18-hour
school load and 25 hours of work a week. "I set out to broaden his
horizons," Bill says thoughtfully. "He's widened mine."

Mike likes to remember the first time he went camping, when
rain turned to snow in the mountains, collapsing the pup tent on

top of them. He remembers his first horseback ride on another camping trip, going fishing, trying bowling, riding behind Bill on his Honda 350, and exploring Fort Casey on nearby Whidbey Island. Even work is fun when it's done in Bill's company, like cutting and piling wood for the fireplace at Bill's house, or helping paint a room.

"It took almost three weeks for SAY to find the right match," Bill admits. "I had never volunteered for anything in my life before. Looking back, though, I think maybe I've changed Mike's goals in this year we've had together.

"When I first met him, he had the idea that he would like to be a police officer; but until that day, all he could see for himself was being on welfare. Now he is interested in forestry, getting a scholarship, and going to college. He has always been interested in guns, and one of the first things we did was to sit down for a four-hour course on gun safety.

"He seems a lot healthier now than when we first met. He didn't eat much then, but now he competes with me for that last taco, and he's grown a lot this past year."

Mike remembers the time shortly before the end of the nine-month period of their association. He was sitting in bed, crying. His mother asked him why he was crying, and he said: "I'm afraid Bill and I will stop being friends." He soon learned that SAY puts no time limit on friendship. "I guess Bill and I are just about perfect friends," Mike says, adding that "we're going to keep on being friends, even when one of us is away."

SAY Seattle is part of a national organization that originated in 1970 with demonstration projects in Santa Rosa, California, and Colorado Springs, Colorado, through the efforts of the Haigh-Scatena Foundation of San Francisco. Since then other SAY projects have been established in several states.

It was in September 1971 that the national organization began studying the feasibility of a SAY Seattle. The target area, in the northwest section of Seattle, was a most likely choice; 40 percent of its inhabitants are middle class, while 60 percent belong to low-income groups, with many people on welfare, many broken homes, and many one-parent households.

Larry Chornyak, 27, is the concerned, articulate director of SAY Seattle. He also has the saving grace of a sense of humor, along with a degree from the University of Washington, and experience that includes teaching kindergarten and four years of working in the juvenile court system.

"At the juvenile court," he says, "I saw volunteers being able to do the kinds of things I would like to be doing, but couldn't because of my job. My professional relationship with the child superseded my ability to form a close, personal relationship, and it is the close, personal relationship that has strength.

"What we're trying to do here in SAY is to provide the opportunity for kids to meet someone who can provide that close caring relationship. That's not always enough. I think there is a need for professional help. Lots of kids have deep emotional problems. They need to be diagnosed in a professional manner.

"But the professional, because of his professionalism, is in a disadvantaged position. So what we are trying to do vicariously is to get professional help to these kids through a medium that kids can accept—that is, a truly committed person."

Larry Chornyak heard about SAY from a teacher friend. Feeling as he did, that the juvenile court system just isn't designed to help kids when they are potential offenders, Social Advocates for Youth had a strong appeal for him.

SAY National thought that Seattle was a fine spot for another SAY branch, and Larry Chornyak became its first director. SAY Seattle was incorporated as a nonprofit corporation late in 1971, and by April 1972 the new project was on its way. Looking back, its director says, "We had no criteria in those early days. There wasn't much rhyme or reason to the way we went about things; it was just helter-skelter."

The Haigh-Scatena Foundation provided the initial seed money. But in 1973 it was decided that Chornyak and his board of directors would have responsibility for funding.

SAY Seattle has a small, closely knit staff. In addition to the director there are Linda McDonald, a social worker, who joined the staff in July 1972; Marilyn Nelson, a family service counselor, who joined in August 1973 to become the project's coordinator of family services and work with volunteers; and a fourth member, Cathy Pryor, who recruits and coordinates the volunteer program and edits the SAY Seattle newsletter.

In the early days of SAY Seattle, the dropout rate for volunteers was 20 percent. Now, with a very careful screening process, which includes three separate interviews, the rate is down to 14 percent.

Volunteers, who range in age from 18 to 32, are recruited constantly through the media and through speeches at meetings and schools, as well as by volunteers telling friends about the program. Volunteer training has evolved into a six-week-cycle workshop geared to the problems and areas of interest of the volunteers, with assistance from outside professional people. And volunteers having problems are also encouraged to turn to SAY's staff for help.

The principal activity of SAY Seattle is the one-to-one matching program aimed at preventing troubled 8–13-year-olds from winding up in the juvenile court system. A total of 49 percent of the youngsters in the program are referred to SAY by the schools. Other sources are the state department of social and health services, the family counselling service, King County juvenile court, and the Seattle Police Department.

To date, SAY Seattle has made 107 matches between needy youngsters and volunteer advocates. Says Linda McDonald: "From what they tell us, 70 percent of the parents feel that the one-to-one program has been a godsend. We do a follow-up to determine the effect, and there is continuous contact between the volunteers, the parents, and the children.

"We do a five-month evaluation of the match and a nine-month evaluation, using the case worker approach to evaluate. In order to make this work, you have to have people who have skills and don't have to have supervision. A volunteer has to be a self-starter. Whoever in the schools knows the kids best and cares about them is the best referral source. You don't have to go to certain titles. You work your school to find out that kind of thing, and you continue to see your referral sources and are visible at meetings. What we do works here because we have the time to do it."

Although the one-to-one program is the main project, SAY Seattle has other projects as well. There is, for instance, the summer recreation and arts and crafts program, which also includes field trips and the widening of cultural horizons. (This project also used to give summer employment to some youngsters through the Job Corps.)

SAY Seattle has gained increasing respect and attention from the local community, and it has benefited from the direct involvement of a number of prominent citizens. William Dering, for example, has been a member of the project's board of directors since 1972. He first heard about SAY when he was volunteer coordinator for juvenile parole services for King County.

"SAY to me was one of those ideas that would nip juvenile delinquency in the bud early," he recalls. "It struck me as being a good thing. I just wish I had more time to put in on the program. I think it's important that people understand the impact an agency like SAY can have on the community. Little boys and girls are being diverted from the big juvenile justice system and being provided an alternative to it."

Edwin Harding, also a SAY board member, is the Seattle manager of Aetna Life and Casualty, a company that has been a solid financial contributor of SAY Seattle. "SAY to me is a very wonderful thing," he says. "I've seen what it has done for those youngsters. Both the volunteers and the youngsters are helped by it. When you hear a volunteer talk about a youngster who had deliberately planned a criminal career for himself because he saw no other way, but who then turned away from it, you know you really have something."

An extension of the SAY national organization is operating in Trinidad, Colorado. With a declining population of about 9,900, Trinidad has problems other than congested inner-city slums, teen gang wars, or rampant juvenile delinquency. In large measure Trinidad is faced with a unique set of problems that rival those of a larger city. The federal government declared Trinidad a "depressed area," and until the summer of 1969 the large juvenile population of this small Colorado town had little to hope for.

It was in this atmosphere that Social Advocates for Youth programs began; and during their fledgling months they had to face three primary problems: gaining the confidence of the local government agencies, families, and children; acquiring a dedicated staff; and building a rich, full reservoir of volunteers.

There were major roadblocks in each of these areas. But VISTA (Volunteers in Service to America) came to Trinidad, bringing energy long depleted in the community. They also brought a wealth of confidence, knowledge, and sophistication that the town did not possess.

The SAY center had its foundations in this energy. The VISTA volunteers talked the city out of an old abandoned city garage with grease-covered floors and sliding doors large enough to permit entry of huge municipal trucks. Out of this old building was created the Trinidad Youth Center, and the Juvenile and Youth Services—now merged into Social Advocates for Youth. Funding was provided from local sources, as well as from a seed grant from the Haigh-Scatena Foundation.

The garage was turned into a recreation center with pottery, leatherwork, sports, and activities that gave a sense of belonging to Trinidad's youth. For some of them it was the first time.

SAY's programs in Trinidad revolve around the youth center and the one-to-one program that proved so successful in Seattle. The primary objective of the SAY one-to-one program is to identify the children who can most benefit from an interpersonal experience. Many of the children have been in trouble and are referred to SAY by the schools, courts, or welfare agencies. The majority of children, though, just need a friend.

SAY has been responsible for many families in Trinidad understanding the need for professional services that are now available in their town. Of SAY, social worker Ray Lutz suggests, "If you can put the children in a big brother program like SAY, then it is easier for them [the families] to accept help."

SAY has also extended its influence to the state junior college located in Trinidad. The school has established a credit course entitled Social Advocates for Youth for which a student can receive full credit for participation in the one-to-one program.

Considering all of this, it is still very difficult to measure the success or failure of a self-help program by conventional methods. As Lutz says, "Service-oriented programs don't keep records like research programs. So when we need data we count heads."

A head count reveals that more than a thousand local youths take advantage of the youth center run by SAY Trinidad, and that 85 youngsters are involved in the one-to-one program.

But it remains difficult to measure how much it means to a child to have a friend who gives special, exclusive, dependable time to that friendship . . . or to measure the genuine value of a volunteer's decision to pursue a career in social work . . . or to be certain what it means to a small child to achieve pride in a piece of pottery he didn't know how to make a week before.

There is always the possibility that the child may have eventually learned how to make pottery anyway, or there is a chance that the troubled young boy would sooner or later find the good influence of a close friend. But then he could run into some bad influence just as easily.

A program like SAY makes the difference between thrusting a child into an uncontrolled, desolate, barren environment, or putting him into a rich atmosphere filled with opportunity.

It is a simple matter of increasing the options, and multiplying the odds.

CHAPTER 8

Community Organization

Power to the People!" was the cry of various groups during the 1960s, but a decade has passed and little power of any kind has reached the people who need it the most—the disadvantaged citizens who need to have at least some control over their own lives and destinies.

Yet some power has changed hands. The residents of low-income communities have begun to discover that they can have a voice in determining and shaping their own social and economic priorities. In some cases they are simply filling the vacuum left by governmental neglect and corporate indifference. In other cases they are actively wresting control away from the outside interests that have long imposed their will on the country's poverty areas.

The key to this changeover has been community organization. Neighborhood people have learned that banding together in a common cause gives strength to a community that has few material resources. They have learned that organization means power—the power to decide, the power to improve, the power to create better lives for themselves.

The self-help community organization project ultimately aims at mobilizing the whole community to deal with all of its problems. But ambition is not sacrificed to practicality, so it starts with limited goals and meets those before expanding. A project may start with a one-day street cleanup, with organizing a civic improvement program on a single block, or with the creation of a small farm co-op. And as other programs are added, the project grows into a multi-service operation encompassing the community.

Housing, schools, jobs, health care, social services, community planning—these and more are all of concern to the self-help projects trying to reshape the country's poverty areas. And as the projects gain strength they find they are able to obtain more cooperation from government officials and private organizations.

The community organization project is giving determined disadvantaged people a better life. More than that, perhaps, it is giving them a sense of accomplishment and pride.

We have power now, but we are well aware that
our power rests solely on the fact that we
represent 45,000 people and have their trust.
The moment we lose or abuse that trust,
we have no power.

The Tremé Community Improvement Association

New Orleans, Louisiana

Tucked away behind New Orleans' fabled French Quarter lies Tremé, a run-down, half-forgotten neighborhood with a past. It was here, around the turn of the century, that jazz was born—the unique product of Tremé's high life and low life, do-gooders and no-gooders, of spirituals and blues. It was Tremé that produced Buddy Bolden, King Oliver, Jelly Roll Morton, Louis Armstrong, and so many of the other great jazz pioneers.

But Tremé's place in history has been largely ignored, as has the neighborhood itself. In fact, even since before the jazz era, it has been Tremé's general condition to be ignored. And the exceptions to this rule have not usually benefited Tremé—as when the city fathers cordoned off part of the neighborhood in the 1890s to create block after block of licensed brothels.

Left behind by the course of progress, present-day Tremé has most of the characteristics of a decaying inner-city neighborhood—not enough good housing, too few job opportunities, too much crime and drug addiction, inadequate city services, and insufficient income (half the families live on less than $3,500 a year).

But Tremé also has a foundation of ethnic and social continuity; most of the people are black, and most come from families that have lived there for half a century or more.

And it has men such as James Hayes and Ronald Chisom.

Hayes and Chisom are the director and co-director respectively of the Tremé Community Improvement Association (TCIA), which is dedicated to improving the quality of life in Tremé.

TCIA evolved from the concern of Hayes, Chisom, and other Tremé residents. In Hayes' words:

"Ron and I grew up in Tremé, and all our life we had seen

people sitting on steps, people shooting dope, people hopeless. We both had jobs at the LSU [Louisiana State University] medical center, and our duties were such that we could move around the city freely. In casual rapping, here and there, we discovered a core of people—some professional, some not, some black, some white—who were of a mind to solve the problems of Tremé.

"We came together, finally, in a committee of six and decided we would hold meetings in Tremé and ask the people what they needed. Our first meeting was in July 1969, and about thirty

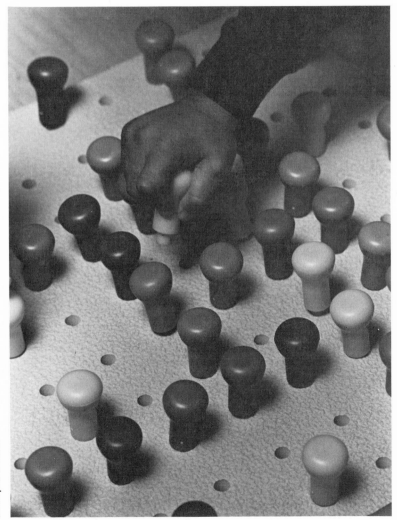

Youngsters in TCIA's preschool classroom learn by doing.

Christopher R. Harris

showed up. We figured this was pretty good, because the people of Tremé didn't trust anybody. The only thing they trusted was their experience that everyone else was on the hustle.

"We decided to do a project to give us visibility. A week later the thirty of us took brooms and shovels and trash cans to a block on Robertson Street and began cleaning it up. It was nine in the morning, and guys came out of the barrooms to laugh. At the middle of the block, one of the hecklers came out of the barroom doorway, took up a rake and used it. Then more came. Guys who hadn't worked in fifteen years got involved. By the end of the cleanup, we were being served lemonade and sandwiches.

"That thing got the community to talking about us. So the next thing we did was choose an issue so we could agitate around it. It is one of the key tactics in organizational strategy.

"Our issue was a double-edged one: abandoned junk cars and the police. Junk cars, dirty and dangerous, and demoralizing, were everywhere in Tremé because the city ignored us.

"And the police paid *too much* attention to Tremé. The people hated them and were afraid of them.

"What we did was have a whole block of people cooperate to push a junk car, the worst magotty car we could find, out in the middle of a street so that it blocked all traffic. Then we stood on the porches and watched. There were hundreds of us.

"A patrol car shows up. He sees all the people, the street blocked, and he takes off with his blue light whirling, whoop-whoop-whoop. Then come more police. They got wreckers. Two wreckers, then three, then four. Now we got a big crowd of police and a big crowd of people. Finally, the big man, the captain of the precinct, shows up in all his gold braid.

" 'What's going on here? Who did this,' he wants to know. Nobody says a word. He doesn't know what to do.

"Ron and I and some others stepped out and gave him our bitch about the junked cars. Well, he made a deal. He took up the bullhorn and asked: 'Will it be all right with you people if we start getting cars removed by 6 a.m.?'

"That was it. We had won. The police had made a deal with the community. And we had shown the power of community action.

"From there on, we—that is, TCIA—were in business. We began monitoring police brutality complaints. We followed those complaints right into city hall. We got results. And now it is virtually eliminated from the Tremé community.

"And throughout all this, we took the position that we would not refer people to other agencies. That is bureaucratic bullshit and it discourages people. If there was any running around to do, any

A young girl plays the role of an adult during a TCIA preschool program.

Christopher R. Harris

phoning to do, and forms to fill out, the staff and volunteers did it. Not the clients. Our slogan became, 'No Problem Is Too Hard For Us To Solve'. We didn't send them somewhere else. We did it."

TCIA's principal activity is representing tenants in their dealings with landlords and the city's public housing authority. Much of this effort is aimed at getting repairs done and rehabilitation undertaken. TCIA has been successful enough so that it is now recognized by both private business and the public housing authority; consequently many housing problems are worked out fairly easily. If necessary, though, TCIA can and does organize rent strikes in order to bring pressure to bear on an uncooperative landlord.

The association's tenant service is valued greatly in a community where much of the housing is in poor condition and where about 90 percent of the people are tenants rather than home owners. It is also valuable to others, too, for, as a member of the National Tenants Organization, TCIA covers all of New Orleans.

TCIA also provides Tremé with a variety of other services. It provides

• counseling and referral services on family planning, medical care, domestic problems, and matters involving government agencies (including advice on filing tax returns)

• a classroom for preschool children that not only begins their scholastic education but also teaches them about such practical

matters as what to do in a grocery store and a post office
- distribution of government-issued welfare checks and food stamps through local TCIA offices
- headquarters for a local Boy Scout troop
- counseling for drug users
- a club and meeting place for senior citizens
- a subagency to secure work for minority contractors and businesses

TCIA's work is accomplished by massive use of volunteers, with the equivalent of 150 full-time workers being drawn from the black population of Tremé and 25 full-time volunteers being drawn from New Orleans' white liberal contingent. The core of the staff consists of Hayes, Chisom, and the four other members of the founding committee.

Hayes, Chisom, and other full-time workers support themselves by holding outside jobs while devoting up to forty hours a week to TCIA. Neither Hayes nor Chisom draws a salary from the association. In fact, the salaries that are paid—most for classroom teaching—average only $600 a year per person.

TCIA operates on a budget of less than $3,600 a year. It has actually spent less than $18,000 over the five-year period since it was founded. Of that amount, $3,000 has been raised through rummage sales and neighborhood fashion shows ($1 admission charge). Other funds have come from the Youth Opportunity program ($4,500), the Council of Jewish Women ($3,500), Project Hope ($3,000), and St. Charles Avenue Presbyterian Church ($3,000).

It is not that TCIA has all the funding it needs for its programs. Rather, it has had difficulty in raising more, largely because of the staff's lack of fund-raising experience. Currently, though, James Hayes and Ronald Chisom are trying to learn the art of obtaining funds, in the hope of being more effective in penetrating the walls of the financial establishment.

In the meantime the association continues to work for the good of Tremé on its customary shoestring budget. And whether or not it does obtain increased financial support, it is already an organization to be reckoned with in New Orleans. As James Hayes says:

"The days of ignoring Tremé, of abusing Tremé are finished. Now, city hall takes no action involving Tremé unless they first confer with TCIA. We, in turn, inform the people. We have power now, but we are well aware that our power rests solely on the fact that we represent 45,000 people and have their trust. The moment we lose or abuse that trust, we have no power."

Urban renewal can be successful only if it has the support of the people who must live through it, and in it.

The South Arsenal Neighborhood Development Corporation

Hartford, Connecticut

In the center of the neighborhood stood an old warehouse, a likely target for a bulldozer. But the people examining the building's 10,000 square feet of floor space had a better idea: why not turn it into a community center?

They answered themselves affirmatively. Since then the former warehouse has been remodeled to accommodate a neighborhood meeting and recreational hall, a grade school for 250 children, and a life center that oversees the delivery of all the community's services. It also houses the offices of the South Arsenal Neighborhood Development Corporation (SAND), the self-help organization that made it all possible.

SAND has accomplished a great deal more by taking charge of the redevelopment of the entire South Arsenal neighborhood, which is situated in the north end of Hartford. And in the process it has demonstrated how community solidarity can generate political power even for the poor.

A decade ago South Arsenal was considered the worst neighborhood in the city. Very few of its residents had high school educations, everyone was poor, and no one knew what to do about it. Symbolic of their plight was the Arsenal School, which had been condemned in 1936 by the board of education. Not only was it still in use but it was dangerously overcrowded.

"Hell, it was a jungle out there when I was in school," says Norman King, SAND's deputy director. "We knew our turf and never strayed from it. Guys were getting knifed and shot all the time. The housing projects were battlegrounds for gangs."

Although poor, South Arsenal residents were far from apathetic. They had been gradually building up a strong neighborhood organization for years. First, there was a tenants' association at the Bellevue Housing Project that staged a successful rent strike and pressured the city into providing better security patrols. Then came the South Arsenal Council, which won increased garbage pickups, managed an ambitious food surplus distribution program, and branched into organizing Cub Scout packs.

The council was watching when, in 1965, the city embarked upon a massive urban renewal program with federal and state funds. The first project was the Windsor Street neighborhood, a slum area just a few blocks from South Arsenal. Area residents initially welcomed the idea. But as the old neighborhood was torn up, long-established shops were closed down, families were shipped off to new neighborhoods with no promise of a return ticket, and the neighborhood seethed with dismay and anger.

South Arsenal residents knew they would be next, and they didn't want their neighborhood destroyed. They were convinced they could do the job themselves better than any outside government agency. So they took the step of forming a neighborhood corporation, SAND. As one of the corporation's workers recalls, "We didn't have the slightest idea how to go about it—everyone chipped in nickels and dimes to pay the $35 registration fee."

But the new corporation knew how to act. Soon it was laying out a redevelopment plan for the neighborhood that indicated the location of playgrounds, housing units, schools, and medical clinics. Thus, when the city announced in November 1967 that South Arsenal was to be an urban renewal area, SAND was ready.

"We went to the city council and told them we had incorporated," says John Banks of SAND. "Boy, were they surprised. I don't think they thought we had the brains to do it. Now we held control over our own destiny—the contractors would be directly answerable to us. We even had architects draw up plans for the neighborhood."

The plans included provisions to minimize hardship on the residents. Renewal was to be phased so that, for each housing project, half of the residents would be moved and then given first priority on space when the new housing was completed. Meantime the corporation would set up activities to maintain contact with the relocated families.

The plans also called for establishing the corporation as a mini-city government, with powers to direct all the community services for the South Arsenal neighborhood.

Not all of SAND's ideas were well received by the officials downtown. It took two years before an overall plan was drawn up that was acceptable to all parties. But in the end, SAND got almost everything it wanted. The influential Greater Hartford Process, a development agency, threw its support behind SAND's plans, and it urged that the neighborhood corporation be given the city, state, and federal money to proceed. With this backing, SAND received the go-ahead to start building its own community.

Conversion of the warehouse to a community center was one of the first steps. And other building is currently under way.

Although urban renewal construction is disrupting lives, a new spirit pervades the neighborhood of South Arsenal.

Consider the new grade school. The classes are kindergarten through third grade, and the children are allowed to progress at their own speed under the Montessori method. It is called the Everywhere School, because it encourages neighborhood youngsters who are temporarily living elsewhere to attend.

The school is funded by the board of education. The teachers are bilingual, speaking both English and Spanish, and many of the paraprofessionals come from the neighborhood.

"Language is not a barrier here," says Josh Smith, a volunteer consultant to SAND. "We are all poor people after all; that is our commonness. It doesn't matter what language we speak, whether we're black, Puerto Rican, or white."

Because the community has organized into a more cohesive unit, and is more sophisticated in the ways of city politics, the quality of life has been improving almost daily. More policemen patrol the streets at night, school crossing guards are at every busy intersection, and when there's a problem in the housing projects, solutions are found more quickly.

The Neighborhood Life Center, a joint venture of SAND and the Greater Hartford Process, oversees all of the community services available to the neighborhood. A resident goes to the center for job counseling, for health and social services.

"The center keeps track of all of a person's needs," says Olive Walker, the chairman of the SAND board of directors. "It has the total picture. If a man is out of work because he is a drunk, we can refer him to competent counselors for both his problems. He doesn't have to fight the red tape of two agencies. It's all here."

SAND has operated since its inception on a year-to-year basis, most recently with the Model Cities program. This has hurt long-range planning, and SAND officials say that, if they had to do it over again, they would prefer funding for three years or more.

Perhaps the biggest lesson to other cities in what SAND has done is that urban renewal can be successful only if it has the support of the people who must live through it, and in it. "Too often," says Banks, "we've had help shoved down our throats, help we didn't want or need."

SAND has long known there is creativity and determination in the ghetto; the City of Hartford now knows too.

I learned how to get things done. And
I learned that patience and persistence
were my two best tactics.

The Allenville Water Company

Allenville, Arizona

Water is running out of the kitchen faucets of nearly all the seventy or so ramshackle homes in the unincorporated community of Allenville, about 35 miles west of Phoenix. The water is unfit for drinking, but it can be used for cooking, washing, and gardening. And no one in the community takes it for granted.

Years of frustration, red tape, and several house burnings lie between the town well and the water that now comes out of the tap through the pipes of the nonprofit Allenville Water Company. Everyone in this community of 500 blacks knows the trouble they have been through.

They also know it wasn't until they interested the mayor of Phoenix and Phoenix's newspaper and television stations in their plight that money finally was found for the water system.

"The old well was almost dried up," says Abraham Harris, 36, president of the Allenville Community for Progress (ACP), which led the effort to raise the $50,000 necessary for a new well and distribution system.

"And we wanted to run pipes from the new well to as many homes as possible," he adds. "Even when the old well was brimming, you still had to go down there to get your water."

Harris means water for washing and cooking. Drinking water has always been purchased in bottled form outside the town.

Allenville, only about four country blocks long, and two blocks wide, was "established" in 1946, about a mile and a half from the small town of Buckeye.

Local residents say that for many years cotton farming was one of the few profitable industries in the outlying Phoenix area, and that hundreds of black fieldworkers were brought in from the South. The only problem, these people claim, was that local ordinances forbade blacks living within Buckeye itself.

Even if there never was such a law, the existence of Allenville is proof that a special area was set aside for the region's blacks.

By the early 1960s, Allenville was still little more than a cluster of houses. It lacked just about all the social and municipal amenities that people in most other towns take for granted. There was no gas station, no school, no corner grocery store, no sidewalk—not even any paved roads. About all the town did have was the old well, located in front of the church. "The only thing we had was the well," Harris says. "And year by year it got drier and drier."

Increased farming and agricultural uses in the surrounding areas, plus a natural depletion factor, caused the well to begin running dry in the 1960s. In 1963 a discussion at the church on some now-forgotten subject turned to water, and the participants decided to see what they could do.

"That's when the burnings started," Harris recalls. "They were never solved. The pastor's house caught fire, there were vague threats. The town forgot about a new well."

Abe Harris points out that 1963 was just one of many racially tumultuous years in which disturbances and riots in many major cities captured headlines nationwide. He thinks that whites in neighboring towns equated any attempts by blacks to better themselves with riots, lootings, and burnings.

"All we did was talk about the need for a new well," he says.

Depressed and discouraged, Harris moved away from Allenville, where he had grown up, and began raising the first of his five children. He moved to Phoenix, working at odd jobs in the city, and in the cotton fields outside the urban area.

"Then in 1965 somebody called up and asked if I wanted to be trained as a community organizer for migrant farm workers," he says. "I said no, but he persisted. Finally I agreed. It changed my life."

And Allenville's. Government money from Washington was being used to help improve working and living conditions for thousands of migrant workers, particularly blacks and Mexican Americans, in the Southwest. As part of his training, Harris was sent back to his old home town of Allenville on behalf of the Migrant Opportunity Program (MOP). His job was to talk to people and determine their single most pressing need.

"The answer was always water," he says.

At the same time some parcels of land became available at the low price of $25 per unit ("low" anywhere else, but not Allenville) and Abe Harris moved his family back home.

"The MOP work," he says, "was a new world to me. I learned how to get things done. And I learned that patience and persistence were my two best tactics."

Harris himself was not immediately accepted by his old town.

As he tells it, some people were suspicious of him coming back home, others were afraid there would be a repeat of the 1963 anti-Allenville violence. His early efforts to get something as simple as a public pay phone installed in town impressed his neighbors.

"When the phone company started stalling me, I simply called them every day."

The public pay phone was installed.

The questions now were—how to get a new well dug, how to run water lines from the well to each house, and how to pay for all this work that had to be done if the town was to have water.

Harris organized town meetings. Elections were held, and officers chosen. Harris and his colleagues, notably James Brown and Clyde Cobbin (all officers in ACP) first approached leaders in Buckeye, and then Maricopa County (which includes Allenville and Buckeye).

"We got nowhere," Abe Harris says. "We got the runaround. There was no city or county money available. Buckeye wouldn't sell us their water. Nothing."

In 1966, Harris decided to try for federal government money. He learned that towns as small as Allenville must work through the U.S. Department of Agriculture's Farm Housing Administration (FHA). So in February 1966, the Allenville Community for Progress applied to the FHA—but the application was returned.

"We didn't have the right estimates, forms, or anything," Harris recalls. "They told us to get a lawyer and an engineer—and they recommended some to us."

A lawyer named David Merkel, together with an engineer with the firm of Williams & Ellis, were both retained on the basis that they would be paid only if Allenville obtained money. They agreed.

An estimate was made that a new 200-foot-deep well and pumping unit, plus water lines to the area's homes, would cost about $50,000, including legal and engineering fees. While Dave Merkel continued the apparently fruitless task of trying to find that much money, Harris and other ACP members began compiling figures on what tap water actually would mean to the community in terms of health, property values, and so forth.

The years between 1966 and 1969, however, were years of frustration marked by the receipt of reams of paper conveying government interest—but no money.

Harris and ACP contacted all of the area's local, state, and national officials, elected and appointed—but not one could or would do anything for the waterless community.

As the town's frustrations continued, its water supply diminished. "The town was going to die without water," Harris says.

During one meeting in 1969 with officials of the Maricopa Area Governments (MAG), lawyer Merkel mentioned Allenville's plight to a MAG official. The official mentioned it to a local reporter. The reporter talked to his editor.

And Allenville was on the way to getting money.

"Public subscription was our last hope," says Dave Merkel, a lawyer who had taken the Allenville case when he was fresh out of law school, and continued to work on it as he rose to become city attorney of Tempe, a small town that is situated just to the east of Phoenix.

The mayor of Phoenix, Hal Graham, posed himself in front of his city's sparkling new water fountain one hot summer day in

Abraham Harris stands beside Allenville's new well and pumping unit.

1969, and was filmed by the city's television news cameras talking about Allenville. He urged that donations be sent to the *Arizona Republic*, the town's leading newspaper, which would collect and then forward the money.

"Allenville had the worst poverty conditions in the state," says Clyde Murray, the reporter who covered much of the Allenville story. "We ran pieces all over the paper. We did everything we could."

Having found nothing but frustration for the four years since 1966, Allenville's citizens were startled to receive nearly $25,000 donated to them within three weeks.

With that money in hand, Merkel could then go back to the FHA and apply for the total $50,000 needed.

Merkel used the initial $25,000 as collateral for an FHA loan of about $25,000—which he promptly repaid. Once the loan was repaid, a matter of days, he could apply for—and receive—a matching grant of about $25,000.

In short order Allenville had a new well, water lines, and water meters at sixty-seven houses. The utility company even sent a man out to explain to the residents how the meters work.

Now that it had truly established its identity as a community, Allenville was able to have the state pave its streets for the first time and put in traffic signs. The school bus now brings kids all the way into town, instead of dropping them off a mile away. And a water supply has meant that most of the residents can have their own flower and vegetable gardens, that some (such as Abe Harris) can keep a few chickens in back, and that nearly all of the people can have the simple convenience of indoor plumbing. Water rates for the Allenville Water Company average about $6 per month.

Allenville still needs drinkable water, and Abe Harris is working now on ways to get the money needed for a purification system. He'd also like to develop some empty land for recreation, as well as find ways of bringing in more jobs and economic opportunities.

Allenville was given half its well money by the charity-conscious people of Phoenix, spurred on by local media—four years after the town had begun its dollar-search. The remaining half came from the federal government—but only after thousands of private citizens had acted.

But Allenville would not have been given any money at all by anyone if it had not shown that it knew how to use that money. It seems rather cruel to say that Allenville had to show that it was worthy enough for charity and grants, but the world is often a cruel place, at least for a time.

"Patience and persistence," Abe Harris says. "That's the key."

*Often people fail in serving the poor because they
don't really want to work at the job. It is
important that you not only tell troubled people
what to do, but do it with them.*

The Davidson Community Center

New York, New York

When people come to the Davidson Community Center they are in trouble.

They have been intimidated and harassed by landlords, or denied their rights to public assistance and justice because they do not speak English. They come in need of jobs, of a place to live, of food. Or because they are ill and frightened. Or because they feel hopelessly lost in a strange city.

That there is such a place to bring problems—and receive help—is almost entirely the doing of Antonia Vazquez, a slight, energetic woman who truly cares about people.

Before the center opened its doors in January 1966, in a storefront on Davidson Avenue in the west Bronx section of New York City, the entire neighborhood, in Toni Vazquez' words, was "crawling toward destruction." Today, because of her courage and purposefulness, as well as the efforts of the many good people she has rallied around her, the signs are more hopeful that the area is crawling in the opposite direction. The area has a population of about 143,000 people, half of whom are black or Puerto Rican migrants who have moved there in the past 10 years from the South or from ghetto neighborhoods in Northern cities. About 47,000 of the people are currently receiving public assistance.

The neighborhood's rapid transition from a mostly white, middle-income community has been marked by an equally rapid decline in housing conditions. The influx of mostly poor and less knowledgeable tenants, plus uncertainty over the future, has caused many landlords to stop maintaining and servicing their buildings. The newcomers, uncomfortable in neighborhoods that offer few or no social amenities, have tended to consider their stay as temporary, so they have mostly not bothered to even try to resist the abuses. Consequently many buildings are deteriorating and many have been abandoned—by the tenants, by the landlords, and by both.

The road to hope began in the basement of 1975 Davidson Avenue, where Toni Vazquez formed a tenants' group in September 1965. That summer she had served as a volunteer block worker for a recreation program—an experience that had opened her eyes to the conditions and problems of the area and to the personal satisfaction of helping people in trouble. At summer's end she found she could not abandon the people she had come to know. At the time she was living in an adjoining apartment house with her husband and 14-year-old son (two older daughters had completed college and were married).

The tenants' group lost its basement meeting place a short while later, but soon found new quarters in a storefront. The owner of the building agreed to rent the burned-out store at 2034 Davidson Avenue for $125 a month.

With a secondhand electric knife as the prize, the group conducted a neighborhood raffle and raised $500—enough for two months' rent and for the paint and materials to fix up the store. The Davidson Community Center was in business—but only just.

From then until 1969 the center operated on a hand-to-mouth, totally volunteer, self-help basis. The bills for rent and utilities were paid with money collected by students on the nearby campus of New York University and donated by local residents and merchants. All supplies, equipment, and furniture were either donated or salvaged. Many times the group had to face the question of whether or not it could continue, and each time it somehow managed to answer affirmatively.

Then, early in 1969, as a condition of accepting a grant of $5,000 from the John Jacob Astor Foundation, the center was incorporated as a nonprofit, tax-exempt organization. Thereafter, foundation grants became the mainstay of the center's financing. And it was also in 1969 that the Davidson Community Center won the prestigious Lane Bryant Award for outstanding voluntary service to the community.

Today, with an annual budget of $23,000, the center is a vital and well-known community resource. With a paid staff of three and many volunteers, supplemented by teachers assigned by the city board of education and recreation leaders provided by various city youth programs, the center maintains an impressive and richly varied program.

It offers information, referral, and counseling to those with problems related to housing, welfare, and employment, as well as to those involved in family crises of every description. Its housing program organizes tenants' groups and secures them legal aid, and it helps relocate families out of abandoned and fire-scarred buildings. And it was recently responsible for having a group of sixteen buildings designated as a target area for rehabilitation by the city's housing and development administration.

The center houses a training program that offers courses in high school equivalency test preparation, English as a second language, and clerical and typing skills. These are all courses that, as taught at the center, are aimed at getting people off welfare.

The Davidson Community Center also serves as the headquarters of a community security patrol. Formed in 1972, the patrol has thirty-five members who patrol neighborhood streets from 5 p.m. to 11 p.m. seven days a week. This program has been credited with lowering street crime in the area by 75 percent, so it is not surprising that it is being used as a showcase in neighborhood crime prevention by the New York Police Department. The department is now working on plans to duplicate the patrol in fifty neighborhoods throughout the city.

At the center there are after-school tutorial and recreational activities for teenagers, and a summer program that offers a play street, bus trips, block parties, and the daily distribution of 1,500 lunches to young and old (the lunches being provided through a program of the U.S. Department of Agriculture).

To Toni Vazquez, Davidson's success has been "a matter of proving ourselves to people, and not a matter of money."

"All you need," she says, "are concerned people who are willing to work. Often people fail in serving the poor because they don't really want to work at the job. It is important that you not only tell troubled people what to do, but do it with them. Many times it is not enough to provide information and instruction. You must go with them to the welfare office, the housing office, the clinic."

Another important element of success, according to Toni Vazquez, has been the effort to racially integrate the program within the center itself. In the beginning there was great hostility among the blacks, Puerto Ricans, and whites who came there. The first step was to have an integrated staff and volunteer group. Often this integration had to be reinforced with the reminder that "we must live for the children."

The center has always maintained a neutral posture toward political candidates and parties. But it keeps informed of the records of candidates and officeholders, and it makes a great effort to assist in voter-registration drives. When it registered a thousand new black and Puerto Rican voters prior to the 1972 elections, a local congressman said to Mrs. Vazquez, "How can we be sure they'll all vote?" She suggested placing a voting machine in the center. This was done, and the new registrants all voted there.

One major problem the center had to deal with early in its history was that of youth gangs, some of which had 100 to 200 members. These gangs took over abandoned apartments, roamed the streets looking for mischief, and generally cowered the local people into being prisoners in their own homes. Toni Vazquez succeeded in getting the leaders of the area's two major gangs to attend a meeting at the center. The leaders came, they explained, "because we want to do something good so people will trust us."

"People won't trust you as long as you frighten them," Mrs. Vazquez told them, and she suggested they stop advertising who they were and take their gang names off their jackets. To her relief the leaders agreed to this.

One member of the "staff" at these meetings was a community relations officer of the New York Police Department, in civilian dress, who was there at Mrs. Vazquez' invitation. He won the confidence of the youths, and in the months that followed he helped many get jobs and become involved in the center's activities.

For all their efforts on behalf of the community, Toni Vazquez and her staff are not professionals. Her co-workers are mothers and housewives like herself. She is the first to tell you that when she started she knew nothing, not even "who was who or where to go." Other than having served several terms as president of a local parent-teachers' association, she had no special preparation for the job she is doing today. And before then her life had been far from easy. Her father died when she was an infant in her native Puerto Rico. And she was 14 years old when her mother died, and she migrated to this country. She completed high school here and went to work in a needlepoint shop until she married. And somewhere along the way she learned to care.

"The people in the community are good people who respond to caring and concern, who are very proud but who can be helped to accept help," she says. "Many simply feel that there is no place for them—that without family, friends, or jobs, they have no chance at all. This is their country, but a strange country, a country where many of them do not know the language.

"You cannot be in a neighborhood like this, with the poor and uneducated, and apply professional methods or standards. You are immediately seen as an outsider, and people resent you. You must act like they do and communicate in simple terms, even in their native language. There is no professional way to reach people. It takes a special way with each and every individual."

We had to organize and select goals for ourselves
that we knew we would be able to attain.

The Scott Area Action Council

Scott, Arkansas

Folksinger Huddie "Leadbelly" Ledbetter created a warm image of "those old cotton fields back home." That sentiment, however, is not shared by the residents of a cotton-farming section of central Arkansas known as the Scott area.

Indeed, Scott area residents have prepared an illustrated brochure, part of a self-help campaign, that is a frank appeal to "*Free Us From Those Old Cotton Fields Back Home.*"

The brochure is the work of the Scott Area Action Council, Inc., a community organization formed in 1970 to aid the 3,500 people (nearly all of them poor blacks) who live in the Scott area and long ago lost their livelihoods on cotton plantations to mechanization. In four years the council has made slow but steady progress in improving housing, creating jobs, training workers in new skills, and establishing such projects as a community-run supermarket.

Much more must be done to get the small community on its feet. But the people of the Scott area are demonstrating what can be achieved with imagination, resourcefulness, and willpower.

The Scott area is situated in one of the most isolated sections of the state. Although its chief community, the town of Scott, is only 15 line-of-sight miles southeast of Little Rock, the driving distance is 47 miles by the only road. Visitors are rare in this 200-square-mile area that lies partly in Pulaski County and partly in Lonoke County.

The people of the Scott area live in "shotgun houses"—tar-papered, tin-roofed shacks that sit starkly on flat, treeless fields along the Arkansas River. (A shotgun house is so constructed that a shot fired through the front door will pass out the back door without hitting anything.) Heating in these houses is primitive; some have butane gas, others depend upon wood-burning stoves to take the chill off the winter weather. Many houses lack electricity. Most of them lack running water and indoor plumbing.

The community has been described as a classic example of a plantation "ghetto."

Members of four wealthy white families own the fertile river bottomlands that are used for growing cotton and soybeans. When they mechanized their farming operations in the 1940s and 1950s, these families left the blacks who had worked the fields by hand to their own devices. Very few blacks had marketable skills. Those who drifted to Little Rock and other cities either were forced to accept menial jobs or stagnate on welfare rolls. Those who remained fought a daily battle with malnutrition and disease, and faced a hopeless future.

Through the second half of the 1960s some tentative aid was offered by the Pulaski County Economic Opportunity Agency (EOA). But this proved ineffective.

The average income per family in Scott (including families with up to twelve members) is still only $178 a month, thereby earning Scott a place among the ten poorest areas in the nation.

In 1970, Thomas McVeigh Smith, a former priest who was then serving as the county EOA director, came to Scott and saw the desperate situation. In conferences with several leaders of the widely scattered community, he came to the conclusion that a self-help program was the only solution. Scott was simply too isolated, too small and unnoticed, to expect help from the outside.

Community leaders and Smith had no difficulty in selecting things that needed to be done. They were obvious.

"Our main concern," Smith now recalls, "Was to go slow. We had to organize and select goals for ourselves that we knew we would be able to attain."

It proved to be a wise course. To have tried for some spectacular goal—such as attracting a major industrial employer to the area—and fail would have simply convinced the Scott residents that their plight was indeed hopeless.

Through the summer and early fall of 1970, community meetings were held at an abandoned schoolhouse. Finally it was decided to form a nonprofit corporation to serve the Scott area.

To make leadership of the project open and democratic, a community election was held involving everyone able to vote and eligible for office. The results of the election were that Roosevelt Wilson, a painter and decorator, became council president, and Annie Bell Boyd became vice-president. Local black residents, of course, dominated the election, but two whites were also voted into office: the Reverend Joe Neckar, a white United Church of Christ minister from Little Rock, was elected treasurer, and Dr. Kenneth Payne, a white physician from Little Rock, was voted a member of the board. The board of directors in turn selected

"Mac" Smith to serve as the executive director of the council.

On October 27, 1970, the enterprise was officially chartered as a nonprofit corporation to be known as the Scott Area Action Council, Inc. The idea was taking tangible form.

A second agency, created to help guide the council—the Scott Residents' Planning Committee—was elected in another community-wide election. Its function would be to select and give priorities to projects. The projects would be recommended to the council, which would be authorized to accept or reject them. No projects could be initiated by the council itself. The planning committee also was given power to recommend funding for various projects. The council could then either accept or reject the recommendations of the committee.

Wayne Bolick

Roosevelt Wilson, president of the Scott Area Action Council, checks out one of the freezer compartments in the council's new supermarket.

"It was important," Smith said, "to give the people control of their projects. The only problem we encountered initially was to get the people to speak up. They had been ignored for so long that some were reluctant to say what they wanted."

That reluctance soon disappeared.

Adhering to its own injunction to proceed slowly and to adopt realistic goals, the council decided to seek volunteer and financial help from the Little Rock community through the churches. Smith and Neckar contacted various area ministers and persuaded them to just come and look.

"We knew," Smith says, "that once they saw the situation at Scott we'd have no trouble getting them to help."

He was right.

During the first year the council obtained about $6,000 for its operations, all from various church groups.

The first project was a pig-raising program started with assistance from Heifer Project International. Any Scott resident who wanted to participate would receive five baby pigs. When the pigs were grown, four would be given back to the council. The participant could keep the fifth pig, either to slaughter for food, sell for profit, or keep for breeding purposes. The council would sell the pigs and use the money as seed money for other projects.

In its second year the pig project realized a profit of $2,471. Skyrocketing feed prices, though, subsequently curtailed this project somewhat (only $800 in profits in 1973), but the project did prove to Scott residents that they could help themselves.

Another project started by the council was a sewing circle, using six donated sewing machines. Neckties and dashikis produced by the women were sold to retail stores in the area. The sewing skills obtained by the women enabled them to get jobs in the many garment-manufacturing plants that have moved into Arkansas during the last few years. This project brought in $1,000 during its first year of operation, and $2,000 during its second.

Profits from the hog and sewing programs were used to finance the first of 1973's breakthrough projects: the purchase of 40 acres of land and the leasing of another 40 acres. On those 80 acres soybeans and cotton were planted and cultivated by 25 men with farming skills who were employed by the council.

An income of $7,000 was realized and the men were able to gain skills in the operation of modern farm machinery. The income they received enabled some of them to purchase their own machinery, which they now will be able to rent to the white landowners during the planting and harvesting seasons.

The 40 acres purchased by the council began to be viewed as an asset for the solution of another basic problem—housing. After suffering a heartbreaking setback from the Farmers Home Administration (which refused to grant a housing loan for the Scott residents because, the inspector said, the area was "too remote"), the council received $100,000 from the Catholic Campaign for Human Development to be used for a housing program.

Neckar decided to resign his pastorate and devote all his time to the housing program as supervisor. Using labor from within the Scott community, the council began building houses in 1974, starting with an initial group of ten structures, all of which would have indoor plumbing and connections to wells.

The ten families moving into the new houses will buy them, making monthly payments to the council. The council will use that money to put into more housing.

Again attacking a major problem at its roots, the council decided to form a profit-making Scott Area Mercantile Corporation, in order to give local people easier access to a food store.

Scott area residents had to travel 25 miles to the nearest grocery store, at North Little Rock. That travel problem was solved in February 1974 with the opening of a small supermarket in the building that houses the Scott Community Center (a replacment for an earlier center that burned under mysterious circumstances, destroying not only the center but the community's food-distribution and storage facilities).

With a $10,000 loan from the Small Business Administration, the corporation equipped the new grocery with modern shelving, refrigeration, and ancillary equipment.

The Scott Area Mercantile Corporation operates the grocery on a multi-purpose basis. These purposes include:

• providing residents with a grocery within the community to sell food at competitive prices

• providing retail store training for the community residents who are being hired to operate the store

• plowing the profits of the store back into council projects planned for the future

The council has purchased a mobile home and set it up as a medical clinic. However this has not improved health care, in that volunteer doctors to staff the clinic are scarce.

The nearest comprehensive medical attention available to Scott residents, most of whom cannot afford it, is at the University of Arkansas Medical Center, 47 miles away.

Through the self-help efforts of the council, much has been accomplished at Scott. But even the most optimistic residents realize the enormity of what remains to be done.

Thomas Smith says the council believes its methods have been successful and plans to continue them. Those methods involve locating people and groups with funds or volunteer help. Then a delegation of Scott residents visits that source of help.

Wayne Bolick

"We've found," says Smith, "that the simple eloquence of these poor people just standing up and telling about their problems is the most effective tool we have. No one who's ever come to Scott and seen our problem has ever refused to offer help. The only people who have refused to help us, other than the Farmers Home Administration, are those who've made their decisions not to help without visiting Scott."

Smith admits that, successful as the project has been, it still has failed to involve the white residents of the Scott area (with one or two exceptions). Even so, as he says, "The wealthy landowners have been convinced, however, that all black men are not worthless souls unable and unwilling to help themselves."

And, while they have not volunteered to help the Scott project, these people have maintained a sort of "benign neglect."

The people of Scott see tangible results of their efforts now, and they have developed the confidence in themselves that will make additional progress certain. They all realize this, and their hopes for the future burn bright.

Sitting nervously in the locked van, the men heard the smashing of metal and glass. Police and national guardsmen were beating their car with rifle butts until it was a disabled wreck. Inside the van, the heater had been turned on full, even though the afternoon temperature was in the 90s. But the worst was yet to come.

The Equal Justice Council

Detroit, Michigan

July 25, 1967, was the third day of the Detroit civil disturbance that was to earn the unenviable distinction of being the worst in the history of any U.S. city.

The city's core area was virtually a battleground. Fires raged. Looting was widespread. Heavily armed police and national guardsmen patrolled the streets, sometimes being challenged by snipers or bands of rock throwers.

Many of the people in the inner city that day were not rioters but victims—terrified, confused, and apprehensive people who often suffered the worst. Most of them sought shelter from the tumult. Some, though, despite the dangers in the streets, went out to check on relatives and friends.

Jim Ingram, a young black man, went out with a friend to check on the friend's sister. They hitchhiked, for bus service had been suspended in the city.

The driver who picked them up when they headed home—another black man—suddenly realized he was almost out of gas. He automatically swung into the next service station before anyone in the car remembered that gasoline sales in the area had been suspended by order of the governor.

As Ingram reminded the driver of this, the three of them realized that the men filling car tanks at the pumps were not station attendants. They had broken the pump locks and were stealing gas.

At that instant police cars arrived. The thieves sped away amidst a hail of police bullets. Ingram and his companions sat mesmerized by the action until police brandishing weapons ordered them out of their car.

As they were being searched, a police van arrived. The men

soon found themselves locked in the van, listening to the smashing of metal and glass. Police and national guardsmen were beating their car with rifle butts until it was a disabled wreck. Inside the van, the heater had been turned on full, even though the afternoon temperature was in the 90s.

But the worst was yet to come.

When the van reached precinct headquarters, a gauntlet of police and guardsmen lined the way into the building. Ingram and his companions were forced to run between the lines of flying rifle and pistol butts.

After being locked up briefly in a small, crowded detention cell, the men were hustled out and ordered downstairs. Another gauntlet of gun- and fist-swinging police lined the stairwell.

In the basement the men were herded into the pistol-shooting range, already jammed with some 80 other black men. And there they were all left.

For two days the men were not even permitted to go to the toilet. At no time were they allowed to phone relatives, friends, or an attorney. No charges were filed against them.

After three days in the hot, stench-ridden shooting range, Ingram was suddenly told he could go. No explanation was given as to why he and the others had been detained.

Today, Jim Ingram is far removed from that nightmarish scene. He is now a public relations executive for an automotive firm, after having established himself as a journalist. But he still vividly recalls his first real experience of how the criminal justice system all too often deals with blacks.

That treatment had been going on for as long as most blacks in Detroit can remember. The injustices that occurred during the 1967 riot—arrests without cause, unlawful detention, denial of due process—were different only in that so many occurred in a brief time span.

As the National Advisory Commission on Civil Disorders pointed out in its 1968 report on the Detroit experience, thousands of people—mostly black and poor—were arrested and processed through the criminal court system without even minimal protection of their constitutional rights.

One group that was already aware of what was happening was a small, informal organization of Christian ministers. Some were pastors of inner-city parishes, and others served congregations outside the areas of the disturbance. What they had in common was a commitment to aid the many distressed families that had suffered through the riot. In attempting to provide counsel and assistance, they were confronted by the chaos that existed in the criminal justice system.

The more they probed, the more they were shocked by the caliousness and indifference shown to poor and minority defendants.

The ministers decided to act. That decision resulted in the conception and creation of what is now the Equal Justice Council, Inc., a project that has been honored nationally for improving the quality of justice for all those who in one way or another become involved with the criminal court system.

The ministers formally organized themselves initially as the Inter-Faith Action Council (IFAC). They decided to begin by launching a program to find out how well justice was being administered in recorder's court. Their choice of court stemmed from the fact that criminal justice in Detroit centers in recorder's court. Prosecution of anyone charged with committing a nonfederal misdemeanor or felony within the city limits take place before one of the twenty recorder's court judges.

As the last echoes of the 1967 civil disturbance were fading away, IFAC members were busy contacting other ministers, telling them of the need to do something constructive about the criminal justice system.

A Methodist bishop, Dwight Loder, listened to IFAC's plea. Deciding it had merit, he announced a $25,000 contribution from his church.

Spurred on by that response, the IFAC effort gained momentum. After some preliminary organizational moves, IFAC set up a justice office, which, in February 1968, was incorporated as a separate entity, the Equal Justice Council, Inc. (EJC).

EJC began with a staff of two. Arnold Mustonen, a young attorney, came from the neighborhood legal services agency to serve as the first executive director. Erma Henderson, a black woman long active in community service work, became executive secretary.

The EJC board of directors—composed of IFAC members and some prominent Detroit attorneys—was convinced that no reform effort would succeed unless people who normally have no contact with the criminal justice system could be made to realize how it worked against many defendants.

As in most cities, the criminal court system in Detroit was and is in effect a self-governing entity quite separate from the other elements of local government. And within the entity operate several factions, each with its own special interests.

These factions include the recorder's court judges, the Wayne County prosecutor's office, the Detroit Police Department, the defense attorneys, and the bail bondsmen.

Although technically adversaries, all of these various factions work closely together. Each needs certain cooperation from the others in order to protect its own interests.

The only faction within the criminal justice system that is routinely treated as an adversary is the very large but powerless faction consisting of the defendants.

If a defendant is affluent or influential, he or she can make some headway. But most defendants are poor, uninfluential, and totally unsophisticated in court procedures. And most of them are black or belong to some other racial or ethnic minority.

EJC's first problem was to find a means of focusing general public attention on the criminal courts. The task fell to Erma Henderson, who by now was executive director, having succeeded Arnold Mustonen who left EJC to pursue his legal career.

Working through the same church contacts that had provided initial support, she set out to recruit people who would be willing to serve as "court watchers." The concept was simple and direct: volunteers would sit in on recorder's court sessions, observing the proceedings and making notes on what happened in each case. Beforehand they would be given a brief, basic course in criminal justice, preferably by some volunteer attorney; this would cover trial procedures, responsibilities of each party, basic defendant's rights, and so forth.

Because court watchers had to be people with free time during the day, most of the early volunteers were middle-class housewives and retirees, many from Detroit's white suburbs. They were people who were responding to pleas from their churches, as well as from the League of Women Voters and other service organizations.

Usually they were people who had never been in a criminal courtroom before. What they saw shocked them. They began talking to their friends, recruiting them as court watchers.

By the summer of 1969, EJC's program was fully operative. The 200 volunteers involved in the first year had increased to nearly 600. Court-watching techniques had been refined, and EJC had been able to set up a formal office in a downtown building.

In July and August of that year, machinery was set in motion for a first formal study that would result in a detailed report on justice in recorder's court.

EJC developed a standardized court watcher's questionnaire. It had a wide range, covering such items as noise in the courtroom;

whether or not the judges and attorneys made use of microphones; age, sex, race, and mode of dress of defendants; whether or not the defendants were represented by counsel; length of the proceedings; and numerous other details.

Using this form, teams of court watchers covered nearly 800 cases from September through December of 1969. Their detailed reports were turned over to the University of Michigan's School of Social Work. Using the school's computer, Donald I. Warren tabulated the data, analyzed it, and in February 1970 issued a copyrighted, 42-page report entitled "Justice in the Recorder's Court of Detroit."

Warren's statistical summaries and charts showed definite patterns of discrimination against blacks and people dressed in work clothes. The discrimination was evident in the types of charges brought, the degree to which judges and attorneys explained defendants' rights, the length of the proceedings, and the sentences imposed.

The study also showed that courtrooms tended to be noisy, that defendants frequently were not clearly informed of their rights, that lack of representation by an attorney led to stiffer sentences.

The study received widespread publicity—nationally as well as locally. People in the middle-class areas of metropolitan Detroit began to raise questions.

From other cities around the country, EJC began to get requests for information and recommendations on how to set a court-watching program into motion.

Court watching is still a flourishing program for EJC. In the six years of its operation, close to 6,200 people have participated. The program has expanded throughout the entire Detroit metropolitan area, with organizations similar to EJC looking into the court systems of some of the suburban cities.

Erma Henderson is much sought after as a speaker by many types of organizations interested in criminal justice. Furthermore, it was her outstanding work with EJC that was clearly an important factor in her winning election to Detroit's city council.

But the Equal Justice Council is now considerably more than just a court-watching organization. It has four other flourishing programs:

1. *The Criminal Justice Public Information & Education Program* (CJPIEP). This is a second step logically following the realization that the courts do not work equally for the poor and minority groups. Using funding from the Model Cities program, CJPIEP

attempts to bring to the inhabitants of Detroit's inner city a better understanding of how the criminal justice system is supposed to work and of how best to deal with it.

EJC recruits people from the inner city, trains them to work as coordinators, and then sends them out to educate the residents of the inner city.

The CJPIEP coordinators spend their time addressing school assemblies, block club meetings, church gatherings, and service club affairs. They tell the groups about the basics of criminal justice, including arrest and arraignment, trial procedures, and the roles of judges, prosecutors, juries, and defense attorneys. They explain the constitutional rights and legal protections to which every citizen is entitled. They identify the government agencies that people can go to for help if they become involved in a criminal matter.

2. *The Jail Ministry.* All prisoners awaiting trial in recorder's court who cannot post bond are detained in the Wayne County jail—including those ultimately proved innocent. Conditions there have been criticized for many years. Previously there had never been anyone connected with the jail to whom prisoners or their relatives and friends could turn for guidance and counseling. Appalled by what she saw when she visited the jail, one of EJC's first court watchers, the wife of a Detroit business executive, set out to get some help for the people trapped there. Working with EJC staffers, she first got ministers to volunteer on a rotating basis to spend time counseling in the jail. That program has broadened. A number of churches agreed to a permanent funding commitment, and those funds now support a full-time minister serving the jail population.

3. *Friends of Equal Justice* (FEJ). The members of FEJ include young people, middle-aged people, housewives, and businessmen. Their common bond is an interest in learning more about the whole spectrum of criminal justice and law enforcement. They meet frequently at EJC headquarters to hear experts. They make visits to the jail, the courts, and other agencies and arms of the criminal justice system, thereby serving in effect as useful intermediaries among the Equal Justice Council, the local authorities, and the inmates. And they are actively involved in a variety of fund-raising activities that are designed to support the work of the Equal Justice Council.

4. *The EJC Referral Service.* Although not a formal program, this

is a vital one. It has grown almost spontaneously as EJC has become widely recognized as a focal point for reform of the criminal justice system.

Staffers now take hundreds of phone calls yearly from people seeking help or advice. It may be a mother wanting to know how she can find out where the police have taken her son, it may be someone wanting an attorney, or a school class that wants an expert speaker.

The Equal Justice Council handles each telephone call as best it can. This means that it sometimes steers the caller to an appropriate service agency, and that it sometimes handles the problem itself.

What has been the effect of EJC and its various programs after some six years of existence?

Erma Henderson is the first to admit there is no definitive way to answer that question by parading masses of hard statistics or other quantitative measures.

There are impressive numbers, of course. There are, for example, the 6,200 people who have served as court watchers; the thousands of citizens who have been reached and influenced by the CJPIEP activities; the hundreds of concerned individuals who have joined Friends of Equal Justice.

But these numbers are not the best indication of EJC's impact.

The council's supporters prefer to point to changes in the recorder's court system. There is, for instance, less chaos in the courtrooms. And more judges have been added to alleviate overcrowded dockets. Furthermore the bail bond system has been overhauled to eliminate many of the discriminatory practices that used to victimize the blacks and the poor. And conditions in the county jail have been markedly improved—one such improvement being that the jail is now used to house only about half as many people as it did in 1968.

The Equal Justice Council does not suggest that it alone is responsible for these and other reforms. But there is solid evidence that the council ranks as one of the most important contributing factors in this change.

The criminal justice system began to change when citizens began to be concerned about how it was working. As Erma Henderson says, "The citizens somehow had never been a part of that system."

But now they are indeed a part of the system, and they are becoming more so every day, thanks to themselves—and in particular to the Equal Justice Council.

This was no shuffling, begging kind of thing.
We were doing hard business. People can
relate to that. Pretty soon the race thing
begins to fade away.

The Arkansas People's Corporation for Self Help

Little Rock, Arkansas

Everett Shelton is a self-styled black militant—militant about the way government money for the poor has been frittered away in high salaries and questionable business practices.

He was angry enough at what he saw during several years of community organization work in New York City and Arkansas to sit down and devise his own special method for assisting the poor. It is known as the Arkansas People's Corporation for Self Help (APCSH).

"My interest has always been to change things for the better, not to tear them down," he says. "I'm not interested in tearing down the government. But I saw all this corruption going on, all this mismanagement; I decided I was not going to be a part of it."

The corporation he started in 1972 is already off to an impressive start in the fields of housing, manpower training, legal counseling, consumer education, drug and alcohol rehabilitation, and health care. The scope and direction of the corporation are in many ways unique, but then so is Shelton.

Everett Shelton was one of seven children born into a poor black family that migrated north to Gary, Indiana, from their scraggy farm in eastern Arkansas. He went to all-black schools, and was nourished by "a system that instills pride in people." He learned about Booker T. Washington and George Washington Carver and felt that, "If they could be great, then I could be great, too. And now my kids know it because they look at me and see I'm doing all right. And *their* kids will believe in themselves, too."

It was in the summer of 1957 that Shelton went down to visit the family's old neighborhood in the East Arkansas farm country. He loved it and loved the people he met. He didn't return "home" again until after a tour of duty in the U.S. Air Force and a staff job

Everett Shelton (left foreground) at a national black conference

with Martin Luther King's Operation Breadbasket office in New York City. This time he stayed. In Arkansas he worked with young people in his church and tackled many of the day-to-day problems of school integration, "especially," as he says, "where the black students were losing their symbols of pride or their positive adult models."

Shelton gradually became more involved in the political process. He led a voter education and registration project, which helped elect blacks to a majority of the public offices in Madison. And he found out, along the way, that the community action agency at Forrest City was ineffective—by both local and national standards—so he decided to run for a seat on the agency's board.

"Once on the inside," he says, "I saw how those agencies in the county were just not doing the job of helping the poor. Those big budgets were heavy on salaries and light on services."

With the aid of a $5,000 grant from the Campaign for Human Development (a Catholic organization), Shelton spent six months putting together an alternative to the government's way of fighting poverty—the Arkansas People's Corporation for Self Help.

The corporation was formally chartered in May 1972 as a non-profit enterprise. Everett Shelton was finally in business—literally—with his own community, the black people of Arkansas.

The time was right and the people were ready. Since 1972, APCSH has embarked on a variety of projects.

A Little Rock bank lent the group enough money to begin a housing project at Lonoke, a community about 25 miles east of Little Rock. "We have bought land and built two houses from the ground up," Shelton says. "It takes time but we hope to build 253 units before we quit.

"We were the first blacks to go into construction at Lonoke. Not everybody took well to the idea—but then the message got through: we were putting $90,000 into that community. This was no shuffling, begging kind of thing. We are doing hard business. People can relate to that. Pretty soon the race thing begins to fade away."

The board members of APCSH are all active in other community organizations, and they bring that experience to the corporation. "This is no free ride," Shelton says. "They participate in Little Rock city planning and they have appeared before the Governor's Land Use Advisory Commission."

APCSH has a contract with the federal Work Incentives program (WIN) to provide job-training and skill-upgrading opportunities for people enrolled in WIN. It also has set up a career counseling program for black students at the Pine Bluff and Little Rock campuses of the University of Arkansas.

Shelton believes deeply in the role that good housing and job opportunities plays in the advancement of not only the community being served by APCSH but also the entire state.

"General Motors passed up Arkansas and set up a new plant in Oklahoma City," he recalls, "because GM wasn't convinced we had enough trained people, and they were also not convinced that Arkansas white workers would let a black worker move up into a supervisory position on the basis of merit. GM was wrong—and we have to prove it to them and to the other corporations as well."

APCSH will probably do it, too. The group's work with the Little Rock bank that provided funds for the Lonoke project has convinced that bank to set up a special department—headed by a black—to deal with the problems of urban blacks. And in June 1973 the corporation held discussions with the top officials of several banks in the area aimed at providing the banking establishment with an increased awareness of the problems and needs and aspirations of the black community in Arkansas.

The list of APCSH's specific accomplishments—real and paid for with sweat and money—includes the following:

● More than 25 families placed in new, decent housing and over 300 people located in better housing as a result of APCSH's

housing information and referral service
- Over 300 people trained for gainful employment
- Legal counseling for more than 150 people
- Immediate assistance with drug and alcoholic rehabilitation followed by placement in the proper programs for 17 people
- Job training and rehabilitation programs for 12 former prison inmates
- Over 150 sick people located by APCSH and provided with transportation to the nearest clinic for treatment
- Consumer education for 300 people as a result of a program to disseminate written information to the community, as well as establishing APCSH as a center for consumer advice

APCSH has also purchased a recording studio known as Little Rock Sound. Through the studio, musicians in the community have a chance to record their work, to listen, and to improve and perhaps market their musical output.

Workmen build one of the first two houses in the Lonoke subdivision.

Through it all runs Everett Shelton's long-held wariness of "giveaway, ripoff" antipoverty programs.

"I don't believe in giving people money and letting them go loose with it," he says. "I believe people have to be accountable. It's another way of building trust and long-range relationships. People understand this and appreciate it.

"And all the people—black and white—that we do business with understand that we're here to stay. We're working in Arkansas to make Arkansas work for us."

What we're working toward is an understanding through human interacting and the solution of problems that don't require just money.

Block Partnership

Dallas, Texas/Birmingham, Alabama

Some of the disparity between the haves and have-nots is fading in two major U.S. cities—Dallas and Birmingham. The reasons for the change are many, but a partial explanation can be found in a program called Block Partnership.

Block Partnership began in Dallas in 1968, when then-Mayor Erik Johnson gathered community and church leaders together with the idea in mind of developing a method whereby affluent whites could be matched with less fortunate partners to work toward solving problems in the minority communities.

Six years later the program is functioning in a manner that has drawn the groups closer together and has produced results few people in Dallas would have predicted.

Working under the auspices and partial sponsorship of the Greater Dallas Council of Churches, Block Partnership forms individual block groups in minority communities throughout Dallas County and pairs them with groups from white churches.

"What we're working toward is an understanding through human interacting and the solution of problems that don't require just money," says Don Johnson, who recently resigned as director of the Block Partnership program.

The success of Block Partnership can be attributed in part to Johnson's personality and the total commitment (16-hour working days) he gave to the program during his five years as director. He has entered private business now, knowing that Block Partnership can sustain itself without his direct leadership.

The original Block Partnership program began in St. Louis, Missouri, but was eventually terminated. Organizers in Dallas went to St. Louis, studied the project, and returned home with some definite objectives in mind.

Funding was and still is provided by the Greater Dallas Council of Churches. Approximately $35,000 is allocated for salaries, rent, expenses, etc. for the Block Partnership staff and headquarters.

When Johnson became director in January 1969, the program was headquartered in the council of churches office in a downtown building, and was strongly influenced by the council staff. A year later, he moved the headquarters into the south Dallas area, one of the largest black communities in the city. The move gave him and the project more independence.

Johnson started out by identifying problems in the low-income communities—poor street lighting, bad paving, lack of day care centers and senior citizen programs, inadequate municipal services, etc.—and then sought the solutions. They had to come largely from the city establishment.

One program was developed in the Roosevelt Heights section of south Dallas, where flooding from the Trinity River has been a way of life for almost 30 years. Through Block Partnership, the residents were able to get the city to include $2.5 million in a $172-million city improvement bond issue to purchase their houses, thereby enabling them to relocate.

One of those who moved after living with flood threats for some twenty-seven years, Mattie Morgan, says, "When it rains now, I can go to bed and go to sleep. I don't see how we came through all those years without someone being drowned."

Others express similar sentiments about Block Partnership programs: new lighting in previously darkened and dangerous neighborhoods, vest-pocket parks where children can play, day care centers that enable mothers to go off to work.

For the participants in the block neighborhoods, the benefits are specific. They can see changes being made, and their neighborhoods are improving. For the city and the county in general, the quality of life is improved.

"When we began, the inner city was deteriorating. Now we have turned that around and we are working toward improvement of the community both in terms of physical appearance and in relationships among the races," Johnson says.

Out of a population of 1.3 million persons in Dallas County, an estimated 150,000 are affected by the problems Block Partnership is seeking to solve. Block Partnership organizers estimate between 5,000 and 10,000 persons have directly participated in the program. The indirect number of beneficiaries may range from 150,000 to 300,000, although many may not know that Block Partnership is responsible.

Volunteer workers to assist the small, full-time paid staff come from the federal agency known as Action. From 1968 through 1973, a total of seventy-five workers volunteered from Action and its predecessors, as well as from a number of colleges and universities located in Dallas and other cities in the area.

But the heart of Block Partnership goes back to the block people themselves. They are the ones who must identify the problems and find the solutions.

When a block group is formed, it is kept at a level of 100 to 300 persons living within a specifically defined area. The block "resident" group and a matching "nonresident" group from one of the white churches are brought together to discuss problems and to get to know one another. If both groups respond well to each other, then a partnership is formed, with representatives of both signing an agreement for a six-month period. At the end of that time, the partnership can be reaffirmed, or the groups can be rematched with other groups.

Sensitivity training is undertaken, in the form of workshops where cultural changes are discussed and where fears are

Block partners discuss problems during a group workshop.

brought out and examined. The people, both the haves and the have-nots, are challenged to meet the problems of difference head-on. "It is a risking of self—a compromise of pride and principles," says one participant.

Block Partnership then take on the problem-solving tasks. "Block Partnership works well where the nonresident partners come in to help and not to rule. It works because the greatest strength is in the minority community," says Dorothy Joiner who's a black "resident" chairwoman of one of the block groups.

Mrs. Joiner says Block Partnership is "a very good thing" to bring the minorities and the establishment people together, but she feels it has not reached all the people that it could. "The people who choose to work with Block Partnership . . . they are already concerned. It doesn't touch the people who are very hard to get to listen. They don't face things until some sort of crisis forces them to."

Her view is shared by some of the white "nonresident" Block Partnership members. "There are people on both sides with hang-ups, but we get together and solve problems. I wish more people would participate," declares George Shelburne.

The offshoot of the Dallas Block Partnership in Birmingham, Alabama, is sponsored by the Greater Birmingham Ministries. The program is located in Jefferson County, where some 23,000 out of 675,000 persons are on welfare.

Sixteen Block Partnership units have been developed since the program began in March 1971. Approximately 2,600 low-income residents have participated, along with nearly 300 white church members. Their combined efforts are credited with easing some of the racial tensions in the city.

City leaders responded to the idea of Block Partnership when it was presented by the Reverend R. H Miles, director of the Greater Birmingham Ministries. Miles views the program as a "thriving urban ministry where people create leadership and are in control of the things that happen to them."

The director, Johnny Coleman, a graduate of the University of Alabama and a former resident of a poverty area in Birmingham, provides the enthusiasm and dedication that makes Block Partnership a viable organization. He is the only paid staff member.

With the help of volunteers, much has been accomplished.

One of the units managed to get the Birmingham city council to block rezoning of black residential districts for industrial use.

Another has cleaned a small creek of sewage, and has got a

large industrial firm not to pollute the air by blowing out its smoke-stacks on Sundays. Block Partnership sponsors recreational programs and projects to feed the city's elderly.

There have been many projects that parallel those in the Dallas Block Partnership program.

In both cities, Block Partnership has become a way for people of different ethnic groups to share themselves and by so doing get to understand each other better.

Not all the fears will be erased, not all the problems solved, but the people of Block Partnership are trying, and they are doing some things that make at least two modern-day urban areas models for bringing about cooperative social change in America.

The heart of Block Partnership is the open citizens' meeting.

*The people know that the money they lay down in
the club is going to stay in the community. . . .
The people understand that and so they've come
by and supported what we're doing, keeping
the money here and sharing this thing with us.*

The People's Club

Rochester, New York

After three years of fighting red tape and shuffling papers in the city's antipoverty agency—and watching the federal money supply dry up—Willie Lightfoot had had enough. So he got together with two old friends, Jackie Caroline and James George, to see if they could all dream up something better. They arrived at the idea of a community program based on an independent enterprise—such an enterprise as a self-supporting, moneymaking people's club.

"We looked at it this way," Caroline recalls. "If we could get a solid business base for our community work, then we would be independent. The priorities and the regulations would be of our own making.

"In a government-funded agency, you are tied down by a lot of bureaucracy and regulations, and you have practically no control over the continuity of your program. If money gets tight, you wind up dumping this or that program. There's nothing else you can do. And a lot of work goes down the drain.

"We had to cut free and do our own thing."

Translating thought into deed, the three of them gave up their jobs in order to establish the nonprofit Monroe County Community Organizers (MCCO) in December 1971.

The three men, all 31 years old and lifelong friends, had grown up in the city's black community, a packed ghetto between Chili Avenue and the Genesee River. They felt they knew its people, its strengths and weaknesses, its spirit, its needs.

Meeting those needs, the three men believed, meant setting up programs that would include job training, education, economic self-reliance—programs that would contribute to the total welfare of the community.

But being determined to steer clear of all government funding, MCCO first had to find money of its own. In considering alternatives, the MCCO trio reasoned that the best source of funds would be a business enterprise. And it would have to be one that, in Jackie Caroline's words, "takes into account the lifestyle of the people in the community. It's always easier to build on or expand something that already exists, rather than bring in something new."

Gradually the idea took shape. MCCO would establish a social club—the People's Club—in the heart of the black community. The club would be more than a money-maker for MCCO. It would be an informal, pleasant, community-oriented place where local residents could meet and talk over their problems—a place where the patrons would be served by friends, counseled by neighbors, and find a renewed sense of community solidarity.

The three friends talked over the idea with other friends, colleagues in community action work, neighbors, relatives—anyone who might be interested. The response was general approval, plus promises of both money and volunteer help.

In March 1972 the MCCO trio found what they were looking for—a two-story brick building, a former laundry, right on Jefferson Avenue, one of the two main business streets in the black community. Making full use of managerial experience and administrative skills, they put together a commercial proposal and then presented it to a local bank. The proposal was accepted, and MCCO obtained a loan of $55,000 for mortgage and rehabilitation costs. This sum, together with $10,000 from people they knew, gave the trio sufficient starting capital. And these and other people, including some from local community organizations, provided the volunteer labor needed to clean out and renovate the old laundry. Then local black artists came in and created a series of murals that reflect the black experience in America and its African roots. At last, in September 1972, came the event everyone had been waiting for—opening day at the People's Club.

The People's Club is a private social club, open only to members and their guests. To be a member, a person must pay a $20 initiation fee, plus dues of $40 per year. Members may bring nonmembers, at a cost of $2.50 per guest per visit.

Despite a high rate of new business failures in the Rochester ghetto, the People's Club has won—and held onto—a sizable clientele. At the close of the first year of operation, for example, the club could boast close to 700 members.

"I think people join for two reasons," says Caroline. "First of all, we have a nice place—good atmosphere, good drinks, live entertainment four nights a week. I think it's the best nightclub in the area, and I'd think that even if it wasn't part of MCCO.

"The second reason, though, is the big one. The people know that the money they lay down in the club is going to stay in the community. It's going to pay for some contracting work we got to have done, for example. And who's the contractor? He's a black

Exterior of the People's Club in Rochester, New York.

guy that lives down the street. And the money will go for waitresses and bartenders and cooks. And who are those folks? They
live right here in Rochester. You go in some of those other places
and they may be nice places, too, but when you slide your dollar
bill across the bar it just keeps on going right out of the community and someplace uptown or even out-of-state. The people understand that, and so they've come by and supported what we're
doing, keeping the money here and sharing this thing with us."

While prices for drinks and food are slightly lower in the
People's Club than in similar public bars and clubs in the community, the difference is too minor to be considered a threat to neighborhood competitors. In any case the use of over-the-counter discounts or giveaways would defeat MCCO's basic concept of a
moneymaking enterprise.

The financial success of the People's Club has stemmed largely
from its popularity (that is, volume business) and its ability to keep
labor costs to a minimum. Most of the staff members are volunteers, and those who are not receive very modest wages. There is
no formal arrangement for long-term employment. If someone
wants to help out at the club, he or she simply works it out with the
manager, James George, on an individual basis. In addition,
MCCO's board members, who oversee the operation of the club,
frequently help out during the peak weekend times when the club
is jammed. As Willie Lightfoot says, "Most of our board members
volunteer time in the club, because that's the way they feel about
the place."

There is more to the building on Jefferson Avenue than the
nightclub. Upstairs, on the second floor of the renovated building,
there are several offices that are leased at low rates to local minority businessmen. There is also a comfortable conference
room, which is available to any community person or group for the
asking. The building has in fact become a community meeting
place—because local people planned it that way, not because an
outside government agency or charitable institution stuck it there
as "a good idea."

In addition to serving as a money-maker and meeting place, the
People's Club manages to find the time and resources, on a limited scale, to serve the community directly instead of through
MCCO. On Thanksgiving Day, for example, the club serves close
to fifteen hundred free meals to needy local families. And in the
summer the club organizes and caters a community picnic that
usually attracts several thousand people.

The initial success of the People's Club led the MCCO board

members to consider starting another business venture to help fuel the parent organization. So it was that MCCO opened the People's Liquor Store, also on Jefferson Avenue, in 1973.

The appearance of these two MCCO enterprises was at first viewed with some apprehension by other businessmen in the area. But that uneasiness soon faded, because, as Caroline says, "We're actually pulling new customers for them into this area." He estimates, in fact, that eight of every ten customers in the People's Club also patronize other local businesses and bars.

The effect of the MCCO enterprises has also been evident in a reawakened sense of community pride among the area merchants. Seeing the good effect on the area of the renovation and general sprucing up of the old laundry building, other building owners have brought out their own paint cans and brushes. This in turn has led to the formation of the Jefferson Avenue Businessmen's Association, the first such association in the community.

The success of the People's Club, as well as the People's Liquor Store, has also led MCCO to set up the MCCO Youth Federation. Headed by 19-year-old Randy Johnson, the federation is dedicated, says Johnson, to "teaching young people responsibility so they can be better able to deal with life." And while the 37-member federation receives an introduction to the world of commerce by way of the MCCO enterprises, Johnson says, "We don't put the value of a dollar over a human being."

As proof of that, Johnson points to a free, citywide picnic that took place in September 1970 sponsored by the federation and held in Genesee Valley Park. The federation members worked hard that day, feeding and entertaining the six thousand people who showed up.

Through its MCCO connections, the youth federation has acquired a house farther down Jefferson Avenue from the People's Club. The young people—under MCCO direction—have renovated the property and now keep it open 24 hours a day as a meeting place and emergency crisis center for local youth.

The People's Club is a money-maker. During its first year of operation, for example, it made more than $32,000, which constituted almost all of MCCO's annual budget. Now joined by the People's Liquor Store, the club promises to provide the capital needed for other community services planned by MCCO. As Caroline says, "Our support comes from the average dude walking down the street. He's got to be the recipient of whatever good things we accomplish. And that's how we want to keep it."

ACORN wins on the issues it deals with because it hangs in there until it does win. If it didn't, it would have been dead.

The Arkansas Community Organizations for Reform Now

Little Rock, Arkansas

Wade Rathke arrived in Arkansas in 1970 to organize welfare recipients into new chapters of the National Welfare Rights Organization (NWRO). The 21-year-old college dropout and his few companions were successful, but that was not enough for them.

"We decided we needed a wider base. We wanted to work with more than just welfare recipients," Rathke says. "About 70 percent of Arkansas' people make less than $6,000 a year. Ideally 70 percent of the people should have 70 percent of the power."

This philosophy led to formation of the Arkansas Community Organizations for Reform Now (ACORN). Initially ACORN served as a statewide coordinating body for NWRO chapters. But as its horizons expanded beyond welfare recipients, it made a decision in April 1971 to sever ties with NWRO.

Since then ACORN has grown to include thirty-two affiliate organizations composed of low-to-moderate-income families. Rathke claims a total membership of 4,700 families operating in groups that refuse to ask for or accept any direct funding from the federal government. It doesn't want federal funding, Rathke says, "because we don't want our flexibility curtailed; we want the right to do what we want." So ACORN is financed by dues from member families ($1 a month per family) and donations from labor unions and churches.

ACORN is in business to deal publicly with issues that affect its members on the state, county, city, and neighborhood level.

One former Little Rock city official credits ACORN "with restoring the neighborhood image" in the inner city. Many of Little Rock's inner-city areas threatened with decay and despair by the flight of the middle class to the suburbs have been rejuvenated in spirit by ACORN-inspired activities. (Half of the ACORN membership is in Pulaski County, the Little Rock area.)

Wade Rathke, the head of ACORN, makes $37.50 a week—after taxes. ▶

WE LIKE
IT HERE

This
HOUSE
is NOT
For Sale

ACORN

JANUARY 1974

		1	2	3	4	5
6	7	8	9	10	11	12
13	14	15	16	17	18	19
20	21	22	23	24	25	26
27	28	29	30	31		

In many instances, ACORN members, acting on the advice and direction of Rathke and his staff of less than twenty paid organizers, have achieved their goals simply by presenting their problems directly to the appropriate officials responsible for a particular social program.

In ACORN's first campaign—to obtain furniture for poor families—a funded program already existed. "But people were sitting around on boxes instead of chairs," Rathke says. "They didn't have an icebox; they didn't have a stove. Informal negotiations failed. We couldn't get the public agencies to respond."

ACORN's tactic to gain that response was direct and effective. The staff sat down with hundreds of persons eligible for furniture and helped them fill out applications. Soon the agency was swamped with paperwork, and within days its officials had agreed to set up new guidelines for distribution of furniture to the needy. ACORN was allowed to help write the new rules.

"We knew we had to win our first campaign," Rathke now says. "We purposely select realistic goals we think we can achieve. We still would rather sacrifice a goal than the organization.

"ACORN wins on the issues it deals with because it hangs in there until it does win. If it didn't, it would have been dead."

Rathke and ACORN prefer to resolve an issue through informal negotiations if possible. Failing that, however, ACORN, with Rathke or another equally astute organizer in the forefront, will resort to activist practices.

ACORN has come a long way since its first campaign, using its combination of tactics to produce an impressive list of successes.

A neighborhood threatened with a white middle-class exodus when blacks began to move in was saved when ACORN members almost matched "For Sale" signs with those that said "WE LIKE IT HERE—This HOUSE is NOT For Sale—ACORN."

ACORN has won reforms in property taxes, including reassessments in Pulaski County and agreement from state authorities to end inequities.

Its campaigns have resulted in more neighborhood parks; installation of safety signs and stoplights for the benefit of school children; jobs for the unemployed; public assistance to families that didn't even know help was available; improved health care; and 10-percent discounts at forty neighborhood stores.

Rathke's organization is not reluctant to take on major opponents. ACORN, for example, has recently been seeking guarantees from a large utility to ensure that emissions from a coal-fired generating station will not harm the air, people, or land.

Director Rathke wanted the campaign motto to be "Only God has a right to change the weather," but he relented when several of the ACORN board members protested, as Rathke reports, that "they didn't think we should bring God into it."

ACORN relies heavily on teaching its members to use the democratic process to operate and achieve its goals. Every group that ACORN organizes elects one member to a one-year term on the ACORN executive board, which meets twice a month to hear what is going on at both the state and local levels.

All major board policies are reported back to the local groups for affirmation before final decisions are made and a campaign begun. The local groups, however, work through their own local leadership in dealing with neighborhood issues.

ACORN, Rathke says, prefers a "low-key image. Our organizers are sort of like car mechanics; they make the car run, but you seldom see them in it."

All ACORN personnel, including Rathke, are paid the same salary, $37.50 a week after taxes. The organization does provide a hospitalization plan for its paid staff and will make emergency loans—in the event, say, a car breaks down. But all loans must be repaid and any disbursement from the emergency fund must be endorsed by four persons, including two board members.

All people accepted for ACORN training as organizers must be dedicated, Rathke says, because "they certainly aren't in it for the money." ACORN and Rathke and his staff have trained more than a score of organizers since 1970.

The average stay for an ACORN organizer has been two years. Some go on to work with similar organizations after their tour with ACORN, and some are sent to other groups around the country at the completion of the one-year training program.

Kaye Jaeger, 24, a graduate of the University of Wisconsin and a veteran of Volunteers in Service to America (VISTA), read an article about ACORN and consequently applied to Wade Rathke.

So Kaye Jaeger was hired, and she now works with the ACORN Food Buyer's Club, an organization that purchases everything from hot salami and cheese to bread from wholesalers once a week, and then sells it below retail to approximately forty families every Saturday morning.

The food club, which Rathke says will work on a small scale but cannot "be turned into a supermarket," is only one of Kay Jaeger's responsibilities. She's also a neighborhood organizer and she helps to program and staff such medical services as eye examinations in ACORN's North Little Rock Service Center.

ACORN's successes have by no means been limited to its central operation at Little Rock, the state's capital city and chief urban center. At Fort Smith, in northwestern Arkansas, for example, ACORN organized a months-long community effort to gain establishment of a school bus system. When private negotiations failed, ACORN got involved in a local school board election, then formed "a three-mile walk" to demonstrate to the city fathers and politicians just how far some children had to walk to school. A school bus system was soon begun.

ACORN now has regional offices at Fort Smith and Pine Bluff, in addition to its main office at Little Rock and its service center at North Little Rock. The ACORN staff serves other areas in Arkansas by sending in organizers to deal with specific problems.

Although Rathke, a Louisiana native, and many of his paid staff are from other states, ACORN does not want to be labeled an outside force. The key, Rathke says, is sticking to neighborhood or community or worker organization. When a neighborhood or group asks for ACORN's help, the staff immediately establishes whether a real problem or real issue exists.

When they move on a problem, the community is organized into a united front. Mrs. Steve McDonald of the Centennial Neighborhood Action Group recounts how this approach succeeded in gaining a new park for her neighborhood. The city had approved conversion of a former school site into the park, but a snag developed when Housing and Urban Development (HUD) funds were frozen in Washington. The neighborhood mailed 250 letters to President Nixon asking him to unfreeze the money, but to no avail.

"We were told there was no way to get the park," says Mrs. McDonald. "When the school board put up the land for sale, we asked for a delay until we could get the funds. We went to city hall, private homes, and to school buildings. They finally got tired of us. Everytime they turned around, ACORN was in their face."

The school board finally agreed that the land would not be sold until the HUD funds were released for the park.

ACORN's chief attribute, most people agree, is its ability to organize a community, neighborhood, or group of people into a united force. Nevertheless, criticism of its tactics, although muted, does exist. For example one state legislator (an ACORN member) complains: "Sometimes they [ACORN] are too provocative."

Replies Wade Rathke: "The problems of our people are what is provocative."

Ideas are easy. The tough part
is making them happen.

Guadalupe Center

Salt Lake City, Utah

Making ideas happen is what it's all about at Guadalupe Center, in the heart of Salt Lake City's low-income neighborhood. And the ideas that have been made to happen include finding jobs for the jobless, making low-interest loans available to high-risk borrowers, providing education for adults who can't read and for preschool children making the transition from a Spanish-language home environment to the English-language public school system, operating a free food market to feed hungry neighborhood families, renovating old houses and building new ones to house low-income families, providing an effective correctional program for delinquent boys, and organizing a social action force that has both political power and respect.

These ideas have all been translated into successful community programs at Guadalupe Center. And each program is designed and operated by the people that it benefits—in response to a need.

Dreams began turning into reality in 1961, when a new Catholic priest, Father Jerald Merrill, was assigned to Salt Lake City's Guadalupe Mission for Spanish-speaking parishioners.

"I was teaching science in the Catholic high school," Merrill says, "but I was spending so much time at the mission that the bishop decided he might as well assign me there."

After his first Sunday sermon, one of the members came to Merrill and said: "Father, I prayed during the Mass that the Holy Spirit would help you speak better Spanish." Merrill's lack of fluency in Spanish was more than compensated for by fluency in hope. He thoroughly believes the dictum laid down by Alexis de Tocqueville: "The evils which are endured with patience so long as they are inevitable seem intolerable as soon as hope can be entertained of escaping them."

There were evils in the city's Spanish-speaking community: low income, lack of opportunity, discrimination, bad housing, conflict between the Catholics and the Mormons, a dearth of self-respect, and too much drugs and crime. Hope was there too, hiding beneath the surface, waiting expression, seeking fulfillment.

Guadalupe Mission had the usual social organizations, and, as was traditional with the people, they were segregated by sex; the men belonged to one group, the women to another. Merrill suggested that they form a "coed" social group, the Guadalupana Society. That's when the ideas began to happen and the hope came forward.

"It's amazing what took place when the men and women met together," Merrill says. "If a man says he will do something when his wife is listening, he intends to do it. And if a woman hears her husband promise to do something, she sees that it gets done."

The Guadalupana Society was only a third of the forty-five families in the mission, but they met regularly, discussed problems, elected leaders, and planned to get things done. One of their first concerns was the neighborhood's young people—they needed a place to meet and socialize, a place to keep them off the streets. The adults also needed a social center. So after much discussion the group decided to rent a 2,000 square-foot room in an old hotel. It was named Guadalupe Center.

Olympus Media

Gaudalupe Center has shown that poor preschoolers can succeed.

During the early days the center devoted time to leadership training. Group meetings were encouraged. Group discussion was open and free. Leaders were elected, and their responsibilities spelled out.

The people tackled small problems—and solved them. They examined larger problems—and found solutions to those.

At one meeting someone said, "Why don't we show those people 'out there' what we can do!" The discussion inevitably turned to the need for funds and where they could be obtained. Other people borrow money, they decided, why not us? And the idea for the Westside Catholic Credit Union was born. But it took a lot of work. The group appointed a committee and it found they would need a state charter. The credit union league was reluctant to support a charter on the city's West Side because the loan delinquency rate was higher there than anywhere else in the state. But the Guadalupe group was confident and their sincerity won out. The credit union league agreed to support the charter and to loan them enough money to get started. The Westside Catholic Credit Union has grown to almost 400 members, with assets exceeding $135,000. Since its inception in 1965 it has loaned more than $1 million to its members.

"Strange things happen around here when loan payments are due," Merrill says, "but the delinquency rate is surprisingly low. I used to be a member of the board of directors, but I was kicked off for not attending the meetings."

Soon, another idea was taking off. Guadalupe Center had moved to a remodeled warehouse after outgrowing its old quarters. But the new center wasn't always open when people wanted to use it. Someone suggested that if a kitchen were available they could have coffee, a little something to eat, and extended hours. This led to the idea of opening a cafe.

The La Morena Cafe was opened in 1966. It had ten tables. Now it occupies most of the space in the center and is one of the city's most popular restaurants, serving lunch and dinner—Mexican food, of course. In 1973 the cafe brought in net profits of more than $35,000, all of which went to the operation of other center projects.

One such project is VIP—the Voluntary Improvement Program of adult education, which began in 1966. Volunteer tutors from the two universities in the city work on a person-to-person basis with adult students who want to learn how to read English or how to handle basic mathematics. The program works because students select their own goals—and because each step is carefully structured so that the student can progress at his own pace.

Profits from the restaurant are also used to fund a community food program. Large families with low incomes need food and occasionally have no money to pay for it. The problem was discussed at the center. An idea happened—Westside Family Market. Twenty-five churches in the Salt Lake area are contacted monthly for donations of food and money to stock the market. When a shopper comes in, he or she is interviewed by the manager and given credit based on need. The customer then shops for whatever he or she wants, up to the assigned limit, and leaves the store with no further obligation.

Another need was for education. Many of the children in the area had trouble in public school. They came from homes where little learning took place during the preschool years or where Spanish was the only language used. School was a frightening experience. The dropout rate of Spanish-surnamed children was nearly fifty percent in Salt Lake City. Guadalupe Early Learning Center was created to demonstrate that poor children *can* succeed and to determine the kinds of conditions necessary to help them succeed. From fifty to a hundred children, ranging in age from preschool to second grade, meet in a converted chapel that the Catholic diocese bought from the Mormon church. Some classes are taught only in Spanish; some are bilingual. The children are bright, eager, excited about learning.

"Some of the parents threaten to keep the kids home from school if they don't behave around the house," the assistant principal says. "We discourage that kind of thing, but it does make us feel a little proud."

Financial support for the early learning center comes from Guadalupe Center, the Catholic diocese, the Holy Cross Sisters, federal funds, and contributions. The first group of "graduates" was recently tested, and their academic performance was on a par with students in other Utah schools.

A persistent need is housing. To accomplish what it wanted, the center called in some outsiders. Representatives from church groups and cooperative associations met at the center and formed the Utah Nonprofit Housing Corporation. They rehabilitated four homes and built seven new ones. All were sold. Recently the corporation secured a loan guarantee from the Federal Housing Administration for $427,000 to build the first 32 units of a 119-unit development in the neighborhood.

Other ideas happen at Guadalupe Center. There was the creation in 1968 of the Spanish-speaking Organization for Community, Integrity, and Opportunity (SOCIO), which brought together all segments of the Spanish-speaking community in a political action organization that is eminently respected by Utah lawmakers. There is the Utah Migrant Council, which began at Guadalupe Center but is now a separately housed, federally-funded program that provides help in health care, education, day care, and man-power training for more than 5,000 migrant farm workers who come into Utah each year. There is Pine Canyon Ranch for Boys, a rehabilitation center for delinquent boys, which began as an idea during a discussion at Guadalupe Center.

If there are lessons to be learned from the Guadalupe experience, they could well be: (1) start small to ensure success and build confidence, (2) let the people identify their own problems, propose their own solutions, and select their own leadership, and (3) define goals often and reward success frequently.

It also helps to have someone around to offer the same kind of practical advice that Jerald Merrill dispenses at Guadalupe Center: "Ideas are easy. The tough part is making them happen."

Olympus Media

West Side children are bright, eager, and excited about learning.

It is a plan which involves individuals from the
grass-roots level up . . . an organized way to
detect and solve problems.

Virginia Assemblies

Petersburg, Virginia

Before Donald Louis Anderson's ideas offered even the faintest glimmer of hope, the rural blacks of Southside Virginia (a geographic area bordering portions of the Virginia-North Carolina state line) were living in a world of poverty and discrimination and neglect. In the six years that it has taken for the glimmer to become a bright ray of hope, the impoverishment has gone unchecked, but the discrimination and neglect have been greatly reduced—thanks to an organization known as Virginia Assemblies.

"Since the assemblies came, people are being treated a little more like human beings," says Ora Clay, the welfare chairwoman of the Nottoway County Assembly. Adds Delegate Ira Lechner, a member of the Virginia state legislature, "You're talking about a potentially powerful political group. . . . Not only political, but economic as well."

The principle purpose of the organization is to deal with the myriad problems of the individuals and communities living in the areas of Southside Virginia (and adjoining portions of North Carolina) where there are substantial numbers of blacks. The organization currently serves some 100,000 people in twenty Virginia counties and two North Carolina counties, all of them at least 35 percent black.

The method used to achieve this purpose is to establish local community organizations, called assemblies, throughout the target areas. A community or whole county is organized into representative districts of 50 people, called conferences. Each conference is represented in a "legislative" body, an assembly. The combined assemblies are served by a parent structure, the Virginia Community Development Organization (VCDO). VCDO is a church-sponsored, tax-exempt, nonprofit, corporation consisting of full-time volunteers and a paid staff that acts as a strategic reserve. VCDO organizes the assemblies, then supplies technical assistance when requested.

"Everybody realizes the need to organize, but previously they had no plan for organization," says the 41-year-old Anderson, a lawyer who has built his home 40 miles north of Roanoke on land that once was part of a plantation on which his ancestors were slaves. He says VCDO is "a plan for organization; it is a plan which involves individuals from the grass-roots level up; it is an organized way to detect and solve problems."

Problems are dealt with on an individual basis. A member of the community fills out a "problem" sheet and gives it to his conference representative. If the representative has no solution, it goes before the assembly leadership or executive council, consisting of 10 to 12 chairmen assigned to different categories of problems, such as welfare, housing, health, education, employment, and so on. If the appropriate chairman cannot solve the problem, it goes to VCDO headquarters in Petersburg, where the staff attempts to find an appropriate and acceptable solution. But the vast majority of problems can be handled on the local level.

To illustrate, Mrs. Clay, a welfare chairwoman, describes the handling of one welfare case: "First, we take a survey to see what this person is eligible for. Then we go to the welfare department and apply. If we do not receive satisfaction, we call to see why this person is denied. If we still do not receive satisfaction, then we seek higher authorities."

"There was this one fellow," she recalls, "who applied for two years but was denied because they said he was able to work. But he had a statement from his doctor saying he couldn't work. He's finally received some social security."

"Sometimes you go to them and you get things," she adds. "Sometimes, you get the runaround."

Welfare assistance can present some very difficult problems, because illiterates sometimes feel intimidated by welfare officials. "The ones who go before the welfare board," explains Garland Davis, the president of Virginia Assemblies, "are questioned in such a way that it puts fear into them. . . . Most come away with no welfare at all. . . . Some of these people come to us, and we straighten it out for them—which is what we can do."

As a result of assembly activity in Southampton County, some 900 persons eligible for welfare were instated on the rolls whereas previously they had been unaware of the fact that they were eligible to receive welfare or had been excluded from receiving such benefits for other, often vaguely defined, reasons.

Virginia Assemblies has also been active in dealing with a variety of other community problems. The organization, for example, has been instrumental is getting paved roads constructed to serve so-called backwoods areas. It has also been active in fighting job discrimination, as well as in providing emergency food supplies for rural families that find themselves without funds or resources.

One of the assemblies' largest projects has been the setting up of a buying club in which participants can obtain food at reduced rates. Two other businesses initiated by the assemblies have been a quilting club and a discount clothing store.

While the assemblies keep a low profile and solve most of their problems on the local level, issues occasionally arise that require the use of confrontation tactics. In the summer of 1972 the Buckingham County Assembly and local voters league combined in a boycott of white merchants "aimed at getting more blacks on the county payroll," reported the Richmond *Times Dispatch.* "We got two black deputy sheriffs," says Buckingham Assembly President Charles White. The boycott tactic also was used in Southampton County to improve employment opportunities for blacks living in that area.

Does the use of confrontation tactics hurt the image of the assemblies? Anderson, the director, thinks not. "I think many groups overemphasize their power," he says. "I say let the image of power grow as the organization itself grows." The assemblies are nonpolitical, in conformity with state laws which prohibit lobbying in the state legislature by tax-exempt organizations.

For an idea that seems to have worked so well, it is difficult to believe Anderson's organizational plan was once rejected by higher-ups. Anderson, as counsel to the U.S. House of Representatives Committee on Education and Labor, in the mid-1960s, offered the idea to a presidential task force, but "they didn't understand it," he says.

When Edwin Lynch, a northern Virginia philanthropist, later gave Anderson his first grant of $10,000, Anderson began devoting full time to the implementation of his goals. He contacted a now-deceased black leader, Dave Gunter, the former head of food service at Virginia State College. Gunter wrote letters to community leaders in six counties, and they called mass meetings in support of the project.

Anderson received additional financial assistance from other foundations and sponsorship from the Commission on Churches and Society of the United Methodist Church, the Campaign for Human Development, the Baptist General Convention of Virginia, and the Episcopal Diocese of Virginia. VCDO started with an estimated $120,000 in funds. Throughout the life of the project, no more than $5,000 has been spent on any single undertaking.

The cost of organizing was low because state selective service rules permitted the use of conscientious objectors as full-time volunteers. A manual by Anderson serves as a training guide for volunteers. Clinics are held for executive council chairmen.

Davis has been the organization's only state president, and was recently reelected. He is well-known in Mecklenburg County and is president of the local voters league. Buckingham Assembly President White, a building contractor with a B.S. in industrial education, holds an executive position with the NAACP. White explains that the assemblies benefit from the "support of the names of other community organizations."

Presently, information concerning the assemblies is circulated by word of mouth or through the organization's monthly newsletter, which has a circulation of 20,000.

Throughout the development of the assemblies, the leaders have shunned publicity for themselves and for the organization. "The more publicity somebody's got, the more discrimination," says Delegate Lechner, a member of the advisory board for the assemblies (the board being primarily a fund-raising group).

However, not all those linked with the assemblies share this view. "I have often expressed that the assemblies should be given more publicity," says White. "Our regular attendance is 50 to 75, depending on the weather. Some people live back in the boondocks."

Not only does State Senator Clive DuVal, a member of the advisory board, feel there should be more publicity, he thinks they should make additional contacts with the legislature. "I think they need to make their needs known. They often need state services such as resurfacing roads. I think they ought to make additional contacts with the legislature and testify on legislation in which they have an interest."

One example of the kind of cooperation DuVal advocates came when the state legislature passed a mortgage foreclosure law on which he and Anderson collaborated. The old law said a trustee could foreclose with the only required advance notice being a legal notice in the classified section of a local newspaper. As a result, many families were unexpectedly thrown out. The new law says an individual must receive a letter 14 days in advance of foreclosure.

Anderson says he sees the assemblies "as the last hope."

"If this doesn't work, there's nobody else in those counties that's doing anything. There's just no one out there. The people would sink into another century, fall farther behind, if we don't make use of this grassroots opportunity."

*It has greatly advanced the idea that . . . a city
should provide funds without smothering the
recipient in controls and regulations.*

The Committee for Community
Controlled Day Care

New York, New York

Day care centers are on the front lines in New York City's battles
for social change.

Disputes over the operation and funding of day care centers
have raised all types of political and social issues. Should the centers be part of the welfare system? Can one center serve equally
well both poor black and middle-class white children? To what extent does government aid mean government control?

In the thick of many of these disputes is the Committee for
Community Controlled Day Care (CCCDC). Functioning out of a
West Side office in Manhattan, the committee is fighting for funding, community control, and economic and racially integrated day
care in more than seventy centers in Manhattan, Brooklyn, and
the Bronx.

Just the sheer force of numbers has made day care a political
and social issue. There are more than 100,000 working women
with young children in the city. Most of the city's day care centers,
perhaps as many as 1,000, are privately operated, often through a
church or community center and usually with active participation
and control from the mothers. Another 500 are run through city
agencies; about 50 operate under the federal Head Start program.

The committee's roots go back to early 1969, when a group of
citizen activists banded together in an emergency coalition to prevent a city agency from trying to impose stiff restrictions on existing day care programs. The department of social services, taking
over day care funding from the antipoverty agency, wanted to tie
the centers to the welfare system and severely limit parental
participation in the day care program.

In one form or another, the CCCDC has been in that fight since.
It won the first round through highly publicized sit-ins and traffic
stoppages. The city agency relented substantially, allowing parent
participation on day care center boards and community selection
of staff members of local centers.

By 1971 the committee was operating on a $10,000 budget, supported by small foundation grants, and relying on a two-person paid staff. It used office space and equipment provided by the West Side Legislative Services Center, maintained by such liberal political leaders as state legislator Albert Blumenthal and Congresswoman Bella Abzug. Besides its coordinators, Shirley Johnson, a black activist, and Robert Gangi, a former Kennedy aide, and its two professionals, the committee relies on volunteer community organizers. Most recently, a steering committee has been established with representatives from the centers.

The CCCDC has three principal goals. It wants accessible day care for the entire population. It wants racially, ethnically, and economically integrated day care. It wants the government to finance—but the community to control—day care centers.

The CCCDC is available to any center seeking technical help or advice and consultation on city government or political issues.

Christopher R. Harris

While working regularly with about seventy day care centers, the committee has aided more than one hundred in the last three years.

It will provide architects, bookkeepers, and lawyers to help centers plan buildings and budgets and to answer legal questions. It helps centers organize more effectively to obtain more money, manpower and technical help. It also runs teacher-training programs and workshops in the humanities and arts.

The objectives sound laudable and not particularly controversial. In some cities they might not be, but New York is a cauldron of controversy; its politics often involve clashes among competing interests and vocal, articulate, and influential groups. Big money rides on many city government decisions.

These controversies occur even in the supposedly mundane world of day care centers. The committee's demands for control of centers and staffing, for example, conflict with the interests of a labor union of day care workers. The union wants fully professional workers, preferably with four-year college degrees. The committee does not think such qualifications are vital and is more concerned with placing community residents in the centers as teachers and staff workers. That struggle has yet to be resolved.

City agencies have interests to protect, as well, although they would claim with some conviction they have the interests of the children at heart. In the eyes of day care center organizers, however, the city and its agencies are personified by representatives of the health department, fire department, buildings department, architects, and early childhood education experts parading through their centers. With rulebooks and checklists in hand, they walk through the rooms in which the little programs are operating, marking down this infringement and that hazard, questioning the bewildered organizers. They complain of unsafe rooms, inadequate teachers, and too many children per class. And they frequently demand changes if the center wants to obtain city funding.

The CCCDC tries to act as a buffer between the city and the community centers. The committee aides and workers know the ropes, are more sophisticated about city hall and the way government works. They have contacts and friends in the right places.

The government demands, despite the committee's attempts to rebuff or channel them, have provoked committee director Johnson into a totally antigovernment stance. Her ideal would be centers completely sustained by the community and cut off from city hall. In some instances she has seen day care programs function effectively on little or no funding, operating like a large family out of a home or church. Once funded however, a number of them have disintegrated over money disputes or they have become too comfortable and less idealistic.

Yet, even among the day care constituency there are splits that make it more difficult to implement the ideal of racially and economically integrated day care centers. Committee organizers have generally found blacks want centers to emphasize discipline, reading and writing, and a structured day. White parents generally want the center to exercise little discipline, to let the children read and write when they are ready, and to let them lead an unstructured life in their time at the center.

Some problems like this seem to defy solution. Nonetheless, in its relatively brief existence the CCCDC can point to a major accomplishment. It has greatly advanced the idea of community control—that a city should provide funds without smothering the recipient in controls and regulations.

Hundreds of parents have taken up this idea as they learn the rudiments of community organizing in the streets and in the day care centers. They are showing that community control *is* a feasible approach to effective local government in a metropolis where city hall is so remote from the people it should serve.

H. Villafana

*They have won the kind of victories usually
achieved at city hall by the rich and
powerful, even though they had little
money or political power.*

People's Free Way

Salt Lake City, Utah

A large number of Salt Lake City's inner-city residents have had the rare and exhilarating experience in recent years of fighting city hall—and winning.

Against stiff odds, members of a group called People's Free Way have successfully thwarted the efforts of land speculators and developers to turn their residential area into commercial property. In the bargain they've forced the city to rethink its zoning, development, and environmental policies. They have won the kind of victories usually achieved at city hall by the rich and powerful, even though they have little money or political power.

The boundaries of the People's Free Way project encompass approximately 5,300 people. At the hub of this community is a center located within the tentacle grasp of a freeway ramp. The center is devoted to the community's needs, and it prides itself on its self-governing grass-roots operation.

At the core of this independence is a block leader program. "Doing for yourself, rather than having others do it for you," says Dorothy Pulley, coordinator and neighborhood specialist for the People's Free Way, "is the key to the success of the block leader program."

There are ninety-seven blocks in the People's Free Way area, and as of now about twenty block leaders. All the block leaders work as volunteers. They have knowledge of the community and neighborhood, its residents and their problems. Specialized technical assistants from the University of Utah train the block leaders to understand the power structure and how to effectively utilize available resources for the desired objectives.

Pleasant Court is a small private "nondedicated street" (which means that the city doesn't recognize it for any services). Residents of the court had appealed to the city for more than two years to maintain the street. Utilizing the block leader program, area representatives took up a collection and bought eighteen tons of gravel and repaired the street themselves. Dramatization of this event by local newspapers brought pressure on the city to examine its policies about nondedicated streets.

Being a block leader has its own personal rewards. Before she became one, Penny Taylor says she was "in a rut and scared to come out." Today she sees the situation differently: "I've learned a lot; I know how to get things done, and I'm no longer afraid. I'm involved instead."

Five years ago, Victor Delgado says, he was a shy and withdrawn man. "By coming to People's Free Way, I have learned to present my case. I'm not bashful anymore; I don't sit in the back of the room, and I have climbed from a man with nothing to a man that someone can respect."

The People's Free Way is fighting to keep the area residential. However, at present, landlords are not compelled to keep up or replace residential structures; they would rather put the land to industrial use. The average house in the area around the People's Free Way center is about fifty-eight years old and in need of repair. In almost eighty percent of the cases, major repair or remodeling is necessary to meet basic housing standards.

Land speculation has been a serious problem since October 1970, when one land owner was instrumental in getting the area zoned C-3A for commercial uses. Since rezoning, there have been eighteen land transactions in the neighborhood, and land values there have soared.

People's Free Way has been trying to curb the encroachment by "being aware of what's going on in each block, who the speculators are, and what they intend to do," says Dorothy Pulley. Since People's Free Way involvement, there has been no new construction of business in the community near the center. An old home built during the pioneer days has been saved from demolition and dedicated as a youth center. A local motel chain has been persuaded to sponsor housing in the area and rent-subsidy money is being made available for building new housing. Currently People's Free Way has plans to petition for a new zoning to preserve local residences.

People's Free Way has been instrumental in some basic changes in policy decisions by city planners. City planners state that "Salt Lake City suffered from over-dependence of extractive industries which tended to be dirty and polluting. Simple overzoning for industrial use will not prove sufficient to attract firms."

The city seems to be serious about its change of policy. New efforts to rezone areas to commercial classifications have been

454

thwarted by the city planning commission.

Vernon F. Jorgensen, planning director for the city, recently replied to a request for rezoning with the following statement: "It is the belief of the planning commission that further rezoning from residential to commercial would result in a worsening of the housing problem in the city and that no evidence of need for such rezoning has been presented."

People's Free Way, like any other poverty organization, has problems. But, unlike many poverty communities, the People's Free Way area has developed a reserve of pragmatic experience to deal effectively with its problems.

Perhaps the spirit of People's Free Way is best captured by a quotation that hangs in the center's offices. The words are those of St. John Chrysostom. He says: "I do not believe in the salvation of one who does not work for the salvation of his neighbor."

With the group's members believing that as they do, the People's Free Way community is in good hands.

Don Busath

Thanks to People's Free Way, says Victor Delgato, "I've climbed from a man with nothing to a man that someone can respect."

We were successful in getting whites to
relinquish leadership interest in our center with a
minimum of friction. We have been able to
concentrate on what we want to do and that
means pulling together different types
of blacks on our board.

The Afro-American
Cultural Center

Omaha, Nebraska

The Near North Side of Omaha looks like a model for black development, and in many ways it is. The neighborhood has a black-
controlled bank, a community credit union, a black-owned and
operated radio station, an Afro-American Cultural Center, and
black-oriented libraries and art collections.

But the neighborhood could just as easily have become a showcase of racial friction and conflict. The reason it has managed to
avoid that fate is a combination of skillful leadership by some
blacks, a well-timed willingness by whites to yield power while
maintaining support, and the ability of blacks to overcome age
and income gaps among themselves in order to cooperate in
working on local projects.

The elements for change stem largely from the shifting residential and ethnic patterns of the neighborhood. In 1967 the Near
North Side was almost half white and half black. Now it is a
neighborhood that is predominately black.

In 1967, Omaha's younger and more outspoken blacks were
chafing at the white dominance of social agencies and financial institutions. A black journalist, Charles Washington, said the city's
blacks lacked "racial self-confidence." Young blacks were leaving. The older black leadership was split.

The chief social agency for the black community in 1967 was
Wesley House, a traditional settlement house funded largely by local Unity Community Services and national and state Methodist
church grants. The house was run by two white ministers and a
mostly white board and staff.

A major change in Omaha's black community came when Wesley House hired as its director a young, Omaha-born black named

Rodney S. Wead. He began promoting the concept of black self-assurance and local black control of community organizations, but allowing for support from whites and blacks living outside the neighborhood. Along with journalist Charles Washington, Wead proposed the idea of an Afro-Cultural Center to give a new direction of black pride to the Wesley settlement house and the black community as a whole.

The Afro-Cultural Center started as a library of black literature, art, history, and music.

A dispute soon developed over the center's name—but it was a dispute that masked some deep-rooted conflicts. The white minister and other white leaders at Wesley House were soon to be eased out. Older, more affluent blacks blamed the younger militants for being responsible for the white exodus from the Near North Side area; they feared that the loss of white leadership would mean the loss of white money in the community. The dispute over the name of the center was resolved by a series of compromises, first calling it the Negro Cultural Center and six months later, on the advice of a white board member, changing it to the Afro-American Cultural Center.

Control of the center shifted gradually to the blacks. Charles Washington became the center president in 1971, and blacks took over all positions on the center's board.

"We were successful," recalls Washington, "in getting whites to relinquish leadership interest in our center with a minimum of friction. We have been able to concentrate on what we want to do and that means pulling together different types of blacks on our board."

The center also moved out of the Wesley House building into its own quarters, a move symbolizing its independence and desire to serve all blacks in the community.

The Washington-Wead team successfully maintained financial support from whites and blacks outside the neighborhood. For the center, this meant modest contributions.

Wead needed more funds to finance his ideas, and he was remarkably successful in obtaining them. Within three years, Wead had started the credit union, radio station, and bank.

The credit union, which makes loans only to community residents, has raised its lending limit from $300 to $2,000 per person. It claims $100,000 in assets and more than five hundred savings-account members. The bank has two hundred shareholders and the radio station has eighty-six. The newest venture for the center is an urban business development program, which has arranged more than $2 million in loans for minority businesses in Omaha.

As vast as these enterprises have become, Washington insists they all have their roots in the cultural center, itself a comparatively low-budget operation running only slightly more than $1,000 annually in expenses.

"This center gave people new confidence that black people would succeed," Washington says. "It was a major factor toward getting some blacks in the community to believe in themselves. I know it served as a springboard for the credit union." Washington mentions, for example, that the credit union idea was stimulated in a discussion at the center about problems concerning loan sharks and pawn shops.

The principal aims of the center continue to be stimulating black pride and awareness. Washington considers these essential elements in dealing with such local problem areas as housing, employment, and education. Consequently center organizers from the start have rejected the concept of an ethnic center serving any groups other than blacks.

"We realized that the focal point had to be black achievements and cultural expression for the center to succeed," says Wead.

Support has come from diverse sources—a loan of 100 books from the Omaha Public Library, a $600 donation from a local public relations executive, a fund-raising committee headed by an insurance executive's wife, contributions from businesses, and proceeds from an Afro-American art exhibition.

The center now has a 700-volume library, used extensively by junior high, high school, and college students. Added to it has been a small art collection and music library. Calendars with pictures of prominent local blacks, including local college graduates, are sold and distributed in local schools. And the center conducts classes and seminars in black culture.

Washington believes that the success of these projects has spurred the black community to attack its major problems with renewed vigor.

"The problems of unemployment, housing, education, and services could not have been effectively fought with the black community attitude like it was in 1967," Washington says.

Community attitudes have certainly changed in Omaha's Near North Side. And the changes have come without disruptive upheaval. Identity has been forged but stability has been maintained, and the black community is now reaping the benefits.

*To tackle the monolithic society, we must
become monolithic ourselves. We would
represent all 90,000 people. . . . And our goal
would be to solve all their economic
and educational problems.*

The Southern Mutual
Help Association

Abbeville, Louisiana

Name: Jada Janise Freeman.
Age: 4 years.
Nationality: American.
*Background: One of the oldest American families. Forebears
date back at least seven generations to French colonial days in
Louisiana. Father, sugar plantation worker; grandfather, same;
great-grandfather, same. Family income: $267 a month, shared
with six other children and two parents. Of this, 53 percent is
spent on food—mostly rice and beans, but milk five times a
week and lean meat four times a month. . . . No rent. The
Freeman shack and outhouse are donated by the plantation.*
*Prospects: Malnutrition, illiteracy, poverty, pregnancy. Life
expectancy is 48 years.*

Jada Janise is not a demographic statistic. She is a bright-
eyed little girl, one of 90,000 children and adults who live and work
on the sugarcane plantations of Louisiana. And to avoid the prospects of malnutrition, illiteracy, poverty, etc., her generation is
breaking out of a poverty-slave cycle that extends back more than
two centuries. It is a breakout being aided and abetted by the
Southern Mutual Help Association, headquartered in the heart of
sugarcane country in Abbeville, Louisiana.

Jada Janise Freeman was born on a plantation named Hard
Times. Her father, Huet Freeman, was born five miles away, at another plantation, the same place where his father and grandfather had been born.

The conditions under which Jada Janise and her family live and
die are virtually as hard as they were back in 1720, when sugar

Huet Freeman and three of his children, including Jada Janise (right) ▶

cultivation began in Louisiana. As a writer of that era observed, "The Negro cabins consist only of badly made slabs through which the winds and rains penetrate at will. Rats circulate freely. . . . The main food is rice and beans. There is very little fresh meat, despite an abundance of game in the countryside."

In two and a half centuries, the sugar workers, including Janise's forebears, have tried several times to break out of the plantation cycle. The first occasion was in 1795, when the slaves revolted and staged a massive march on New Orleans to burn it. They were routed by the militia 30 miles from the city.

The second breakout came in the early 19th century. Rather than a revolt, it was a class evolution. Slaves, trained in carpentry and other skills on the plantation, began to work in the towns and cities. Their masters found it more profitable to rent them out as skilled labor, rather than to use all of them for field labor. As a result a remarkable transition occurred in U.S. economic life.

By 1840, in New Orleans, 85 percent of all carpenters, mechanics, tinsmiths, bakers, cooks, wheelwrights, were black people, and most of them were former plantation slaves. Being allowed to keep part of their wages, many thousands of them had bought their own and their children's freedom. Some were opening schools; some were even sending their children north to college.

Among these skilled workers was Janise's great-great-great grandfather, who bought his freedom and took the surname, "Freeman."

This breakout, too, was crushed. For in 1840 the south began to experience a massive influx of German and Irish immigrants, as well as white Northerners. These newcomers strongly opposed black employment. By 1860 virtually all of the black skilled labor and artisan class had been dispersed back to agricultural jobs.

The Civil War, except for the legal and morale implications of Emancipation, did not greatly affect the Freeman family. The Freemans were not caught up again until 1879, when sugar workers attempted to organize a union and strike for higher wages. The movement was crushed by brutal use of the state militia, and its leaders were jailed. In one incident, the "Thibodeaux Massacre," at least thirty blacks were killed.

This marked the end of the third breakout effort in 84 years. First armed revolt, then economic effort, and finally labor organizing. All had failed.

The trauma of defeat was so deep, so well learned, that the sugar workers did not try again for 74 more years. Then, in 1953, they made their fourth effort.

Assisted by Roman Catholic priests and nuns, 15,000 sugar workers attempted to organize as part of the National Agricultural Workers Union. Janise's father, Huet, was 10 years old. He saw strikers evicted from their homes. He saw his own family's credit cut off at the store. He saw the police used to break the strike. He saw violence. The 1953 effort was beaten. The workers went back to their old ways. And the priests and nuns were rebuked by their bishop who, bowing to pressures of politicans and sugar growers, transferred many out of the state.

Sixteen more years passed during which time Huet Freeman, baby and boy on a plantation, became a man on a plantation and married a plantation worker, Viola. In 1969 their seventh child was born, and they called her Jada Janise.

In the year of the seventh child, the Biblical symbol of wisdom and good fortune, the fifth and current breakout began. Huet Freeman and his family would be caught up in it.

The breakout of 1969 began with a plantation survey commissioned by the Amalgamated Meat Cutters Union, which was hoping to organize the workers. To do the survey, what amounted to an all-star team of social workers was pulled together from southern Louisiana. These experienced veterans would become the nucleus of Southern Mutual Help Association. They included:

● Sister Anne Catherine Bizalion, a Dominican nun, citizen of France, and for 15 years a social worker in the sugarcane country

● Father Frank Ecimovich, a long-time white civil rights figure

● H. L. Mitchell, white organizer for the Amalgamated Meat Cutters Union

● Henry Pelet, a white sugar mill worker, union organizer, and veteran of the 1953 strike

● Frank La peyrolerie, a black union organizer, and 1953 veteran

● Gustave Rhodes, a black plantation worker and another 1953 veteran (and later president of the association)

● William Westerbrook, a black plantation worker

● Marion Overton White, a black lawyer and civil rights activist

● Murphy Wright, a black minister

Despite the differences of color, nationality, occupation, and even religious conviction, it was a natural team. Each member respected and knew each other, at least by reputation. Each had passionate social concern. And each had had bitter experience in federal poverty program projects, having seen them emasculated and appropriated by local political and economic forces.

"The union survey showed us what we already knew," declares

Sister Anne Catherine, now the executive director of Southern Mutual Help. "Union organizing was virtually impossible. And to help the workers in any manner, we would have to be as big as the sugarcane economic interests themselves."

The sugarcane industry is a pervasive, monolithic establishment in Louisiana, embracing 17 parishes or nearly 20 percent of the state's land area.

The large landowner controls jobs and the economic life of the people. His power is greater because they live in *his* cabins on *his* land. Often the store to which they are indebted is *his*. His ownership is also apt to extend into the nearest towns, to control stores, theaters, service stations, banks. And then there is his influence on local schools, hospitals, and government.

The sugar baron even controls the most intimate matters, sometimes by arrangement with local medical doctors. To see a dentist or physician, a worker must obtain a written "pass," like a slave, from the owner. Then the doctor's fee is, or was, automatically deducted from his paycheck. The worker may never see his own money.

The grower's connection with neighboring landowners is close, sometimes by marriage, always by economics, culture, and skin color. To be blacklisted by one employer is to be outlawed by all. The same employing class hold seats in the legislature, local government, and the courts.

This monolithic society regards the worker with attitudes unchanged since slave days:

● A landowner says, "There isn't hardly a payday that some darkie doesn't ask me to let him have $20 or $25 and then he'll come along the next payday and say, 'please don't take it out'."

● A sugar grower says, "All they live for is an automobile, a television set, and getting drunk. This is what they want. . . . Most of the blacks have no responsibility, and they're laughing at the public, with giving them food stamps, welfare payments, and everything else. The father has no responsibility."

These comments may sound like caricature, but they are real—and typical. And they are made by the people in power.

"The survey was completed in the summer of 1969," says Sister Anne Catherine. "And we asked ourselves, 'Now that we've come together, what next?' "

The group took took a full year to devise a philosophy, but what they arrived at was, in Sister Anne Catherine's words, "size, numbers." They decided that, "To tackle the monolithic society, we must become monolithic ourselves. We would represent *all* 90,000 people dependent upon sugar plantation paychecks in *all* 17 parishes. And our goal would be to solve *all* their economic and educational problems."

Sister Anne Catherine recollects that "this sheer decision to represent 100,000 people gave us an implied political power. We were immediately bigger than parish governments, congressional districts, and town-sized economic powers. We could go to Washington or to New York and be received, for we represented a sizable economic and political population.

"We made two other philosophical or strategic decisions.

"The second was *not* to follow the old OEO [Office of Economic Opportunity] formula of one-third's [that is, agency boards should include one-third poor, one-third local business class, and one-third politicians]. We had all found that that didn't work. Each board and each agency became a cockpit for a power struggle between the factions as to which one would control the board. As a consequence, energies that should go to social work were used up on infighting. We therefore decided to keep power firmly within the hands of the organizing cadre, which was us."

The group's third decision, as Sister Anne Catherine recalls, "was to be 'sophisticated' about grant applications. Our goal was to help the workers with all problems, and to be physically present so they could call on us. Therefore it didn't matter if we were funded to do health surveys, or compile wage statistics, or operate a school. Any of these would keep us on the scene. So our design was simply to learn which projects could be funded, and then to develop a program for those funds.

"Our first $500 was spent on travel to Washington and New York to make ourselves known, to learn about fund raising, and learn which programs could be funded."

The strategy of size, the political power implied by uniting 90,000 people, and fund-raising sophistication, has worked. And since it was formed in 1970, Southern Mutual has had personal contact with virtually every one of the 90,000 men, women, and children that it represents.

Southern Mutual's first project was a health survey. It acquainted them with the people, and the people with them. The Southern Mutual staff and volunteers learned and acted:

- The people needed a health clinic. A clinic was funded.
- The people in the Tabbit Hill community, near Abbeville, needed a road. A road was subsequently built.
- The people needed representation—and, most importantly,

expert statistics—in their annual applications to the U.S. Department of Agriculture to determine the hourly wage rate. Southern Mutual provided such statistics and representation.

• Adult education was needed—and so programs were begun. Not easily, however.

Every advance took months, sometimes years, of persuasion and political lobbying—sometimes in Abbeville, sometimes elsewhere in Louisiana, sometimes in Washington. The health clinic was opposed by doctors, for instance, on grounds it amounted to socialized medicine.

"Only by being present," says Sister Anne Catherine, "could we learn the needs." For instance, one of the needs was housing. Southern Mutual obtained funding for a project whereby teams of sugar workers are trained to build their own houses at an average cost of $8,800 for a three-bedroom house. And maintenance is low-cost, because plantation workers having built their houses know how to repair them.

Education is another critical area, with 40 percent of the residents of some parishes having less than a fourth-grade education. Teams of college student volunteers are conducting classes at night, and making progress attacking ignorance.

Henry Pelet, a mill worker and director of a Southern Mutual education program, says, "I've lived in this cane area all my life, and I haven't liked the things I've seen. Today, we are starting to change it."

Southern Mutual began on a budget of $550 in its first year. The entire amount was spent on fund-raising liaison. The 1973 budget is $528,364. This is not to say that fund raising is easy, but knowing how to do it has solved a problem that has sunk many other worthwhile agencies.

Furthermore the results are not confined to the sugarcane workers. For instance, Huet Freeman—the father of Jada Janise—was aided by Southern Mutual in suing the U.S. Department of Agriculture for a wage increase. He won, and in the year 1972 the sugar workers collectively were awarded an extra $7.5 million in regular pay, plus another $5 million in back pay. It amounted to $850 more that year per working family—and the money was spent in the sugarcane towns.

Two men—both white, young, and up-and-coming political stars in southern Louisiana—have commented on Southern Mutual's fallout benefits to the community of Abbeville.

● Assistant District Attorney Frank Summers: "Southern Mutual came to help blacks at a time when there was a great black-white upheaval, and Southern Mutual has helped us weather that situation. They've brought leadership and ability and bright, talented people. And they have caused Abbeville to recognize that having poor blacks was a community problem, and that it was in the community interest—morally and economically—to solve it."

● Daniel Noel, chief of police: "Southern Mutual has generated a political reform. It, and it directly, has changed the attitude of white officialdom toward the problems of the poor."

It was not always thus. But the early days of threats, vilification, and violence have now given way to respect, credibility, and power—through the efforts of Southern Mutual.

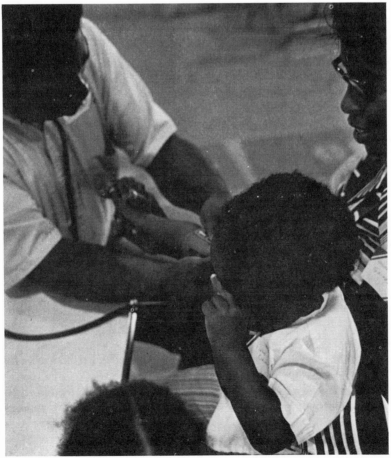

Christopher R. Harris

All patients receive personalized care at Southern Mutual's health clinic.

Printed by
The William Byrd Press, Inc.
Richmond, Virginia

Typesetting by
BRU-EL Graphic, Inc.
Springfield, Virginia

Book design by
Steven R. Christensen

Cover design by
Litho Services, Inc.
Richmond, Virginia

Cover photos by
Al Clayton and Christopher R. Harris

LITTLE BLUE BEN

PHOEBE GILMAN

SCHOLASTIC

ISBN 0-590-73317-6

9 8 7 6 5 4 3 2 1   Printed in Hong Kong   9/8 0 1 2 3 4 5 6 /9

Little Blue Ben
lives in the glen

4

with his brother, Blue Cat,
and their mother, Blue Hen.

5

Their little blue house
is filled to the door
with eggs the hen lays
by the dozens and more.

She boils eggs for breakfast,
she fries eggs for lunch.
For supper she toasts them
to give them a crunch.

"Just wait till you taste
this new treat for the tummy.
These shishkabobed eggs
are deliciously yummy."

11

"Oh, yuck!" says Blue Ben.
"These eggs are *not* yummy!
They're sticky and icky.
They're bluey. They're crummy!"

"Let's play hide and seek,
and when I am the winner,
then *you'll* have to eat
my blue eggs for your dinner."
As little Blue Ben
disappears in the book,
search high and low
to help the cat look.

"Little Blue Ben,
I know you're not far.

16

Come out, come out,
wherever you are!"

"He must have gone this way.
He's sure to be near.

I'll never give up,
if it takes me all year."

"Where, oh where
can he possibly be?

Is he under that mushroom
or inside this tree?"

21

"Would he hide in the water?
How dumb can he get?

He can't be in there.
It's too cold. It's too wet."

23

"He's here in the grass...
No, he's under that stone.

24

I missed him again,"
says the cat with a moan.

"He won't ever find me,"
says Ben, full of glee.

"Who's tinier? Who's tougher?
Who's trickier than me?"

27

"Ho, ho! I'm the greatest!
I knew I'd be winner!

Guess who'll be eating
blue eggs for his dinner?"

29

"Not I!" says the cat.
"All my troubles are past.
Little Blue Ben,
I've found you at last."

But they make such a noise
with their quarrelling then,
that it reaches the ears
of the wise old Blue Hen.

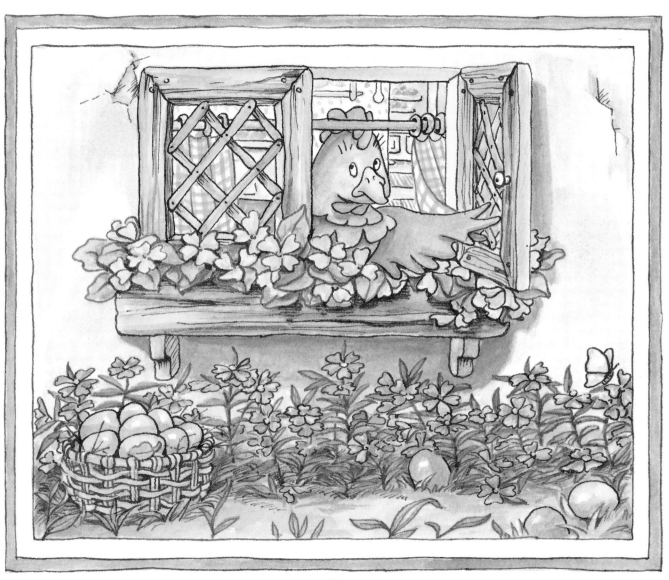

"I'm ashamed of you both
for making me scold.
Where have you been?
Your eggs are all cold."

"If you don't eat your eggs,
you won't grow up to be
as big and as strong
and as clever as me!"

Then Little Blue Ben,
and Blue Pussycat too,
are marched up to bed...

39

Goodbye. Toodle-oo!